Preface

After a period of relative calm, injunctions were suddenly in the headlines again in the week in which this edition went to press. Five employees of a company had made allegations of discreditable conduct against its chief executive. The complaints were compromised; the terms of the settlement in each case included a non-disclosure agreement (NDA). The Daily Telegraph obtained details of the allegations. An application by the chief executive for an interlocutory injunction preventing publication pending a full trial was refused by Haddon-Cave J but granted by the Court of Appeal: *ABC v Telegraph Media Group Ltd* [2018] EWCA Civ 2329. Two days later the Claimant was named in Parliament. Meanwhile the Prime Minister had announced an inquiry into the use of NDAs.

Another high-profile injunction case, earlier in the life of the last edition, was the decision of the Supreme Court in *PJS v News Group Newspapers* [2016] AC 1081. The Supreme Court held that the fact that information about a claimant's private life can be found on the internet does not necessarily mean that an injunction to restrain publicity should be refused. Staying with the internet but turning from private lives to trade marks, *Cartier International AG v British Telecommunications plc* confirmed that the courts have power to grant injunctions requiring internet service providers (ISPs) to block access to websites advertising counterfeit goods, although the holder of the intellectual property rights will generally have to pay the ISP's costs.

Over the course of many editions this book has drawn readers' attention to the duty of a claimant making an injunction application without notice to make full and frank disclosure of matters adverse to his case. Any immigration practitioners who thought that this rule did not apply in the Administrative Court have been told in no uncertain terms that it does by the judgment of the Lord Chief Justice in *R. (SB) (Afghanistan) v SSHD*.

As in recent editions I have had the great advantage of assistance from Her Honour Judge Isabel Parry, Designated Family Judge at Cardiff, who has single-handedly updated the chapter on injunctions in the family courts; and from Andrew Burns QC, a distinguished practitioner in the field of employment and commercial law. Readers who have suggestions or who spot errors or omissions are warmly encouraged to write to me at the Royal Court of Justice. The law is stated as at 29 October 2018.

David Bean
Royal Courts of Justice

TABLE OF CONTENTS

PART A: JURISDICTION

1. INTRODUCTION

2. CRITERIA: PERMANENT INJUNCTIONS

INJUNCTIONS

INJUNCTIONS

13TH EDITION

DAVID BEAN MA (Cantab)
Of the Middle Temple,
A Lord Justice of Appeal

ASSISTED BY

ANDREW BURNS MA (Cantab)
Of the Middle Temple,
One of Her Majesty's Counsel;
Recorder of the Crown Court

PART C (MATRIMONIAL AND DOMESTIC PROCEEDINGS) BY

ISABEL PARRY MA (Cantab)
Of Gray's Inn,
A Circuit Judge, Wales and Chester Circuit

SWEET & MAXWELL

 THOMSON REUTERS

Published in 2018 by Thomson Reuters, trading as Sweet & Maxwell.
Thomson Reuters is registered in England & Wales, Company No.1679046.
Registered Office and address for service: 5 Canada Square, Canary Wharf,
London E14 5AQ.

For further information on our products and services, visit
www.sweetandmaxwell.co.uk

Computerset by Sweet & Maxwell.
Printed and bound by CPI Group (UK) Ltd, Croydon, CR0 4YY.
No natural forests were destroyed to make this product: only farmed timber
was used and re-planted.
A CIP catalogue record of this book is available for the British Library.

ISBN: 978-0-414-07013-4

PART B: PRACTICE AND PROCEDURE

5. INTERIM APPLICATIONS

6. OTHER PROCEEDINGS

PART C: MATRIMONIAL AND DOMESTIC PROCEEDINGS

10. FAMILY INJUNCTIONS AND PROTECTIVE ORDERS

PART D: PRECEDENTS

CONTENTS

TABLE OF CASES

TABLE OF STATUTES

TABLE OF STATUTORY INSTRUMENTS

TABLE OF CIVIL PROCEDURE RULES

TABLE OF EUROPEAN LEGISLATION

List of Abbreviations

A.C.	Appeal Cases
All E.R.	All England Reports
B.C.C.	British Company Cases
C.A.T.	Court of Appeal (Civil Division) Transcript
C.L.Y.	Current Law Year Book
CC	County Council
CCR	County Court Rules
Ch.	Law Reports, Chancery Division
Com. L.	Commercial Law Reports
CPR	Civil Procedure Rules
E.M.L.R.	Entertainment and Media Law Reports
ECHR	European Convention on Human Rights
F.C.R.	Family Cases Reports
F.L.R.	Family Law Reports
F.S.R.	Fleet Street Reports
Fam.	Law Reports, Family Division
FPC	Family Proceedings Courts
FPR	Family Proceedings Rules
I.C.R.	Industrial Cases Reports
I.R.L.R	Industrial Relations Law Reports
L.S.G.	Law Society Gazette
LBC	London Borough Council
MBC	Metropolitan Borough Council
NICA	Northern Ireland Court of Appeal
N.P.C.	New Property Cases
Q.B.	Law Reports, Queen's Bench Division
R.P.C.	Reports of Patent, Design and Trademark Cases
RSC	Rules of the Supreme Court
W.L.R.	Weekly Law Reports

PART A: JURISDICTION

CHAPTER 1

Introduction

1 DEFINITION, CLASSIFICATION AND EFFECT

An injunction is an order of a court requiring a party either to do a specific act **1-01** or acts (a *mandatory* or positive injunction) or to refrain from doing a specific act or acts (a *prohibitory* or negative injunction).

Injunctions may be further classified according to the period of time for which the order is to remain in force. A *final* or *perpetual* injunction is a final judgment, and for that reason is usually only granted (except by consent of the defendant) after a trial on the merits. An *interim* injunction, by contrast, is a provisional measure taken at an earlier stage in the proceedings, before the court has had an opportunity to hear and weigh fully the evidence on both sides.

An injunction may be granted even though the claimant's legal rights have not as yet been infringed; in such a case the claimant is described as having obtained the injunction quia timet—"because he fears"—that wrong will be done to him if the order is not made. In *Redland Bricks Ltd v Morris* [1970] A.C. 652, Lord Upjohn said at 664G:

> "[T]o prevent the jurisdiction of the courts being stultified equity has invented the quia timet action, that is an action for an injunction to prevent an apprehended legal wrong, though none has occurred at present."

It may be noted at this stage that mandatory injunctions (see para.2-20) are less common than the prohibitory type and are likely, all things being equal, to be more drastic in their effect. A mandatory injunction is seldom granted as an interim measure (though see para.3-35 and following). Courts prefer to hear full evidence on both sides before attempting to compel positive action.

An injunction carries the sanction of contempt of court if it is disobeyed (see **1-02** para.9-01 and following). It must therefore always be expressed with precision and clarity. As it was put in a Scottish case in 1874, cited by Lord Hope in *Attorney General v Punch Ltd* [2003] 1 A.C. 1046, "if an injunction is to be granted at all, it must be in terms so plain that he who runs may read". In *O (A Child) v Rhodes* [2016] A.C. 219 the Supreme Court held that an injunction granted by the Court of Appeal prohibiting the publication by the appellant of "graphic accounts" of the abuse he suffered as a child infringed this basic rule (see per Lady Hale at [79] and Lord Neuberger at [98]-[100]).

Once an injunction is granted or undertaking given, it remains in force and must be obeyed until it is discharged by the court, however stale the litigation (*Isaacs v Robertson* [1985] A.C. 97), and even if the order should not have been made in the first place (*Johnson v Walton* [1990] 1 F.L.R 350; *M v Home Office* [1994] 1 A.C. 377).

2   REQUIREMENT OF A SUBSTANTIVE CLAIM

1-03   The injunction is an equitable remedy and originally could only be granted by the High Court of Chancery. Nowadays both the High Court (all divisions) and the County Court have a broad discretionary jurisdiction, by virtue of s.37(1) of the Senior Courts Act 1981 (formerly the Supreme Court Act 1981) and s.38 of the County Courts Act 1984 respectively, to grant an interim or final injunction "in all cases in which it appears to the court to be just and convenient to do so". The order may be made unconditionally or on such terms and conditions as the court thinks just (Senior Courts Act 1981 s.37(2)).

Strictly, as Lord Scott explained in *Fourie v Le Roux* [2007] 1 W.L.R. 320 at [46]: "The power of a judge sitting in the High Court to grant an injunction against a party to proceedings properly served is confirmed by, but does not derive from, section 37 of the [Senior Courts] Act 1981 and its statutory predecessors. It derives from the pre- Supreme Court of Judicature Act 1873 (36 & 37 Vict c 66) powers of the Chancery courts, and other courts, to grant injunctions (see section 16 of the 1873 Act and section 19(2)(b) of the 1981 Act).

There is one overriding requirement: the applicant must normally have a cause of action in law entitling him to substantive relief (see *Fourie v Le Roux* [2007] 1 W.L.R. 320). An injunction is not a cause of action (like a tort or a breach of contract) but a remedy (like damages). "They are a supplementary remedy, granted to protect the efficacy of court proceedings, domestic or foreign" (Lord Bingham in *Fourie* at [2]). For example, the law does not recognise a right of exclusive property in the name of a house (*Day v Brownrigg* (1878) 10 Ch. D. 294) nor of a political party (*Kean v McGivan* [1982] F.S.R. 119). Neither does it recognise a right of exclusive property in the names of people; a peer failed to obtain an injunction restraining his ex-wife, after her remarriage, from continuing to call herself "Countess Cowley" (*Cowley (Earl) v Cowley (Countess)* [1901] A.C. 450). A private citizen cannot obtain an injunction to prevent the commission of a criminal offence unless he can prove that he personally has suffered or will suffer damage amounting to an actionable tort as a result (*Gouriet v Union of Post Office Workers* [1978] A.C. 435; see also paras 4-42 to 4-44). An individual cannot obtain an injunction restraining the BBC from broadcasting anti-German programmes (*Thorne v BBC* [1967] 1 W.L.R. 1104). In each case there is *no cause of action*.

"A right to obtain an interlocutory injunction is not a cause of action. It cannot stand on its own. It is dependent upon there being a pre-existing cause of action against the defendant arising out of an invasion, actual or threatened by him, of a legal or equitable right of the plaintiff for the enforcement of which the defendant is amenable to the jurisdiction of the court. The right to obtain an interlocutory injunction is merely ancillary and incidental to the pre-existing cause of action. It is granted to preserve the status quo pending the ascertainment by the court of the rights of the parties and the grant to the plaintiff of the relief to which his cause of action entitles him, which may or may not include a final injunction." (Per Lord Diplock in *The Siskina* [1979] A.C. 210 at 254.)

"Although the words of section 37(1) and its forebears are very wide it is firmly established by a long history of judicial self-denial that they are not to be taken at their face value and that their application is subject to severe constraints: see *The Siskina* [1979] A.C. 210 ... the doctrine of *The Siskina*, put at its highest, is that the right to an interim injunction cannot exist in isolation, but is always incidental to and dependent on the enforcement of a substantive right, which usually although not invariably takes the shape of a cause of action." (Per Lord Mustill in *Channel Tunnel Group Ltd v Balfour Beatty Construction Ltd* [1993] A.C. 334 at 360–362.)

1-04   There are a few exceptions to the cause of action rule: they include applications to restrain the institution of proceedings in the High Court or overseas courts and, pursuant to the Civil Jurisdiction and Judgments Acts 1982 and 1991 and Orders in Council made under the 1982 Act, applications when there is litigation between the parties in the courts of another country (see paras 4-53 and 7-47 and following). An injunction can be granted even if a cause of action (in its strict sense) does not yet exist, if it is nevertheless possible to issue a contribution notice. If a co-defendant is entitled to issue and serve a contribution notice, he has a cause of action for so doing. In a proper case a freezing injunction can be issued in support of a valid contribution notice (*Kazakhstan Kagazy plc v Zhunus* [2017] 1 W.L.R. 1360).

An interim injunction must be ancillary to a substantive claim made in the action, but it need not be in a form which could be granted after final judgment. For example, in *Fresh Fruit Wales Ltd v Halbert, The Times,* 29 January 1991, the claimants claimed delivery up of 22 rugby season tickets. At a trial, they would either succeed entirely or fail entirely. The Court of Appeal held that s.37(1) conferred a discretion on the court to grant an interim injunction ordering delivery up of half the tickets (though such an order was in fact refused).

A party seeking a permanent injunction must claim it in his pleadings; an interim injunction may be granted even though the equivalent final order has not been specifically claimed (CPR r.25.1(4)).

In *Re Channel Four Television Co Ltd* [1988] C.L.Y 2864, the Court of Appeal, **1-05** Criminal Division, made an order on an application by the Attorney General prohibiting a television "re-enactment" of an appeal from being broadcast until after judgment in the appeal. This was said to derive from the inherent power of a superior court of record to grant an injunction to protect its own process.

In the *parens patriae* jurisdiction exercised by the Family Division of the High Court over children or patients with a mental disability, the concept of a substantive cause of action is wide, but not infinite. In *Re V (A Minor) (Injunction: Jurisdiction)* [1997] 2 F.C.R. 195, Johnson J had held that both a declaration and an injunction could be granted in favour of a man approaching his 18th birthday, mentally competent but with severe physical disabilities, who sought to restrain his parents (whether before or after he reached the age of 18) from interfering with his right to choose where he was to live and with whom he was to associate. Both the injunction and the declaration were set aside; the Court of Appeal held that there was no evidence of the parents seeking to interfere with V's legal rights and, in the absence of an issue affecting his legal rights, no order could be made. Contrast this with *Re S (Hospital Patient: Court's Jurisdiction)* [1996] Fam. 1, where the Court of Appeal upheld an interim injunction granted by Hale J to a woman caring for an elderly patient who had suffered a severe stroke, to prevent his relatives from removing him from the jurisdiction until the court could make a declaration as to what course of treatment was in his best interests.

In *Broadmoor Special Hospital Authority v Robinson* [2000] QB 775, the defendant, an inmate at Broadmoor who had been convicted of manslaughter, wrote a book identifying other patients and discussing their mental states. The Court of Appeal held by a majority that a public body required to exercise a statutory responsibility in the public interest could, in the absence of an implication to the contrary in the statute, apply to the court to prevent interference with the performance of those responsibilities; it held unanimously, however, that the hospital authority could not bring proceedings to protect other patients' rights to confidence or privacy (such claims had to be in the patients' names), nor to prevent distress to victims' families, and that therefore an injunction had rightly been refused on the facts. The dissenting judgment of Morritt LJ on the jurisdiction point is powerfully argued.

1-06   In *Governor and Company of the Bank of Scotland v A* [2001] 1 W.L.R. 751, a bank, faced with a difficulty caused by the legislation on money laundering, applied for an injunction against itself prohibiting it from making payments from a customer's accounts. The Court of Appeal held that it was impossible to envisage circumstances in which it would be appropriate to grant an injunction against the only party seeking relief. (An interim declaration under CPR r.25.1(1)(b) might be appropriate: see para.5-29).

In *Maclaine Watson & Co v ITC (No.2)* [1989] Ch. 286, the Court of Appeal was faced with the problem of how to compel a judgment debtor (the International Tin Council), which was an unincorporated association, to disclose its UK assets, since the usual powers under rules of court to examine a judgment debtor did not apply. It held that the court had power under s.37(1) of the Senior Courts Act 1981 to grant a mandatory injunction ordering such disclosure, on either of two bases. First, the defendants' failure to meet the money judgment in favour of the claimants was a breach of their obligations to the claimants and thus an invasion of the claimants' legal rights. Secondly, it was also a failure to comply with an order of the court, and there was power under s.37(1) to make any ancillary order, including a mandatory order, to ensure the effectiveness of any other order made by the court. This second point in particular is of great importance. See also *Re Oriental Credit Ltd* [1988] Ch. 204, where Harman J granted an injunction under s.37(1) restraining a company director from leaving the country until he had complied with a registrar's order to attend for oral examination. However in *B v B (Injunction: Jurisdiction)* [1998] 1 W.L.R. 329, Wilson J held that an injunction cannot be granted to compel a party against whom an order for costs has been made (or money judgment given) to remain in this country until the sum due has been paid.

3   "JUST AND CONVENIENT"

1-07   The words "just and convenient" in s.37(1) of the Senior Courts Act 1981 re-enact similar provisions in statutes of 1873 and 1925. This expression must be taken to mean "just, as well as convenient" (*Day v Brownrigg* (1878) 10 Ch. D. 294). It is not a licence for a judge to grant an injunction whenever he dislikes what the defendant is doing—that would be palm tree justice.

In *South Carolina Insurance Co v Assurantie Maatschappij* [1987] A.C. 24, a majority of the House of Lords stated that the power of the High Court to grant injunctions under s.37(1) "has been circumscribed by judicial authority dating back many years", and that it is limited (with the exception of injunctions to restrain proceedings overseas) to two situations:

(a)   where one party to an action can show that the other party has invaded, or threatens to invade, a legal or equitable right of the former, for the enforcement of which the latter is amenable to the jurisdiction of the court;

(b)   where one party to an action has behaved, or threatens to behave, in a manner which is unconscionable.

1-08   In *Pickering v Liverpool Daily Post* [1991] 2 A.C. 370, the House of Lords unanimously followed *South Carolina* and reaffirmed the traditional view that the power to grant injunctions is circumscribed by judicial authority. Subsequent dicta in the House of Lords indicated an unwillingness to restrict in any way the scope of the power to grant injunctions under s.37(1). In the *Channel Tunnel* case (above), three members of the House expressed doubts as to whether the power is restricted to exclusive categories, as the majority in *South Carolina* had indicated. In *Kirklees*

MBC v Wickes Building Supplies Ltd [1993] A.C. 227, Lord Goff, with the agreement of all members of the House, stated:

"The power to grant injunctions, which now arises under section 37 of the Supreme Court Act 1981, is a discretionary power, which should not as a matter of principle be fettered by rules."

This debate exercised the House of Lords in a number of cases after *The Siskina* [1979] A.C. 210, but the modern trend is towards finding jurisdiction if the ends are thought to justify the judicial means.

In his dissenting judgment in the Privy Council in *Mercedes-Benz AG v Leiduck* [1996] 1 A.C. 284, Lord Nicholls said that dicta in previous cases were:

"highly persuasive voices that the jurisdiction to grant an injunction, unfettered by statute, should not be rigidly confined to exclusive categories by judicial decision ... The court habitually grants injunctions in respect of certain types of conduct. But that does not mean that the situations in which injunctions may be granted are now set in stone for all time. The grant of *Mareva* injunctions itself gives the lie to this. As circumstances in the world change, so must the situations in which the courts may properly exercise their jurisdiction to grant injunctions. The exercise of the jurisdiction must be principled, but the criterion is injustice. Injustice is to be viewed and decided in the light of today's conditions and standards, not those of yester-year."

However, the fact that jurisdiction is established does not mean that an injunction must be granted. The discretionary nature of the jurisdiction was emphasised in *South Bucks DC v Porter* [2003] 2 A.C. 558. In a series of cases, injunctions were sought against gypsies under s.187B(2) of the Town and Country Planning Act 1990, which provides that on an application by a local authority to restrain breaches of planning control, "the court may grant such an injunction as the court thinks appropriate for the purpose of restraining the breach". The claimant authorities argued that such injunctions should issue effectively as of right upon a breach being proved (citing cases predating *Lawrence v Fen Tigers* [2014] A.C. 822 see para.2.12). Rejecting this, Lord Bingham of Cornhill said:

1-09

"It is indeed inherent in the concept of an injunction in English law that it is a remedy that the court may but need not grant, depending on its judgment of all the circumstances. Underpinning the court's jurisdiction to grant an injunction is section 37(1) of the Supreme Court Act 1981, conferring power to do so 'in all cases in which it appears to the court to be just and convenient to do so'. Thus the court is not obliged to grant an injunction because a local authority considers it necessary or expedient for any actual or apprehended breach of planning control to be restrained by injunction and so makes application to the court.

The court's discretion to grant or withhold relief is not however unfettered ... The discretion of the court under section 187B, like every other judicial discretion, must be exercised judicially ... In [some] cases the task of the court may be relatively straightforward. But in all cases the court must decide whether in all the circumstances it is just to grant the relief sought against the particular defendant."

For an example of the court taking a broad view on whether a claimant had a cause of action, see *Re V (A Minor) (Injunction: Jurisdiction)*, discussed above. Sir Thomas Bingham MR observed ([1996] Fam. 1 at 19):

"If it is necessary for the [claimant] to demonstrate in herself a specific legal right which is liable to be infringed by the proposed action of the wife and the son, then in my view the [claimant] does so. But to insist on demonstration of a specific legal right in this sensitive and socially important area of the law is in my view to confine the inherent jurisdiction of the court within an inappropriate straitjacket. The matters which the judge listed in her judgment are in my view quite enough to show that the [claimant] is far from being a stranger or an officious busybody: and that is in my view enough to give the court jurisdiction."

In *Cartier International AG v British Sky Broadcasting* [2017] Bus. L.R. 1 (on an issue which did not go to the Supreme Court) the Court of Appeal had to consider whether the court has power to grant a website blocking injunctions against internet service providers (ISPs) who are aware that their services are being used by third parties to infringe registered trade marks by offering counterfeit goods for sale and intellectual property rights. The trade mark owners had no conventional cause of action against the ISPs, who were not themselves infringing the trade marks; nor were they engaged in a common design with the website operators offering the counterfeited goods; and they owed no common law duty of care to the trade mark owners. Nevertheless, the court held that such an injunction could and should be granted. Kitchin LJ drew an analogy with the equitable protective duty described in the *Norwich Pharmacal* case. He held that restricting injunctions to the particular situations described in *The Siskina* or *South Carolina* [1987] A.C. 24 would impose a straitjacket on the court and its ability to exercise its equitable powers. That was not warranted by principle. Instead, pursuant to general equitable principles, injunctions may be issued in new categories when this course appears appropriate.

4   JUDGES AND COURTS

1-10   The old law prohibiting masters and district judges from granting injunctions in civil proceedings was largely swept away in 2015. Search orders, freezing injunctions and orders for disclosure of assets ancillary to freezing injunctions may only be granted by a judge or deputy judge of the High Court or (except for search orders) by an authorised circuit judge in the county court. District judges and masters have jurisdiction to deal with other types of injunction application, although guidance issued by the Chancellor of the High Court on 12 June 2015 states that masters will not usually hear applications for interim injunctions where the *American Cyanamid* test must be applied. If such an application is made to a master it will be referred to a judge unless there are good reasons for the master to hear it. Masters may hear interim injunction applications if the injunction is secondary to the main relief sought; and may vary or discharge an injunction by consent.

Under s.3 of the Courts and Legal Services Act 1990, the County Court has the power to make any order in any proceedings which the High Court could make, except in judicial review and such other cases as may be prescribed by regulations. The County Courts Remedies Regulations 2014 (SI 2014/982) prescribe search orders as excepted for the purposes of s.38 and, accordingly, county courts have no power to make such orders, save that by consent. However in major county courts it is common to find that the designated civil judge (or the local mercantile judge, if there is one) is authorised ("ticketed") under s.9 of the Senior Courts Act 1981 to sit as a deputy judge of the High Court, so that the same result can be achieved in the same building, but under the flag of the High Court.

Practitioners intending to make an immediate application for a search order should therefore issue proceedings in the High Court. Where county court proceedings are required for jurisdictional reasons or are already on foot, application may nevertheless be made for such orders pursuant to CPR Pt 23, but only in the High Court: see regs 4 to 5 of the 2014 Regulations.

1-11   The Crown Court has no general power to grant injunctions, but by s.45(4) of the 1981 Act is given the same powers as the High Court to grant orders to prevent contempt of court: see para.4-38 and *In Re Trinity Mirror Plc* [2008] QB 770. A youth court may grant an injunction to restrain anti-social behaviour against a defendant aged under 18: s.1(8)(a) of the Anti-Social Behaviour, Crime and Policing Act 2014, discussed at para.4-65, below.

The full width of the s.37 power is available to the Supreme Court, no less than to a High Court judge (*Attorney General's Reference (No.3 of 1999)* [2010] 1 A.C. 145 at [57]).

5 PARTIES

An injunction is usually granted only against a named defendant, but certain **1-12** types of order are made *contra mundum*, that is, against the whole world: *Venables v News Group Newspapers Ltd* [2001] Fam. 430; *X (a Woman formerly known as Mary Bell) v SO* [2003] 2 F.C.R. 686: see para.4-22. There is also a discretion to make an order against a person or persons unknown if justice requires it, although the court must "keep a watchful eye on claims brought against persons unknown, to guard against any abuse of the facility to bring claims in this way" (per Warby J in *GYH v Persons Unknown* [2017] EWHC 3360(QB)). In *Bloomsbury Publishing Group Ltd and JK Rowling v News Group Newspapers Ltd* [2003] 1 W.L.R. 1633, copies of a forthcoming book in the Harry Potter series had been stolen from the printers. Morritt VC granted injunctions against four named defendants and accepted undertakings from another, but he also continued an injunction granted against "the person or persons who have offered the publishers of the Sun, Daily Mail and Daily Mirror newspapers a copy of the book ..." The crucial point, he held, is that

> "the description used must be sufficiently certain as to identify both those who are included and those who are not. If the test is satisfied it does not seem to me to matter that the description may apply to no one, or to more than one person, nor that there is no further element of subsequent identification whether by service or otherwise."

The title of the case of *X and Y v The Person or Persons who have offered and/or provided to the publishers of the Mail on Sunday, Mirror and Sun newspapers information about the state of the claimants' marriage* [2006] EWHC 2783 speaks for itself. Eady J, granting an injunction against the defendants, said that the claimants were required to use their best endeavours to effect service on the primary wrongdoers; otherwise the litigation would go to sleep indefinitely, and what was supposed to be a temporary holding injunction would become a substitute for a full and fair adjudication. Another example is *Kerner v (1) WX (2) YZ (Persons Unknown responsible for pursuing and/or taking photographs of the Claimant and her son at their home on 22 January, 2015)* [2015] EWHC 1247 (QB). In the internet age, injunctions have been granted against anonymous online publishers. In *Brett Wilson LLP v Persons Unknown* [2016] 4 WLR 69 the defendants were "Persons unknown responsible for the operation and publication of the website" when a final injunction was granted. The relevant procedural safeguards had to be respected, which included ensuring the unknown defendants had been duly served (at a specified email address) with the proceedings and any application for interim or final relief (*Smith v Unknown Defendants* [2016] EWHC 1775 (QB)). In *LJY v Persons Unknown* [2018] E.M.L.R. 19 the injunction had to be served by a series of text messages to the number provided in a letter from a blackmailer. *British Pregnancy Advisory Service v The Person using the alias "Pablo Escobar"* [2012]

EWHC 572 (QB) is an example of an injunction against an individual using an assumed name.

In a number of cases, an injunction has been granted prohibiting the occupation of land in breach of planning controls by "persons unknown", for example in *South Cambridgeshire DC v Persons Unknown* [2004] EWCA Civ 1280, approved by Lord Rodger of Earlsferry in *Secretary of State for Environment, Food and Rural Affairs v Meier* [2009] 1 W.L.R. 2780. A person moving on to the land who learns of the terms of such an injunction is bound by it and is in contempt of court if he remains there (*South Cambridgeshire DC v Gammell* [2006] 1 W.L.R. 658). There have also been many cases involving protesters sued as "persons unknown": see *Ineos Upstream Ltd v Persons Unknown and others* [2017] EWHC 2945, in which the claim form named five categories of persons unknown as well as two individual defendants.

1-13   In appropriate cases, an injunction may be granted against named defendants as representatives of a larger group (*Michaels (M) (Furriers) Ltd v Askew* (1983) 127 S.J. 597; *EMI Records Ltd v Kudhail* [1985] F.S.R. 36; *Oxford University v Webb* [2006] EWHC 2490 (QB)), but not if there is a conflict of interest between the members of the group (*UK Nirex Ltd v Barton, The Times,* 14 October, 1986) or if there are no individuals before the court who can properly be treated as representatives of the group (*EDO MBM Technology Ltd v Campaign to Smash EDO* [2005] EWHC 837 (QB)). There is a useful review of the authorities in *SmithKline Beecham Plc v Avery* [2007] EWHC 948 (QB). A judge may properly exercise a discretion not to frame an injunction in terms which would make it enforceable against persons who are not parties to the claim (*Astellas Pharma Ltd v Stop Huntingdon Animal Cruelty* [2011] EWCA Civ 752: see para.4-63). Ward LJ commented that "difficult issues arise from seeking to join unknown defendants and to enforce injunctions against them".

Although it is less frequent, an injunction may also be granted to a representative claimant, as in *The Law Society (in a representative capacity on behalf of all the solicitors and law firms in England and Wales and other individuals and organisations that are at serious risk of being named on the website www.solicitorsfromhell.co.uk) v Kordowski* [2011] EWHC 3185 (QB). In this case the title of the case tells the story. In *Emerson Developments Ltd and others v Avery* [2004] EWHC 194 an injunction against harassment was granted in favour of five companies and their employees, the sixth claimant being one employee who represented all other employees of the claimants.

For cases on the grant of freezing injunctions against persons, such as a defendant's spouse, against whom there is no substantive cause of action, see para.7-11.

6   SCOPE OF THE REMEDY

1-14   Provided that the applicant has a substantive cause of action, the court's discretion to grant or refuse an injunction is almost unlimited. The following are some of the purposes for which an injunction may be granted (the list is not comprehensive). It will be observed that the number of mandatory injunctions mentioned is very small.

(a) Real property

1-15   (a) To restrain trespass to land by persons or structures; to compel the removal of overhanging structures;

(b) to restrain trespass by a hunt (*League Against Cruel Sports Ltd v Scott* [1986] QB 240);

(c) to exclude a defendant from his home so as to stop serious nuisance committed against a neighbour (*Liburd v Cork* [1981] C.L.Y. 1999 CA; see para.4-65 and following for injunctions against anti-social behaviour);

(d) to prohibit the defendant from entering an "exclusion zone" around the claimant's home (*Burris v Azadani* [1995] 1 W.L.R. 1372);

(e) to order removal of a tree whose roots are causing damage to a wall (*Elliott v Islington LBC* [1991] 10 E.G. 145);

(f) to restrain infringement of a right to light; to compel the removal of structures so built (*Pugh v Howells* (1984) 48 P. & C.R. 298);

(g) to restrain building in breach of covenant; to compel the demolition of structures so built;

(h) to protect a licence to occupy premises;

(i) to restrain the sale of land to a third party when the vendor has already agreed to sell it to the applicant;

(j) to enforce a local authority tenant's right to buy (*Dance v Welwyn Hatfield DC* [1990] 1 W.L.R. 1097).

(b) Environmental harm

(a) To restrain nuisance by noise, smells, vibration or pollution; **1-16**

(b) to enforce a planning obligation (Town and Country Planning Act 1990 s.106); to restrain breaches of planning control (s.187B of the same Act), damage to protected trees (s.214A of the same Act) or damage to listed buildings (s.44A of the Planning (Listed Buildings and Conservation Areas) Act 1990).

(c) Landlord and tenant

(a) By a landlord: to restrain subletting or assignment in breach of the terms of a **1-17** lease;

(b) by certain types of landlord: to restrain anti-social behaviour by tenants or their visitors (Housing Act 1996 s.152: see para.4-65 and following);

(c) by a tenant: to restrain harassment, to compel the landlord to allow peaceful re-entry, to enforce the landlord's liability to repair under the Defective Premises Act 1972 (*Barrett v Lounova Ltd* [1989] 1 All E.R. 351).

(d) Employment and industrial relations

(a) To restrain an ex-employee from breaking the terms of a valid restrictive **1-18** covenant (see para.4-05);

(b) to restrain an employee or ex-employee from revealing trade secrets, or an employee from revealing other confidential information (see para.4-07);

(c) to restrain interference with contractual rights;

(d) to restrain certain forms of picketing;

(e) to restrain a trade union from expelling a member (an injunction will *not* generally lie to compel the performance of a contract of employment: see, however, para.4-02);

(f) to prevent the dissipation of assets by the respondent to an employment tribunal claim (*Amicus v Dynamex Friction Ltd* [2005] I.R.L.R. 724).

(e) Intellectual property

1-19   (a) To restrain infringement of a patent, registered design or trade mark;
         (b) to restrain breach of copyright;
         (c) to restrain passing off;
         (d) to restrain the misuse of ideas disclosed in confidence (*Seager v Copydex* [1967] 1 W.L.R. 923);
         (e) to require a defendant to allow a claimant to enter premises to search for and remove material infringing the claimant's copyright and documents evidencing such infringement (see Ch.8, "Search Orders");
         (f) to require an internet service provider to prevent access to a "pirate" website see paras. 1-09 and 4-72.

(f) Commercial

1-20   (a) To restrain the transfer of assets or chattels out of the jurisdiction, or their disposal within the jurisdiction so as to render them unavailable or untraceable (see Ch.7, "Freezing Injunctions");
         (b) to restrain a dishonest debtor from leaving the country and to compel delivery up of his passport, but only pending compliance with orders for disclosure (see para.7-42);
         (c) to restrain a bankrupt from leaving the country until he has co-operated with the trustee's enquiries and attended an application to commit him for contempt (*Morris v Murjani* [1996] 1 W.L.R. 848);
         (d) to restrain improper activity by a partner;
         (e) to restrain a defendant from inducing breach of a future contract (*Union Traffic v TGWU* [1989] I.R.L.R 127);
         (f) to restrain the carrying on of unauthorised investment business (see para.4-59);
         (g) to restrain the use of a ship the subject of a time charter outside the "pool" (*Lauritzencool AB v Lady Navigation Inc* [2005] 1 W.L.R. 3686).

(g) Companies

1-21   (a) To restrain the presentation of a winding-up petition (see para.4-51);
         (b) to restrain ultra vires acts by a company;
         (c) to restrain a defendant shareholder from voting in general meeting so as to dissipate his assets (*Standard Chartered Bank v Walker* [1992] 1 W.L.R. 561);
         (d) to compel the exercise of votes in general meeting in accordance with an agreement.

(h) Fiduciaries

1-22   (a) To restrain an executor from continuing to act;
         (b) to restrain a trustee from committing a breach of trust.

(i) Publications (see Ch.4)

1-23   (a) To restrain the publication of defamatory statements;
         (b) to restrain the publication of information which would breach the claimant's right to privacy;
         (c) to restrain the publication of Cabinet secrets;
         (d) to restrain publicity which would identify a ward of court;

(e) to protect the anonymity of an adult who committed a notorious murder as a child and whose life or personal safety would otherwise be endangered;

(f) to prevent the processing of personal data likely to cause substantial damage or distress;

(g) to restrain false statements of fact about election candidates.

(j) Harassment and anti-social behaviour

(a) To restrain harassment by "paparazzi" photographers (*Tin Lang Hong v XYZ* [2011] EWHC 2995 (QB)); **1-24**

(b) to prohibit anti-social behaviour (see Ch.4.9)

(c) to exclude members of a violent gang from a particular area (see para.4-69)

(k) Family (see Ch.10)

(a) To restrain molestation; **1-25**

(b) to compel a spouse or partner to leave the matrimonial or family home; to restrain a spouse or partner from returning to the matrimonial or family home;

(c) to compel an unruly member of the family to leave a house (*Egan v Egan* [1975] Ch. 218);

(d) to protect elderly and vulnerable parents from molestation by their son (*Re L (Vulnerable Adults with Capacity: Court's Jurisdiction* [2011] Fam.189);

(e) to restrain the removal of a child from the care of the person with whom he or she is living;

(f) to restrain the removal of a child from England and Wales;

(g) to restrain the removal of an elderly patient from the jurisdiction (*Re S (Hospital Patient: Court's Jurisdiction)* [1996] Fam. 1);

(h) to restrain dealings with property by a spouse;

(i) to restrain a parent from leaving the country pending the completion of blood tests (*Re J (A Minor) (Wardship)* [1988] 1 F.L.R. 65).

(l) Discrimination (see para.4-58)

To restrain acts of discrimination (Equality Act 2006 s.24) on the application of the Commission for Equality and Human Rights. **1-26**

(m) Public law

(a) To restrain the commission of a crime (but see paras 4-42 to 4-44); **1-27**

(b) to restrain ultra vires acts of a local authority;

(c) to restrain the unlawful holding of a public office;

(e) to restrain a person from receiving a debt due to him from the Crown;

(f) to restrain a struck-off solicitor from practising (*Law Society v Shah* [2015] 1 W.L.R. 2094).

(n) Litigation (see paras 4-51 to 4-53)

(a) To restrain proceedings in another jurisdiction (an anti-suit injunction) if England is the appropriate forum, if there is an exclusive jurisdiction clause, or if the proceedings are brought in bad faith; **1-28**

(b) to prevent vexatious litigation; to restrain a vexatious litigant from entering the Royal Courts of Justice;

(c) to restrain the use in litigation of documents protected by legal professional privilege (*Derby v Weldon (No.8)* [1991] 1 W.L.R. 73);

(d) to restrain the use in litigation of "without prejudice" communications (*Instance v Denny* [2000] F.S.R. 869);

(e) to restrain the use by a party to a civil action of a document seized from another party by the police (*Marcel v Commissioner of Police of the Metropolis* [1992] Ch. 225);

(f) to restrain a police officer from interfering with potential witnesses for the defence in criminal proceedings (*Connolly v Dale* [1996] QB 120).

The areas in which the scope of the remedy is limited will be discussed in Ch.4.

CHAPTER 2

Criteria: Permanent Injunctions

The procedure for obtaining an injunction will be considered in Part B of this book, but it will be useful to discuss first whether the court is likely to grant an injunction at all. A permanent injunction is a remedy that may be granted at the end of a final hearing. The criteria for interim injunctions are different and will be the subject of Ch.3. Certain considerations are peculiar to individual areas of the law and will be dealt with in Ch.4, but there are also criteria which apply generally. **2-01**

It should be noted that the court must make its decision by reference to the state of the law at the date when the question has to be resolved, and not at the date when the claim was issued (*Application des Gaz SA v Falks Veritas Ltd* [1974] Ch. 381). Likewise, the factual evidence should be up to date, and need not refer to the position as at the commencement of proceedings.

1   A DISCRETIONARY REMEDY

If a claimant suffers personal injury, damage to his goods or financial loss from a breach of contract, he has the remedy of damages as of right; that is to say, if he brings his action within the limitation period, follows the proper procedures and proves his case against the defendant and the extent of his loss, he will be entitled to an award of damages. The same is not true of an injunction which, being an equitable remedy, is within the court's discretion. Even where the claimant has shown that his rights are being infringed he may be refused an injunction and left to his remedy in damages, or his behaviour may have been such as to disqualify him from obtaining equitable relief. Fraud or dishonest conduct entitles the court to refuse an injunction. Acquiescence and laches may cause a claimant to lose his eligibility to an injunction and require special consideration: see para.2-16. **2-02**

Where the claimant has established that a legal wrong such as a nuisance has been committed, then he will prima facie be entitled to an injunction to restrain the defendant from committing that legal wrong in the future. However, ever since Lord Cairns' Act (the Chancery Amendment Act 1858), now found in s.50 of the Senior Courts Act 1981, the court has had power to award damages instead of an injunction in any case. Such damages are conventionally based on the reduction in the value of the claimant's rights as a result of the continuation of the legal wrong. The jurisdiction remains discretionary even where the defendant (in disciplinary proceedings, for example) has acted in breach of the rules of natural justice; the court may still decline to grant an injunction in such cases (*Glynn v Keele University* [1971] 1 W.L.R. 487).

As Lord Neuberger said in *Lawrence v Fen Tigers* [2014] A.C. 822, the approach to be adopted by a judge when being asked to award damages instead of an injunction is a "classic exercise of discretion" which should be unfettered and much more flexible than that suggested in the recent cases. In those cases (*Regan v Paul*

Properties DPF No. 1 Ltd [2007] Ch. 135 and *Watson v Croft Promosport Ltd* [2009] 3 All E.R. 249) the Court of Appeal had suggested that an injunction should be refused in favour of damages only in "very exceptional circumstances".

2-03   One of the defendants in *Lawrence* obtained planning permission for a motocross track next to his motor racing stadium limiting the frequency of racing, but not noise levels. The claimant neighbours alleged that the noise was unacceptable despite reduction measures and successfully brought a claim for nuisance against the defendants and obtained an injunction from the judge limiting sports activities on the track. It was argued that there was no discretion to refuse an injunction as the four tests in *Shelfer v City of London Electric Lighting Co* [1895] 1 Ch. 287 were not fulfilled, namely that damages in substitution for an injunction may only be given where the injury to the claimant's legal rights is small, is capable of being estimated in money and adequately compensated by a small money payment, and it would be oppressive to the defendant to grant an injunction.

The Supreme Court disagreed. It held that caution must be exercised when applying the long-standing 'good working rule' in *Shelfer*. This rule was said by Lord Sumption to be "out of date" (*Lawrence* at [161]) and Lord Neuberger held that it should only be applied subject to the following modifications. First, these four tests are not a fetter on the exercise of the court's discretion. Secondly, if the four tests were satisfied it would normally be right to refuse an injunction (unless there were other countervailing circumstances). Thirdly, the fact that those tests are not all satisfied does not mean that an injunction should be granted (*Lawrence* at [123]). As the prima facie position is that an injunction should be granted, the legal burden is on the defendant to show why it should not (*Lawrence* at [121]).

Where the injury cannot fairly be compensated by money or if the defendant has acted in a high-handed manner, endeavoured to steal a march upon the claimant or to evade the jurisdiction of the court an injunction will normally be necessary, in order to do justice to the claimant and as a warning to others (*Colls v Home & Colonial Store Ltd* [1904] A.C. 179).

2-04   In cases where the interference with the claimant's right is trivial, an injunction may be refused (*Imperial Gas Light & Coke Co v Broadbent* (1859) 74 H.L. Cas. 600). The claimant may also be confined not merely to damages, but to nominal damages (*Armstrong v Sheppard & Short Ltd* [1959] 2 QB 384). This applies even where the wrong complained of is continuing trespass on the claimant's land; while an injunction will usually be granted in such cases (*Patel v WH Smith (Eziot) Ltd* [1987] 1 W.L.R. 853), if there is no injury to the landowner, the claimant may obtain nominal damages and no injunction (*Behrens v Richards* [1905] 2 Ch. 614). In this last case, Buckley J described one head of the claimant's claim as a "petty contest" and a "matter for the application of reason, common sense and ordinary forbearance, not for an injunction". These cautionary observations should be kept in mind. In *Fielden v Cox* (1906) 22 T.L.R. 411, the court refused an injunction against lepidopterists who had committed a technical trespass to land but who had desisted on request. In *Radford v Campbell* (1890) 6 T.L.R. 488 an injunction was refused where its real object would have been to gratify the pride of Nottingham Forest FC by restraining the defendant from playing for Blackburn Rovers FC. The modern approach is likely to be different now that sport is big business (e.g.. *Araci v Fallon* [2011] EWCA Civ 668; [2011] L.L.R. 440 in which the Court of Appeal granted an injunction preventing a jockey from riding a rival owner's horse at the Epsom Derby).

Where travellers had established an unauthorised encampment on one site owned by the claimant, there was no reason in law why both a possession order extending to potential additional sites and an injunction prohibiting trespass on such sites should not be granted. The question whether an injunction would be an effective remedy in any case would depend on the facts at the time of enforcement. Although the grant of an injunction is discretionary, the court should grant an injunction necessary to uphold legal rights against a threatened invasion unless there is some factor sufficiently weighty to displace the general rule (*Secretary of State for the Environment, Food and Rural Affairs v Meier* [2009] 1 W.L.R. 828).

The claimant's behaviour

The behaviour of the claimant may argue against an injunction. "He who comes to equity must come with clean hands"; accordingly, the application of a party with unclean hands is likely to fail. The uncleanliness may consist of untruthful evidence (*Armstrong v Sheppard & Short Ltd* [1959] 2 QB 384) or the use of "deplorable means" in pursuing an objective (*Hubbard v Vosper* [1972] 2 QB 84), but there is no universal rule that a claimant whose behaviour is open to criticism on moral or other grounds is thereby barred entirely from equitable relief. The cleanliness required is to be judged in relation to the relief that is sought. A claimant applying for an injunction to prevent her ex-husband from selling the secrets of their married life to a Sunday newspaper was not barred by the fact that her own adultery had contributed to the ultimate breakdown of the marriage (*Argyll (Duchess) v Argyll (Duke)* [1967] Ch. 302). In *Ford v Foster* (1872) L.R. 7 Ch. App. 611, the defendant had clearly and "most improperly" violated the claimant's trademark "Eureka", referring to a type of shirt; the claimant had, in invoices and advertisements, wrongly described himself as the "patentee" of the shirt, but this did not prevent him from obtaining a permanent injunction against the defendant.

The scope of the application of the 'unclean hands' doctrine is limited as the misconduct or impropriety of the claimant must have an immediate and necessary relation to the equity sued for. Attempts to mislead a court in the course of the litigation may present good grounds for refusing equitable relief, not only where the purpose is to create a false case, but also where it is to bolster the truth with fabricated evidence. Ultimately in each case it is a matter of assessment by the judge, who has to examine all the relevant factors in the case before him to see if the misconduct of the claimant is sufficient to warrant a refusal of the relief sought (*Royal Bank of Scotland plc v Highland Financial Partners* [2013] EWCA Civ 328, [2013] 1 C.L.C. 596).

In *Kazakhstan Kagazy plc v Zhunus* [2017] 1 W.L.R. 1360) Longmore LJ said that one fraudster should not be entitled to freezing relief against another fraudster on the basis that "the court would never order an account between two highwaymen who successfully rob passengers crossing Bagshot Heath: see *Upsdell v Stewart* (1793) Peake 255". However where it was impossible to determine relative fault and misconduct at the preliminary stage and where the court could later have the power to order contribution even between fraudsters, it was appropriate to 'hold the ring' with a freezing order until trial.

The relevance of malice

A defendant cannot be restrained from doing an inherently lawful act merely because he acts deliberately or maliciously and to the detriment of the claimant (*Bradford Corp v Pickles* [1895] A.C. 587). However, where what the defendant does is capable of constituting a cause of action in law, malice or spite on the part of the defendant may properly influence the court to exercise its discretion in favour

2-05

2-06

of granting an injunction (*Christie v Davey* [1893] 1 Ch. 316, a case of nuisance by noise; *Hollywood Silver Fox Farm Ltd v Emmett* [1936] 1 All E.R. 825).

Whether the injunction will be ineffective

2-07   "When granting an injunction, the court does not contemplate the possibility that it will be disobeyed ... Apprehension that a party may disobey an order should not deter the court from making an order otherwise appropriate: there is not one law for the law-abiding and another for the lawless and truculent. When making an order, the court should ordinarily be willing to enforce it if necessary. The rule of law is not well served if orders are made and disobeyed with impunity. These propositions, however, rest on the assumption that the order made by the court is just in all the circumstances and one with which the defendant can and reasonably ought to comply, an assumption which ordinarily applies both when the order is made and when the time for enforcement arises ... The court should ordinarily be slow to make an order which it would not at that time be willing, if need be, to enforce by imprisonment. But imprisonment in this context is intended not to punish but to induce compliance, reinforcing the requirement that the order be one with which the defendant can and reasonably ought to comply." (Per Lord Bingham of Cornhill in *South Bucks DC v Porter* [2003] 2 A.C. 558 at [32].)

Although the court should not normally make orders which it would be unable to enforce, it is appropriate to grant an injunction if it is considered that it would have a real deterrent effect on the particular defendants (*Secretary of State for the Environment, Food and Rural Affairs v Meier* [2009] 1 W.L.R. 2780).

In *PJS v News Group Newspapers* [2016] A.C. 1081 the Court of Appeal had set aside an interim injunction on the grounds that the protected information was now in the public domain and therefore the injunction served no useful purpose. However the Supreme Court held that there was a difference between information being available on the internet on websites based overseas and the details being on the pages of a British newspaper. If the purpose of an injunction were to preserve a secret, it would have failed and would be futile, but it could still prevent intrusion or harassment (Lord Mance citing *CTB v News Group Newspapers Ltd* [2011] EWHC 1326 (QB); [2011] EWHC 1334 (QB)).

Minors and protected parties

2-08   The Court of Appeal has held that an injunction should not be granted against a protected party or patient incapable of understanding it, nor against a minor if there are no effective means of enforcing the order (*Wookey v Wookey; Re S (A Minor)* [1991] Fam. 121). However in *Nottingham City Council v Zain (A Minor)* [2002] 1 W.L.R. 607, where *Wookey* was not cited, an injunction was granted prohibiting a 17-year-old defendant from entering a housing estate. Parliament has now specifically provided that gang-related violence injunctions (see para.4-69) may be granted against anyone aged 14 or over.

2   ADEQUACY OF DAMAGES

2-09   "The very first principle of injunction law is that prima facie you do not obtain injunctions to restrain actionable wrongs for which damages are the proper remedy" (per Lindley LJ in *London & Blackwall Railway Co v Cross* (1886) 31 Ch. D. 354 at [369]).

If the claimant can be fully compensated by an award of damages, no injunction will normally be granted. In particular, where the wrongdoing has ceased and there is no likelihood of its recurring, an injunction will generally be refused (*Proctor v*

Bayley (1889) 42 Ch. D. 390); a permanent injunction requires the prospect of *continuing or recurring injury to the claimant*. However where the defendant's conduct was high-handed an injunction could be granted even for a minor infringement which could be addressed by damages (*Ottercroft Ltd v Scandia Care* [2016] EWCA Civ 867). In that case the defendant built a fire escape staircase in flagrant breach of an undertaking to the court; so it was not oppressive to make an order.

It is comparatively unusual for the defendant to be able to say that damages are the only available remedy in the case and that the court does not even have a discretion to grant an injunction. The more common defence is that although the claimant has made out a prima facie case for an injunction, nevertheless the court, weighing all the circumstances in the balance, should exercise its discretion against granting one.

There is a general power under s.50 of the Senior Courts Act 1981 to award damages in lieu of an injunction (even where there is no separate claim for damages), and it is here that the discretionary nature of the injunction jurisdiction becomes most apparent. The readiness of the court to refuse an injunction varies according to the branch of the law and the nature of the claimant's rights which have been infringed.

An injunction will not lie to enforce private rights, restricting the use of land against a statutory body discharging functions (such as the provision of community care) in the public interest, where a statutory compensation scheme provides the proper remedy (*Brown v Heathlands NHS Trust* [1996] 1 All E.R. 133). **2-10**

As to restrictive covenants contained in contracts of employment, see paras 4-05 to 4-06; if a covenant is found to be invalid (on the ground, for example, of restraint of trade), it will obviously not be enforced by injunction. If the covenant is enforceable there is still the question of discretion. As Cox J held in *TFS Derivatives Ltd v Morgan* [2005] IRLR 246:

"Even if the covenant is held to be reasonable, the court will then finally decide whether, as a matter of discretion, the injunctive relief sought should in all the circumstances be granted, having regard, amongst other things, to its reasonableness as at the time of trial."

Where the defendant has wrongfully interfered with the claimant's rights as an owner of property and intends to continue that interference, the claimant is prima facie entitled to an injunction (*Pride of Derby and Derbyshire Angling Association Ltd v British Celanese Ltd* [1953] Ch. 149). Special circumstances may occur in which the remedy of damages will adequately compensate the claimant for the loss he has suffered and may in the future suffer. However it is for the wrongdoer to satisfy the court that such special circumstances exist (*Mackinnon Industries v Walker* [1951] W.N. 401). The proper remedy for the occupant of a dwelling ejected contrary to the Rent Act 1977 is a mandatory injunction requiring the ejector to allow him access and occupation; he is not limited to damages, since this would encourage the very mischief which security of tenure under the Rent Act 1977 was designed to prevent (*Luganda v Service Hotels* [1969] 2 Ch. 209).

Shelfer is not completely redundant as shown by the Court of Appeal in *Jaggard v Sawyer* [1995] 1 W.L.R. 269. The defendants built a house at the end of a private cul-de-sac. When the building work was beginning the claimant threatened, but did not make, an application for an interim injunction to enforce covenants prohibiting access over her part of the cul-de-sac. By the time of the trial, the building was completed and an injunction would have been oppressive to the defendants. The judge's decision to refuse an injunction on the principles in *Shelfer* and award the claimant less than £700 in lieu was affirmed by the Court of Appeal. Millett LJ observed that if the claimant had applied for an interlocutory injunction at an early **2-11** stage, she would almost certainly have obtained it, just as claimants who apply promptly for injunctions to restrain oversailing cranes and other trespasses to airspace are generally successful; the grant of an injunction merely restores the parties to the same position, with the same relative bargaining strength, as before the trespass began.

In some cases, a money payment is not an available alternative because the claimant is a public authority or the Attorney General, and the injury is to the public at large. Where a property company had built an extension to a house which projected beyond the building line, in contravention of a statute requiring local authority consent for such a development, and the Attorney General, on the relation of the local authority, sought a mandatory injunction directing the extension to be pulled down, the court could not give damages in lieu (*Attorney General v Wimbledon House Estate Co Ltd* [1904] 2 Ch. 34). "It is an injury to the public", said Farwell J, "and there is no one to whom compensation can be made".

Discretionary factors

2-12   The public interest must be considered, but if substantial damage will be done to the claimant in the absence of an injunction, the claimant's rights should prevail over the public interest. This appears to be the result of the contrasting decisions in *Miller v Jackson* [1977] QB 966 and *Kennaway v Thompson* [1981] QB 88. In *Miller v Jackson* the claimants, whose property adjoined the village cricket field, sought an order restraining the defendants, members of the cricket club, from committing nuisance; the effect of this would be that cricket on that ground would have to stop. The Court of Appeal weighed the claimants' prima facie entitlement to quiet enjoyment of their property against the public interest in cricket being played on the ground. Although damages could not entirely compensate the claimants, the court (by a majority) exercised its discretion against the grant of an injunction. In *Kennaway v Thompson*, the claimant owned land adjacent to an artificial lake where very noisy motor boat racing and other water sports took place almost daily from April to October. The Court of Appeal granted an injunction to restrict the use of the lake, for activities creating more than 75 decibels of noise, to a small number of events covering a total of 10 days each year. However, where the defendant is a body exercising statutory functions in the public interest, no injunction will be granted: see *Brown v Heathlands NHS Trust* [1996] 1 All E.R. 133, above.

Damages may be awarded under s.50 in lieu of an injunction for future infringements of the claimant's human rights (*Marcic v Thames Water Utilities Ltd (No.2)* [2002] QB 1003).

Where the defendant is in breach of a valid express negative covenant, an injunction will normally be granted but the judge still has and must exercise a discretion. The earliest cases suggested that there is no question of the balance of convenience or inconvenience, or the amount of damage or injury; the injunction merely gives the court's sanction to what the parties have already contracted for (*Doherty v Allman* (1878) 3 App. Cas. 709). This led to suggestions in cases that such injunctions issue "as of course" and there must be special or exceptional circumstances or particular hardship before the court will exercise its discretion to refuse an injunction (see e.g. *Insurance Company v Lloyds Syndicate* [1995] 1 Lloyds Rep 272 at 277 and *Araci v Fallon* [2011] EWCA Civ 668; (2011) 155(23) S.J.L.B. 39).

2-13   Although *Lawrence v Fen Tigers* concerned a nuisance claim rather than breach of covenant, it was held in *Prophet v Huggett* [2014] I.R.L.R. 618 (at first instance) that the Supreme Court's intention to preserve the court's discretion was "equally apposite" to cases about covenants. Whilst expressing reservations about the direct applicability of *Lawrence*, Sir Colin Rimer in *D v P* [2016] ICR 688 agreed that phrases such as "exceptional circumstances" were not helpful, although he otherwise endorsed the approach in *Insurance Company v Lloyds Syndicate*. He said that the starting point is that the ordinary remedy to enforce a negative covenant is an injunction. But as an injunction is a discretionary remedy, that is not the finishing point and the categories of circumstances under which an injunction may be refused "are never closed and every case will turn on its own facts" (*D v P* at [21]). The approach to the exercise of the discretion is not a mechanistic one and the burden of showing why an injunction should not be granted is on the person who would otherwise be enjoined. The Court held that these principles were consistent with *Lawrence* and the earlier authorities.

D v P confirms that the factors identified in previous cases are still relevant, but are not the exhaustive factors for granting or refusing an injunction and should not be applied mechanistically. However courts will remain alert to prevent a defendant trying to buy the privilege of infringing the claimant's rights. A submission that damages should be awarded in lieu of an injunction on the ground that an injunction will not benefit the claimant comes ill from a defendant who has himself created that situation by acting in breach of obligations freely undertaken.

The test for granting an injunction is stricter where the injunction sought is mandatory (see below at para.2-20 and *Charrington v Simons & Co Ltd* [1971] 1 W.L.R. 598), but the question is one of substance, not form, and does not depend on the use of positive or negative forms of expression (*Lord Strathcona Steamship Co v Dominion Coal Co* [1926] A.C. 108 at [121]).

Quia timet injunctions: damages in lieu

Generally damages are only awarded in respect of injury actually committed before the court case is brought. Quia timet applications for an injunction provide an exception. The claimant has not yet suffered injury but "fears" that injury will occur. If the court feels that damages are more appropriate than an injunction, or should be given in addition to an injunction, it may award damages even though the wrongdoing remains in the future (*Leeds Industrial Co-operative Society Ltd v Slack* [1924] A.C. 851; see also *Attorney General v Blake* [2001] 1 A.C. 268 at [281], per Lord Nicholls). This does not, however, dispense with the need in all quia timet applications for the claimant to show a substantial likelihood of damage occurring, which is both imminent and real (*Elliot v Islington LBC* [2012] 7 E.G. 90 (C.S.) and, as Chadwick LJ described it in *Lloyd v Symonds* [1998] EWCA Civ 511, "irreparable harm—that is to say, harm which, if it occurs, cannot be reversed or restrained by an immediate interlocutory injunction and cannot be adequately compensated by an award for damages". **2-14**

Damages in addition

The court may, of course, make an award of damages in addition to granting an injunction in a proper case. However where the claimant in an action for nuisance by noise or vibration successfully claims an injunction (or obtains an undertaking), that being the real remedy in the action, and also asks for general damages without being able to prove any special damage, his damages may be limited to a nominal amount (*Lipman v Pulman (George) & Sons Ltd* (1904) 91 L.T. 132). **2-15**

3   ACQUIESCENCE OR LACHES

2-16   These two terms are often used interchangeably, but it is better practice to refer to them distinctly. They overlap, but neither is wholly included in the other. Both involve *inaction* on the part of the claimant.

Acquiescence

2-17   "If a person having a right, and seeing another person about to commit, or in the course of committing an act infringing upon that right, stands by in such a manner as really to induce the person committing the act, and who might otherwise have abstained from it, to believe that he assents to its being committed, he cannot afterwards be heard to complain of the act. This ... is the proper sense of the term 'acquiescence'." (per Thesiger LJ in *De Bussche v Alt* (1878) 8 Ch. D. 286 at 314.)

Acquiescence, then, involves the claimant standing by while the act complained of is still taking place, or has not yet taken place. It does require that the claimant should know that the act is being done, for otherwise he cannot be said to be acquiescing in it (*Re Pauling's Settlement Trusts* [1964] Ch. 303). Moreover, he must be aware that his legal rights are involved. Where a householder raised no objection to the construction of a sewer under a pathway behind his house and garden, but did not realise (his title deeds being in the possession of mortgagees) that the pathway was his own property, he was not debarred by acquiescence from bringing an action for an injunction to restrain the discharge of effluent through his land (*Armstrong v Sheppard & Short Ltd* [1959] 2 QB 384). Misleading assurances by the defendant may also excuse what might otherwise amount to acquiescence on the part of the claimant (*Isenberg v East India House Estate Co Ltd* (1863) 3 De G.J. & Sm. 263). The Privy Council in *Singh v Rainbow Court Townhouses* [2018] UKPC 19 approved the dicta in *Chatsworth Estates Co v Fewell* [1931] 1 Ch 224:

"It is in all cases a question of degree. It is in many ways analogous to the doctrine of estoppel, and I think it is a fair test to treat it in that way and ask, 'Have the plaintiffs by their acts and omissions represented to the defendant that the covenants are no longer enforceable...?'"

A claimant who has acquiesced is only debarred from relief altogether where it would be dishonest or unconscionable for him, after the delay, to seek to enforce his rights. However even if seeking an injunction after acquiescence falls short of being dishonest or unconscionable, the court still has a discretion to refuse an injunction and award damages in lieu.

2-18   Expense incurred or goodwill built up by the defendant and a failure by the claimant to apply for interlocutory relief at an early stage may all properly be taken into account as weighing against the grant of an injunction. Where the defendant installed amusement machines in his tea room premises in breach of covenant and the claimants (assignees of the benefit of the covenant), confused as to the extent of their rights, took no action for three years during which time the defendant spent large sums and built up his business, the court refused an injunction but awarded damages (*Shaw v Applegate* [1977] 1 W.L.R. 970). Buckley LJ nevertheless noted (at [978E]) that delay caused by a claimant's doubts about his rights should not be conclusive against him:

"It should not, I think, be the policy of the courts to push people into litigation until they are really sure that they have got a genuine complaint and have got a case in which they are likely to be able to succeed."

Delay is particularly likely to be fatal when the claimant has waited until the eleventh hour before taking action. In *Bates v Lord Hailsham of St Marylebone* [1972] 1 W.L.R. 1373, the applicant sought at two hours' notice to restrain the Lord Chancellor and others from making an order with regard to solicitors' remuneration; the tardiness of the application was not sufficiently explained. Even litigation launched with several weeks to go before the prospective act complained of may be too late if the claimant had notice earlier. In *Morecambe and Heysham Corp v Mecca Ltd* [1962] R.P.C. 145, the claimants' object was to stop the holding of the "Miss Britain" competition in June; they knew all the relevant facts by mid-December but did not give notice of motion until April. Interim relief was refused.

Sometimes the claimant's acquiescence takes a more active form, so as to debar him from complaining of the breach. If, for example, the claimant seeks to enforce a restrictive covenant prohibiting the use of premises as a shop, his case will be fatally weakened by the emergence of evidence that he patronised the shop (*Sayers v Collyer* (1884) 28 Ch. D. 103):

> "The sale of beer by the defendant began in 1879, only four doors from the house where the claimant lived, and went on till the commencement of the action [in 1882]... and during some part of that period the claimant himself bought beer at the defendant's house. I can hardly imagine a stronger case of acquiescence than this." (Per Baggallay LJ at 107.)

Laches

This is unreasonable inaction by the claimant *after* the infringement of his rights had already taken place, such as to make it unjust to the defendant that an injunction should be granted. There are two elements: the delay, and the consequent injustice. Delay in bringing an action is not of itself (subject to the operation of the Limitation Acts) a reason for sending the claimant away empty handed; a litigant who issues his claim form one day short of the limitation period is within his rights at law. However since the injunction is, as we have seen, an equitable remedy, the doctrine of laches may be pleaded as a defence. Although it is not an immutable requirement, some form of detrimental reliance is usually an essential ingredient of laches (per Lord Neuberger of Abbotsbury in *Fisher v Brooker* [2009] 1 W.L.R. 1764, a case of infringement of copyright). Two important factors to be weighed in the balance are the length of the delay and the nature of the acts done in the interval (*Lindsay Petroleum Co v Hurd* (1874) L.R. 5 P.C. 221). In some laches cases it is not the length of the delay which matters but "the circumstances in which it occurred and, to a significant extent, the reason why it occurred" (per Edis J in *Legends Live v Harrison* [2017] I.R.L.R. 59). Where there are numerous claimants and concerted action by them is difficult, laches will be less readily imputed (*Legg v ILEA* [1972] 1 W.L.R. 1245).

2-19

Laches is most effective as a defence at the interlocutory stage. Mere delay in bringing an action (as opposed to acquiescence) does not bar a claim for a permanent injunction or any other permanent relief in respect of a cause of action where there is a statutory period of limitation within which claims must be brought (*Archbold v Scully* (1861) 9 H.L. Cas. 360 at [383]; *Re Pauling's Settlement Trusts* [1962] 1 W.L.R. 86 at [115]). Nonetheless, as Lord Neuberger observed in *Fisher v Brooker*, if the court is satisfied that it would be oppressive to grant an injunction in the particular circumstances because of prejudicial delay, it may refuse an injunction and leave the claimant to his remedy in damages.

4   MANDATORY AND QUIA TIMET INJUNCTIONS AT TRIAL

Mandatory injunctions

2-20   Special considerations apply to mandatory injunctions, which the courts are traditionally more reluctant to grant. The rules as to the discretionary nature of the remedy, and the relevance of the claimant's conduct, still apply, but there are also important distinctions. By granting a prohibitory injunction, the court does no more than prevent for the future the continuance or repetition of the conduct of which the claimant complains. However, a mandatory injunction goes further than that.

In *Co-operative Insurance Society Ltd v Argyll Stores (Holdings) Ltd* [1998] A.C. 1 the claimants, owners of a shopping centre, sought a mandatory injunction to enforce a covenant to keep a supermarket open. The House of Lords held that the claimants should be confined to a remedy in damages. The speech of Lord Hoffmann contains a valuable review of the law relating to mandatory injunctions. Two types of case should be distinguished: where the order requires the defendant to achieve a result, and where it requires him to carry on an activity such as a business over a period of time. Lord Hoffmann listed four arguments:

(1) *The need for constant supervision.* This is the usual objection to orders to carry on a business. (It has less force where the order is to achieve a result.) There is the risk of repeated applications to the court. The defendant, who *ex hypothesi* did not think it in his economic interests to continue with the business, is being required to do so "under a sword of Damocles". However this did not prevent a court in *Schillings International LLP v Scott* [2018] EWHC 1210 (Ch) making an interim injunction against a partner to comply with the LLP agreement until his retirement on the basis that it did not lie in his mouth to say that "an injunction would be oppressive if it made him comply with parts of his bargain".

(2) *The expense of enforcement.* Because an injunction carries the contempt sanction, an application to enforce the order is likely to be "a heavy and expensive piece of litigation". In cases of carrying on an activity, this may occur repeatedly.

(3) *The need for precision.* "The court must be careful to see that the defendant knows exactly what he has to do, and this means not as a matter of law but as a matter of fact" (per Lord Upjohn in *Morris v Redland Bricks Ltd* [1970] A.C. 652). However, Lord Hoffmann went on:

> "[P]recision is of course a matter of degree and the courts have shown themselves willing to cope with a certain degree of imprecision in cases of orders requiring the achievement of a result in which the [claimant]'s merits appeared strong. Like all the reasons which I have been discussing it is, taken alone, merely a discretionary matter to be taken into account. It is, however, a very important one."

> In *Haederle v Thomas* [2016] EWHC 1866 (Ch) Henderson J held that a typing error in a freezing injunction made the order unclear and uncertain to the defendant, a German speaker then acting in person (though it would have been obvious to a English practitioner familiar with freezing injunctions) and that the defendant should not be at risk of imprisonment for contempt when the order served upon him was deficient in this material respect.

(4) *Unjust enrichment of the claimant.* The grant of a mandatory injunction, said
Lord Hoffmann:

> "may cause injustice by allowing the [claimant] to enrich himself at the
> defendant's expense. The loss which the defendant may suffer through having to
> comply with the order (for example, by running a business at a loss for an
> indefinite period) may be far greater than the [claimant] would suffer from the
> contract being broken."

In exceptional cases, the discretion to grant an order requiring the continuation   **2-21**
of an activity remains. The "settled principles" laid down in *CIS v Argyll Stores*,
however, make it clear that such cases will be few and far between.

It has been said that injunctions should be "confined to cases where the injury
done to the claimant cannot be estimated and sufficiently compensated by a pecuni-
ary sum" (*Isenberg v East India Estate Co Ltd* (1863) 3 De G.J. & Sm. 263). In that
case, an injunction was unsuccessfully sought to compel the defendant to pull down
part of a new building which interfered with the claimant's right to light. Lord
Westbury LC held that instead, there should be an inquiry as to damages.

If the defendant presses on with building operations after receiving notice that   **2-22**
an action for nuisance or disturbance of an easement has been or may be commenced, he does so at the risk of an injunction ordering demolition (*Smith v Day*
(1880) 13 Ch. D. 651); he is not entitled to buy his way out of his wrongdoing
(*Wakeham v Wood* (1981) 125 S.J. 608). However even where the defendant has
continued building in breach of a restrictive covenant in the face of protest or the
issue of proceedings, there is no rule that the claimant will be granted an injunction if he succeeds at the trial (*Wrotham Park Estate Co v Parkside Homes Ltd*
[1974] 1 W.L.R. 798). In the last-named case, the judge refused to order the demolition of houses built in breach of a restrictive covenant, saying that

> "it would be an unpardonable waste of much needed houses to direct that they now be
> pulled down ... without hesitation I decline to grant a mandatory injunction." (See also
> *Jaggard v Sawyer* [1995] 1 W.L.R. 269, cited at para.2-11.)

By contrast, where the defendant had significantly trespassed on the claimant's
land by building a garage, the Court of Appeal held that damages could not be
awarded in lieu of an injunction; the only choice was between an order for possession and an order for demolition (*Harrow LBC v Donohoe* [1993] C.L.Y. 4041).

A mandatory injunction will not be granted to require an employee to carry out
work under his contract of employment (see paras 4-01 to 4-04), and only rarely
to compel an employer to provide work (see paras 4-10 to 4-13).

Quia timet mandatory injunctions

A mandatory injunction may also be sought where no damage has yet occurred.   **2-23**
Such orders may not involve the undoing of what has *already* been done, but may
still be troublesome and costly for the defendant. The principles to be considered
in a quia timet application for a mandatory injunction were laid down authoritatively
by Lord Upjohn in *Redland Bricks Ltd v Morris* [1970] A.C. 652 at [665G]–
[666G]. He began by noting that the grant of a mandatory injunction is entirely
discretionary, and unlike a negative injunction it can never be "as of course"; every
case must depend essentially upon its own particular circumstances, but the following general principles apply:

(1) "A mandatory injunction can only be granted where the claimant shows a
     very strong probability upon the facts that grave damage will accrue to him

in the future. As Lord Dunedin said in 1919, it is not sufficient to say 'timeo' (*A-G of Canada v Ritchie Contracting and Supply Co Ltd* [1919] AC 999, 1005). It is a jurisdiction to be exercised sparingly and with caution but in the proper case unhesitatingly." This was applied in *Secretary of State for the Environment v Drury* [2004] 1 W.L.R. 1906 CA, where Wilson J, giving the leading judgment, approved at [20] the proposition that the applicant "must prove that there is an imminent danger of very substantial damage". Imminent in these circumstances is used in the sense that the circumstances must be such that the remedy sought is not premature (*Hooper v Rogers* [1975] Ch. 43, Russell LJ at [50]).

(2)   The claimant must also show that damages will not be a sufficient or adequate remedy if such damage does happen.

> "Unlike the case where a negative injunction is granted to prevent the continuance or recurrence of a wrongful act, the question of the cost to the defendant to do works to prevent or lessen the likelihood of a future apprehended wrong must be an element to be taken into account."

Lord Upjohn went on to give two contrasting examples. Where the defendant has acted without regard to his neighbour's rights or, to sum it up, "wantonly and quite unreasonably", he may be ordered to restore the status quo even if the expense to him is disproportionate to the advantage to the claimant. But where he has acted "reasonably, though in the event wrongly", the court can bear in mind that the damage may never occur, or that if it does occur the claimant can claim damages, and refuse to make a mandatory order involving the defendant in heavy expenditure. The court may also adopt a compromise course by ordering the defendant not to fully restore the status quo, but to take steps which will reduce the likelihood of damage to the claimant.

(3)   Finally, Lord Upjohn mentioned an important factor—the need for precision in a positive injunction (see the dictum cited in para.2-20). In *Redland Bricks Ltd v Morris* itself, the county court judge had granted a mandatory injunction directing the defendants to restore support to the claimant's land. This order was set aside by the House of Lords, partly on the grounds of hardship to the defendants, and partly because it gave the defendants no indication of exactly what was to be done. The requirement of precision applies to prohibitory injunctions as well (and indeed to all orders of a court), but it is in the field of mandatory orders that the problem is most acute in practice.

The overarching principle remains a discretionary balancing act. Russell LJ said in *Hooper v Rogers* [1975] Ch. 43 (a claim for damages in lieu of a mandatory injunction to compel a farmer to reinstate some land) at p.50: "In truth it seems to me that the degree of probability of future injury is not an absolute standard: what is to be aimed at is justice between the parties, having regard to all the relevant circumstances." Similarly in *Network Rail Infrastructure v Williams* [2018] EWCA Civ 1514 Sir Terence Etherton C said that it is possibly "too prescriptive" to say that there must be proof of imminent physical injury for a quia timet injunction to be granted, and that what matters is "the probability and likely gravity of damage rather than simply its imminence"). It is also useful to have regard to the cases on interim mandatory injunctions (see para.3-36) as there is much overlap in the approach taken and the factors mentioned in *Nottingham Building Society v Eurodynamics Systems Plc* [1993] F.S.R. 468, Chadwick J as approved in *Zockoll Group Ltd v Mercury Communications Ltd* [1998] F.S.R. 354.

CHAPTER 3

Criteria: Interim Injunctions

1 SIGNIFICANCE OF INTERIM INJUNCTIONS

The hearing of an application for an interim injunction is not a trial on the merits. **3-01**
There is usually no oral evidence and no opportunity for cross-examination. The
full pre-trial processes of disclosure and inspection of documents have not occurred; indeed the statements of each side's case may not yet have been served. An
interim hearing is often only listed for an hour and rarely lasts longer than one court
day. The criteria applied must inevitably be different, because neither side's case
can be "proved" as at a final hearing. The function of an interim injunction is often
described as a process which is designed to "hold the ring" (see e.g. *United States
of America v Abacha* [2015] 1 W.L.R. 1917) pending final determination of the
merits or other disposal of the dispute.

Nevertheless, it must not be thought that interim injunctions are in any way a
secondary or temporary remedy in practice. Quite the reverse is the truth. The courts
grant far more interim than final injunctions each year, simply because, as Lord
Denning MR put it:

> "Nearly always ... these cases do not go to trial. The parties accept the prima facie view
> of the court or settle the case. At any rate, in 99 cases out of 100, it goes no further." *Fel-
> lowes & Son v Fisher* [1976] QB 122 at [129G].)

The effective finality of an interim injunction depends on the area of law **3-02**
involved. Cases involving the rights of owners of real property, such as nuisance
claims, often reach final judgment because the dispute is permanent. Conversely,
the grant of an interim injunction in an industrial dispute (if it is available: see
para.4-14) or in matrimonial litigation is usually the end of the matter, since by the
time the claim comes on for trial months later the factual position may have changed
substantially and the assistance of the court may no longer be required. Many cases
are settled once the claimant obtains, or fails to obtain, an interim injunction,
although the increasing availability and practicality of the speedy trial process
means that the court can now decide a dispute at a final hearing within a matter of
weeks.

Where the injunction sought may refer to a single occasion which will be long
past by the time a trial (even a speedy trial) on the merits could be held, so that if
the claimant succeeds, the "interim" injunction will have effect once and for all,
interim relief may still be available (*Woodford v Smith* [1970] 1 W.L.R. 806). If
there is plainly no defence to the claim and the only object in raising a defence is
delay, an injunction should issue even if it gives the claimant his whole remedy
before the trial (*Manchester Corp v Connolly* [1970] 1 Ch. 420). Where the granting of the injunction would amount to a final determination at the interim stage, the
court will take into account the strengths and weaknesses of the respective cases

and the likelihood of the claimant's eventual success at trial (*Araci v Fallon* [2011] EWCA Civ 668).

2   UNDERTAKING IN DAMAGES

3-03   If the claimant obtains an interim injunction but subsequently the case goes to trial and he fails to obtain a final order, the defendant will meanwhile have been restrained unjustly and will generally be entitled to damages for any loss he has sustained. The practice has therefore grown up, in almost every case where an interim injunction is to be granted, of requiring the claimant to undertake to pay any damages subsequently found due to the defendant as compensation if the injunction cannot be justified at trial.

An undertaking or cross-undertaking in damages in favour of the defendant will be inserted automatically in the order of the court (save in family proceedings or in Competition Appeal Tribunal fast-track cases) unless the judge specifies otherwise (Practice Direction PD 25A 5.1(1)). There is no jurisdiction to compel a claimant to give an undertaking in damages, but in most non-family cases, if he refuses to give one he is unlikely to obtain an interim injunction. If a claimant misrepresents the position as to his financial position or fails to disclose some material fact in his statement or affidavit, then that may be grounds for an application to discharge the injunction (see para.6-13).

In *SmithKline Beecham Plc v Apotex Europe Ltd* [2007] Ch 71 Jacob LJ said:

> "The practice of requiring a cross-undertaking from a plaintiff who sought an interlocutory (now called 'interim') injunction developed in the 19th century. The reason was that the court at the interlocutory stage did not know who the ultimate winner would be. So if an injunction was granted but the case ultimately failed, the person enjoined would have a remedy.
>
> The legal justification of the practice stems from the discretion of the court to grant or withhold an injunction given by what is now s.37 of the [Senior Courts] Act 1981 ... The court in effect says to the plaintiff (now 'claimant') seeking an interim injunction: 'I will not grant you an interim injunction unless you give the cross-undertaking,' see e.g. F. *Hoffmann-La Roche v Secretary of State* [1975] A.C. 295 at 361 per Lord Diplock. It follows that the court cannot impose a cross-undertaking on a claimant against his will—it is the 'price' he must 'pay' for the grant of the injunction.
>
> A party who is granted an interim injunction but who ultimately loses the full trial is not regarded as a wrongdoer because he got an interim injunction. Sometimes, for convenience and want of a better term, the expression 'wrongful injunction' is used, but in truth there is nothing wrongful about it. The decision whether or not to grant it is made on the basis of a necessarily incomplete picture. The decision depends on all the circumstances of the case, generally whether or not damages to an ultimately victorious claimant would be an adequate remedy, whether the claimant can show a serious issue to be tried and so on. There is no need here to recite all the various considerations which may arise— *American Cyanamid v Ethicon* [1975] A.C. 396 and the many other cases about grant or refusal of an interim injunction are discussed in all the books. Lord Diplock put it broadly in *NWL v Woods* [1979] 3 All E.R. 614 at 624:
>
> > 'In assessing whether what is compendiously called the balance of convenience lies in granting or refusing interlocutory injunctions in actions between parties of undoubted solvency the judge is engaged in weighing the respective risks that injustice may result from his deciding one way rather than the other at a stage when the evidence is incomplete.'
>
> But a number of particular considerations do call for mention in the context of this case. First is that the existence of the cross-undertaking in damages is a very material considera-

tion in whether or not an injunction should be granted. The fact that an ultimately unsuccessful claimant will have to compensate the defendant for having 'wrongly' stopped his proposed activity is a major factor in assessing the balance of risk.

Second is that the position of third parties or the public who may be affected by the injunction is a matter which the court can take into account in exercising its discretion. This is so in limited circumstances even for a final injunction, see e.g. *Miller v Jackson* [1977] 1 QB 966 and *Chiron v Organon (No.10)* [1995] F.S.R. 325."

This undertaking is regarded as the price for interfering with the defendant's **3-04** freedom before he has been found liable for anything. It is fairness rather than likelihood of loss that leads to the requirement of a cross-undertaking (*JSC Mezhdunarodniy Promyshlenniy Bank v Pugachev* [2015] EWCA Civ 139 citing *Financial Services Authority v Sinaloa Gold plc* [2013] 2 AC 28). As Lord Toulson observed in *Les Laboratoires Servier v Apotex Inc* [2015] A.C. 430:

> "Cross-undertakings are a standard and valuable feature of litigation, particularly but not only in commercial litigation. There is a public interest in their enforceability in bona fide disputes. It saves the court from having to make a more detailed—and therefore time consuming and expensive—assessment of the merits at an interlocutory stage than might otherwise be necessary, since the cross-undertaking is designed to protect the defendant against the applicant gaining a financial advantage from obtaining an injunction which is later set aside on the claim failing."

The same principle is followed if, instead of an interim injunction being granted, the defendant has undertaken to the court not to do the act or acts complained of pending final determination of the case. Despite the superficially voluntary nature of such an undertaking, the unjustified damage to the defendant if the claim fails at trial is just the same as if an interim injunction had been granted. The claimant will therefore be required to give a cross-undertaking in damages.

The general principles for assessing damages payable under an undertaking or cross-undertaking in damages were outlined by Norris J in *Les Laboratoires Servier v Apotex Inc* [2009] F.S.R. 3 and approved by the Court of Appeal in *AstraZeneca AB v KRKA dd Novo Mesto* (2015) 145 B.M.L.R. 188 [2015] EWCA Civ 484: see 6-05, below.

In each of two cases in 1990, the claimants sought a final injunction in their **3-05** pleadings but did not seek an interim injunction since an undertaking in damages would have been required and the potential liability if the undertaking were to be enforced was enormous. The defendants applied to strike out the claim for a final injunction unless the claimant was willing to apply for an interim injunction and give an undertaking in damages. In *Blue Town Investments Ltd v Higgs & Hill Ltd* [1990] 1 W.L.R. 696, the injunction claimed was for the demolition of buildings supposedly infringing the claimants' right to light. The right to light had been valued at £7,500; the cost of complying with an injunction at trial would be up to £1 million. Browne-Wilkinson VC held that the prospects of an injunction being granted at trial were "minimal" and granted the defendants' application. In *Oxy Electric Ltd v Zainuddin* [1991] 1 W.L.R. 115, however, the claimants had a seriously arguable case for a final injunction restraining building in breach of a restrictive covenant, and Hoffmann J refused to force them to apply for an interim injunction.

An undertaking in damages in the event of a successful appeal is not generally required from a party who is granted an injunction at trial, but there is a discretion to do so (*Gwembe Valley Development Co Ltd v Koshy (No.4) The Times,* 28 February, 2002, Rimer J).

The affidavit or statement in support of an injunction application should deal with **3-06** the claimant's ability to honour the undertaking in damages; if there is a subsequent change in the claimant's financial position affecting his ability to honour the undertaking, especially in a freezing order case, he is under a duty to disclose it to the defendant (*Staines v Walsh* [2003] EWHC 1486 (Ch), *The Times,* 1 August, 2003). The fact that a claimant is legally aided or of limited means does not preclude the grant of an injunction in a proper case, with an undertaking in damages being given even though it is likely to prove of very little worth (*Allen v Jambo Holdings Ltd* [1980] 1 W.L.R. 1252).

Fortifying the undertaking

3-07   Where, however, there are doubts about the claimant's resources, the court has discretion to require either security or the payment of money into court to "fortify" the undertaking, or (as an alternative) an undertaking from a more financially secure person or body. In cases where the claimant is a subsidiary of a large company and apparently lacking funds, it is common for the parent company to be invited to guarantee the undertaking in damages in writing. The applicant for fortification must show a sufficient level of risk of loss to require fortification and that the contemplated loss would be caused by the injunction. Someone with extensive and substantial assets may reasonably suppose that substantial damage will be incurred if he is unable to deal freely and properly with those assets (*JSC Mezhdunarodniy Promyshlenniy Bank v Pugachev* [2016] 1 W.L.R. 160).

In a freezing injunction case, if the defendant can show that it has a good arguable case that it will suffer loss in consequence of the order, it should be protected by requiring fortification of the undertaking. "It is completely contrary to principle to require proof on the balance of probabilities on such an [interlocutory] application and to do so would encourage wasteful satellite litigation" (per Tomlinson LJ in *Energy Venture Partners Ltd v Malabu Oil and Gas Ltd* [2015] 1 W.L.R. 2309 at [53]). As to the amount of the cross-undertaking or fortification, the court must make "an intelligent estimate to be made of the likely amount of any loss which may be suffered by the applicant for fortification… by reason of the making of an interim order" (ibid.).

It is too late to apply for security to fortify an undertaking in damages when the relevant interim injunction has been discharged (*Commodity Ocean Transport v Basford Unicorn Industries; The Mito* [1987] 2 Lloyd's Rep. 197). A respondent to an anti-suit injunction which gave undertakings to the court could not be required to fortify such undertakings (*Orient Express Lines v Peninsular Shipping Services* [2013] EWHC 3855 (Comm)).

In whose favour does the undertaking operate?

3-08   It was held by Morritt J that in a case with more than one defendant, the undertaking operates in favour of all defendants, even if the injunction is sought against only one of them (*Dubai Bank v Galadari (No.2), The Times,* 11 October, 1989, following *Tucker v New Brunswick Trading Co* (1890) 44 Ch. D. 249).

However in two cases, an attempt was made, based on a previous version of the Practice Direction, to argue that an undertaking in damages should routinely operate in favour of anyone, whether a party or not, who may sustain loss by reason of the grant of an interim injunction. In *Miller Brewing Co v The Mersey Docks and Harbour Co* [2004] F.S.R. 5 (cited by Lewison J in *SmithKline Beecham plc v Apotex Europe Ltd* [2006] 1 W.L.R. 872 at 889), Neuberger J rejected the contention. The judge pointed out that this would require the claimant to sign not merely a blank cheque in the defendant's favour, but "a series of blank cheques in favour of third parties of whose interests and existence he might be unaware and for whose losses he might find himself liable even though he might be entitled to his injunction"

If a third party was detrimentally and unfairly affected by an interim injunction, his interests could be put before the court by the defendant or the third party himself could apply to the court to vary or discharge the injunction or to have the benefit of the undertaking in damages extended to him.

The same approach was taken by the Court of Appeal in the *SmithKline Beecham* case. Jacob LJ said:

3-09

"....[T]hird parties unconnected with the dispute ('neutrals') who may incur expense in complying with the order may specifically be covered by a cross-undertaking. This was first required by Robert Goff J in a freezing order case, *Searose v Seatrain* [1981] 1 W.L.R. 894. The practice in freezing order cases of requiring from the plaintiff an express undertaking to indemnify any third party affected by the order against all expenses reasonably incurred in complying with the order and all liabilities flowing from such compliance was endorsed by this court in *Z v A-Z* [1982] QB 558 ...

[U]ntil this case, it has always been assumed that an outsider (as I will call a legal entity which is not a party to the proceedings) does not have a claim as of right against a party who obtained a 'wrongful' interim injunction which caused him expense or damage. The only possible exception to that is Lord Denning MR's statement that a party who gives notice of a freezing injunction to a bank or innocent third party enters into an implied contract whereby he will pay for the costs of that party complying with the order—see *Z v A-Z* at p.575... [But the] Court has jurisdiction to require a party seeking an interim injunction to give a cross-undertaking for the benefit of third parties affected by the injunction, see *Allied Irish Bank v Ashford Hotels* [1997] 3 All E.R. 309. This stems from the discretionary nature of the jurisdiction conferred by s.37 of the 1981 Act."

Dispensing with the undertaking

The court has a discretion to grant an interim injunction without requiring an undertaking in damages. There are a number of types of case in which an undertaking is generally dispensed with. They include:

3-10

(a) matrimonial and domestic proceedings concerning personal conduct (see Ch.10); however where an injunction was sought in a family case restraining the disposal of property allegedly vested in a third party, an undertaking in damages was required (*W v H* [2001] 1 All E.R. 300);

(b) where the Crown applies for an injunction to enforce what is prima facie the law of the land (*F Hoffmann-La Roche & Co AG v Secretary of State for Trade and Industry* [1975] A.C. 295; *Director General of Fair Trading v Tobyward Ltd* [1989] 1 W.L.R. 517) or to uphold the proper administration of justice (*Attorney General v News Group Newspapers Ltd* [1987] QB 1). If the Crown is seeking to enforce its proprietary rights, this rule does not apply. In a case where the Attorney General sued to recover funds belonging to a charity, an undertaking in damages was required from the receiver of the charity, limited to the amount of the fund (*Attorney General v Wright* [1988] 1 W.L.R. 164);

(c) where a local authority or other public authority seeks to enforce what is prima facie the law of the land (*Kirklees MBC v Wickes Building Supplies Ltd* [1993] A.C. 227);

(d) where a City regulatory body seeks an injunction using its statutory powers (*SIB v Lloyd-Wright* [1993] 4 All E.R. 210; *Financial Services Authority v Sinaloa Gold Plc* [2011] EWCA Civ 1158); likewise where the United

States Securities and Exchange Commission seeks a freezing injunction in support of proceedings against alleged fraudsters in the United States (*United States Securities and Exchange Commission v Manterfield* [2009] 2 All E.R. 1009). So long as the public authority is willing to meet the costs and expenses incurred by third parties in complying with the order, it is not usually required to give a cross-undertaking in damages as well (*FSA v Sinaloa Gold Plc*);

(e) in a fast-track application under rule 58 of the Competition Appeal Tribunal Rules 2015 the CAT has a discretion to dispense with the cross-undertaking.

3-11 Where a company in liquidation or receivership applies for an interim injunction, the usual practice is to require an undertaking in damages from the liquidator or receiver, limited to the amount of the assets available to him or to a specified sum which is a reasonable estimate of those assets (*Re DPR Futures Ltd* [1989] 1 W.L.R. 778). However the extent of the cross-undertaking is a matter of discretion and the mere fact that litigation is being brought by a liquidator of an insolvent company does not require the cross-undertaking to be capped, although it is a highly relevant factor (*JSC Mezhdunarodniy Promyshlenniy Bank v Pugachev* [2016] 1 W.L.R. 160).

In *R. v Inspectorate of Pollution Ex p. Greenpeace Ltd* [1994] 1 W.L.R. 570, the Court of Appeal, refusing a stay pending judicial review proceedings, took into account that the applicant had given no undertaking in damages.

3 THE AMERICAN CYANAMID CASE

3-12 The decision of the House of Lords in *American Cyanamid Co v Ethicon Ltd* [1975] A.C. 396 clarified, or (in the opinion of some practitioners) revolutionised, the approach of the courts to interim applications on notice for prohibitory injunctions. The guidelines laid down by Lord Diplock are still regarded as the leading source of law on the subject, although as the Court of Appeal pointed out in *Cayne v Global Natural Resources Plc* [1984] 1 All E.R. 225, they are based on the proposition that there will be a trial on the merits at a later stage when the rights of the parties will be determined; in reality this happens only in a very small percentage of cases. Therefore although the *Cyanamid* guidelines are normally closely followed in interim injunction applications, there may be room to argue that a more stringent test is required in some circumstances before relief is granted. Support for this approach comes from Kerr LJ in *Cambridge Nutrition Ltd v BBC* [1990] 3 All E.R. 523 at [534j]:

"It is important to bear in mind that the *American Cyanamid* case contains no principle of universal application. The only such principle is the statutory power of the court to grant injunctions when it is just and convenient to do so. The *American Cyanamid* case is no more than a set of useful guidelines which apply in many cases. It must never be used as a rule of thumb, let alone as a straitjacket ... The *American Cyanamid* case provides an authoritative and most helpful approach to cases where the function of the court in relation to the grant or refusal of interim injunctions is to hold the balance as justly as possible in situations where the substantial issues between the parties can only be resolved by a trial. In my view ... the present case is not in that category. Neither side is interested in monetary compensation, and once the interim decision has been given little, if anything, will remain in practice."

The guidelines may be conveniently discussed under the following headings:

(a) a serious question to be tried;

(b) inadequacy of damages to either side;
(c) balance of convenience;
(d) special cases.

A serious question to be tried

The claimant does not need to show a prima facie case, in the sense of convinc-   **3-13**
ing the court that on the evidence before it he is more likely than not to obtain a
final injunction at trial:

> "The evidence available to the court at the hearing of the application for an interim injunc-
> tion is incomplete. It is given on affidavit and has not been tested by oral cross-
> examination. The purpose sought to be achieved by giving to the court discretion to grant
> such injunctions would be stultified if the discretion were clogged by a technical rule
> forbidding its exercise if on that incomplete untested evidence the court evaluated the
> chances of the claimant's ultimate success in the action at 50 per cent or less, but permit-
> ting its exercise if the court evaluated his chances at more than 50 per cent ... there is no
> such rule ... The court no doubt must be satisfied that ... there is a serious question to be
> tried ..." (*American Cyanamid* at [406G-407G].)

> "If the extent of the uncompensatable disadvantage to each party would not differ widely,
> it may not be improper to take into account in tipping the balance the relative strength of
> each party's case as revealed by the affidavit evidence adduced on the hearing of the
> application. This, however, should be done only where it is apparent on the facts disclosed
> by evidence as to which there is no credible dispute, that the strength of one party's case
> is disproportionate to that of the other party. The court is not justified in embarking on
> anything like a trial of the action on conflicting affidavits in order to evaluate the strength
> of either party's case." (*American Cyanamid* at [409B].)

The last-quoted paragraph led, at least in some courts, to a new technical rule   **3-14**
instead of the old one. The old one had been that the claimant had to show a better
than 50 per cent chance of success; now it was thought to have been replaced by a
rule that, once the claimant showed a serious question to be tried, any further reference to the relative strength of the parties' cases was prohibited. This placed a
weapon for injustice in the hands of claimants with weak but arguable cases (just
as the "adequacy of damages and ability to pay" criterion—see below—favours parties with ample resources), all the more so at a time when, in both Chancery and
Queen's Bench Divisions, there were substantial delays in hearing trials.

This interpretation, widely held in the 20 years after *American Cyanamid*, of what
the case meant was subjected to a detailed and devastating analysis by Laddie J in
Series 5 Software v Clarke [1996] 1 All E.R. 853. The judge held that where on an
application for an interim injunction the court is able from reading the evidence to
form a clear view as to the relative strengths of the parties' cases, it should take that
view into account in deciding whether to grant or refuse the injunction. The proper
approach, he held, was as follows:

> "(1) The grant of an interim injunction is a matter of discretion and depends on all the facts
> of the case. (2) There are no fixed rules as to when an injunction should or should not be
> granted. The relief must be kept flexible. (3) Because of the practice adopted on the hear-
> ing of applications for interim relief, the court should rarely attempt to resolve complex
> issues of fact or law. (4) Major factors the court can bear in mind are (a) the extent to
> which damages are likely to be an adequate remedy for each party and the ability of the
> other party to pay, (b) the balance of convenience, (c) the maintenance of the status quo,
> and (d) any clear view the court may reach as to the relative strength of the parties' cases."

The judge added (correctly, it is submitted) that there is great value to most parties in having an early, non-binding view of the merits from a judge, and giving such a view assists in reducing the costs of litigation. On the facts, he found the claimants' case arguable, but weak, and refused an injunction.

On the face of it, this judgment was revolutionary, even heretical. However in truth it represented what many judges had been doing already, and since 1996 it has stood the test of time. In the passing-off case of *Guardian Group v Associated Newspapers* (CA, 20 January 2000, Unreported) Robert Walker LJ said that in applying the *American Cyanamid* principles the court may give "proper weight to any clear view which the court can form at the time of the application for interim relief (and without the need for a mini-trial or copious affidavit evidence) as to the likely outcome at trial".

3-15   An authoritative review of *American Cyanamid* a third of a century on was given by Lord Hoffmann in *National Commercial Bank Jamaica Ltd v Olint Corp Ltd* [2009] 1 W.L.R. 1405:

> "It is often said that the purpose of an interlocutory injunction is to preserve the status quo, but it is of course impossible to stop the world pending trial. The court may order a defendant to do something or not to do something else, but such restrictions on the defendant's freedom of action will have consequences, for him and for others, which a court has to take into account. The purpose of such an injunction is to improve the chances of the court being able to do justice after a determination of the merits at the trial. At the interlocutory stage, the court must therefore assess whether granting or withholding an injunction is more likely to produce a just result. As the House of Lords pointed out in *American Cyanamid Co v Ethicon Ltd* [1975] AC 396, that means that if damages will be an adequate remedy for the plaintiff, there are no grounds for interference with the defendant's freedom of action by the grant of an injunction. Likewise, if there is a serious issue to be tried and the plaintiff could be prejudiced by the acts or omissions of the defendant pending trial and the cross-undertaking in damages would provide the defendant with an adequate remedy if it turns out that his freedom of action should not have been restrained, then an injunction should ordinarily be granted.
>
> In practice, however, it is often hard to tell whether either damages or the cross-undertaking will be an adequate remedy and the court has to engage in trying to predict whether granting or withholding an injunction is more or less likely to cause irremediable prejudice (and to what extent) if it turns out that the injunction should not have been granted or withheld, as the case may be. The basic principle is that the court should take whichever course seems likely to cause the least irremediable prejudice to one party or the other. This is an assessment in which, as Lord Diplock said in the *American Cyanamid* case [1975] AC 396, 408:
>
>> 'It would be unwise to attempt even to list all the various matters which may need to be taken into consideration in deciding where the balance lies, let alone to suggest the relative weight to be attached to them.'
>
> Among the matters which the court may take into account are the prejudice which the plaintiff may suffer if no injunction is granted or the defendant may suffer if it is; the likelihood of such prejudice actually occurring; the extent to which it may be compensated by an award of damages or enforcement of the cross-undertaking; the likelihood of either party being able to satisfy such an award; and the likelihood that the injunction will turn out to have been wrongly granted or withheld, that is to say, the court's opinion of the relative strength of the parties' cases."

3-16   Sir Terence Etherton C said in *Sukhoruchkin v van Bekestein* [2014] EWCA Civ 399 that "the general principle is now well established that, on an application for an interim injunction, the court should not attempt to resolve critical disputed questions of fact or difficult points of law on which the claim of either party may ultimately depend, particularly where the point of law turns on fine questions of fact which are in dispute or are presently obscure" (citing *Derby v Weldon* [1990] Ch

48, 58F-G, 63G-H). This is clearly right in respect of points of law which really do turn on seriously disputed questions of fact. But a defendant is entitled to argue at the interim injunction stage that even if the claimant's evidence is accepted, there is still no serious question to be tried. Indeed a 'serious issue to be tried' has been said to be the same as a 'real prospect of success' (although the phrase "good arguable case" was not appropriate): *Protomed Ltd v Medication Systems Ltd* [2013] EWCA Civ 1205. The hierarchy of such terms was discussed in *Alternative Power Solution Ltd v Central Electricity Board* [2015] 1 W.L.R. 697 when it was said (on an injunction application to prevent a banker from making payment under a letter of credit) that the special test in such cases was whether it was 'seriously arguable' that the only realistic inference was fraud and that the bank was aware of it and; that the expression 'seriously arguable' was intended to be a more stringent test than 'good arguable case', let alone 'serious issue to be tried'.

The *American Cyanamid* guidelines are primarily directed to applications where **3-17** the facts are in dispute. Where the issues are of law and do not require lengthy argument the court frequently does resolve them at the interim stage, and the court will not, save in very special circumstances, refuse to determine a question of law if substantial hardship to one of the parties may result from that refusal (*City of Bradford Metropolitan Council v Brown* (1986) 84 L.G.R. 731). The decisions of the House of Lords in *Associated British Ports Ltd v TGWU* [1989] 1 W.L.R. 939 and of the Supreme Court in *O (A Child) v Rhodes* [2016] A.C. 219 show that courts should not be too easily talked out of deciding questions of law at the interim stage in appropriate cases.

In a case where the defendant has not raised any arguable defence, there is no serious question to be tried and an interim injunction should generally be granted without considering the adequacy of damages or the balance of convenience (*Official Custodian for Charities v Mackey* [1985] Ch. 168; *Patel v Smith Ltd* [1987] 1 W.L.R. 853). Conversely, a claimant who does not show even a serious question to be tried should fail irrespective of the balance of convenience.

If, but only if, the parties have shown that there is a serious question to be tried, the case goes on to the second stage.

Inadequacy of damages to either side

"The court should go on to consider whether ... if the claimant were to succeed at the trial   **3-18**
in establishing his right to a permanent injunction, he would be adequately compensated
by an award of damages for the loss he would have sustained as a result of the defendant's
continuing to do what was sought to be enjoined between the time of the application and
the time of the trial. If damages ... would be an adequate remedy and the defendant would
be in a financial position to pay them, no interim injunction should normally be granted,
however strong the claimant's claim appeared to be at that stage." (*American Cyanamid*
at [408B-C].)

If, however, damages would *not* adequately compensate the claimant for the temporary damage, *and* he is in a financial position to give a satisfactory undertaking as to damages, *and* an award of damages pursuant to that undertaking would adequately compensate the defendant in the event of the defendant succeeding at trial, an interim injunction may be granted. If the claimant *is not* in a financial position to honour his undertaking as to damages, and appreciable damage to the defendant is likely, an injunction will usually (*Morning Star Co-operative Society Ltd v Express Newspapers Ltd* [1979] F.S.R. 113) but not always (*Allen v Jambo Holdings Ltd* [1980] 1 W.L.R. 1252) be refused. The question has been suggested to be more accurately posed in this way: "Is it just, in all the circumstances, that a [claimant] should be confined to his remedy in damages?" (*Evans Marshall & Co*

Ltd v Bertola SA [1973] 1 W.L.R. 349).

3-19   This stage follows from the principle that equitable relief is not usually available where damages are an adequate remedy (Millett LJ's dissenting dicta in *Co-operative Insurance Society Ltd v Argyll Stores (Holdings) Ltd* [1996] Ch 286 at [304] being cited with approval by the Supreme Court in *Lawrence v Fen Tigers* [2014] A.C. 822). In some cases the defendant could not be compensated by an award of damages, whatever the parties' means. In *Cambridge Nutrition Ltd v BBC* [1990] 3 All E.R. 523, for example, the Court of Appeal held that the BBC could not be usefully compensated in damages if an interim injunction delayed the broadcasting of a topical programme. Where a contract stipulates that damages will be limited or capped in the event of a breach, it does not follow that a payment of those limited or capped damages would be an adequate remedy, indeed it is a circumstance which tends to favour the grant of an injunction (*AB v CD* [2015] 1 W.L.R. 771; *Bath and North East Somerset DC v Mowlem Plc* [2004] EWCA Civ 115; [2015] 1 W.L.R. 785).

A claimant is not entitled to an injunction to prevent damage which, if suffered, would be too remote (*Peaudouce SA v Kimberley-Clark Ltd* [1996] F.S.R. 680). The test in any event is whether damages would be an *adequate* remedy, not whether they would be a perfect remedy (per Robert Walker J). Finally it should be noted that "while adequacy of damages as a remedy is a reason to refuse an injunction, you cannot turn the argument on its head and say that inadequacy of damages is a positive reason to grant an otherwise inappropriate injunction" (per Lord Toulson in his dissenting judgment in *PJS v News Group Newspapers* [2016] A.C. 1081).

Balance of convenience

3-20   "It is where there is doubt as to the adequacy of the respective remedies in damages available to either party or to both, that the question of balance of convenience arises." (*American Cyanamid* at [408E].)

By definition, once the investigation has reached this third stage, the decision of the court, whether in favour of or against an injunction, will inevitably involve some disadvantage to one or the other side which damages cannot compensate. The extent of this "uncompensatable disadvantage" either way is a significant factor in determining the balance of convenience. In many cases it has been the decisive question. Where, for example, in a restraint of trade case, an injunction would have deprived the defendant of his job, this was held to be more serious than the prejudice caused to the claimants by the defendant's continuing to work for a rival firm pending trial (*Fellowes & Son v Fisher* [1976] QB 122); similarly, where the defendants set up a factory and were manufacturing products, allegedly in breach of covenant, it would have been "catastrophic" to compel them to close before the merits had been finally determined (*Potters-Ballotini v Weston Baker* [1977] R.P.C. 202). Conversely, in *Hubbard v Pitt* [1976] QB 142, it was the claimant firm of estate agents which was able to show the greater potentially uncompensatable disadvantage; if the picketing outside their office was allowed to continue they would suffer irreparable damage, whereas the defendant pickets, if restrained by injunction, could continue to press their point of view elsewhere. The Court of Appeal granted an injunction.

The wider public interest may in some cases be an important or even decisive factor: see, for example, paras 4-70 to 4-72 for decisions relating to new drugs allegedly infringing a patent.

3-21   The fact that the defendant has other business interests which he could pursue pending trial is not a conclusive argument in the claimant's favour (*Conder*

International Ltd v Hibbing Ltd [1984] F.S.R. 312). Where a buyer seeks an interim injunction to restrain a bank from paying under a letter of credit on the grounds of fraud within the knowledge of the bank, the ordinary balance of convenience is not the correct test (*Alternative Power Solution Ltd v Central Electricity Board* [2015] 1 W.L.R. 697) as it would almost always militate against the grant of an injunction.

If, by the time a letter before action is written, the defendant is already substantially committed to the launch of a new product or publication, that is a factor against the grant of an interim injunction (*Management Publications Ltd v Blenheim Exhibitions Group Plc* [1991] F.S.R. 550; cf. *Belfast Ropework Co Ltd v Pixdane Ltd* [1976] F.S.R. 337).

The phrase "balance of convenience" lays itself open to criticism. It is a useful shorthand, but

3-22

> "the balance that one is seeking to make is more fundamental, more weighty, than mere 'convenience'. I think it is quite clear ... that, although the phrase may well be substantially less elegant, the 'balance of the risk of doing an injustice' better describes the process involved." (Per May LJ in *Cayne v Global Natural Resources Plc* [1984] 1 All E.R. 225 at [237h].)

In another case, *Francome v Mirror Group Newspapers Ltd* [1984] 1 W.L.R. 892, Sir John Donaldson MR preferred "a balance of justice". More recently Butcher J discussed the different ways of describing the important balancing process required in all interim relief cases in the context of a rare application for an interim declaration:

> "...I consider that it must be the case, when considering the grant of an interim declaration that the court has to have regard to the balance of justice or injustice to the parties... Whether that exercise is properly called the "balance of convenience" may not matter greatly; it is necessary to consider what degree of prejudice the grant or refusal of the interim remedy would impose upon each side, bearing in mind that, being interim, any remedy granted may turn out to have been wrongly granted." (*BALPA v British Airways Cityflyer Ltd* [2018] EWHC 1889 (QB))

An example of apparently even balance is where there will be substantial uncompensatable disadvantage to one or other party whichever way the interim decision goes. However where there is only a *risk* of unquantifiable damage to the claimant from the refusal of interim relief, as against a *certainty* of unquantifiable damage to the defendant from the grant of it, it cannot be said that the scales are evenly balanced and an injunction should generally be refused (*Walker (John) & Sons Ltd v Rothmans International Ltd* [1978] F.S.R. 357; however cf. *Mirage Studios v Counter-Feat Clothing Co Ltd* [1991] F.S.R. 145).

Status quo

> "Where other factors appear to be evenly balanced it is a counsel of prudence to take such measures as are calculated to preserve the status quo." (*American Cyanamid* at [408F].)

3-23

This advice of Lord Diplock illustrates how essential it is for the claimant to move quickly. In many cases prompt action may mean that the preservation of the status quo favours the claimant as the defendant's activities are still at the preliminary stage. Conversely, if the defendant has proceeded a long way, he may be able to claim that preservation of the status quo involves allowing him to continue manufacturing the product or polluting the river or continuing to distribute the publication, as the case may be. This argument will not avail a defendant, however, who has rushed on with his work in order to defeat the claimant's attempts to stop him: *Shepherd Homes Ltd v Sandham* [1971] Ch. 340. If preserving the status quo for a short period whilst there is an expedited trial would not be disproportionate an injunction may be appropriate (*NATS v Gatwick Airport* [2015] P.T.S.R. 566).

The relevant status quo is the state of affairs existing during the period immediately preceding the issue of proceedings or, if there is unreasonable delay between the issue of the claim and the application for an interim injunction, the period immediately preceding the application. The duration of that period since the state of affairs last changed must be more than minimal, having regard to the total length of the relationship between the parties in respect of which the injunction is granted; otherwise the state of affairs before the last change would be the status quo (*Garden Cottage Foods Ltd v Milk Marketing Board* [1984] A.C. 130 at [140C]). On an application to enforce a restrictive covenant in an employment case, the status quo to be preserved is that which was obtained before the breach, not at the date of the hearing (*Unigate Dairies Ltd v Bruce, The Times*, 2 March, 1988). However for an interim injunction to restrain use of a trade mark it was said that *Garden Cottage Foods Ltd* [1984] A.C. 130 was not trying to lay down a universal test. Such a case was different from a confidential information or privacy case in which the status quo may be very important and once breached there is no going back. Where there was no irrevocable long-term consequences the status quo was less significant (*Interflora Inc v Marks & Spencer Plc* [2015] F.S.R. 13).

3-24   Delay by the claimant is a factor in the defendant's favour, but by itself is not a bar to an interim injunction. Such injunctions are not "awarded as a prize for the vigilant and automatically withheld from the less vigilant ... Each case turns on its own facts" (per Rimer J in *Law Society v Society of Lawyers* [1996] F.S.R. 739). In most cases it is reasonable for the claimant to seek suitable undertakings from the defendant before issuing proceedings.

After Nike commenced a global advertising campaign using the claimant's trademark in mid-January, a 'cease and desist' letter in late January was followed by an injunction application in late February. In the meantime Instagram, YouTube and live events carried the disputed logo. The Court of Appeal held that the interval before the application was so short that the relevant status quo was that which pertained before the start of Nike's campaign and Nike could not improve its position "by pushing on in the face of reasoned complaints" (*Frank Industries Pty UK v Nike Retail BV* [2018] F.S.R. 24).

Special cases

3-25   Lord Diplock concluded his discussion of principle in *American Cyanamid* by adding that "there may be many other special factors to be taken into consideration in the particular circumstances of individual cases". Since the *American Cyanamid* decision, a number of special categories of case have been formulated by the Court of Appeal and judges of first instance. In some of these, the claimant is still required to show something like a prima facie case if he is to obtain an injunction; in others the balance of convenience is not considered.

Trade dispute defence

3-26   One special case was prescribed by statute shortly after the *American Cyanamid* decision. Section 221(2) of the Trade Union and Labour Relations (Consolidation) Act 1992 provides as follows:

"Where—

(a)   an application for an interim injunction is made to a court, pending the trial of an action, and

(b) the party against whom it is sought claims that he acted in contemplation or furtherance of a trade dispute,

the court shall, in exercising its discretion whether or not to grant the injunction, have regard to the likelihood of that party's succeeding at the trial of the action in establishing any matter which would, under sections 219–220 of the Act, afford a defence to the action under section 219 (protection from certain tort liabilities) or section 220 (peaceful picketing)."

This clearly lays down a different approach from *American Cyanamid* in that the court is specifically directed to estimate the likelihood of the action being successfully defended at trial in strike and industrial action injunctions (see paras 4-14 to 4-15).

An important additional restriction is imposed by statute on the power to grant without notice injunctions in industrial disputes. Section 221(1) of the Trade Union and Labour Relations (Consolidation) Act 1992 provides:

"Where an application for an injunction or interdict [the Scottish equivalent] is made to a court in the absence of the party against whom the injunction or interdict is sought or any representative of his and that party claims, or in the opinion of the court would be likely to claim, that he acted in contemplation or furtherance of a trade dispute, the court shall not grant the injunction or interdict unless satisfied that all steps which in the circumstances were reasonable have been taken with a view to securing that notice of the application and an opportunity of being heard with respect to the application have been given to that party."

Actions against a public authority

Actions brought against a public authority provide another example of a special case. A local authority should not be restrained by interim injunction from exercising its statutory powers unless the claimant has shown a real prospect that his claim for a permanent injunction will succeed at trial. The *public interest* is a legitimate factor to be considered in assessing where the balance of convenience lies (*Smith v ILEA* [1978] 1 All E.R. 411). Where the defendant was the Crown and the claimant was seeking to have a statute declared incompatible with the Treaty of Rome, an interim injunction could be granted only if the claimant's challenge to the validity of the Act was "soundly based" (*R. v Secretary of State for Transport Ex p. Factortame Ltd (No.2)* [1991] 1 A.C. 603). **3-27**

Where the grant or refusal of an injunction will dispose of the action

American Cyanamid **3-28**

"was not dealing with a case in which the grant or refusal of an injunction at [the interim] stage would, in effect, dispose of the action finally in favour of whichever party was successful in the application, because there would be nothing left on which it was in the unsuccessful party's interest to proceed to trial" (per Lord Diplock in *NWL Ltd v Woods* [1979] 1 W.L.R. 1294 at [1306]).

Where the grant or refusal of an interim injunction will have the practical effect of putting an end to the action, the court should approach the case on the broad principle of what it can do in its best endeavour to avoid injustice, and to balance the risk of doing an injustice to either party. In such a case the court should bear in mind that to grant the injunction sought by the claimant would mean giving him judgment in the case without permitting the defendant the right of trial. Accordingly, the guidelines on the balance of convenience do not apply in such a case since, whatever the strengths of either side, the defendant should not be precluded by the grant of an interim injunction from disputing the claimant's claim at a trial (*Cayne v Global Natural Resources Plc* [1984] 1 All E.R. 225; see also *Cambridge Nutrition Ltd v BBC* [1990] 3 All E.R. 523). The court should take into account the strengths and weaknesses of the respective cases and the likelihood of the claimant's eventual success at trial (*Araci v Fallon* [2011] L.L.R. 440).

Applications to restrain litigation (see para.4-50) are an obvious example of this. In *Bryanston Finance Ltd v de Vries (No.2)* [1976] Ch. 63, the claimant company sought an injunction restraining the defendant shareholder from presenting a petition to wind up the company. The court held that the company was only entitled to interim relief if, on the available evidence, it could be said that presentation of a petition would prima facie be an abuse of process. Another example is where the injunction is only being sought for a very short period, as in *Associated Newspapers Group Plc v News Group Newspapers Ltd* [1986] R.P.C. 515, where the time span was only a few days.

No dispute on the facts

3-29   In *Office Overload Ltd v Gunn* [1977] F.S.R. 39, a covenant in restraint of trade was upheld and the "balance of convenience" test not applied, in a case which was "plain and uncontroversial" on the facts. Bridge LJ said that *American Cyanamid* dealt with

> "the principle which ought to govern the grant of interim injunctions where there is either an unresolved dispute on the affidavit evidence before the court, or a question of law to be decided."

Restraint of trade

3-30   See paras 4-05 to 4-06.

Covenants between neighbours

3-31   Prohibitory injunctions enforcing negative covenants between the parties have already been considered in the context of *Lawrence v Fen Tigers* [2014] A.C. 822 and its review of the case law which suggests that at trial although it may be overstating it to say that such injunctions will issue "as of course", they will normally be granted (see para.2-12). In *Hampstead & Suburban Properties Ltd v Diomedous* [1969] 1 Ch. 248, it was held that the same principle applied at the interim stage where a covenantor was in clear breach of an express prohibition against playing music in such a way as to cause nuisance or annoyance to his neighbours. The defendant was in flagrant breach of covenant and his argument on the balance of convenience was without merit. Restrictive covenants between neighbours continue to be treated as prima facie enforceable by interim injunction as the balance of convenience will normally fall in favour of preventing nuisance or interference with property rights.

Defamation

3-32   See para.4-26.

Matrimonial and domestic proceedings

See Ch.10.   **3-33**

Injunctions pending a reference to the European Court of Justice

In *International Transport Workers' Federation v Viking Line ABP* [2006]   **3-34**
I.R.L.R. 58, the respondent shipowners sought an injunction to prevent industrial
action against "flags of convenience". The case raised issues of European law which
the Court of Appeal referred to the Court of Justice in Luxembourg, a process which
almost invariably takes more than two years. An interim injunction would therefore
have come close to giving the shipowners a remedy which should only be available after a trial. Waller LJ considered that they had shown a serious case to be tried
but took its weaknesses into account in concluding that interim relief should be
refused.

It will be observed that a high proportion of actions in which interim injunctions are sought can be classified under one of the above headings of "special
cases".

4   MANDATORY INJUNCTIONS

At an interim stage a court may order a mandatory injunction compelling the   **3-35**
respondent to do something. The statutory authority for the grant of mandatory and
prohibitory injunctions stems alike from s.37 of the Senior Courts Act 1981 and a
"balance of injustice" test still applies (*Leisure Data v Bell* [1988] F.S.R. 367), but
the courts recognise that a mandatory injunction is normally more drastic in its
effect. As Megarry J said in *Shepherd Homes v Sandham* [1971] Ch. 340:

> "the court is far more reluctant to grant a mandatory injunction than it would be to grant
> a comparable prohibitory injunction. In a normal case the court must, inter alia, feel a high
> degree of assurance that at the trial it will appear that the injunction was rightly granted;
> and this is a higher standard than is required for a prohibitory injunction."

Megarry J added that "the case has to be unusually strong and clear before a mandatory injunction will be granted, even if it is sought to enforce a contractual
obligation". This is because prohibitory injunctions look to the future, whereas
mandatory injunctions tend to look to the past by providing a means of undoing
what has already been done and taking positive steps to dismantle it, which would
waste time and money if it was later established that that was not legally necessary (*Frank Industries Pty UK v Nike Retail BV* [2018] F.S.R. 24).

This has certainly been the traditional view in respect of any mandatory interim
injunction. In cases where the interim application is for, say, demolition of a fence
(as in *Shepherd Homes Ltd v Sandham* itself), a stringent test is always applied;
likewise where the relief sought is the payment of money. However the dictum of
Megarry J cited above is qualified by the words "in a normal case"; he also said (at
[349A]) that "the subject is not one in which it is possible to draw firm lines or
impose any rigid classification". This element of flexibility was seized on in *Films
Rover International Ltd v Cannon Film Sales Ltd* [1987] 1 W.L.R. 670 by Hoffmann
J. He held that the "high degree of assurance" test does not have to be satisfied in
all cases, and that the fundamental principle on interim applications for prohibitory and mandatory injunctions alike is that the court should take whichever course

appears to carry the lower risk of injustice if it should turn out at trial to have been "wrong".

3-36   In *Nottingham Building Society v Eurodynamics Systems Plc* [1993] F.S.R. 468, Chadwick J said that the principles to be applied were these:

"Firstly, this being an interlocutory matter, the overriding consideration is which course is likely to involve the least risk of injustice if it turns out to be 'wrong' in the sense described by Hoffmann J.

Secondly, in considering whether to grant a mandatory injunction the court must keep in mind that an order which requires a party to take some positive step at an interlocutory stage may well carry a greater risk of injustice if it turns out to have been wrongly made than an order which merely prohibits action, thus preserving the status quo.

Thirdly, it is legitimate, where a mandatory injunction is sought, to consider whether the court does feel a high degree of assurance that the [claimant] will be able to establish his right at a trial. That is because the greater the degree of assurance the [claimant] will ultimately establish his right, the less will be the risk of injustice if the injunction is granted.

But finally, even when the court is unable to feel any high degree of assurance that the [claimant] will establish his right, there may still be circumstances in which it is appropriate to grant a mandatory injunction at an interlocutory stage. Those circumstances will exist where the risk of injustice if this injunction is refused sufficiently outweigh the risk of injustice if it is granted."

The Court of Appeal approved these observations in *Zockoll Group Ltd v Mercury Communications Ltd* [1998] F.S.R. 354, adding that they should be regarded as "all the citation that should in future be necessary". Nevertheless, few courts would deprive themselves of the convenient summary of the law given by Lord Hoffmann, in the *National Commercial Bank Jamaica* case, above:

"There is ... no reason to suppose that, in stating [the *American Cyanamid*] principles, Lord Diplock was intending to confine them to injunctions which could be described as prohibitory rather than mandatory. In both cases, the underlying principle is the same, namely, that the court should take whichever course seems likely to cause the least irremediable prejudice to one party or the other: see Lord Jauncey in *R v Secretary of State for Transport, Ex p Factortame Ltd (No 2)* (Case C-213/89) [1991] 1 AC 603, 682–683. What is true is that the features which ordinarily justify describing an injunction as mandatory are often more likely to cause irremediable prejudice than in cases in which a defendant is merely prevented from taking or continuing with some course of action: see *Films Rover International Ltd v Cannon Film Sales Ltd* [1987] 1 WLR 670, 680. But this is no more than a generalisation. What is required in each case is to examine what on the particular facts of the case the consequences of granting or withholding of the injunction is likely to be. If it appears that the injunction is likely to cause irremediable prejudice to the defendant, a court may be reluctant to grant it unless satisfied that the chances that it will turn out to have been wrongly granted are low; that is to say, that the court will feel, as Megarry J said in *Shepherd Homes Ltd v Sandham* [1971] Ch 340, 351, 'a high degree of assurance that at the trial it will appear that the injunction was rightly granted.'

For these reasons, arguments over whether the injunction should be classified as prohibitive or mandatory are barren: see *Films Rover* [1987] 1 WLR 670, 680. What matters is what the practical consequences of the actual injunction are likely to be. It seems to me that both Jones J and the Court of Appeal proceeded by first deciding how the injunction should be classified and then applying a rule that if it was mandatory, a 'high degree of assurance' was required, while if it was prohibitory, all that was needed was a 'serious issue to be tried'. Jones J thought it was mandatory and refused the injunction while the Court of Appeal thought it was prohibitory and granted it. Their Lordships consider that this type of box-ticking approach does not do justice to the complexity of a decision as to whether or not to grant an interlocutory injunction."

This balance of injustice or prejudice approach was taken in *Actial Farmaceutica Lda v De Simone* [2015] EWCA Civ 1032. The Court said that the principles in *Novartis AG v Hospira (UK) Ltd* [2014] 1 W.L.R. 1264 (see para.6-22) were of general application and the judge was right to assess whether greater harm would be incurred by failing to grant the interim relief than by granting it. Kitchin LJ commented:

> "No doubt the nature of the relief sought will, in most if not all cases, be a relevant consideration and if an order is of a mandatory nature, then, as Chadwick J indicated [in *Nottingham Building Society v Eurodynamics Systems Plc* cited above], it may well carry a greater risk of injustice if it turns out to have been wrongly made than an order which merely prohibits action. But in all cases, the critical question is whether the risk of injustice if the injunction turns out to have been wrongly refused sufficiently outweighs the risk of injustice if it turns out to have been wrongly granted."

These principles were applied in *MM v BC, RS, Facebook Ireland Ltd* [2017] NIQB 127 when refusing a mandatory interim injunction against Facebook to block further distribution of "revenge porn" images. Citing the above authorities and a passage in this book with approval, Maguire J held that there was no strong probability of further dissemination or that the plaintiff would sustain "grave damage", whilst the order sought was onerous, time consuming and expensive and disproportionate to any gains which might result.

Chambers v British Olympic Association [2008] EWHC 2028 (QB) was an at- **3-37** tempt by the sprinter Dwain Chambers, who had been banned for using performance-enhancing drugs, to obtain an interim mandatory injunction compelling his inclusion in the British team at the 2008 Olympic Games. Mackay J refused an injunction, holding that: (a) he was not satisfied to a high degree of assurance that the British Olympic Association's actions would be shown at a trial to be invalid; and (b) the risk of injustice to Mr Chambers if an interim injunction were refused but he succeeded at trial did not outweigh the risk of injustice to the British Olympic Association if an injunction were granted and he failed at a trial. The balance of injustice test meant that, although the courts had jurisdiction to grant an interim mandatory injunction requiring HM Revenue and Customs to restore a company's registration as an owner of duty-suspended goods, that power should only be exercised in exceptional cases where the decision was arguably an abuse of power, improper or taken in bad faith (*CC&C Ltd v Revenue and Customs Commissioners* [2014] EWCA Civ 1653).

A case may justify an immediate mandatory injunction by being in the nature of an emergency. Where the landlords of a block of flats had begun taking down one of the staircases in breach of the claimant's rights as a tenant, he obtained a mandatory injunction, ordering the landlords to restore the staircase, on the hearing at the interim stage (*Allport v Securities Corp* (1895) 64 L.J. Ch. 491). Such an order was effectively final, but it was unlikely that the defendants would find any stronger evidence for the trial than they had already adduced. Damages would not adequately compensate the claimant, and his rights were being interfered with in a high-handed manner.

Relief may certainly be granted if the defendant has hurried on with, for example, building works after receiving notice of the hearing (*Daniel v Ferguson* [1891] 2 Ch. 27) or after learning that a claim had been issued and the claimant was trying to effect service of it upon him (*Von Joel v Hornsey* [1895] 2 Ch. 774). In both these cases interim injunctions were granted for the demolition of buildings. (See also cases on suspension of injunctions at para.6-10.)

An interim mandatory injunction may issue to enforce specifically a contractual **3-38** obligation, such as a duty to allow a valuer to enter premises (*Smith v Peters* (1875) L.R. 20 Eq. 511), or an obligation to sign a document necessary for the operation of a letter of credit (*Astro Exito Navegacion SA v Southland Enterprise Co Ltd (No.2)* (1983) 127 S.J. 461). This is especially so when the defendant is the only source of supply available to the claimant and the refusal of an injunction would be likely to force the claimant out of business (*Sky Petroleum Ltd v VIP Petroleum Ltd* [1974] 1 W.L.R. 576). In charterparty withdrawal cases, injunctions are granted restraining the owners from using the ship otherwise than in accordance with the terms of the charter; this is a mandatory order in effect (because the owner is compelled to continue providing the ship to the charterer), even though prohibitory in its wording.

In an action claiming delivery up of banknotes being held by the police pending a criminal trial, the grant of an interim mandatory injunction shortly before the trial directing the police to hand over the banknotes is equivalent to summary judgment. Since such a mandatory injunction disposes of the action, it should not be granted unless there is clearly no defence to the action (*Malone v Metropolitan Police Commissioner* [1980] QB 49). A similar test is applied to an interim application for an order directing the payment of wages (*Jakeman v SW Thames RHA* [1990] I.R.L.R. 62).

3-39   A defendant's objections to the grant of an interim injunction on the grounds that it would be mandatory in effect will not carry much weight if the only possible remedy under a statute is mandatory. In an action by a retailer against a manufacturer under competition law alleging wrongful withholding of supplies, the remedy at the interim stage was to order the manufacturer to resume supplies pending the trial; the fact that this was a mandatory order did not make it objectionable in principle (*Comet Radiovision Services v Farnell-Tandberg Ltd* [1971] 1 W.L.R. 1287).

It requires a still more exceptional case for a mandatory injunction to be granted without notice, even where the claimant gives a proper undertaking in damages. A without notice application for an order requiring the defendant to pay a sum of money to a bank was refused by Megarry J in *Felton v Callis* [1969] 1 QB 200, the learned judge observing that such an injunction would establish "a vigorous new jurisdiction ... of a promptitude and strength that would put ... summary judgment in the shade". In addition to the cautionary notes sounded above, the caveats against the grant of any mandatory orders apply, e.g. the need for the defendant to know exactly what he has to do (see para.2-20).

5   ECHR ARTICLE 6

3-40   Until 2009 the European Court of Human Rights regarded interim injunctions as outside the ambit of Article 6 of the Convention. But in *Micallef v Malta* [2009] ECHR 1571 the Court held that "whenever an interim measure can be considered effectively to determine the civil right or obligation at stake, notwithstanding the length of time it is in force, Article 6 will be applicable", although it added that "in exceptional cases—where, for example, the effectiveness of the decision-measure sought depends on a rapid decision-making process—it may not be possible immediately to comply with all of the requirements of Article 6". As Sir Stanley Burnton observed in *Perry v Nursing and Midwifery Council* [2013] EWCA Civ 145, it is not easy to understand from the judgment what test is to be applied to determine whether interim proceedings result in an order determinative of a civil right. It does not appear that this decision is likely to change the approach of the English courts to injunction applications. However the *Practice Guidance (Interim Non-disclosure Orders)* [2012] 1 WLR 1003 cites *Micallef v Malta* when giving guidance that the general rule is that interim injunction hearings are carried out in, and judgments and orders are, public.

CHAPTER 4

Special Cases in the Law of Injunctions

1 CONTRACTS OF EMPLOYMENT AND OTHER BUSINESS RELATIONSHIPS

Express covenants

The courts will not grant an injunction to restrain breaches of a covenant in a **4-01** contract of employment if:

(a) this would amount to indirect specific performance;
(b) it would perpetuate a relationship based on mutual trust and confidence which no longer exist;
(c) the covenant is invalid under the restraint of trade doctrine.

Indirect specific performance

The rule against indirect specific performance is incorporated, so far as concerns **4-02** cases where the defendant is an employee of the claimant, in the Trade Union and Labour Relations (Consolidation) Act 1992 s.236, which provides:

"No court shall, whether by way of—

(a) an order for specific performance or specific implement [the Scottish equivalent] of a contract of employment, or
(b) an injunction or interdict [the Scottish equivalent] restraining a breach or threatened breach of such contract,

compel an employee to do any work or attend at any place for the doing of any work."

Many reported cases illustrate how the prohibition against indirect specific performance is interpreted. Thus, in *Whitwood Chemical Co v Hardman* [1891] 2 Ch. 416, the court refused to grant an injunction restraining breach of an undertaking by an employee "to give his whole time to the company" and, in *Ehrman v Bartholomew* [1898] 1 Ch. 671, a promise "not to engage in any other business for ten years" was likewise held to be unenforceable. However, in the leading case of *Lumley v Wagner* (1852) 1 De G.M. & G. 604, an injunction was granted to restrain the defendant, who had contracted to sing at the Covent Garden Opera for a season lasting three months, from using her talents as a singer elsewhere during that period.

In the celebrated case of *Warner Bros v Nelson* [1937] 1 K.B. 209, Branson J granted an injunction restraining the defendant (Bette Davis), who had agreed for very large sums to take part in the claimants' films and no others, from working for a rival film company. This decision was criticised by Oliver J in *Nichols Advanced Vehicle Systems Inc v Angelis* (unreported 1979, but cited in *Warren v Mendy*, below), on the grounds that the injunction "did not in practice leave the defendant ... much choice if she wanted to pursue her chosen profession".

The basis for the refusal to grant an injunction amounting to specific performance was explained in *Chappell v Times Newspapers Ltd* [1975] 1 W.L.R. 482: "if one party has no faith in the honesty or integrity or the loyalty of the other, to force him to serve or to employ that other is a plain recipe for disaster". However Lord Wilson in *Geys v Societe Generale* [2013] 1 A.C. 523 raised the "big question whether nowadays the more impersonal, less hierarchical, relationship of many employers with their employees requires review of the usual unavailability of specific performance". He referred to Stephenson LJ in *Chappell* who held that there may be exceptions to the general rule "in accordance with the general principle on which discretionary remedies are granted, namely, where, and only where, an injunction is required by justice and equity in a particular case, and, at the interim stage, by the balance of convenience". Where a big employer has sufficient confidence in the employee's ability and other necessary attributes it may be reasonable to order relief (*Powell v Brent LBC* [1988] I.C.R. 176) but it was not where the producers of the play 'War Horse' decided to dispense with its live band (*Ashworth v Royal National Theatre* [2014] I.R.L.R. 526).

4-03   Analogous considerations were discussed in *Page One Records Ltd v Britton* [1968] 1 W.L.R. 157 where the claimants, the managers of the "Troggs" pop group, sought to enjoin the singers from changing to a new manager in breach of their contract with the claimants. The evidence showed that the group would be unable to pursue their joint career successfully without a manager. Stamp J refused an injunction on the grounds that to grant it would mean forcing the group to choose between continuing to employ managers in whom they no longer placed their trust and confidence or giving up their livelihood altogether.

It has long been held that an injunction should not be granted against working for a new employer in breach of covenant if it would force the ex-employee into "starvation or idleness". A technique which attempts to meet the starvation point, if not the idleness point, is the "garden leave" clause, under which a departing employee is kept on the payroll of the old employer for a period of months, given no work, and prohibited from working for anyone else. It was held by the Court of Appeal in *Provident Financial Group Plc v Hayward* [1989] 3 All E.R. 298 that there is a discretion to enforce a clause of this kind if there would otherwise be a real prospect of serious or significant damage to the claimants. However there is no rule requiring employers to give some form of undertaking as to remuneration which goes beyond their obligations under the contract, in order that they should be entitled to obtain an injunction (*Sunrise Brokers LLP v Rodgers* [2015] I.C.R. 272 citing *Standard Life Health Care Ltd v Gorman* [2010] I.R.L.R. 233).

Covenants restraining an employee from working for a competitor during his employment are not subject to the doctrine of restraint of trade, and do not need to pass any test of reasonableness in order to be enforceable, but the court will be astute to recognise that the practice of long periods of garden leave is obviously capable of abuse (*J M Finn & Co Ltd v Holliday* [2014] I.R.L.R. 102 per Simler J). The issue in such a case is whether the court should exercise its discretion to enforce the contractual prohibition by injunction, rather than by an award of damages (*Elsevier Ltd v Munro* [2014] I.R.L.R. 766).

4-04   If the proposed new employer's business has nothing to do with that of the old employer, an injunction is inappropriate as an injunction may only be granted to protect a legitimate business asset of the old employer. The duration of the garden leave period is also material. In *Evening Standard v Henderson* [1987] I.C.R. 588, the claimants obtained an injunction for a 12-month period by offering the defendant—unusually—the choice between returning to his old job for that period or spending it on garden leave on full pay. See also *Credit Suisse Asset Management Ltd v Armstrong* [1996] I.R.L.R. 450.

An injunction may be granted to prevent a defendant from fulfilling contracts made in breach of covenant (*PSM International Ltd v Whitehouse* [1992] I.R.L.R. 279).

No injunction should be granted against a third party which would have the indirect effect of specifically enforcing a contract of employment, or a boxer's contract with his manager (*Warren v Mendy* [1989] 3 All E.R. 103).

Restraint of trade

Where a restrictive covenant is held to fall foul of the restraint of trade doctrine, **4-05** no injunction to restrain its breach (and, indeed, no damages) can be obtained. This enormous subject is fully covered in other textbooks. Some basic points are that a covenant will only be enforced against an ex-employee if it is no wider than reasonably necessary to protect the employer's customer connection or trade secrets, that it will not be enforced at all if the employer has repudiated the contract and that the courts will not rewrite an invalid covenant (*Prophet plc v Huggett* [2014] I.R.L.R. 797), although in certain circumstances objectionable parts will be "severed" and the remainder enforced (see the classic summary in *Office Angels v Rainer-Thomas* [1991] I.R.L.R. 214 and that in *Coppage v Safety Net Security Ltd* [2013] I.R.L.R. 970). However severance to save an unreasonable restraint can only be applied to separate covenants and not to parts of a single covenant: *Tillman v Egon Zehnder* [2018] I.C.R. 574.

A problem which arises very frequently in practice is whether the *American Cyanamid* guidelines (see para.3-12) apply to such cases. In *Dairy Crest Ltd v Pigott* [1989] I.C.R. 92 and *Lawrence David Ltd v Ashton* [1991] 1 All E.R. 385, the Court of Appeal (in each case Fox and Balcombe LJJ) held that they do. The curious result of this, if applied literally, would be that an employer seeking an interim injunction to enforce a two-year restrictive covenant (as in both *Dairy Crest* and *Lawrence David*) might only need to show a serious question to be tried as to the validity of the covenant, whereas an employer seeking to enforce a three-month restraint would need to go rather further. So nowadays the courts generally adopt the approach of Chadwick LJ in *Arbuthnot Fund Managers Ltd v Rawlings* [2003] EWCA Civ 518:

> "Unless the court is satisfied that there are disputed facts which bear on the construction of the relevant contractual terms, and that those facts cannot be resolved without a trial, the court at the interim stage is as well able to construe the relevant contractual terms as a court will be at a trial."

For example, where the claimant is seeking an injunction to enforce a covenant for a three-month period, so that in practice there is no possibility of the trial taking place, the court should consider whether the claimant would be likely to succeed at trial, rather than merely whether there is a serious issue to be tried (*Phoenix Partners Group LLP v Asoyag* [2010] I.R.L.R. 594). Similarly in a springboard injunction application (see para.4-07 below) a court needs to form a provisional view on the merits and as to the likely length of any final injunction (*MPT Group v Peel* [2017] I.R.L.R. 1092) and consider the balance of convenience and discretionary matters in that light (*Aquinas Education v Miller* [2018] I.R.L.R. 518).

The High Court is much more willing now than at the time of the *Dairy Crest* **4-06** and *Lawrence David* cases to give directions for an expedited or speedy trial to take place within a few months or indeed a few weeks of the interim injunction, or to exercise its discretion to give rulings on preliminary issues of law. Although the existence of an injunction is a factor to be taken into account when setting a timetable for trial, a speedy trial does not follow as a matter of course. The issue of whether to grant expedition is a matter for the judge's discretion (*Warner-Lambert Co LLC v Teva UK Ltd* [2011] F.S.R. 44). The discretionary case management factors (articulated in *WL Gore v Geox Spa* [2008] EWCA Civ 622) as to when to order a speedy trial were discussed in *Petter v EMC Europe* [2015] EWCA Civ 480.

Breach of confidence

4-07   An employee is under an obligation to his employer not to disclose confidential information obtained by him in the course of and as a result of his employment. The obligation arises from an implied term of his contract, quite apart from any express restrictive covenants (*Bents Brewery Co Ltd v Hogan* [1945] 2 All E.R. 570) and by virtue of a free-standing equitable duty of confidence (*BBC v HarperCollins Publishers Ltd* [2011] E.M.L.R. 6 concerning the secret identity of The Stig from the BBC's "Top Gear"). It applies during the period of employment to all confidential information, and continues after the employment has ended to the extent that the confidential information can be regarded as a trade secret or equivalent to a trade secret (*Faccenda Chicken Ltd v Fowler* [1987] Ch. 117; *Lancashire Fires Ltd v SA Lyons & Co Ltd* [1996] F.S.R. 629); the latter category includes the contents of a list of customers which the employee has made, copied or memorised during his employment. The fact that copied information could have been pieced together legitimately is no defence (*Johnson & Bloy v Wolstenholme Rink* [1987] I.R.L.R. 499). No injunction should be granted unless the confidential information can be defined with some precision (*Lock International Plc v Beswick* [1989] 1 W.L.R. 1268). However an injunction does not always follow from every breach of confidence as, in the words of Lord Neuberger in *Vestergaard Frandsen A/S v Bestnet Europe Ltd* [2013] 1 W.L.R. 1556:

> "... in a modern economy, the law has to maintain a realistic and fair balance between (i) effectively protecting trade secrets (and other intellectual property rights) and (ii) not unreasonably inhibiting competition in the market place. The importance to the economic prosperity of the country of research and development in the commercial world is self-evident, and the protection of intellectual property, including trade secrets, is one of the vital contributions of the law to that end. On the other hand, the law should not discourage former employees from benefiting society and advancing themselves by imposing unfair potential difficulties on their honest attempts to compete with their former employers."

An injunction lies both against the employee and against the third party who seeks to employ him in a capacity in which he may misuse confidential information; the cause of action in the latter case is inducing a breach of contract (*Hivac Ltd v Park Royal Scientific Instruments Ltd* [1946] Ch. 169). In some cases it may be appropriate to limit to one year the period for which an injunction restraining an ex-employee from misusing trade secrets should run; this prevents him from obtaining a "springboard" (*Fisher Karpark Industries Ltd v Nichols* [1982] F.S.R. 351). Such an injunction to protect the claimant's interests should not normally extend beyond the period for which the unfair advantage may reasonably be expected to continue (*Bullivant (Roger) Ltd v Ellis* [1987] I.C.R. 464). Springboard injunctions can also be granted in relation to breaches of contractual and fiduciary duties

(*UBS Wealth Management (UK) Ltd v Vestra Wealth LLP* [2008] I.R.L.R. 965). They are available to prevent economic loss to a previous employer caused by former staff members taking an unfair advantage, and "unfair start", of any serious breaches of their contract of employment. The remedy of injunction is, as usual, discretionary. In some cases it is a question of balancing the claimant's interest in maintaining the confidence against the public interest in knowing the truth, or the defendant's right to freedom of expression under art.10 of the European Convention on Human Rights (ECHR): see paras 4-17 to 4-22. Springboard relief has to be sought and obtained at a time when the unlawful advantage is still being enjoyed by the wrongdoer and should have the aim simply of restoring the parties to the competitive position they would have occupied but for the misconduct. Such relief is not intended to punish the wrongdoer, but to provide fair and just protection from unlawful harm on an interim basis (*QBE Management Services (UK) Ltd v Dymoke* [2012] I.R.L.R. 458).

The risk of misuse of confidential information often provides a justification for the grant of an injunction as damages may not be an adequate remedy. As Warby J said in *Elsevier Ltd v Munro* [2014] I.R.L.R. 766 "the misuse of confidential information can be and often is insidious and hard to prove and the difficulties of establishing causation are considerable". Where confidential information has already been published by the defendant, the court will nevertheless grant an injunction restraining further publication if that would give the claimant real protection and injunctive relief is appropriate (*Speed Seal Products Ltd v Paddington* [1985] 1 W.L.R. 1327). A mandatory injunction may be granted for the imaging and inspection of an ex-employee's computers following concerns about misuse of confidential information (*Warm Zones v Thurley* [2014] I.R.L.R. 791). **4-08**

In *Attorney General v Blake* [2001] 1 A.C. 268, the "notorious, self-confessed traitor" George Blake had written his memoirs, parts of which were based on information he had acquired in his career in the intelligence service. The book had been published. He had acted in breach of confidence, but it was too late to obtain an injunction preventing publication and a private law damages claim failed since the Crown could suffer no loss. The House of Lords held that the Attorney General was not entitled to an injunction to restrain Blake from receiving royalties from the publishers of the book—although an interim injunction in form, it was in effect a confiscation order for which there was no statutory power. However they achieved the same result by holding that the Attorney General had a private law claim to an account of profits, and that until the profits were paid over, an injunction should remain in force prohibiting their payment to Blake.

Barring-out relief

Where a professional has provided services to a former client and has therefore acquired confidential information, that client may apply for a "barring-out" injunction to prevent him from working for another client with an adverse interest: *Prince Jefri Bolkiah v KPMG (a firm)* [1999] 2 A.C. 222. A solicitor or accountant may be restrained if such a restriction is necessary to avoid a significant risk of the disclosure or misuse of confidential information belonging to a former client. This does not normally apply to the relationship of employer and employee (*Caterpillar Logistics Services (UK) Ltd v Paula Huesca De Crean* [2012] I.C.R. 981), although it does apply to patent attorneys (*Generics (UK) Ltd v Yeda Research & Development Co Ltd* [2011] EWHC 3200 (Pat)) and to some fiduciaries (for example trustees, company directors or liquidators). If barring out relief is sought against a former employee, it is essential that it should be based on an express and **4-09** reasonable covenant by which the employee agrees to such a barring out, although the absence of such a covenant will not prevent the employer from obtaining injunctive relief to enforce the former employee's continuing obligation to respect the confidentiality of information provided to him by the employer (*Personnel Hygiene Services v Rentokil Initial UK* [2014] EWCA Civ 29 analysing the ratio of *Caterpillar Logistics Services*).

Injunctions against dismissal

4-10   The court will not usually restrain an employer from terminating an employee's contract, but will leave the employee to his remedy in damages (*Chappell v Times Newspapers Ltd* [1975] 1 W.L.R. 482); in *Cresswell v Board of Inland Revenue* [1984] 2 All E.R. 713 at 719, Walton J stated that "damages and not an injunction is the proper remedy in virtually every case of breach of contract, especially one relating to master and servant". The basis for this rule is the need for mutual trust and confidence, mentioned above.

Two exceptions to the general rule have been developed. The first is where the employer retains confidence in the employee's integrity and ability; an injunction may then be granted if it is clear that it would be just to do so (*Hill v Parsons* [1972] Ch. 305; *Powell v Brent LBC* [1988] I.C.R. 176). The second is where the claimant's contract of employment requires a particular procedure to be followed as a precondition of dismissal, and that procedure has not been followed. On these facts in *Jones v Lee* [1980] I.C.R. 310 and *Robb v Hammersmith and Fulham LBC* [1991] I.R.L.R. 72, employees obtained injunctions even though they had lost the confidence of the employer; in the *Robb* case an interim injunction against dismissal pending the outcome of a contractual disciplinary procedure was granted on the "workable" basis of the claimant being suspended on full pay and the defendants being allowed to appoint a temporary substitute. In *Mezey v SW London and St George's Mental Health NHS Trust (No.2)* [2010] I.R.L.R. 512, an injunction was granted to stop a disciplinary hearing from proceeding at all.

4-11   There have been attempts in a number of cases to obtain an injunction based on the "contractual procedure" exception against a private sector employer who has lost trust and confidence in the claimant. In *Alexander v Standard Telephones & Cables Ltd* [1990] I.R.L.R. 55, for example, the claimants were refused an injunction to restrain redundancy dismissals which were alleged to be in breach of a procedure agreement; Aldous J held that the employers had less confidence in the dismissed men than in those who were retained, and could not be compelled by injunction to reinstate those who had been selected for redundancy. In *R. v BBC Ex p. Lavelle* [1983] I.C.R. 99, on the other hand, Woolf J granted an injunction to restrain the dismissal of an employee until she had been afforded the disciplinary hearing which her contract permitted; in another judicial review case, *R. (Arthurworrey) v Haringey LBC* [2002] I.C.R. 279, Jackson J granted an injunction prohibiting the employer from carrying out domestic proceedings before the employee had given evidence at a public inquiry concerning the same facts. Courts have also granted injunctions to restrain a suspension, as in *Mezey v SW London and St George's Mental Health NHS Trust (No.1)* [2007] I.R.L.R. 244. In cases where an employer is proposing to hold a disciplinary inquiry or tribunal, the courts will not intervene to remedy minor irregularities (*Kulkarni v Milton Keynes Hospital NHS Foundation Trust* [2009] I.R.L.R. 829). However an injunction may be granted where there is a substantial breach of contract and damages would be limited (*West London Mental Health NHS Trust v Chhabra* [2014] I.C.R. 194; *Edwards v Chesterfield Royal Hospital NHS Foundation Trust* [2012] I.R.L.R. 129) or where the domestic tribunal has acted improperly or it is inevitable that it will do so (*Ali v Southwark LBC* [1988] I.C.R. 567, following *Longley v NUJ* [1987] I.R.L.R. 109, a case involving a trade union internal tribunal). An appeal hearing was restrained by injunction where the employer proposed to consider increasing the disciplinary sanction in breach of contract (*McMillan v Airedale NHS Foundation Trust* [2014] I.R.L.R 803). The breaches of contract or procedural errors must be sufficiently serious to make the continued pursuit of the disciplinary process unfair in a manner which cannot be remedied within the proceedings themselves (*Hendy v Ministry of Justice* [2014] I.R.L.R. 856).

Injunctions to restrain other breaches of contract by an employer

In *Hughes v Southwark LBC* [1988] I.R.L.R. 55, the claimants alleged that the defendant council was unreasonably requiring them to do work which was not part of their contractual duties. Taylor J held that the *American Cyanamid* guidelines applied and that damages would not be an adequate remedy for the claimants. He granted an interim injunction preventing the council, pending a trial, from requiring compliance with the instruction. **4-12**

An injunction will not be granted to an employee who has failed to exhaust a domestic appeals procedure (*Longden v Bedfordshire CC* [1987] I.R.L.I.B. 323). Nor should an interim injunction lie to require an employer to allow access to his premises by an employee suspended on suspicion of gross misconduct, even when such access is sought to carry out the employee's duties as a shop steward (*City and Hackney Health Authority v National Union of Public Employees* [1985] I.R.L.R. 252).

Interim reinstatement

Sections 128–132 of the Employment Rights Act 1996 contain provisions for interim relief in unfair dismissal cases before employment tribunals where it is alleged that an employee has been dismissed for making protected disclosures or for carrying out certain health and safety, trade union or representative functions or activities (for trade union activities see the Trade Union and Labour Relations (Consolidation) Act 1992 ss.161 to 166). Application for interim relief must be made to the tribunal not later than seven days after the effective date of termination of employment. The tribunal may request the employer to reinstate the employee or re-engage him in another job pending the hearing and, in the event of the employer refusing to do this or failing to attend, the tribunal may make an order for the continuation of the contract of employment. The aim of this interim procedure is to preserve the status quo as it was before the dismissal until the full hearing. The tribunal's order is not an injunction and does not carry the contempt sanction. **4-13**

Interim reinstatement may not be ordered unless it appears "likely" that the applicant will succeed in establishing that his dismissal was for the specified reason or principal reason. The tribunal must make a summary assessment of whether it is likely that the claimant will succeed at a final hearing (*Mihaj v Sodexho Ltd* [2014] I.C.R. D25). The Employment Appeal Tribunal in *Taplin v Shippam Ltd* [1978] I.C.R. 1068 interpreted this as meaning that the employee must show not merely a reasonable prospect of success, not only a 51 per cent chance, but a "pretty good chance"—something more than 51 per cent. Although in other contexts the word "likely" means no more than "more likely than not" (e.g. *Bailey v Rolls Royce Ltd* [1984] I.C.R. 688), context is everything and there are good reasons for having a "comparatively high test in relation to interim relief" (*Dandpat v University of Bath* [2010] EWCA Civ 305). It is clearly a different and more stringent test than the "serious question to be tried" in *American Cyanamid* (see para.3-12).

Trade disputes

4-14   Certain acts which would otherwise give rise to liability in tort are protected from such liability by ss.219 to 220 of the Trade Union and Labour Relations (Consolidation) Act 1992, if done "in contemplation or furtherance of a trade dispute". Subsequent legislation has greatly reduced the range of acts to which the protection of this phrase, known as the "golden formula", is available, but the formula itself remains important for any strike or other industrial action: see, e.g. *P v NASUWT* [2003] 2 A.C. 663. For the trade dispute defence to succeed there must be a trade dispute, as widely defined by s.244, and the acts in question must be done in contemplation or furtherance of that dispute (*ISS Mediclean Ltd v GMB* [2015] I.R.L.R. 96).

There are two special statutory provisions regarding injunctions in this class of action. Section 221(1) of the Trade Union and Labour Relations (Consolidation) Act 1992 states that such injunctions should not be granted without notice, unless all reasonable steps have been taken to notify the defendant of the hearing and to give him an opportunity to be heard. Section 221(2) of the Act directs the court, in exercising its discretion whether or not to grant an injunction, to have regard to the likelihood of the defendant establishing the defence at trial—in contrast with the guidelines laid down in the *American Cyanamid* case, which would almost inevitably lead to the grant of an injunction on the basis of the balance of convenience. The test for granting an injunction is whether it is likely that the defendant would establish a defence to actions based on inducement to breach of contract; the court is not concerned with the merits of the underlying dispute, nor the balance of convenience between the parties, nor the convenience of the public (*London Underground Ltd v Associated Society of Locomotive Engineers and Firemen* [2012] I.R.L.R. 196).

In *Govia Thameslink Railway Ltd v ASLEF* [2017] I.C.R. 497, an employer sought an injunction to restrain industrial action on the basis that it infringed its EU freedoms of establishment and services. The Court of Appeal confirmed that the American Cyanamid guidelines applied in such a case, but refused the injunction on the basis that the train company had failed to establish an arguable case.

4-15   An injunction should ordinarily be refused where the defendant has shown that the defence of statutory immunity is more likely than not to succeed; in exceptional cases, however, where the consequences to the claimant or others of refusing an injunction may be disastrous, the defendant may be required to show a higher degree of probability that the defence will succeed before an injunction is refused (*NWL Ltd v Woods* [1979] 1 W.L.R. 1294).

In *NWL Ltd v Woods* Lord Diplock said:

> "[I]t is in the nature of industrial action that it can be promoted effectively only so long as it is possible to strike while the iron is still hot; once postponed it is unlikely that it can be revived ... [accordingly], the grant or refusal of an interim injunction generally disposes finally of the action; in practice actions of this type seldom if ever come to actual trial."

Despite these observations, the courts in many trade dispute cases, especially in the 1970s and 1980s, adhered to the fiction that the interim decision is merely a temporary measure to preserve the status quo (i.e. no strike) pending a trial: see, e.g. the decision of the Court of Appeal in *Associated British Ports Ltd v TGWU*

[1989] 1 W.L.R. 939 (reversed on other grounds in the House of Lords). Trade dispute litigation has been revived in recent years and employers became quick to seek injunctions from the High Court, but the Court of Appeal has reduced the scope for granting an interim injunction based on the purported failure of a trade union to adhere to the "golden formula" for ballot notices and strike notices set out in Part V of the Trade Union and Labour Relations (Consolidation) Act 1992, suggesting that substantial compliance may be sufficient to defeat an injunction application: *RMT v Serco; ASLEF v London Midland* [2011] I.R.L.R. 399.

As the statute prescribes a maximum liability of a trade union to pay damages to an employer arising out of industrial action, the claimant can usually argue that damages would therefore be an inadequate remedy (*Mercury Communications Ltd v Scott-Garner* [1984] Ch. 37).

Disclosure orders

An interim order for disclosure may be made in addition to an interim injunc-   **4-16**
tion in a breach of fiduciary duty claim. The rationale for this is to correct the misrepresentation sown in the minds of the claimant's clients that the defendants had been entitled to solicit them (*Intelsec Systems v Grech-Cini* [2000] 1 W.L.R. 1190, in which the claimant sought disclosure of names and addresses of all those the defendants had contacted). Interim disclosure is an exceptional and not a routine order and matters relevant to the exercise of discretion include the inability of the claimant to plead a case without disclosure, the width of the order sought, the saving of costs, the adequacy of damages as a remedy, the need to take pragmatic steps to protect the business from future and further loss and the need to police the injunction order (*Aon Ltd v JCT Reinsurance Brokers Ltd* [2010] I.R.L.R. 600).

2   RESTRAINT OF PUBLICATION

On August 1, 2011 Lord Neuberger MR issued the document Practice Guidance: **4-17**
Interim Non-Disclosure Orders, which is considered in Ch.5. The following paragraphs of this chapter consider the relevant statutory provisions and some of the case law.

The impact of the Human Rights Act

Prior restraint of publication by injunction is a contentious topic. Articles 8 and   **4-18**
10 of the ECHR come into conflict. Article 8(1) states that "everyone has the right to respect for his private and family life, his home and correspondence". Article 10(1) states that "everyone has the right to freedom of expression", but art.10(2) permits restrictions which are

> "prescribed by law and necessary in a democratic society in the interests of national security, territorial integrity or public safety, for the prevention of disorder or crime, for the protection of health or morals, for the protection of the reputation or rights of others, for preventing the disclosure of information received in confidence, or for maintaining the authority and impartiality of the judiciary."

In *Re S (a child) (identification: restriction on publication)* [2005] 1 A.C. 593 Lord Steyn, speaking of the conflict between arts 8 and 10, said that the court's approach should be as follows: (a) neither article takes precedence over the other; (b) an intense focus on the comparative importance of the specific rights being claimed in the individual case is necessary; (c) the justifications for interfering with or restricting each right must be taken into account; and (d) the proportionality test must be applied to each.

4-19   Lord Nicholls said in *Attorney General v Punch Ltd* [2003] 1 A.C. 1046 at [27], after referring to art.10:

> "Restraints on the freedom of expression are acceptable only to the extent they are necessary and justified by compelling reasons. The need for the restraint must be convincingly established. Restraints on the freedom of the press call for particularly rigorous scrutiny."

Section 12 of the Human Rights Act 1998 provides:

> "(1)   This section applies if a court is considering whether to grant any relief which, if granted, might affect the exercise of the Convention right to freedom of expression.
>
> (2)   If the person against whom the application for relief is to be made ('the respondent') is neither present nor represented, no such relief is to be granted unless the court is satisfied—
>
>   (a)   that the applicant has taken all practicable steps to notify the respondent; or
>   (b)   that there are compelling reasons why the respondent should not be notified.
>
> (3)   No such relief is to be granted so as to restrain publication before trial unless the court is satisfied that the applicant is likely to establish that publication should not be allowed.
>
> (4)   The court must have particular regard to the importance of the Convention right to freedom of expression and, where the proceedings relate to material which the respondent claims, or which appears to the court, to be journalistic, literary or artistic material (or to conduct connected with such material) to—
>
>   (a)   the extent to which—
>   (i)   the material has, or is about to, become available to the public; or
>   (ii)   it is, or would be, in the public interest for the material to be published;
>   (b)   any relevant privacy code.
>
> (5)   In this section 'court' includes a tribunal; and 'relief' includes any remedy or order (other than in criminal proceedings)."

4-20   In *Cream Holdings Ltd v Banerjee* [2005] 1 A.C. 253, the House of Lords considered in detail the meaning of "likely" in s.12(3) of the Human Rights Act. Lord Nicholls said that Parliament's main purpose in enacting s.12(3) was to set a higher threshold for the grant of interlocutory injunctions against the media than the *American Cyanamid* guideline of a serious question to be tried or a real prospect of success at the trial. However he rejected the defendants' submission that "likely" in s.12(3) means "more likely than not" in every case. For example, he observed, the test of probability of success clearly does not apply to an interim injunction for a matter of hours or longer pending a hearing on notice, nor to interim relief pending an appeal, since confidentiality, once breached, is lost forever. He continued (at [19], [20] and [22]):

> "The matter goes further than these procedural difficulties. Cases may arise where the adverse consequences of disclosure of information would be extremely serious, such as a grave risk of personal injury to a particular person. Threats may have been made against a person accused or convicted of a crime or a person who gave evidence at a trial. Disclosure of his current whereabouts might have extremely serious consequences. Despite the potential seriousness of the adverse consequences of disclosure, the applicant's claim to confidentiality may be weak. The applicant's case may depend, for instance, on a disputed question of fact on which the applicant has an arguable but distinctly poor case. It would be extraordinary if in such a case the court were compelled to apply a 'probability of success' test and therefore, regardless of the seriousness of the

possible adverse consequences, refuse to restrain publication until the disputed issue of fact can be resolved at the trial.

These considerations indicate that 'likely' in section 12(3) cannot have been intended to mean 'more likely than not' in all situations. That, as a test of universal application, would set the degree of likelihood too high. In some cases application of that test would achieve the antithesis of a fair trial. Some flexibility is essential. The intention of Parliament must be taken to be that 'likely' should have an extended meaning which sets as a normal prerequisite to the grant of an injunction before trial a likelihood of success at the trial higher than the commonplace *American Cyanamid* standard of 'real prospect' but permits the court to dispense with this higher standard where particular circumstances make this necessary ...

Section 12(3) makes the likelihood of success at the trial an essential element in the court's consideration of whether to make an interim order. But in order to achieve the necessary flexibility the degree of likelihood of success at the trial needed to satisfy section 12(3) must depend on the circumstances. There can be no single, rigid standard governing all applications for interim restraint orders. Rather, on its proper construction the effect of section 12(3) is that the court is not to make an interim restraint order unless satisfied the applicant's prospects of success at the trial are sufficiently favourable to justify such an order being made in the particular circumstances of the case. As to what degree of likelihood makes the prospects of success 'sufficiently favourable', the general approach should be that courts will be exceedingly slow to make interim restraint orders where the applicant has not satisfied the court he will probably ('more likely than not') succeed at the trial. In general, that should be the threshold an applicant must cross before the court embarks on exercising its discretion, duly taking into account the relevant jurisprudence on article 10 and any countervailing Convention rights. But there will be cases where it is necessary for a court to depart from this general approach and a lesser degree of likelihood will suffice as a prerequisite. Circumstances where this may be so include those mentioned above: where the potential adverse consequences of disclosure are particularly grave, or where a short-lived injunction is needed to enable the court to hear and give proper consideration to an application for interim relief pending the trial or any relevant appeal."

The correct approach on an application for an interlocutory injunction to restrain the publication of information on the basis of breach of confidence is to consider first whether art.8 of the ECHR is engaged, secondly, whether art.10 is engaged, and thirdly, whether the claimant has shown, in accordance with s.12(3) of the Human Rights Act 1998, that he is likely to establish at trial that publication should not be allowed; in respect of the third question, the court should be "exceedingly slow" to make interim restraint orders where the court is not satisfied that he is more likely than not to succeed at trial once the balancing exercise between his art.8 rights and the defendants' art.10 rights has been carried out (*Lord Browne of Madingley v Associated Newspapers Ltd* [2008] QB 103).

The Supreme Court in the celebrated case of *PJS v News Group Newspapers* [2016] A.C. 1081 considered an interim injunction restraining publication of a story alleging extra-marital sexual activities involving a famous couple in the entertainment business. After the injunction was granted the story was widely published overseas and on internet websites and social media so the defendant applied to set aside the injunction as the protected information was in the public domain. The Supreme Court endorsed the approach in *Banerjee* holding, in relation to the interplay between art.8 and art.10, that:

"(i) neither article has preference over the other, (ii) where their values are in conflict, what is necessary is an intense focus on the comparative importance of the rights being claimed in the individual case, (iii) the justifications for interfering with or restricting each right must be taken into account and (iv) the proportionality test must be applied".

The impact of s.12 and art.10 on injunction cases is not confined to claims for **4-21** breach of privacy, defamation and the like. An example is the trade mark case of *Interflora Inc v Marks and Spencer plc* [2014] EWHC 4168 (Ch); [2015] F.S.R. 13. The claimants sought an interim injunction to prohibit the defendant from using the search word "Interflora" in internet advertising. Birss J said:

> "In my judgment in this case, the Article 10 right of the defendant is engaged. What the defendant wishes to do is publish an advertisement, and, to that extent, this injunction could engage its freedom of speech rights.
>
> But it is important not to overstate the importance of the defendant's Article 10 rights in a case like this. First, it is, indeed, commercial speech. It is not about artistic or political freedom to express facts or opinions or to speak unwelcome truths to power. This case is really about competition, fair or unfair; and that is how the CJEU analysed it.
>
> The important collision of rights here is between the claimant's intellectual property right, its trade mark, and the defendant's right to compete fairly with the claimants. Although the advertisement complained of is an advertisement and, in that sense, engages Article 10, a key element of it, which is an important part of the real dispute, is the fact that a user clicks on it and then is linked to the Marks and Spencer website. In that sense, it is not merely an advertisement; it is a link to a shop, and selling flowers can be the result. However, since Article 10 is, in my judgment, engaged, it seems to me that section 12(3) does apply.
>
> I turn to *Cream Holdings Ltd v. Banerjee.* [Birss J considered the speech of Lord Nicholls at paragraphs [22]-[23], and continued:] It is clear from this that, in general, the threshold for the test of likelihood means "probably will win", "more likely than not", but there are clear exceptions and in the end, the court has to conduct a careful balancing of rights and freedoms…
>
> It seems to me that … it is impossible to say that Interflora are more likely than not to win [at trial]. So, if a proper approach under section 12(3) to this case requires the balance to tip in favour of the claimant on the merits, then I should not grant an injunction.
>
> However, it seems to me that in a case like this, it is not enough to stop there. Cream Holdings shows that the balance of rights and of harm, and so on, may well mean that an interim injunction is appropriate even if the court cannot say that the claimant will probably win. In my judgment, this is especially so where, as here, this is in no sense a weak case by the claimant. As I said, the merits are finely balanced. It is clear to me that the merits come well past satisfying the American Cyanamid level."

After a detailed analysis of the parties' arguments Birss J dismissed the application for an interim injunction.

However obvious the breach of confidence involved in a publication, if it contains material which engages art.10 on a matter of public concern a balancing exercise has to be undertaken and an injunction may be refused: see, e.g. *London Regional Transport v Mayor of London* [2003] E.M.L.R. 4. On the other hand, in carrying out that exercise, it is arguable that a duty of confidentiality expressly assumed under a contract carries more weight, when balanced against the restriction of the right of freedom of expression, than a duty of confidentiality not buttressed by express agreement (*Campbell v Frisbee* [2003] I.C.R. 141).

Injunctions contra mundum

4-22   An injunction to restrain publication is occasionally granted *contra mundum*, that is to say, against the whole world (see para.1-12). In *Venables and Thompson v News Group Newspapers Ltd* [2001] Fam. 430 the claimants, the murderers of two-year-old James Bulger, were granted permanent injunctions (extending beyond their 18th birthdays) preventing disclosure of their identities. One ground was the real risk that, given the public detestation of their crime, their lives might be in danger: see the later proceedings brought by the first claimant, *Venables v News Group Newspapers Ltd* [2010] EWHC B18 (QB); see also *X (a Woman formerly known as Mary Bell) v SO* [2003] 2 F.C.R. 686, and Ch.10.

However, it is the duty of the court to examine with care each application for a departure from the ordinary rule that the press can report everything which takes place in a criminal court. In *Re S (A Child) (Identification: Restrictions on Publication)* [2005] 1 A.C. 593, a mother had been charged with the murder of one of her sons. The guardian of another son, S, then aged five, obtained an injunction from a judge of the Family Division preventing not merely the identification of S and the school he attended, which was not controversial, but also publication of the names and photographs of the mother and her deceased son, which was. The House of Lords held that the freedom of the press, subject to existing statutory restrictions, to report proceedings at criminal trials is a valuable check on the criminal process and promotes public confidence in the administration of justice. The injunction, in respect of the mother and the dead boy, was discharged.

Re Trinity Mirror Plc [2008] QB 770 is another example of the same principle.   **4-23**
A man had pleaded guilty in the Crown Court to child pornography offences. The Crown Court judge made an order restraining the media from protecting his identity. The reason given was to protect his children, even though they had been neither victims of nor witnesses to his offences. A five-judge Court of Appeal, Criminal Division, held that the Crown Court had had no jurisdiction to grant an injunction for the protection of the defendant's children. The High Court would have had jurisdiction, but it would have been wrong in any event for an injunction to have been granted. Sir Igor Judge P said that it was impossible to over-emphasise the importance to be attached to the ability of the media to report criminal trials. However, in *R. (Press Association) v Cambridge Crown Court* [2012] EWCA Crim 2434 Lord Judge CJ accepted that anonymity might be granted to a defendant in an extreme case where to identify him would imperil his life or safety or that of his family. In the Northern Irish case of *ZY v Higgins and Northern Ireland Courts and Tribunal Service* [2013] NIQB 8 McCloskey J granted anonymity to a defendant who had pleaded guilty to sexual offences and blackmail and been sentenced to 21 months' imprisonment, where there was evidence of a real risk of suicide if his name was publicised.

Reporting restriction orders *contra mundum* are regularly granted in Family Division cases involving children: see *Re Jane* [2010] EWHC 3221 (Fam), discussed at para.10-77; *Re J (A Child)* [2013] EWHC 2694 (Fam) and Precedent 28.

The form of order and its effect on third parties

David Shayler was a former MI5 officer who wrote newspaper articles using   **4-24**
confidential material about MI5's intelligence activities (see *R. v Shayler* [2003] 1 A.C. 247). The Attorney General sought and obtained from Hooper J an interim injunction restraining Mr Shayler from disclosing to any newspaper:

> "any information obtained by him in the course of or by virtue of his employment in and position as a member of the Security Service (whether presented as fact or fiction) which relates to or which may be construed as relating to the Security Service or its membership or activities or to security or intelligence activities generally."

There were provisos for material disclosed with the written agreement of the Attorney General and for the repetition of information disclosed in a published newspaper article. Even with the provisos, however, the form of order was capable of catching material that was plainly not confidential and still less a threat to national security, such as information about the quality of food served in the MI5 canteen. In subsequent contempt proceedings against *Punch* and its editor for aiding and abetting a breach of Hooper J's order (*Attorney General v Punch Ltd* [2003]

1 A.C. 1046), Lord Nicholls said (at [35]–[36] and [46]):

"An interlocutory injunction, like any other injunction, must be expressed in terms which are clear and certain. The injunction must define precisely what acts are prohibited. The court must ensure that the language of its order makes plain what is permitted and what is prohibited. This is a well-established, soundly-based principle. A person should not be put at risk of being in contempt of court by an ambiguous prohibition, or a prohibition the scope of which is obviously open to dispute. An order expressed to restrain publication of 'confidential information' or 'information whose disclosure risks damaging national security' would be undesirable for this reason.

For the same reason an order restraining publication of material whose disclosure '*arguably* risks damaging national security', or words to the like effect, would not be satisfactory. Its ambit would not be sufficiently certain. An injunction against Mr Shayler drawn in such terms would clearly exclude from its scope some information whose disclosure would be harmless. But such a formula would still not produce a clear boundary line. Including the word 'arguably' in the injunction would not render clear a boundary which otherwise would lack certainty in its application. There may well be matters where it would not be readily obvious whether disclosure would or would not 'arguably' risk damaging national security ... An interlocutory order ought not be drawn in terms where it is apparent that such a dispute may arise over its scope ...

This discussion does, of course, underline how important it is for courts to seek to ensure that injunctions are not drawn in wider terms than necessary. This is of particular importance when the terms of the injunction may, in practice, affect the conduct of third parties."

The House held that the proper remedy of a third party (such as a newspaper or magazine) affected by the order was to apply to the court for the injunction to be varied. The order should make it clear that the party enjoined and anyone else whose conduct is affected by the order has that right. Indeed, the modern practice set out in the 2011 Practice Guidance: Interim Non-Disclosure Orders (see Appendix to Ch.5) is to require the media to be given notice of an application for an injunction of this kind.

Public domain exception

4-25   There is no purpose in granting an interim injunction restraining publication unless it will (at least arguably) prevent further material damage to the claimant's interests (see, e.g. *Lord Advocate v Scotsman Publications Ltd* [1990] 1 A.C. 812, the *Inside Intelligence* case). Where allegations have already been widely disseminated, an interim injunction will usually be refused for that reason. An exception, dating from a time before the internet, was *Attorney General v Guardian Newspapers Ltd* [1987] 1 W.L.R. 1248, where the House of Lords, by a 3:2 majority, upheld an interim injunction against the publication in England and Wales of the book *Spycatcher*, or of the allegations contained in it, despite the fact that it was by then heading to the bestseller lists in New York. (The interim injunction was discharged at trial [1990] A.C. 109.)

An interim order restricting the communication of ideas and information should therefore generally include a proviso that it will not apply to information which has already entered the public domain: see *Attorney General v Times Newspapers Ltd* [2001] 1 W.L.R. 885, where the proviso read:

"Nothing in this [order] prevents the Defendants or any of them from republishing anything which at the date of publication or intended publication by the Defendant or Defendants ... has previously been published in any other newspaper, magazine or other publication, whether within or outside the jurisdiction of the Court, to such an extent that the information is in the public domain (other than in a case where the only such publication was made by or was caused by the Defendants or any of them); [or] has previously been published by or through the internet or other electronic media to such an extent that the information is in the public domain (other than in a case where the only such publication was made by or was caused by the Defendants or any of them)."

In *CTB v News Group Newspapers Ltd* [2011] EWHC 1326 (QB) an interim injunction was granted to restrain a story about an alleged sexual relationship involving a married footballer who was then named on Twitter and the internet. The defendants argued that privacy injunctions ceased to serve any useful purpose in the internet age and the court should beware of acting like King Canute. However Eady J continued the injunction saying that the "modern law of privacy is not concerned solely with information or 'secrets': it is also concerned importantly with intrusion" ... "Wall-to-wall excoriation in national newspapers, whether tabloid or 'broadsheet', is likely to be significantly more intrusive and distressing for those concerned than the availability of information on the Internet or in foreign journals to those, however many, who take the trouble to look it up."

The fact that confidential documents have appeared briefly on the internet before the grant of an injunction is not a bar to an order: *Barclays Bank Plc v Guardian News Media Ltd* [2009] EWHC 591; (2009) 153(13) S.J.L.B. 30 QB; *AB v Sunday Newspapers* [2014] NICA 58. Even widespread publication of sexual allegations across the internet worldwide does not mean that an injunction has no purpose. In *PJS v News Group Newspapers* [2016] A.C. 1081 the Supreme Court endorsed the *CTB* approach and continued an interim injunction despite the story and the names of those involved appearing in overseas and Scottish newspapers and on the internet saying that it was quite different for the information "to be recorded in eye-catching headlines and sensational terms in a national newspaper, or to be freely available on search engines". The Court gave particular attention to the utility of protecting the couple's children by preventing domestic publication.

Defamation

In *Bonnard v Perryman* [1891] 2 Ch 269, a five-judge Court of Appeal held that **4-26** an interim injunction will not be granted to restrain publication of an allegedly defamatory statement if the defendant adduces evidence that he will seek to justify the statement (in other words, prove that it is true) at trial. This great case, still good law to this day, remains a pillar of the right to free speech in this jurisdiction.

As a result of the *Bonnard v Perryman* principle, it used to be extremely unusual for claimants to apply for, or be granted, interim injunctions to restrain the publication of a slander or libel. Nowadays interim injunctions to restrain defamatory publications are becoming more frequent. This is because defendants can easily publish false and malicious allegations on the internet, and some people choose to do so as a means of extortion, harassment or revenge, or for other motives. The Protection from Harassment Act 1997 s.7(4) provides that speech can amount to harassment (see 4-62). Interim injunctions are increasingly granted to restrain harassment in the form of campaigns of vilification. Some of these campaigns involve the publication of defamatory allegations (others involve indecent images, or the publication of private or personal information). However, before granting an interim injunction on the basis of harassment, the court considers first whether reliance on the law of harassment is an attempt to by-pass the law on freedom of speech, and will only grant the injunction if satisfied that that is not the case (*ZAM v CFW* [2013] EWHC 662 (QB), per Tugendhat J).

It applies to cases where the defendant intends to justify the "sting" of the allegations even though he cannot prove the precise facts stated (*Khashoggi v IPC*

Magazines Ltd [1986] 1 W.L.R. 1412); it also applies where the defendant intends to plead fair comment on a matter of public interest (*Fraser v Evans* [1969] 1 QB 349 at 360, per Lord Denning MR), and likewise if the publication is prima facie privileged. However, an injunction may be granted if the defence is a sham or clearly has no chance of success at trial, or (in the case of qualified privilege) if there is "absolutely overwhelming" evidence of malice (*Harakas v Baltic Mercantile and Shipping Exchange Ltd* [1982] 1 W.L.R. 958; *Herbage v Pressdram Ltd* [1984] 2 All E.R. 769).

4-27   The rule in *Bonnard v Perryman* as to the defence of justification is unaffected by the *American Cyanamid* case or by s.12(3) of the Human Rights Act 1998 (*Greene v Associated Newspapers Ltd* [2005] QB 972). An interim injunction against alleged defamation will not be granted where the defendant is saying what he honestly believes to be true. This principle has been further emphasised by the incorporation of art.10 of the ECHR into English law. An injunction can only be granted if the court is satisfied that a plea of justification *must* fail (per Stocker LJ in *Williams v Wolman* Unreported January 30, 1990 CA).

The same rule applies to cases of injurious falsehood ("trade libel") (*Bestobell Paints Ltd v Bigg* [1975] F.S.R. 421), but not to trademark infringement or passing off cases (*Boehringer Ingelheim Ltd v Vetplus Ltd* [2007] F.S.R. 29), nor to a claim based on unlawful interference with contractual rights (*Microdata Information Services Ltd v Rivendale Ltd* [1991] F.S.R. 681). If the claimant's principal purpose, however the cause of action may be framed, is to protect his reputation, an interim injunction should be refused (*Sim v Heinz Ltd* [1959] 1 W.L.R. 313). For example, where the tort alleged is conspiracy to injure the claimant's interests and an interim injunction application is made, the court will scrutinise it carefully to ensure that the allegation of conspiracy is not simply an attempt to circumvent *Bonnard v Perryman* (*Gulf Oil Ltd v Page* [1987] Ch. 327). The public interest in freedom of speech is one of the most important factors to be taken into account (*Femis-Bank (Anguilla) Ltd v Lazar* [1991] Ch. 391).

On the other hand, once a final judgment has been entered, whether after a trial, or summarily, a defendant's right to freedom of expression does not preclude the grant of an injunction. On the contrary, a claimant who succeeds in obtaining a final judgment is normally entitled to a permanent injunction to vindicate the right that he has proved that he has. So where a defamatory allegation has been proved to be false there is no public interest in allowing it to be republished, and a strong public interest in preventing the public from being further misinformed. Final or permanent injunctions to restrain defamatory statements are routinely granted after final judgments. (*ZAM v CFW*, above). But the claimant must show that there is a threat or a real risk of further publication by the defendant; there is no general rule that permanent injunctions will always be granted to successful claimants in defamation actions (per Tugendhat J in *Citation Plc v Ellis Whittam Ltd* [2012] EWHC 549 (QB)).

Misuse of private information

4-28   The courts have, at least since *Prince Albert v Strange* (1851) 41 E.R. 1171, granted injunctions restraining the publication of offending material in a claim for breach of confidence, whether it be to protect commercial information (*Hivac Ltd v Park Royal Ltd* [1946] Ch. 169), marital secrets (*Argyll (Duchess) v Argyll (Duke)* [1967] Ch. 302), royal secrets (*Attorney General v Barker* [1990] 3 All E.R. 257), Cabinet secrets (*Attorney General v Jonathan Cape Ltd* [1976] QB 752 (the *Crossman diaries* case)), or documents disclosed in civil litigation (*Distillers Co Ltd v Times Newspapers Ltd* [1975] QB 613). As Buxton LJ observed in *McKennitt v Ash*

[2008] QB 73, there is no English domestic law tort of invasion of privacy. Accordingly, in developing a right to protect private information, the English courts have to proceed through the tort of breach of confidence, into which the jurisprudence of arts 8 and 10 of the ECHR has to be "shoehorned". In the traditional breach of confidence claim there is a pre-existing relationship of confidence between the parties, but the cause of action also arises where the defendant has acquired by unlawful or surreptitious means information which he should have known he was not free to use. In *Campbell v MGN* [2004] 2 A.C. 457 (see below), Lord Nicholls suggested that the tort might be renamed "misuse of private information". The claimant must identify clearly the precise information sought to be protected; this may be contained in a confidential schedule.

Where an injunction was sought against a blackmailer, although this still affected the right to freedom of expression it was said that blackmail constituted a misuse of free speech rights and reduced the weight to be attached to free speech and increased the weight in favour of restraint as the court would not encourage blackmailers. The grant of a privacy injunction to block blackmail was a legitimate aim of preventing crime and where an allegation was being used to blackmail someone, its truth would not necessarily be considered an obstacle to the grant of an injunction based on misuse of private information (*LJY v Persons Unknown* [2018] E.M.L.R. 19).

Since the Human Rights Act came into force, the courts have seen a long-running battle between individuals, especially those in the public eye, seeking to develop a law of privacy, and the media who resist it. The claimants in *Douglas v Hello! Ltd* [2001] QB 967 (Michael Douglas and Catherine Zeta-Jones), who had entered into an exclusive contract with *OK!* magazine for publication of photographs of their wedding, sought interlocutory injunctions to prohibit the publication of unauthorised pictures of the same event by *OK!*'s rivals, *Hello!* The Court of Appeal discharged an injunction granted by Hunt J. A damages claim went to trial before Lindsay J, and on appeal from that decision a differently constituted Court of Appeal expressed the view ([2006] QB 125 at [251]–[259]) that the interlocutory decision of their predecessors had been wrong.

A v B Plc [2003] QB 195 was a much publicised (and unsuccessful) attempt by a professional footballer to obtain an injunction to prevent publication of details of his extra-marital affairs. The judgment of the court, delivered by Lord Woolf CJ, laid down a series of guidelines, covering several pages, as to whether judges should grant interim injunctions to restrain publication before trial where the claimant alleges breach of confidence and the defendant relies on the right to freedom of expression. They included the following:

    4-29

(a) Interference with press freedom has to be justified even when there is no identifiable special public interest in the material in question being published, since the existence of a free press is desirable in itself. Regardless of the quality of the material which it is intended to publish, prima facie the court should not interfere with publication.

(b) Where protection of privacy is justified, an action for breach of confidence will provide the necessary protection; it is unnecessary, at least at first instance, to consider whether there is a separate tort of infringement of privacy.

(c) A duty of confidence will arise whenever the defendant is in a situation where he knows or ought to know that the claimant can reasonably expect his privacy to be protected. This will depend on all the circumstances of the relationship between the parties at the time of the threatened or actual breach of the alleged duty of confidence.

(d) The fact that the information has been obtained by unlawful means such as bugging does not necessarily mean that an injunction should be granted, but it may be a compelling factor in the exercise of discretion.

(e) The more stable a sexual relationship, the greater its significance in determining whether the claimant has the right to have the confidence in it respected.

(f) A public figure is entitled to a private life, but high profile individuals may be role models, and "if you have courted public attention you will have less ground to object to the intrusion which follows". In many situations, the public have "an understandable and so a legitimate interest in being told the information".

Holding that it was most unlikely that a permanent injunction would be granted at trial, the Court of Appeal discharged the interim injunction granted at first instance. The claimant could then be identified as the footballer Gary Flitcroft.

The phrase "an understandable and so legitimate interest in being told the information" attracted widespread criticism; it appears to equate whatever interests the public with the public interest. However in *Campbell v MGN Ltd* [2003] QB 633 at [40], a differently constituted Court of Appeal expressed the view that it had been misunderstood. The Lord Chief Justice had not been speaking of "private facts which a fair-minded person would consider it offensive to disclose". The *Campbell* case itself was a claim for damages, not for an injunction, and was taken to the House of Lords ([2004] 2 A.C. 457); it is an important authority on the balancing exercise between ECHR arts 8 and 10 in breach of confidence cases.

4-30   *A v B Plc* was more directly criticised by Buxton LJ, giving the leading judgment in the Court of Appeal in *McKennitt v Ash* [2008] QB 73 as being irreconcilable with the subsequent decision of the European Court of Human Rights in *Von Hannover v Germany* (2004) 40 E.H.R.R. 1, in which the Strasbourg Court held that Princess Caroline of Monaco had been deprived of a proper remedy to protect her privacy when the German courts allowed photographs of her taken without her consent to be published. Buxton LJ said that "it seems clear that *A v B Plc* cannot be read as any sort of binding authority on the content of Articles 8 and 10".

Gross LJ said in *Hutcheson (formerly known as "KGM") v News Group Newspapers Ltd* [2012] E.M.L.R. 38:

> "There is an important distinction between the desire to keep information private and invoking the full panoply of the Court's jurisdiction in order to do so. It is and should remain a strong thing to impose a prior restraint on publication."

An illustration of the last proposition is *McClaren v News Group Newspapers Ltd* [2012] EWHC 2466 (QB), in which a former manager of the England football team failed to obtain an injunction preventing *The Sun* from publishing a "kiss and tell" story of a sexual relationship. Lindblom J noted that the claimant had previously disclosed an earlier extra-marital relationship in a national newspaper, telling its readers that he was happily married and that his marriage would survive. Another, also from the world of football, is *Ferdinand v MGN Ltd* [2011] EWHC 2454 (QB).

4-31   The claimant in *K v News Group Newspapers Ltd* [2011] 1 W.L.R. 1827, a well-known personality in the entertainment industry and a married man with teenage children, had had an affair with a work colleague. When a newspaper sought to publish the fact of the affair and that it was the real cause of the colleague subsequently losing her job, the claimant sought an injunction restraining publication, supported by both his wife and his former colleague. The Court of Appeal granted an injunction. It held that the benefits to be achieved by publication in the interests of free speech were wholly outweighed by the harm which would be done through the interference with the right to privacy of all those affected, especially where the rights of children were in play.

In the *K* case the claimant had a cause of action for misuse of his private information: the effect on his children reinforced his claim, but did not give the children a cause of action of their own. In *OPO v MLA* the claimant child, acting through his mother as litigation friend, sought an injunction to prohibit publication of his father's autobiography on the grounds (put forward by the mother) that publication would traumatise the child. It was held both by Bean J ([2014] EWHC 2468 (QB)) and in the Court of Appeal ([2014] EWCA Civ 1277) that there was simply no cause of action under this heading: the information about the father's life was his own, not the child's. (The Court of Appeal granted an injunction on other grounds which was discharged by the Supreme Court: *Rhodes v OPO* [2015] 2 W.L.R. 1373.) On the other hand, in *Murray v Express Newspapers* [2009] Ch 481, it was held that photographers who took pictures of the 19-month old son of the author J.K. Rowling against the wishes of his parents were (at least arguably) violating the child's right to privacy.

Where personal safety is at stake the balancing exercise may be entirely different, as in *AB v Sunday Newspapers* [2014] NICA 58, where the Northern Ireland Court of Appeal granted an injunction restraining the naming of the claimant as a police informer, and did so notwithstanding that he had already been named in a blog.

Super-injunctions

In a few privacy cases claimants have sought interim injunctions not only prohibiting the publication of material about them but also prohibiting anyone from disclosing the existence of the injunction itself. In one case (*RJW v Guardian News and Media Ltd* [2009] EWHC 2540 (QB)) a corporate claimant, Trafigura Plc, was granted an interim injunction of this type which prohibited the disclosure by anyone with notice of the order not only from repeating certain allegations, said to originate from a "whistleblower", about the dumping of toxic waste, but also from reporting the fact of the litigation. The matter became one of constitutional importance when a Member of Parliament tabled a question to the Secretary of State for Justice disclosing the existence of the injunction. The injunction was amended, by consent, to make it clear that it did not prevent the publication or reporting of proceedings in Parliament. However the widespread concerns which the case had caused led Lord Neuberger MR to establish and chair a "committee on super-injunctions".

The committee's report, published on 20 May 2011 on the judiciary website, drew attention to the distinction between super-injunctions and anonymised injunctions. A super-injunction is an interim injunction which restrains a person from: (i) publishing information which concerns the applicant and is said to be confidential or private; and (ii) publicising or informing others of the existence of the order and the proceedings (the "super" element of the order). This is to be contrasted with an anonymised injunction, which is an interim injunction which restrains a person from publishing information which concerns the applicant and is said to be confidential or private where the names of either or both of the parties to the proceedings are not stated. The committee noted that there had only been a handful of super-injunction cases.

The proper approach to an application for a super-injunction, properly so called, is that of Tugendhat J in *John Terry (previously referred to as LNS) v Persons Unknown* [2010] 1 F.C.R. 659. He said at [138]–[139]:

"The reason why, on some occasions, applicants wish for there to be an order restricting

4-32

4-33

reports of the fact that an injunction has been granted is in order to prevent the alleged wrongdoer from being tipped off about the proceedings before an injunction could be applied for, or made against him, or before he can be served. In the interval between learning of the intention of the applicant to bring proceedings, and the receipt by the alleged wrongdoer of an injunction binding upon him, the alleged wrongdoer might consider that he or she could disclose the information, and hope to avoid the risk of being in contempt of court. Alternatively, in some cases, the alleged wrongdoer may destroy any evidence which may be needed in order to identify him as the source of the leak. Tipping off of the alleged wrongdoer can thus defeat the purpose of the order. If a prohibition of the disclosure of the making of the injunction is included in an order for the purpose of preventing tipping off, and if the order provides for a return date (as the Practice Direction envisages) then the prohibition on disclosure may normally be expected to expire once the alleged wrongdoer has been served with an injunction, or at the return date (whichever is earlier)."

In *Donald v Ntuli (Guardian News and Media Ltd intervening)* [2011] 1 W.L.R. 294 the claimant, a member of the "boy band" Take That, had been granted a super-injunction against the defendant, with whom he had previously been in a relationship. The Court of Appeal upheld some of the substantive elements of the injunction restricting publication of information about the claimant, but discharged the super-injunction (and also an order for anonymity).

Anonymised injunctions

4-34   Anonymised injunctions have been more frequent and, in some cases, just as controversial. An order for anonymity and reporting restrictions is a derogation from the principle of open justice, as to which see *A v BBC* [2014] 2 W.L.R. 1243, SC. There are some cases in which anonymity must be given to a respondent, because if it is not, the naming of a respondent may indirectly enable readers who already know other information about the case to identify the claimant, a process known as jigsaw identification (*G v G and Wikimedia Foundation Inc* [2009] EWHC 3148 (QB)).

An order for anonymity cannot be made simply because the parties consent. The court should only make such an order after closely scrutinising the application, considering whether a degree of restraint on publication is necessary and, if so, whether there is any less restrictive or more acceptable alternative than that which is sought. If the claimant is refused anonymity, that will mean that significantly less other information about the case will be publishable than if the proceedings had been anonymised (*JIH v News Group Newspapers Ltd* [2011] 2 All E.R. 324, where the claimant was granted anonymity by the Court of Appeal). In *Goodwin v NGN Ltd* [2011] EWHC 1437 (QB), Tugendhat J refused anonymity to the claimant, the chief executive of a major banking group, but granted it to the colleague with whom he had been having a sexual relationship.

4-35   In some cases anonymity cannot be maintained. The claimant in *CTB v News Group Newspapers Ltd and Imogen Thomas* [2011] EWHC 1232, 1326 and 1334 (QB) obtained an interim injunction restraining publication of the fact that he was having an affair, together with an order for anonymity. It then became widely known on the internet that he was the footballer Ryan Giggs. Subsequent events were described by Tugendhat J at a later hearing (*Giggs (previously known as CTB) v News Group Newspapers Ltd and Imogen Thomas* [2012] EWHC 431 (QB)):

"There can be few people in England and Wales who have not heard of this litigation. The initials CTB have been chanted at football matches when Mr Giggs has been playing for Manchester United. And Mr Giggs has been named in Parliament, raising questions as to the proper relationship between Parliament and the judiciary ... What is famous or notorious about this litigation is that the order to be anonymised did not achieve its purpose."

But, he added, the injunction *had* achieved its purpose of restraining publication of any further account of the sexual relationship between Mr Giggs and Ms Thomas.

If the defendant is a blackmailer different considerations are likely to apply. As Tugendhat J explained in *AMM v HXW* [2010] EWHC 2457 (QB) at [38]–[39]:

> "The fact that a person is making unwarranted demands with threats to disclose information does not of itself mean that that person has no right to freedom of expression. As Lord Atkin pointed out in *Thorne v Motor Trade Association* [1937] AC 797, 817, the blackmailer may even be under a duty to disclose the information. But if a person is making unwarranted demands with threats to publish, that is a factor in deciding whether that person has any Art 10 rights, and, if so, then the weight to be accorded to them in balancing them with the applicant's Art 8 rights.
>
> In my judgment, the need to have regard to the Art 8 rights of the Claimant, and to promote the public interest in preventing and punishing blackmail are both factors which weigh strongly in favour of the grant of an anonymity order. There is a strong case that Defendant has no right to publish the information which she seeks to publish about her relationship with her former husband. On this view her Art 10 rights are not strong. And as an alleged blackmailer, her Art 10 rights are much weaker. ...."

Warby J, in *BUQ v HRE* [2015] EWHC 1272 (QB), said at [50] that where a blackmailer responds to a claim for an injunction by claiming that he never intended to carry out his threat, the court will inevitably take a good deal of persuading that the threat was and is an entirely false one.

Hearing in public

Even in privacy cases, proceedings should be held in public save in the most **4-36** unusual circumstances. Documents and submissions should be prepared in a way which facilitates that approach; confidential material can be placed in an annex which the court can readily identify and order not to be disclosed. Counsel are expected to avoid revealing private information in their oral submissions; if it is really necessary to do so, the court can be asked to sit in private temporarily. If private information is revealed in open session, an appropriate order can be made preventing its reporting (*Ambrosiadou v Coward* [2011] EWCA Civ 409; see also the Practice Guidance appended to Ch.5).

Preventing contempt of court

Publication of material calculated to prejudge an issue in pending litigation is a **4-37** contempt of court (see Ch.9) and may be restrained by injunction in order to protect the proper administration of justice (*Attorney General v Times Newspapers Ltd* [1974] A.C. 273; *Attorney General v Punch Ltd* [2003] 1 A.C. 1046). Moreover, when the proximity of a trial means that there is a substantial risk of the publication causing serious prejudice to the trial, the "strict liability rule" imposed by s.2 of the Contempt of Court Act 1981 prevails over the principle of *Bonnard v Perryman* and allows the court to grant an injunction restraining the publication (*Attorney General v News Group Newspapers Ltd* [1987] QB 1). However injunctions of this kind are exceptional, since it is not usually possible to determine in advance what kind of comment will create such a risk (*Pickering v Liverpool Daily Post and Echo Newspapers Ltd* [1991] 2 A.C. 370 at 425). In *Harris v Harris; Attorney General v Harris* [2001] 2 F.L.R. 895, Munby J said:

> "The freedom to publish things which judges might think should not be published is all the more important where the subject of what is being said is the judges themselves. Any judicial power to punish such publication requires the most cogent justification. Even more cogent must be the justification for giving the judges a power of prior restraint."

In *Attorney General v BBC, The Times,* 14 March 2007, an injunction restraining the BBC from broadcasting details of injunction proceedings relating to a high-profile police investigation was discharged on appeal. The alleged risk of substantial prejudice to the investigation was regarded by the court as speculative.

The Attorney General is the usual claimant when an injunction is sought to prevent contempt of this kind. However, in *Peacock v London Weekend Television* (1986) 150 J.P. 71, six police officers involved in the arrest of a man who died in custody obtained an injunction to prevent the broadcast of a "reconstruction" of the incident, on the grounds that it would involve a possible contempt of the coroner (whose inquest had been adjourned sine die). The Court of Appeal relied on s.37 of the Senior Courts Act 1981 as giving it jurisdiction. The nature of the claimants' cause of action is far from clear. The principal sanction in most cases is not prior restraint but the threat of a contempt prosecution: *Leary v BBC* Unreported 29 September 1989 CA, in which Lord Donaldson MR said:

> "No one should think that on a speculative basis you can go to the courts and call upon the publisher or printed material or television or radio material to come forward and tell the court exactly what it is proposed to do, and invite the court to act as a censor. That is not the function of the court. It is different, of course, if there is solid evidence as to what the content of the publication will be and that evidence leads the court to conclude that prima facie there will be a contempt of court."

4-38   The Crown Court has by virtue of s.45(4) of the Senior Courts Act 1981 power to grant orders to prevent contempts of court, but the proposed injunction must be directly linked to the exercise of the Crown Court's jurisdiction. In the *Trinity Mirror* case [2008] QB 770 (see para.4-23), an order prohibiting publication of the defendant's name had been made on that basis. The Court of Appeal held that s.45(4) did not apply. Sir Igor Judge P said that

> "the Crown Court has no general power to grant injunctions. There is no inherent jurisdiction to do so on the basis that it is seeking to achieve a desirable, or indeed a 'just and convenient' objective. Unless the proposed injunction is directly linked to the exercise of the Crown Court's jurisdiction and the exercise of its statutory functions, the appropriate jurisdiction is lacking. The order was not incidental to the defendant's trial, conviction and sentence. Accordingly, the ambit of s.45(4) of the Supreme Court Act 1981 did not extend to protect the children from the consequences of the identification of their father in the criminal proceedings before the Crown Court."

The court, however, described as "unimpeachable" a decision of Aikens J in the Crown Court in *Ex p. HTV Cymru (Wales) Ltd* [2002] E.M.L.R. 11, restraining a television company from interviewing witnesses who had given evidence in a criminal trial until all the evidence was complete. The injunction was granted under s.45(4) to prevent a potential contempt of court, since witnesses might have to be recalled. In *R. v Harwood* Unreported 20 July 2012, Fulford J made an order during a Crown Court trial requiring the publishers of the *Mail Online* to remove from their website two articles revealing past allegations of misconduct against the defendant which had not been adduced in evidence before the jury. See also *In Re British Broadcasting Corp and In Re Attorney General's Reference No.3 of 1999* [2010] 1 A.C. 145, in which the House of Lords held that the BBC were free to broadcast a programme about a previously acquitted defendant against whom the Crown were contemplating a fresh prosecution pursuant to Pt 10 of the Criminal Justice Act 2003. An existing anonymity order was discharged.

In *Attorney General v Channel Four Television Co Ltd* [1988] Crim. L.R. 237 the Court of Appeal, Criminal Division made an order, on an application by the Attorney General, prohibiting a television re-enactment of an appeal from being broadcast until after judgment in the appeal. This was said to derive from the inherent power of a superior court of record to grant an injunction to protect its own process. It must be doubted whether such an order would be made today in a case not involving a jury.

Criticism of court decisions

In *Re J (a child)* [2013] EWHC 2694 (Fam) Sir James Munby P said:　　　　4-39

"It is not the role of the judge to seek to exercise any kind of editorial control over the manner in which the media reports information which it is entitled to publish ... Comment and criticism may be ill-informed and based, it may be, on misunderstanding or misrepresentation of the facts. If such criticism exceeds what is lawful there are other remedies available. The fear of such criticism, however justified that fear may be, and however unjustified the criticism, is, however, not of itself a justification for prior restraint by injunction of the kind being sought here, even if the criticism is expressed in vigorous, trenchant or outspoken terms. If there is no basis for injuncting a story expressed in the temperate or scholarly language of a legal periodical or the broadsheet press there can be no basis for injuncting the same story simply because it is expressed in the more robust, colourful or intemperate language of the tabloid press or even in language which is crude, insulting and vulgar. A much more robust view must be taken today than previously of what ought rightly to be allowed to pass as permissible criticism ... The publicist—I speak generally, not of the present case—may be an unprincipled charlatan seeking to manipulate public opinion by feeding it tendentious accounts of the proceedings. But freedom of speech is not something to be awarded to those who are thought deserving and denied to those who are thought undeserving."

The Data Protection Act 1998

This Act creates two powers to grant orders in the nature of injunctions. Under　　4-40
s.10, where an individual has given notice in writing to a data controller to cease processing personal data of which he is the data subject on the grounds that continued processing of that data would cause him unwarranted damage or distress, and the data controller has not complied with the notice, a court may (if it considers the notice to be justified) order the data controller to take such steps to comply with the notice as the court thinks fit (s.10(4)). Section 14 confers a power to order a data controller to rectify, block, erase or destroy personal data which are inaccurate (s.14(1)), or where there has been a contravention of the requirements of the Act and there is a substantial risk of further contravention (s.14(4)).

Election statements

By s.106(3) of the Representation of the People Act 1983, a person making or　　4-41
publishing any false statement of fact in relation to the personal character or conduct of a candidate at a parliamentary or local government election

"may be restrained by interim or perpetual injunction of the High Court or the county court from any repetition of that false statement or a false statement of a similar character in relation to the candidate and, for the purpose of granting an interim injunction, prima facie proof of the falsity of the statement shall be sufficient."

Clearly both *American Cyanamid* and *Bonnard v Perryman* are inapplicable to a case within this statutory provision.

3   PUBLIC LAW

Restraining the commission of a crime

4-42   Subject to two exceptions noted below, only the Attorney General may be a claimant in an action to restrain the commission of a criminal offence or an interference with a public right. He may act either on his own initiative or at the request of a private individual willing to bear the costs of the case (a "relator"). In either case his discretion to proceed or not is absolute (*London City Council v Attorney General* [1902] A.C. 165) and, if he refuses his consent to relator proceedings, that is an end of the matter (*Gouriet v Union of Post Office Workers* [1978] A.C. 435). Injunctions have been sought in relator actions, for example, to restrain persistent breaches of a statute which imposes a wholly inadequate penalty on summary conviction (*Attorney General v Harris* [1961] 1 QB 74), or to restrain the use of premises as a hotel without a fire certificate pending a magistrates' court hearing which could not take place for several weeks (*Attorney General v Chaudry* [1971] 1 W.L.R. 1614). Once a clear breach of a statute is proved and the Attorney General applies to the High Court for an injunction as being the most effective method open to him of enforcing that right, the court will refuse to grant the injunction only in exceptional circumstances (*Attorney General v Bastow* [1957] 1 QB 514).

The Local Government Act 1972 s.222 empowers a local authority to bring civil proceedings in its own name where it considers this to be expedient for the promotion or protection of the interests of the inhabitants of the area. This enabled a local authority, without having to obtain the Attorney General's consent, to apply for an injunction, for example, against then illegal Sunday trading (*Stoke-on-Trent City Council v B&Q (Retail) Ltd* [1984] A.C. 754). Similarly, an injunction was granted to prohibit a suspected drug dealer from entering a housing estate (*Nottingham City Council v Zain (A Minor)* [2002] 1 W.L.R. 607; see now the power under the Antisocial Behaviour, Crime and Policing Act 2014, para.4-65). However, the claimants must show something more than infringement of the criminal law for an injunction to be granted:

> "[T]he essential foundation for the exercise of the court's discretion to grant an injunction is not that the offender is deliberately and flagrantly flouting the law but the need to draw the inference that the defendant's unlawful operations will continue unless and until effectively restrained by the law and that nothing short of an injunction will be effective to restrain them." (Per Bingham LJ in *City of London Corp v Bovis Construction Ltd* [1992] 3 All E.R. 697.)

4-43   In *Guildford BC v Hein* [2005] L.G.R. 797, an animal cruelty case, the Court of Appeal again held that it was not necessary under s.222 for a local authority to establish that there had been "deliberate and flagrant flouting" of the criminal law. The question to be asked was whether criminal proceedings were likely to prove ineffective to achieve the public interest purpose for which the legislation had been enacted, but an injunction should only be granted in an exceptional case.

The defendants in *Worcestershire County Council v Tongue* [2004] Ch. 236 had likewise been convicted of cruelty to animals, the prosecution being brought by the local authority. It was held that despite this, the court had no jurisdiction to grant the authority an injunction under s.222 allowing them to enter the defendant's land and remove the animals, though an injunction was granted prohibiting the defendants from keeping animals other than cats and dogs.

4-44   The fact that a reference has been made to the European Court of Justice on a challenge to the validity of provisions of the criminal law is not a reason for refusing to grant an interim injunction restraining breaches of that law (*Portsmouth City Council v Richards* (1989) 87 L.G.R. 757).

The court may, however, in its discretion, properly decline to exercise its jurisdiction to grant an interim order in aid of the enforcement of disputed legislative measures where it is necessary to invoke the court's assistance in order to secure their enforcement (*R. v Secretary of State for Transport Ex p. Factortame Ltd (No.1)* [1990] 2 A.C. 85 at [141]).

Where a private or corporate person can show that a property interest of his is being interfered with by a criminal act, *and* that the statute creating the offence was passed for the benefit or protection of a particular class of individuals including the claimant, the court may grant a prohibitory injunction restraining the defendant from damaging the claimant's interest (*Ex p. Island Records Ltd* [1978] Ch. 122, as interpreted in *Lonrho Ltd v Shell Petroleum Co Ltd (No.2)* [1982] A.C. 173 at [187]). If the claimant is not among those protected by the statute, no injunction can be granted (*RCA Corp v Pollard* [1983] Ch. 135; cf. *Rickless v United Artists Corp* [1988] QB 40).

Applications for judicial review

An application for an injunction may be made in public law cases in the course of an application for judicial review. The appropriate time to make an interim application is when seeking permission to apply for judicial review. Where an interim injunction is sought, the application must contain a request for urgent consideration, a draft order and a statement of the grounds for seeking an injunction; these will be placed before a judge who will decide whether to make an immediate interim order or to direct an oral hearing of which the proposed respondents have been given notice (*Practice Statement: Administrative Courts: Listing and Urgent Cases*). For a mandatory order, a strong prima facie case is required (see para.3-35 and following). Even for a prohibitory injunction, the public interest must be taken into account (see *Smith v ILEA* [1981] 1 All E.R. 411; *Sierbein v Westminster City Council* (1987) 86 L.G.R. 431).

4-45

Injunctions against the Crown

For centuries it was settled law that an injunction could not be granted against the Crown. This rule was swept away so far as judicial review cases are concerned by the House of Lords in *M v Home Office* [1994] 1 A.C. 377: it was held that there is jurisdiction to grant injunctions (interim or final) against a minister, government department or officer of the Crown and to enforce it by contempt proceedings. Where the court considers it inappropriate to grant an injunction against the Crown, a similar result is achieved in many cases by a "stay of proceedings" which the court may grant in the event of giving permission to apply for judicial review (CPR r.54.10). A "stay of removal directions" is a remedy routinely granted in immigration cases. As the editors of the *White Book* drily observe, "the criteria for granting a stay and, in particular, the relationship between stays and interim remedies, remains to be worked out" (para.54.10.4).

Even before *M v Home Office*, an injunction against the Crown had been granted in one area, namely EU law. In *R. v Secretary of State for Transport Ex p. Factortame Ltd (No.2)* [1991] 1 A.C. 603, it was held (following a reference to the European Court of Justice) that, where a statute is alleged to contravene the Treaty of Rome, an interim injunction may be granted to restrain its enforcement if the challenge to the validity of the statute is "sufficiently firmly based to justify so exceptional a course". Since the applicants would suffer obvious and immediate

4-46

damage if denied interim relief, an interim injunction was granted, for the first time in English legal history, restraining the Secretary of State from enforcing certain provisions of an Act of Parliament, and on the grounds, not that the statute *was* invalid, but that it *might well be* invalid.

4-47   In *R. v Secretary of State for the Environment Ex p. Royal Society for the Protection of Birds* (1995) 7 Admin. L.R. 434, the RSPB sought an interim declaration in judicial review proceedings where a reference was being made to the European Court of Justice. The House of Lords refused the application; even assuming that there was such a thing as an interim declaration (which there now is: see above), it would be wrong to grant one so as to give the applicants the same benefit as an interim injunction, without the risk of very substantial liability on the undertaking in damages which would be a condition of an injunction. In *R. v Inspectorate of Pollution Ex p. Greenpeace Ltd* [1994] 1 W.L.R. 570 the Court of Appeal, refusing a stay pending judicial review proceedings, took into account that the applicant had given no undertaking in damages.

In *R. v HM Treasury Ex p. British Telecommunications Plc* [1994] 1 C.M.L.R. 621, the Court of Appeal held that on an application for an interim injunction to disapply legislation, the *Factortame* test ("sufficiently firmly based to justify so exceptional a course") is not a universal formula. The court will only disapply legislation by injunction with great circumspection, but its approach may differ according to whether, for example, the law in question is a major statute on which an election has been fought, or a minor piece of subordinate legislation affecting few people other than the parties.

4-48   A judge of the Family Division cannot in the exercise of family jurisdiction (whether under the Children Act 1989, in wardship or under the court's inherent jurisdiction) grant an injunction restraining the Home Secretary from removing from the jurisdiction a child subject to immigration control. However a judge nominated to sit in the Administrative Court may do so in judicial review proceedings to challenge directions for the child's removal on the grounds of failure to take into account all relevant matters, including orders made by the family court: *R. (Anton) v Secretary of State for the Home Department* [2005] Fam. Law 442.

Section 30 of the Senior Courts Act 1981 provides that an injunction may be granted to restrain a person from acting in a public office in which he is not entitled to act. Such an order may only be sought by way of application for judicial review.

4   DEFENDANTS OUTSIDE THE JURISDICTION

4-49   The Court of Appeal held in *In re Liddell's Settlement Trusts* [1936] Ch 365 that:

"In granting injunctions the Court operates *in personam*. The person to whom its orders are addressed must be within the reach of the Court or amenable to its jurisdiction. But the Court will not suffer any one within its reach to do what is contrary to its notions of equity, merely because the act to be done may be, in point of locality, beyond its jurisdiction.

As a consequence of the rule, that in granting an injunction the Court operates *in personam*, the Court may exercise jurisdiction independently of the locality of the act to be done, provided the person against whom relief is sought is within the reach and amenable to the process of the Court. This jurisdiction is not grounded upon any pretension to the exercise of judicial or administrative rights abroad, but on the circumstance of the person to whom the order is addressed being within the reach of the Court."

Sir James Munby P said in *Re J (a child)* [2013] EWHC 2694 (Fam) that *In re Liddell* establishes two further propositions. The first is that a defendant outside the jurisdiction is, for this purpose, "within the reach of the court" if properly served in accordance with the relevant rules of court (in *re Liddell* itself because the defendant was a British subject ordinarily resident within the jurisdiction). The second is that where following such service the defendant is within the reach of the court, the court has jurisdiction to grant an injunction irrespective of the locality of the act to be done.

If the defendant is a company incorporated abroad with assets in this jurisdiction, an injunction can be granted so as to stop its agents from doing acts in breach of contract either here or abroad; if they disobey the injunction, it can be enforced by sequestration against the company's assets here (*Hospital for Sick Children v Walt Disney Productions Inc* [1968] Ch. 52).

For a discussion of freezing injunctions in support of proceedings abroad, see para.7-44. As to injunctions in cases where children are about to be or have been removed from the jurisdiction, see para.10-70.

5   RESTRAINT OF LEGAL PROCEEDINGS

Litigation in English courts

A case pending in the High Court may not be restrained by injunction, as opposed to a stay, but this rule only applies once proceedings have begun. There is no bar to an injunction being granted to restrain the *institution* of proceedings. The basis for orders of this kind is the inherent jurisdiction of the court to prevent abuses of its own process (*Forte (Charles) Investments Ltd v Amanda* [1964] Ch. 240); *Essex Electric Ltd v IPC Computers (UK) Ltd* [1991] F.S.R. 690). There is accordingly no substantive claim to which the injunction has to be ancillary (*Masri v Consolidated Contractors Ltd* [2009] QB 503). The criteria laid down in the *American Cyanamid* case do not govern applications for an interim injunction of this special kind, designed to stop the commencement of proceedings *in limine*.   **4-50**

The most common type of injunction restraining litigation is the injunction to prevent the presentation of a petition in the Companies Court of the Chancery Division to wind up a limited company, which is made to a judge by the issue of an originating application in a prescribed form (*Practice Direction: Insolvency Proceedings* [1999] B.C.C. 421). Such a petition is an abuse of process and will be restrained by injunction if presented in respect of a debt which is shown to be disputed on substantial grounds (*Stonegate Securities Ltd v Gregory* [1980] Ch. 576). If, however, the defendant proves that he does have substantial grounds for presenting a petition, it is immaterial that his shareholding is small or that he may be actuated by personal malice (*Bryanston Finance Ltd v de Vries (No.2)* [1976] Ch. 63).

The Attorney General may apply to a Divisional Court for a civil proceedings order against a vexatious litigant under s.42 of the Senior Courts Act 1981; while the final hearing of that application is pending, the court may grant an interim injunction preventing the allegedly vexatious litigant from issuing any further claims or applications until it has been heard (*Re Blackstone* [1995] C.O.D. 105; *Attorney General v Campbell* [1997] C.O.D. 249).   **4-51**

The High Court or a designated civil judge in the county court also has jurisdiction to prohibit a litigant from abusing the process of the court by one of the methods set out in *Bhamjee v Forsdick* [2004] 1 W.L.R. 88 at para.53:

(a)   making applications within a single set of existing proceedings without permission (a civil restraint order);

(b)   making applications in any court concerning any matters related to speci-
      fied proceedings without permission applied for and granted on paper (an
      extended civil restraint order);

(c)   initiating any civil proceedings or making any applications, whether in the
      High Court or county courts, without permission applied for and granted on
      paper (a general civil restraint order).

4-52   Any of these orders may be made for a period of up to two years on the application of another party to the proceedings or of the court's own motion, and a penal
notice may be attached. In extreme cases, orders have been made prohibiting an
individual from entering the Royal Courts of Justice to litigate on behalf of other
people (*Paragon Finance v Noueiri* [2001] 1 W.L.R. 2357) or at all (*Attorney
General v Ebert* [2002] 2 All E.R. 789).

The High Court has jurisdiction to restrain proceedings in a county court or
magistrates' court, although such injunctions have been very rarely granted. In
Thames Launches Ltd v Trinity House Corp [1961] Ch. 197, the defendants were
restrained by injunction from proceeding with a prosecution in a magistrates' court
under the Pilotage Act 1913 on the ground that an action was pending between the
same parties in the Chancery Division which involved the same question of law as
to the construction of a statute. It must not be deduced from this that prosecutions
in magistrates' courts will regularly be stopped by High Court injunctions.

Litigation abroad

4-53   An injunction may be granted to restrain civil litigation in another jurisdiction,
provided that the defendant is properly amenable to the jurisdiction of the English
courts. As a general rule, however, before an anti-suit injunction of this kind is
granted, comity requires that the English forum should have a sufficient interest in,
or connection with, the matter to justify interfering indirectly with the foreign court
(*Airbus Industries GIE v Patel* [1999] 1 A.C. 119, where an injunction restraining
British citizens from litigating in Texas in respect of an air crash which had occurred in India was discharged by the House of Lords).

An injunction to prevent forum shopping should not be granted unless the applicant shows that the case could be tried in England with substantially less
inconvenience and expense and that the foreign proceedings would be vexatious or
oppressive (*SNI Aerospatiale v Lee Kui Jak* [1987] A.C. 871). More recently, the
key principles in considering an application for an anti-suit injunction were set out
by the Court of Appeal in *Michael Wilson and Partners Ltd v Emmott* [2018]
EWCA Civ 51 at [34]–[40].

An anti-suit injunction must be sought promptly, before the foreign proceedings are too far advanced (*The Angelic Grace* [1995] 1 Lloyd's Rep 87). A foreign
defendant cannot allow foreign proceedings to continue practically to judgment and
then seek last minute relief in England, even where the delay has caused no
prejudice (*Ecobank Transnational Inc v Tanoh* [2016] 1 W.L.R. 2231). That would
offend the principle of comity.

4-54   If the facts alleged disclose no cause of action justiciable in an English court, an
injunction will only be granted if it would be unconscionable on the part of the
defendant to pursue the foreign litigation (*British Airways Board v Laker Airways
Ltd* [1985] A.C. 58).

The Judgments Regulation (Council Regulation 44/2001) and its predecessor the
Brussels Convention preclude the grant of an anti-suit injunction against defendants who are threatening to commence or continue proceedings in another Convention country, even when those defendants are acting in bad faith with the intent and

purpose of frustrating or obstructing proceedings properly before an English court
or tribunal (*Turner v Grovit* [2005] 1 A.C. 101). The European Court of Justice has
also held that it is not open to an English court to order a party before it to
discontinue proceedings begun by that party in another Member State on the ground
that the parties had agreed to refer any disputes between them to arbitration in
London (*West Tankers Inc v Allianz SpA* [2009] 1 A.C. 1138, also known as the
Front Comor case). It held that the preliminary issue concerning the applicability
of an arbitration agreement, including in particular its validity, comes within the
scope of the Judgments Regulation and does not fall within the arbitration
exclusion. With this substantial exception, an injunction may be granted to restrain
proceedings brought in breach of an exclusive jurisdiction clause (see *Donohue v
Armco Inc* [2002] 1 All E.R. 749) or in breach of contract (*The Tropaioforos* [1962]
2 Lloyd's Rep. 469), or to restrain enforcement of a foreign judgment obtained by
fraud (*Ellerman Lines Ltd v Read* [1928] 2 K.B. 144). *The Front Comor* does not
impact upon the court's jurisdiction to order an anti-arbitration injunction restraining an arbitration in another Member State: *Claxton Engineering Services Ltd v
TXM Olaj-Es Gazkutato Kft* [2011] 1 Lloyd's Rep. 510. What the impact on these
principles of UK withdrawal from the European Union would or will be remains
to be seen.

With the substantial exception established in *The Front Comor*, an injunction may   **4-55**
be granted to restrain proceedings brought in breach of an exclusive jurisdiction
clause (see *Donohue v Armco Inc* [2002] 1 All E.R. 749) or in breach of contract
(*The Tropaioforos* [1960] 2 Lloyd's Rep. 469).

It will be a rare case in which an injunction will be granted in England which
would prevent reliance on, or compliance with, a foreign judgment. But:

> "it is consistent with principle for an English court to restrain re-litigation abroad of a
> claim which has already been the subject of an English judgment. There is long-
> established authority that protection of the jurisdiction of the English court, its process and
> its judgments by injunction is a legitimate ground for the grant of an anti-suit injunction."
> (Per Lawrence Collins LJ in *Masri v Consolidated Contractors International UK Ltd
> (No.3)* [2009] QB 503; reversed on the facts [2010] 1 A.C. 90.)

So an injunction may be granted to restrain enforcement of a foreign judgment
obtained by fraud (*Ellerman Lines Ltd v Read* [1928] 2 K.B. 144), or in breach of
an exclusive jurisdiction clause (*Bank St Petersburg OJSC v Arkhangelsky* [2014]
1 W.L.R. 4360), though the power is to be sparingly exercised.

There is no principle that an anti-suit injunction will not be granted so as to
prevent a foreign litigant from resorting to the courts of his own country. So where
a company is being wound up in the jurisdiction in which it has been incorporated
(in the case in question, the British Virgin Islands), an anti-suit injunction should
be issued to prevent a creditor from pursuing proceedings in another jurisdiction
calculated to give him an unjustifiable priority: *Stichting Shell Pensioenfunds v Krys*
[2014] UKPC 41. In England and Wales the Companies Court has special powers
under s.126(1) of the Insolvency Act 1986, after the presentation of a winding-up
petition against a company, to grant an injunction restraining proceedings against
it in another jurisdiction.

Arbitration

By s.44(2)(e) of the Arbitration Act 1996, the High Court has the same power   **4-56**
to grant an interim injunction for the purpose of and in relation to a reference to
arbitration as it has in an action in the High Court. Such an injunction enables the
court to preserve the parties' rights while the arbitration is under way, but may not

extend to a final anti-suit injunction due to the express reference to "interim" injunctions in s.44(2)(e): *Cetelem SA v Roust Holdings Ltd* [2005] 1 W.L.R. 3555. It may permit interim anti-suit injunctions: *Starlight Shipping Co v Tai Ping Insurance Co Ltd Hubei Branch* [2008] 1 All E.R. (Comm) 593 at [2], but certainly s.37 of the Senior Courts Act 1981 can be used to support arbitration by requiring parties to refer their disputes to arbitration: *The Angelic Grace* [1995] 1 Lloyd's Rep 78. The limitations of s.44 of the Arbitration Act 1996 cannot be circumvented by s.37, but where no arbitration has been commenced and none is intended, the court has discretion to consider whether or not to protect a right to arbitrate using s.37: but even where no arbitration has been commenced and none is intended, the court may grant an injunction restraining foreign proceedings brought in violation of an agreement to resolve disputes by arbitration in England: *AES Ust-Kamenogorsk Hydropower Plant LLP v Ust-Kamenogorsk Hydropower Plant JSC* [2013] 1 W.L.R. 1889.

The court also has power under s.37 of the Senior Courts Act 1981 to restrain an arbitration from proceeding, although such anti-arbitration injunctions are only to be granted in exceptional circumstances: *Claxton Engineering Services Ltd v TXM Olaj-Es Gazkutato Kft* [2011] 1 Lloyd's Rep. 510. The power may be exercised if two conditions are satisfied, namely that: (a) the injunction would not cause injustice to the claimant in the arbitration; and (b) the continuance of the arbitration would be oppressive, vexatious, unconscionable or an abuse of process (*Elektrim SA v Vivendi Universal SA* [2007] 2 Lloyd's Rep. 8). The court's discretion to grant such an injunction is only exercised very sparingly and delay in applying for it may in some cases be fatal (*J Jarvis & Sons Ltd v Blue Circle Dartford Estates Ltd* [2007] EWHC 1262 (TCC); [2007] B.L.R. 439, Jackson J).

An applicant for an anti-suit injunction has to show a 'high degree of probability' that there was an arbitration agreement that governed the dispute in question (*Midgulf International Ltd v Groupe Chimiche Tunisien* [2009] 2 Lloyd's Rep 411). The same threshold is appropriate for an anti-enforcement injunction (*Ecobank Transnational Inc v Tanoh* [2016] 1 W.L.R. 2231).

Anti-enforcement injunctions

4-57   Examples of anti-enforcement injunctions are few and far between because an applicant for anti-suit relief needs to act promptly and such injunctions can breach the principle of comity between legal systems. Waiting until after judgment is given in the foreign proceedings means that an application is not likely to succeed unless the respondent has acted fraudulently (e.g. *Ellerman Lines Ltd v Read* [1928] 2 KB 144), if the relevant agreement was reached post judgment or because he had no means of knowing that the judgment was being sought until it was served on him (*Ecobank Transnational Inc v Tanoh* [2016] 1 W.L.R. 2231). Unreasonable delay is a bar to an anti-enforcement injunction even where the respondent has not been prejudiced by the delay. The grant of an injunction will mean that the cost of the other proceedings and the resources of the rival court will (unless the injunction is discharged) have been wasted.

6   DISCRIMINATION

4-58   A designated county court may, under s.24 of the Equality Act 2006, grant an injunction restraining certain discriminatory acts or practices. Such an injunction may *only* be applied for by the Commission for Equality and Human Rights, and it must appear to the Commission that, unless restrained, the defendant is likely in the future to do an unlawful discriminatory act. Private citizens have no standing to apply for injunctions of this kind.

7 FINANCIAL SERVICES AND CONSUMER CONTRACTS

The Secretary of State or the appropriate regulator may apply for an injunction under ss.380–381 of the Financial Services and Markets Act 2000 to restrain certain contraventions of the Act, to require a person to take steps to remedy such contraventions, and to restrain him from disposing of or otherwise dealing with his assets. The effect of these sections is to give the Secretary of State and the regulator a statutory cause of action to apply for a freezing injunction for the protection of investors (*Securities and Investment Board v Pantell SA* [1990] Ch. 426, a case under the previous statute). Private citizens have no standing to apply for an injunction on the basis of these provisions.

4-59

A regulatory body in the United States seeking the disgorgement of assets obtained by fraud may be granted a freezing order over such assets in this jurisdiction (*US Securities and Exchange Commission v Manterfield* [2009] 2 All E.R. 1009).

The Director General of Fair Trading may apply for an injunction under reg.12 of the Unfair Terms in Consumer Contracts Regulations 1999 against any person appearing to be using, or recommending the use of, an unfair term drawn up for general use in contracts concluded with consumers. This may extend to the continuing use of unfair terms in an existing contract (*Office of Fair Trading v Foxtons Ltd* [2010] 1 W.L.R. 663).

8 STATE IMMUNITY

No injunction may be granted against a foreign state (State Immunity Act 1978 s.13(2)(a)). This rule does not apply where the defendant consents in writing to the grant of relief; such consent may be contained in a prior agreement (s.13(3)). Where a defendant resists an interim injunction on the grounds of state immunity and there is a dispute as to whether the claim for immunity is well founded, the court is bound to decide finally at the interim stage whether such immunity exists; it cannot, for example, grant a freezing injunction on the basis only of a good arguable case (see *A Co Ltd v Republic of X* [1990] 2 Lloyd's Rep. 520). The court should give effect to state immunity even if the state does not appear (*ETI Euro Telecom International NV v Republic of Bolivia* [2009] 1 W.L.R. 665).

4-60

9 HARASSMENT AND ANTI-SOCIAL BEHAVIOUR

Since the mid-1990s, Parliament has enacted legislation providing for injunctions against harassment and anti-social behaviour. In each case civil proceedings may be brought for an injunction with the usual civil burden of proof and hearsay evidence being admissible, and a power of arrest can be attached to the order. There is an important distinction between them: any individual claimant can seek an injunction (and damages) under the Protection from Harassment Act 1997, whereas the Anti-social Behaviour Crime and Policing Act 2014 and the Policing and Crime

4-61

Act 2009 restrict claims to local authorities and (under the 2014 Act) other social landlords, and the police.

The Protection from Harassment Act 1997

4-62   Section 1 of the 1997 Act states that a person must not pursue a course of conduct which amounts to harassment of another, and which he knows or ought to know amounts to harassment of the other. "Harassment" includes alarming or causing distress to the victim (s.7(2)); a "course of conduct" must involve conduct on at least two occasions (s.7(3)), and "conduct" includes speech (s.7(4)). The Act is frequently used in family disputes, and there is a full discussion of the substantive provisions of the Act at paras 10-63 to 10-69.

Breaches of s.1 can give rise to criminal and civil sanctions. Prosecutions may be brought under s.2, and one of the sanctions available to the criminal court is a restraining order under s.5; this is not an injunction carrying the contempt sanction, but breach of it is a further offence. Harassment intended to dissuade people (including third parties) from carrying on lawful activities is prohibited by s.1(1A) of the Act, introduced by amendment in 2005: see para.10-65.

Claims may be issued and applications made in anticipation of harassment. Section 3(1) provides (emphasis added):

"An actual *or apprehended* breach of section 1 may be the subject of a claim in civil proceedings by the person who is *or may be* the victim of the course of conduct in question."

4-63   Civil proceedings may be brought by the issue of a claim under the CPR Pt 8 procedure, either in the Queen's Bench Division or in the county court where the claimant or the defendant resides or carries on business (CPR r.65.28). The potential remedies are damages, an injunction, or both. The standard of proof is the civil standard (*Hipgrave v Jones* [2005] 2 F.L.R. 174).

Any victim or potential victim may apply. A corporate entity is not a "person" entitled to bring a claim under the Act (*Daiichi UK Ltd v Stop Huntingdon Animal Cruelty* [2004] 1 W.L.R. 1503). However a director of a company may sue on behalf of employees of the company if that is the most convenient and expeditious way of enabling the court to protect their interests (*Emerson Developments Ltd v Avery* [2004] EWHC 194 (QB)). Similarly a chief constable may claim on behalf of the officers under his command. In such a case a "course of conduct" may be established without showing that any individual officer has been harassed more than once (*Chief Constable of Surrey Police v Godfrey* [2017] EWHC 2014 (QB)).

In many cases orders under the Act have been made against animal rights activists. However the Act was not intended by Parliament to be used to clamp down on the discussion of matters of public interest or upon the rights of political protest and public demonstration, which are so much part of our democratic tradition (per Eady J in *Huntingdon Life Sciences Ltd v Curtin, The Times,* 11 December 1997). An exclusion zone order may be made against protesters, but only if a less drastic form of injunction has been put to the test and found to be inadequate (per Owen J in *Hall v Save Newchurch Guinea Pigs Campaign* [2005] EWHC 372 (QB), *The Times,* 7 April 2005). In *Astellas Pharma Ltd v Stop Huntingdon Animal Cruelty* [2011] EWCA Civ 752, the court granted an injunction to prevent protests at certain specified locations by the defendants, some of whom were representative, but refused to add a declaration that it was enforceable against "protesters" under the 1997 Act.

Quia timet interim injunctions were granted and continued against persons unknown restraining a range of activities relating to protests against fracking opera-tors and third party contractors in *Ineos Upstream Ltd v Persons Unknown* [2017] EWHC 2945 (Ch). Morgan J applied the test of likelihood as the injunction potentially affected the defendants' freedom of expression (s.12(3) Human Rights Act 1998 and *Cream Holdings Ltd v Banerjee* [2005] 1 A.C. 253: see para.4-20 above).

If an injunction is granted and the claimant considers that it has been breached, an application may be made (substantiated by sworn evidence) to a judge or district judge for a warrant of arrest (s.3(3)–(5)). The application, which may be made without notice, must state whether the police have been informed of the defendant's conduct and whether criminal proceedings are being pursued (CPR r.65.29(2)). The judge before whom the defendant is brought following his arrest may determine whether the facts, and the circumstances which led to the arrest, amounted to disobedience of the injunction, or may adjourn the hearing for a maximum of 14 days, with the defendant being given at least two days' notice of the adjourned hear-ing (CPR r.65.30). **4-64**

Breach without reasonable excuse of an injunction granted under the Act may be treated as an offence or as a contempt of court, but once the defendant has been punished for contempt he cannot be convicted in the criminal courts for the of-fence, and vice versa (s.3(6)–(8)). If contempt proceedings are brought, the usual two-year maximum applies (see Ch.9), but on conviction in the Crown Court for breach of the injunction, the maximum penalty is five years' imprisonment, a contrast emphasised by Lord Woolf CJ in *Murray v Robinson* [2006] 1 F.L.R. 365.

Since the special criminal sanctions for breach have no lower age limit, it would appear that injunctions under this Act may be granted against persons under 18. The power of arrest under s.3 and the option of criminal sanctions for breach, do not ap-ply if an undertaking has been accepted in lieu of an injunction; so an undertaking is very much a second-class remedy under this statute.

Injunctions under the Anti-social Behaviour, Crime and Policing Act 2014

An injunction under Part 1 of the Anti-social Behaviour, Crime and Policing Act 2014 is a civil power which can be applied for to deal with anti-social individuals The Home Office statutory guidance provides that such an injunction: **4-65**

> "can offer fast and effective protection for victims and communities and set a clear standard of behaviour for perpetrators, stopping the person's behaviour from escalating. Although the injunction is a civil power, it is still a formal sanction and many profession-als will want to consider informal approaches before resorting to court action, especially in the case of under 18s. However, where informal approaches have not worked or profes-sionals decide that a formal response is needed more quickly, they should be free to do so."

Under s.1 of the 2014 Act the High Court or county court (or youth court for someone between 10 and 18 years) may grant an injunction if a person has engaged or threatens to engage in anti-social behaviour and it is just and convenient to grant an injunction to prevent such behaviour. Such an injunction may be prohibitory or mandatory in form, but must, so far as practicable, avoid any interference with at-tendance at work, school or other educational establishment (s.1(5)). It must specify the period for which it has effect (or state that it has effect until further order) and can last no longer than 12 months if the respondent is under 18 years old. The injunction may include a power of arrest if the anti-social behaviour involves any threat or use of violence and there is a significant risk of harm (s.4) in which case the application must be personally served (CPR r.65.49). In cases of violence and risk of harm an adult respondent may be excluded by the order from the place where he or she normally lives (s.13).

4-66   Anti-social behaviour means conduct that has caused, or is likely to cause, harassment, alarm or distress to any person (s.2). Where a housing provider, local authority or the police apply for an injunction the behaviour includes conduct capable of causing nuisance or annoyance to a person in relation to that person's occupation of residential premises. It also includes conduct capable of causing housing-related nuisance or annoyance to any person in relation to the housing management functions of a housing provider or local authority.

This means that there is a two tier approach to anti-social behaviour with a lower test of nuisance and annoyance for housing-related cases and a higher test of harassment, alarm or distress for non-housing cases such as behaviour in a public place, town or city centre, shopping mall, or local park.

Only public authorities specified in s.5 may apply for an injunction (after consulting the local youth offending team if the respondent is a youth: s.14). Applications are made by a CPR Part 8 claim form (stating the terms of the injunction sought) supported by a witness statement in accordance with CPR Part 65 and PD 65. Applications for interim injunctions may be made without notice being given to the respondent, but cannot then require the respondent to participate in particular activities (s.7). Under previous legislation (the Housing Act 1996) it was held that exceptional circumstances are required for a without notice order, involving a risk of significant harm if the order is not made immediately, and the order must be no wider than is necessary and proportionate as a means of avoiding the apprehended harm (*Moat Housing Group South Ltd v Harris* [2006] QB 606). The courts are likely to take a similar restrictive approach under the 2014 Act, although, as with anti-social behaviour orders, it is likely that a without notice order is compatible with Art.6 ECHR (*R. on the application of M) v Lord Chancellor* [2004] 1 W.L.R. 2298).

4-67   Unlike the previous anti-social behaviour orders, injunctions under the 2014 Act are obtainable on a civil standard of proof and there is no need to prove necessity. Breach is not itself a criminal offence and the statutory guidance issued by the Home Office points out that there is more scope for positive requirements to focus on long-term solutions.

Under CPR r.65.44 every provision to which a power of arrest is attached must be set out in a separate paragraph of the injunction. The injunction must specify an individual or an organisation responsible for supervising compliance with the requirements of the order, who must give evidence to the court about its suitability and enforceability and who must make any necessary arrangements in connection with the requirements (s.3). The supervisor must inform the applicant and the police if there is any failure to comply with any relevant requirement and the respondent has a duty to keep in touch with the supervisor and notify him of any change of address.

4-68   The court which granted the injunction (or the county court if granted by a youth court, but where the respondent is now aged 18 years) may vary or discharge an injunction, including by adding an additional prohibition or requirement, extending its period or by attaching or varying a power of arrest. However section 8 provides that after an unsuccessful application to discharge or vary, no further application can be made without the consent of the court or the agreement of the other party. Before applying to vary or discharge an injunction against a youth, the local youth offending team must be consulted about the application. In any case the applicant must inform any other body or individual the applicant thinks appropriate about the variation or discharge (s.14).

If the applicant has cause to suspect a breach, he may apply for a warrant for the respondent's arrest and under s.10 such application to be supported by an affidavit or oral evidence (CPR r.65.46). Alternatively, under section 9 if the police have reasonable cause to suspect that the respondent is in breach then he may be arrested without warrant and within 24 hours must be brought before a judge (or magistrate where the respondent is a youth) for a remand hearing.

Gang-related violence injunctions under the Policing and Crime Act 2009

Sections 34–45 of the Policing and Crime Act 2009 as amended by s.51 of the **4-69** Serious Crime Act 2015 allow the police and local authorities to apply to the High Court or a county court for an injunction against a respondent aged 14 or over who has engaged in, encouraged or assisted gang-related violence or gang-related drug dealing. For the purposes of this legislation something is gang-related if it occurs in the course of, or is otherwise related to, the activities of a group that consists of at least three people, and has one or more characteristics that enable its members to be identified by others as a group (s.34(4) of the 2009 Act, as amended).

The application may be made with or without notice and may be heard by a district judge. The order can include any reasonable prohibition or requirement which is necessary either to prevent the respondent from engaging in, encouraging or assisting such violence, or to protect him from them, and a power of arrest may be attached to it. Any prohibition or requirement in the order is limited to a maximum period of two years (s.36(1)).

The Home Office document *Injunctions to prevent gang-related violence and drug dealing: statutory guidance*, available on the Home Office website, is required reading for anyone acting for parties to this type of litigation. Reference should also be made to CPR rr.65.42 to 65.49.

It is not necessary when granting an injunction under the 2009 Act that the court should first consider whether an anti-social behaviour order would provide an adequate remedy: *Birmingham CC v James* [2014] 1 W.L.R. 23.

The use of the civil standard of proof on the balance of probabilities in applications for gang-related injunctions is compatible with Article 6 of the ECHR (*Jones v Birmingham City Council* [2018] EWCA Civ 1189).

10   PATENTS AND TRADEMARKS

"In intellectual property cases a plaintiff is concerned not only to stop exact repetition of **4-70** the defendant's current activity which can be described with particularity, but to prevent fresh invasions of his rights in ways which cannot be foreseen or described exactly. The ingenuity of those who infringe copyright and trade marks and engage in passing off is boundless, and plaintiffs cannot be adequately protected by orders which are cabined or confined. That is the reason for the standard forms of injunctions in such cases, with their inevitable references to 'otherwise infringing,' 'substantial part,' 'to like effect,' 'colourable imitation,' and 'otherwise passing off.' Where a defendant, faced with such an order, acts honestly and reasonably, this will mitigate and even excuse a breach of the order; but if a breach is proved, it will be for him to mitigate or justify it, and his excuse may need to be thoroughly probed if the circumstances are suspicious." (Per Millett J in *Spectravest Inc v Aperknit Ltd* [1988] F.S.R. 161.)

If the proprietor of a registered trademark establishes that a defendant has infringed that mark then, as a general rule, an injunction will be granted against him because he has evinced an intention to engage in an infringing activity. On the other hand, injunctive relief is a discretionary remedy and if it appears from all the circumstances that the defendant presents no such threat and there is no risk of further infringement, then an injunction will be refused (*Stretchline Intellectual Properties v H&M Hennes & Mauritz UK (No. 3)* [2016] R.P.C. 15). The court will also be concerned to ensure that any injunction is appropriate and proportionate in the light of all the facts of the case and is drafted in such a way as to define as clearly as possible what it is that the defendant may not do. The court will always have in mind that the scope of any injunction must be fair to the defendant and should not extend any further than necessary. If, for example, an injunction in general form would have the practical effect of stifling a legitimate business, then it may be appropriate to craft a qualified injunction. All must depend upon the circumstances of the particular case (*Specsavers International Healthcare Ltd v Asda Stores Ltd* [2012] EWCA Civ 494).

4-71   Injunctions will usually be granted to a successful patent claimant:

> "[I]f the effect of an injunction is not oppressive, the defendant cannot buy his way out of it, even if the price, objectively ascertained, would be modest." (*Navitaire Inc v EasyJet Airline Co Ltd (No.4)* [2006] R.P.C. 4.)

However, a court may be willing to grant carve-outs or conditional injunctions where it would be grossly disproportionate to impose a total prohibition (*Virgin Atlantic Airways Ltd v Premium Aircraft Interiors UK Ltd* [2011] F.S.R. 27, which also held that where a patent has been amended, the court will not enforce an injunction obtained before the amendment as a means of preventing future alleged infringements of the amended patent).

Chiron v Organon (No.10) [1995] F.S.R. 325 applied the principles for declining an injunction set out in *Shelfer v City of London Electric Lighting Co* [1895] 1 Ch. 287 that the damages must be capable of being adequately compensated by a small money payment and that it would be oppressive to grant an injunction. It doubted *Roussel-Uclaf v GD Searle* [1977] F.S.R. 125, where an interim injunction was refused on public interest grounds where the infringing product was a lifesaving drug, suggesting that the research exception in the Patents Act 1977 was sufficient to protect the public.

There are statutory powers under ss.97A and 191JA of the Copyright, Designs and Patents Act 1988 (as amended) to grant injunctions against internet service providers where the service provider has actual knowledge that its service is being used in order to infringe copyright or a performer's property rights: see *Twentieth Century Fox Film Corp v British Telecommunications plc* [2011] EWHC 1981 (Ch).

4-72   The court has jurisdiction to grant a website blocking injunction against an internet service provider in a trade mark case—interpreting s.37(1) Senior Courts Act 1981 in compliance with Directive 2004/48 art.11 (*Cartier International AG v British Sky Broadcasting Ltd* [2017] 1 All E.R. 700: reversed in the Supreme Court only in relation to costs: [2018] 1 W.L.R. 3259). The claimant trade mark owners of Cartier, Mont Blanc etc. applied for orders requiring the biggest UK ISPs to prevent access to specified websites which advertised and sold counterfeit goods. Provided the court has *in personam* jurisdiction over the person against whom an injunction was sought, there was jurisdiction to grant it (following *Fourie v Le Roux* [2007] 1 W.L.R. 320) which could be exercised in new ways (*Samsung Electronics (UK) Ltd v Apple Inc* [2012] EWCA Civ 1339, [2013] E.C.D.R. 2).

Injunction applications in intellectual property cases may engage Article 10 considerations: see the judgment of Birss J in *Interflora Inc v Marks and Spencer plc* [2014] EWHC 4168 (Ch), discussed at para.4-24 above.

Injunctions in patent and trade mark infringement cases have traditionally been granted in broad general terms: see *Coflexip SA v Stolt Comex Seaway MS Ltd*

[2000] EWCA Civ 242; *Specsavers International Healthcare Ltd v Asda Stores Ltd* [2012] EWCA Civ 494. But Kitchin LJ said in the latter case at [10] that "the court will always have in mind that the scope of an injunction must be fair to the defendant and should not extend any further than necessary. If, for example, an injunction in general form would have the practical effect of stifling a legitimate business then it may be appropriate to craft a qualified injunction.....All must depend on the circumstances of the particular case."

Where a party breached a settlement agreement not to infringe an intellectual property right, the same principles were to be applied to the grant of injunctive relief as if it been a successful action for patent infringement (*Stretchline Intellectual Properties v H&M Hennes & Mauritz UK (No. 3)* [2016] R.P.C. 15 applying *Cantor Gaming v GameAccount Global* [2008] F.S.R. 4).

11 COMPETITION

The Consumer Rights Act 2015 came into force on 1 October 2015 and gives a new jurisdiction to the Competition Appeal Tribunal ("CAT") to grant injunctions in accordance with the Competition Appeal Tribunal Rules 2015. The CAT was previously restricted to follow on claims based on a finding of regulatory infringement. The intention of the Act is to improve access for claimants to obtain redress for cartel and other competition infringements and so that injunctions can be granted to both consumers and businesses to restrain abuse of dominance or other anti-competitive conduct. **4-73**

The CAT may grant interim and final injunctions in all cases in which it appears to be just and convenient to do so (rule 67 of the 2015 Rules). Any such order may be made either unconditionally or on such terms and conditions as the CAT thinks just. Under rule 68 interim injunctions may be granted at any time, including before proceedings are started (in which case directions requiring a claim may be given) and after judgment has been given. Interim injunctions may only be granted if the matter is urgent or it is otherwise necessary to do so in the interests of justice (rule 68(3)).

The significant innovation is that in proceedings subject to the fast-track procedure under rule 58 of the Competition Appeal Tribunal Rules 2015 the CAT may grant an interim injunction without requiring the applicant to provide an undertaking as to damages or subject to a cap on the amount of the undertaking as to damages. A small business without the financial means to get an injunction against a cartel in the High Court may be able to seek redress without having to offer a potentially crippling cross undertaking. Apart from this, the procedure follows standard lines. If the application is made without notice, the evidence must set out the reasons why notice has not been given ('good reasons' are required by rule 69). In the ordinary case where a cross undertaking in damages is required the evidence in support must include the ability to pay. **4-74**

The CAT has no power to commit for contempt of court. If the respondent to an injunction fails to comply with its terms, the applicant may apply to the CAT with supporting evidence for certification of the matter to be enforced in the High Court (rule 70). After giving the parties an opportunity to be heard, the CAT must make directions as it thinks fit for determining whether to certify the matter to the High Court.

PART B: PRACTICE AND PROCEDURE

CHAPTER 5

Interim Applications

The procedure for obtaining a *permanent* injunction, whether in the Chancery or the Queen's Bench Division, does not differ greatly from the procedure in any other claim. The hearing will consist of oral evidence with cross-examination and speeches in the usual way. It is in dealing with interim applications that the practice and procedure relating to injunctions require special attention. Most injunction cases stop at the interim stage and go no further (see Ch.3). Certainly it is only a small minority of cases which go directly to trial without the claimant applying for interim relief early in the proceedings.

5-01

During normal court hours, application for a hearing in London should be made:

(a) in the Queen's Bench Division general list, to the listing office for the Interim Applications Judge (Room WG08; Tel. 020 7947 6924);

(b) in the Admiralty and Commercial Courts, to those courts' listing office (Rolls Building, Fetter Lane, London EC4A 1NL; Tel. 020 7947 6826);

(c) in the Administrative Court, to that court's listing office (Room C315; Tel. 020 7947 6655);

(d) in the Chancery Division, to the clerk to the Chancery Interim Applications Judge, identified in each edition of the daily Court Hearings List on HM Courts and Tribunal Service's website, or to the Chancery Judges' Listing Office at the Rolls Building (7 Rolls Building, Fetter Lane, London EC4A 1NL; Tel. 020 7947 6690);

(e) in the Family Division (see Ch.10), to the office of the Clerk of the Rules (Room TM 9.08; Tel. 020 7947 6543);

(f) in the Technology and Construction Court, to that court's listing office at the Rolls Building, Fetter Lane, London EC4A 1NL; Tel. 0207 947 7987.

Outside normal court hours and at weekends, a duty judge system is operated. The judge may conduct the hearing at home or, indeed, anywhere else; jurisdiction is neither conferred nor excluded by locality (*St Edmundsbury & Ipswich Diocesan Board of Finance v Clark* [1973] Ch. 323, per Megarry J).

Urgent applications should be made in liaison with the relevant listing officer. In cases where a hearing cannot be arranged, applications for injunctions may be made by telephone, but only by counsel or solicitors. Between 10.00 and 17.00 on weekdays the caller should ring the Royal Courts of Justice switchboard (Tel. 020 7947 6000) and ask to be put in contact with a High Court judge of the appropriate division available to deal with an emergency application in a High Court matter. A district registry or county court may be similarly contacted through the switchboard of each local county court during working hours (all listed on the HMCS Court Finder website). Outside these hours the call should be to the Royal Courts of Justice switchboard, who will contact the relevant duty High Court judge's clerk or the appropriate area circuit judge, or alternatively to the local

5-02

Urgent Court Business Officer (CPR PD 25A para.4). A list of contact telephone numbers is given at the end of this book.

1 JURISDICTION

5-03   Interim injunctions are the first of 15 types of interim remedy catalogued in CPR r.25.1(1). Leaving aside domestic or matrimonial litigation (see Ch.10), which may be conducted in the Family Division or in the county court, there are three possible courts of trial: the Chancery Division of the High Court, the Queen's Bench Division of the High Court (the general list or, in appropriate cases, the Commercial Court) and the county court.

In deciding between Chancery and Queen's Bench the following factors may be considered:

(1)   Where the subject matter is assigned to a particular division by statute (such as the Senior Courts Act 1981 Sch.1) or by rules of court, the claimant has no choice and must commence proceedings in that division. Matters assigned to the Chancery Division relevant to the law of injunctions include patents and registered designs, bankruptcy, the sale of real property, the performance of contracts for leases and the execution of trusts. Copyright and passing off cases should also be conducted in the Chancery Division (*Swedac Ltd v Magnet & Southerns Plc* [1989] 1 F.S.R. 243; *APAC Rowena Ltd v Norpol Packaging Ltd* [1991] F.S.R. 273; see also CPR r.63). A few highly specialised types of case are assigned to the Queen's Bench Division (see the *Queen's Bench Guide*, para.1.5.5), including proceedings for the registration of foreign judgments.

(2)   In the Chancery Division, the applications judge will hear cases of up to two hours in length. In the Queen's Bench general list, applications estimated to last more than an hour are placed in the Interim Hearings List rather than being dealt with by the Interim Applications Judge. However, it is usually possible, depending on the pressure of work, for a very urgent case to be heard at short notice by the Queen's Bench Interim Applications Judge, or at least for an expedited hearing to be ordered with interim relief being granted meanwhile.

2 WITHOUT NOTICE APPLICATIONS

5-04   CPR r.23.4 provides that the general rule is that notice must be given of an application, with a copy of the application notice being served on each respondent. An application may be made without notice if this is permitted by a rule, Practice Direction or court order.

"Practice Direction PD 23A, para.3" provides:

"An application may be made without serving an application notice only:

(1)   where there is exceptional urgency;
(2)   where the overriding objective is best furthered by doing so;
(3)   by consent of all parties;
(4)   with the permission of the court;
(5)   where para.2.10 applies [date fixed for hearing but insufficient time to serve application notice]; or
(6)   where a court order, rule or practice direction permits."

Paragraph 4 states:

"4.1   Unless the court otherwise directs or paragraph 3 of this practice direction applies the application notice must be served as soon as practicable after it has been issued and, if there is to be a hearing, at least 3 clear days before the hearing date (CPR r.23.7(1)(b)).

4.1A   Where there is to be a telephone hearing the application notice must be served as soon as practicable after it has been issued and in any event at least 5 days before the date of the hearing.

4.2   Where an application notice should be served but there is not sufficient time to do so, informal notification of the application should be given unless the circumstances of the application require secrecy." (CPR PD 25A para.4.3(3) uses the phrase "except in cases where secrecy is essential".)

The effect of these paragraphs is, it is submitted, to codify previous practice in injunction applications. Three types of case may be distinguished:

(a)   *No notice at all*: cases requiring secrecy, notably freezing and search orders.
(b)   *Informal notice*: where the case is too urgent to wait for three clear working days, but secrecy cannot be justified. This covers a large proportion of injunction applications. The defendant may, and if present generally does, take part in the hearing.
(c)   *Three clear working days' notice in writing*: all other cases.

In *Re First Express Ltd* [1991] B.C.C. 782, a case which deserved but did not achieve inclusion in the main series of law reports, Hoffmann J said: **5-05**

"It is a basic principle of justice that an order should not be made against a party without giving him the opportunity to be heard. The only exception is when two conditions are satisfied. First, that giving him such an opportunity appears likely to cause injustice to the applicant, by reason either of the delay involved or the action which it appears likely that the respondent or others would take before the order can be made. Secondly, when the court is satisfied that any damage which the respondent may suffer through having to comply with the order is compensateable under the cross-undertaking or that the risk of uncompensateable loss is clearly outweighed by the risk of injustice to the applicant if the order is not made.

There is, I think, a tendency among applicants to think that a calculation of the balance of advantage and disadvantage in accordance with the second condition is sufficient to justify an ex parte order. In my view this attitude should be discouraged. One does not reach any balancing of advantage and disadvantage unless the first condition has been satisfied. The principle *audi alteram partem* does not yield to a mere utilitarian calculation. It can be displaced only by invoking the overriding principle of justice which enables a court to act at once if it appears likely that otherwise injustice may be caused."

In *National Commercial Bank Jamaica v Olint Corp Ltd* [2009] 1 W.L.R. 1405, Lord Hoffmann as he by then was, said that:

"a judge should not entertain an application of which no notice has been given unless *either* giving notice would enable the defendant to take steps to defeat the purpose of the injunction (as in the case of a *Mareva* or *Anton Piller* order) *or* there has literally no time to give notice before the injunction is required to prevent the threatened wrongful act."

Failure to appreciate this is the most frequent mistake in injunction litigation. To take as an example injunctions in the harassment jurisdiction (see para.4-66) prohibiting a defendant from entering his own home, in the leading case of *Moat Housing Group South Ltd v Harris* [2006] QB 606 Brooke LJ emphasised that exceptional circumstances are required for such an order to be made without notice, with a risk of significant harm if the order is not made immediately; the order must   **5-06** be no wider than is necessary and proportionate as a means of avoiding the apprehended harm.

Without notice applications should only be granted in very limited circumstances where to give notice would enable the defendant to take steps to defeat the purpose of the injunction, or where there was some exceptional urgency which meant literally that there was no time to give notice (*CEF Holdings Ltd v Mundey* [2012] EWHC 1524 (QB)). In *FZ v SZ* [2011] 1 F.L.R. 64 (see para.10-15), Mostyn J criticised the volume of spurious ex parte applications in the Family Division. In *O'Farrell v O'Farrell* [2012] EWHC 123 (QB) Tugendhat J, the judge then in charge of the lists, said that he had been "shocked at the volume of spurious ex parte applications that are made in the Queen's Bench Division". He noted:

> "In these days of mobile phones and emails it is almost always possible to give at least informal notice of an application. And it is equally almost always possible for the Judge hearing such an application to communicate with the intended defendant or respondent, either in a three way telephone call, or by a series of calls, or exchanges of e-mail. Judges do this routinely, including when on out of hours duty. Cases where no notice is required for reasons given in PD 25A para 4.3(3) are very rare indeed. The giving of informal notice of an urgent application is not only anelementary requirement of justice. It may also result in a saving of costs. The parties may agree an order, thereby rendering unnecessary a second hearing on a return date."

5-07 If the applicant has unreasonably delayed in making an application after he has knowledge of the facts an injunction will be refused, even where the defendant would not be greatly inconvenienced by the restraint—promptness is essential (*Bates v Lord Hailsham* [1972] 1 W.L.R. 1373). However a party can also be unreasonably precipitate—for instance inappropriately bringing proceedings without any prior complaint to the defendant or attempt to explore an amicable resolution (*Caterpillar Logistics Services (UK) Ltd v Paula Huesca de Crean* [2012] 3 All E.R. 129).

It is fundamental to any without notice application for an injunction that the party applying for it should show the utmost good faith in making the application (see para.5-12 and para.7-04 for full and frank disclosure in freezing orders).

An injunction restraining the publication of confidential information may be applied for and granted for a very short period without notice where the defendant is allegedly blackmailing the claimant (examples being *ASG v GSA* [2009] EWCA Civ 1574 and *SKA v CRH* [2012] EWHC 766 (QB)), or there is a real risk of the information being widely disseminated if notice is given. However where an order is sought against the media, notice must be given: see the *Practice Guidance: Interim Non-Disclosure Orders* [2012] 1 W.L.R. 1003; White Book paragraph B13-001.

5-08 *Trent Strategic Health Authority v Jain* [2009] 1 All E.R. 957 concerned the closure of a care home on the basis of an application wrongly made without notice. Although the case was not about an injunction, the House of Lords drew analogies with injunction applications. Lord Neuberger of Abbotsbury said that the case:

> "provides an object lesson ... for any judge to whom any application is made, where no prior notice of the application has been given to the respondent against whom an order is being sought. In any such case, before entertaining the application, the judge should, really as a matter of course, ensure that it is simply not possible or that it is inappropriate to give the respondent any notice. Impossibility would arise where there was extreme urgency or where the respondent cannot be contacted within the requisite time-scale; the classic case where it might be inappropriate would be in the case of some freezing injunctions, where there is a real risk of dissipation or concealment being effected very quickly by the respondent. However, even in many cases where it is impossible or inappropriate

to give written notice as required by the rules relating to applications on notice, it may well be possible and not inappropriate to give informal notice, even by telephone or e-mail, to inform the respondent of the application, before the applicant seeks such an order—or even after the application has been made and before the order is pronounced. If such a course is possible and not inappropriate, then the Judge should normally require it to be taken. And the more draconian the effect of the order applied for or to be made, the more necessary it is for the Judge to be satisfied that it is simply impossible or inappropriate to give the respondent any notice that the application is being sought before he or she makes the order. Furthermore, it is wholly unsatisfactory for an applicant to contend before the Judge that an application must be heard at once without any, or even very limited, notice to the respondent, in circumstances where the applicant has been preparing the application for some time, and could therefore have given notice, possibly only of an informal nature, to the respondent to warn that the application was being, or even might be, made."

A very common type of without notice application in the Administrative Court is for an injunction or stay to restrain the Home Secretary from carrying out removal directions in an immigration case. In *R (on the application of SB (Afghanistan))* [2018] EWCA Civ 215 the Court of Appeal, Lord Burnett of Maldon CJ presiding, emphasised that in this type of case the claimant's lawyers are under the same obligation as in other civil proceedings to act promptly (para.50); to give notice of the intended application to the defendant, via the Government Legal Department (para. 61); and that any order is liable to be discharged if the claimant and his lawyers have not complied with their duty of candour (para.79).

The claimant may not adduce evidence in the defendant's absence which he is **5-09** not prepared to reveal in the defendant's presence (*WEA Records Ltd v Visions Channel 4 Ltd* [1983] 1 W.L.R. 721; *Kelly v BBC* [2001] 1 All E.R. 323).

The Court of Appeal has held that it is "wholly wrong", during a trial or other hearing on notice, for one party to make a without notice application to the trial judge for an injunction, thus having the opportunity to make allegations in the other party's absence (*Re All Starr Video Ltd, The Times*, 25 March 1993).

In cases of extreme urgency, the facts may have to be outlined to the judge orally by counsel; in that event, however, they must then be repeated in the form of witness statements with a declaration of truth so that there can be no dispute about what evidence was before the court (*Attorney General v BBC, The Times*, 14 March 2007). Normally an application for an injunction sought without proper notice should include a statement explaining fully and honestly why proper notice could not have been given. Witness statements on a without notice application should contain a statement setting out the duty to give full and frank disclosure (*CEF Holdings Ltd v Mundey* [2012] EWHC 1524 (QB)).

It is advisable for solicitors acting on without notice applications to obtain the **5-10** specific authority of their clients to give the usual undertaking in damages. In cases where it is feared that the client may later "forget" giving this authority, it may be useful to recite the undertaking in the draft statement to be signed or the affidavit to be sworn in support of the application. A corporate claimant, unless a well-known public company, should give evidence of its assets available to honour the undertaking.

The costs of a without notice application should, as a general rule, be reserved.

A prohibitory injunction is binding on the defendant and carries the sanction of committal for breach as soon as he is notified of it. Personal service is not a prerequisite unless the injunction is mandatory (see para.9-07).

Full notes of the hearing without notice should be provided to the defendant **5-11** (*Interoute Telecommunications UK Ltd v Fashion Group Ltd, The Times*, 10 November 1999; *Cinpres Gas Injection Ltd v Melea Ltd, The Times*, 21 December

2005), especially in a freezing order case, where the notes should be provided whether or not they are requested (*Thane Investments Ltd v Tomlinson, The Times,* 10 December 2002). It is wrong as a matter of principle to rely on the existence of a transcript.

Where an application for an injunction without notice has been refused, the court has a discretion to consider a second application if material new evidence has become available (*Laemthong International Lines Co Ltd v Artis* [2005] 1 Lloyd's Rep. 100, Colman J). Such an application should, if practicable, be made to the same judge. If the original judge is not available, there is plainly a heavy duty on the applicant to disclose to the second judge everything said by the first judge, both in giving judgment and during the hearing.

3   WITHOUT NOTICE HEARINGS: DUTIES TO THE COURT

5-12   There is a duty of disclosure on both lawyers and clients in compiling the evidence on applications for injunctions without notice. The duty was explained in *Siporex Trade SA v Comdel Commodities Ltd* [1986] 2 Lloyd's Rep. 428. An applicant for relief must:

> "identify the crucial points for and against the application, and not rely on general statements, and the mere exhibiting of numerous documents ... He must disclose all facts which reasonably could or would be taken into account by the judge in deciding whether to grant the application. It is no excuse for an applicant to say that he was not aware of the importance of matters he has omitted to state. If the duty of full and fair disclosure is not observed the court may discharge the injunction even if after full inquiry the view is taken that the order made was just and convenient and would probably have been made even if there had been full disclosure." (Per Bingham J at 437.)

There is also a duty imposed on advocates to ensure that all the paperwork, including the draft order, is correct, and that the court is assisted fairly in the absence of the defendant. In *Memory Corp Plc v Sidhu* [2000] 1 W.L.R. 1443, counsel had obtained a freezing injunction without notice including a clause which he and the judge were unaware had been disapproved in a recent case. Mummery LJ said at 1460:

> "It is unsatisfactory for an advocate to hand to the court for the first time during the course of an urgent hearing a long and complex draft order which requires close reading and careful scrutiny by the court. If the advocate is unable to produce a draft order for the judge to read before the oral hearing starts then the application should not be made, save in the most exceptional circumstances, until the order has been drafted and lodged.
>
> I emphasise the special responsibility of the advocate for the preparation of draft orders for the use of the court. There may be a convenient precedent to hand on the word processor of the instructing solicitors or in their files or in counsel's chambers, but it is the duty of the advocate actually presenting the case on the oral hearing or the application to settle the draft order personally so as to ensure that he is thoroughly familiar with the detail of it and is in the best possible position to respond to the court's concerns and to assist the court on the final form of the order.
>
> Applications of this kind should never be treated by the advocate and those instructing him as involving routine pieces of paper work containing common form orders to be printed out from a computer and rubber stamped by the court. The urgency of the application and the absence of the other side necessarily mean that the court is even more reliant than it normally is on the scrupulous and meticulous assistance of the advocate in deciding whether or not to make extreme orders of this kind in the circumstances of the particular case.

In this case I am sorry to say that [the judge] did not receive from counsel as much careful assistance as he was entitled to expect on the detailed form of the freezing order. That lack of assistance contributed to the judge making an order in a form which I am confident he would not have made if counsel had performed his functions to the high standard required of the profession of an advocate."

Hughes LJ said in *In Re Stanford International Ltd* [2011] Ch. 33:

"In effect a prosecutor seeking an ex parte order must put on his defence hat and ask himself what, if he were representing the defendant or a third party with a relevant interest, he would be saying to the judge, and, having answered that question, that is precisely what he must tell."

That case concerned a restraint order, but if one substitutes the word "claimant" for "prosecutor", it describes aptly the duty of the advocate on any without notice application. A serious breach of the duty to make full and frank disclosure on a without notice application gives grounds to discharge even a meritorious order (*Orb A.R.L. v Fiddler* [2016] EWHC 361 (Comm)). It may turn on whether there is an immediate and necessary relation between the misconduct and the injunction applied for (*Boreh v Republic of Djibouti* [2015] EWHC 769 (Comm)).

The duty of full and frank disclosure continues to apply if the applicant gives informal notice (less notice than that laid down in CPR PD 25A r.2.2, which is not less than three days), even if the defendant is represented: *CEF Holdings Ltd v Mundey* [2012] EWHC 1524 (QB). This is subject to one qualification. If the respondent who has been given inadequate notice appears and is able to present all the relevant factual and legal issues to the court himself, then the applicant for the interim relief is discharged from the obligation to provide the same information.

The Practice Direction at para. 25APD.5 requires a usual injunction order to contain an undertaking by the applicant to serve the application notice, the evidence in support and the order made at a without notice hearing. Notes of a without notice hearing should be taken and provided to the respondent. In a freezing injunction the applicant is usually required to swear an affidavit containing all or the substance of what was said to the court by the applicant's counsel or solicitors and serve copies of the evidence and other documents provided to the court.

4 DOCUMENTS

The three basic documents required for a hearing without notice or on informal notice are (in addition to the stamped application notice) two copies of the claim form, one or more signed witness statements, and two copies of the draft order sought. For freezing and search orders an affidavit is required in place of a witness statement.

Whenever possible, a draft of the order sought should be filed with the application notice and a disk containing the draft should also be available to the court in a format compatible with the word processing software used by the court. This will enable the court officer to arrange for any amendments to be incorporated and for the speedy preparation and sealing of the order (Practice Direction PD 25A para.2.4). If the interim application is being made in the Chancery Division, an electronic draft of the order sought, in Word (.doc) format, should be sent to chanceryinterimorders@justice.gov.uk.

If a claim form has been issued but an application notice has not, a draft order should be produced at the hearing and the application notice and evidence in sup-

5-13

port must be filed with the court on the same or the next working day, or as ordered by the court (CPR PD 25A para.4.3(2)).

If no claim form has been issued, the applicant must undertake to issue one immediately (or as directed) and the claim form should, wherever possible, be served with the injunction order (CPR PD 25A para.4.4(2)).

In cases where the claimant seeks leave to issue a claim for service out of the jurisdiction, there will only be a draft claim form in any event; in all other cases where time permits, the claimant should issue his claim form before the hearing. Failure by a solicitor to comply with an undertaking to issue a claim constitutes a contempt of court (*Refson & Co Ltd v Saggers* [1984] 1 W.L.R. 1025) and may be grounds for discharging the injunction (*Siporex Trade SA v Comdel Commodities Ltd* [1986] 2 Lloyd's Rep. 428). When an undertaking has been given, time is of the essence; pressure of work is not a valid excuse for non-compliance (*Re S (A Child)* [2001] 1 All E.R. 362).

The claim form

5-14   This will be in the usual form (see Precedent 11). It is not necessary to claim an injunction specifically unless the obtaining of it is a substantial object of the claim, but it is advisable nonetheless to include it in most cases (except for injunctions which will not be claimed as substantive relief, notably freezing injunctions).

If particulars of claim are not contained in or served with the claim form, they must be served within 14 days in accordance with CPR r.7.4(1) —even if an interim injunction has meanwhile been granted, unless the defendant expressly agrees otherwise (*Hytrac Conveyors Ltd v Conveyors International Ltd* [1983] 1 W.L.R. 44) or the court grants an extension of time. In *Caterpillar Logistics Services UK Ltd v Crean* [2012] EWCA Civ 156, the Court of Appeal emphasised that the fixing of a hearing on notice more than 14 days ahead is not an excuse for failure to serve particulars of claim.

Evidence

5-15   Applications for search orders and freezing injunctions must be supported by affidavit evidence. Applications for other interim injunctions must be supported by evidence set out in either a witness statement (Precedent 13), a statement of case verified by a statement of truth, or the application if that is verified by a statement of truth. These various possibilities will be referred to as "statements".

A statement in support of an application for an injunction should contain a clear and concise statement of the following:

(a)   the facts relied on for the claim;
(b)   if the application is made without notice, the reasons for giving none;
(c)   all material facts of which the court should be aware, including any answer asserted by the defendant (or which he is thought likely to assert) either to the substantive claim or to the claim for interim relief, and any facts known to the applicant which might lead the court not to grant relief without notice.

The third requirement reaffirms the long-established duty of an applicant for without notice relief to make full and frank disclosure of all material facts known to him (*R. v Kensington Income Tax Commissioners Ex p. Princess Edmond de Polignac* [1917] 1 K.B. 486); for the discharge of injunctions following a failure to comply with this rule, see paras 6-13 to 6-14 and 7-34 to 7-36.

5-16   Note also that:

"the place to disclose the facts, both favourable and adverse, is in the affidavit [or witness statement] and not in the exhibits. No doubt it will usually be convenient to exhibit a few key documents where it is necessary to do so to explain the case. But the recent tendency to overload the case at the without notice stage and to burden the Judge with masses of documents in case something is left out, ought to be firmly resisted. If the facts are not fairly stated in the affidavit, it will not assist the Claimant to be able to point to some exhibit from which that fact might be extracted. If they are fairly stated then it should not avail the Defendant to show that some document, relevant on [disclosure], has been omitted. At the hearing [on notice] it is different. But even at that stage, restraint must be exercised." (*National Bank of Sharjah v Dellborg* [1993] 2 Bank L.R. 109 at 112, per Lloyd LJ)

Evidence used in interim proceedings may contain statements of information or belief with the sources and grounds thereof. Some witnesses omit to state the source of their information, merely saying "I am informed and believe". This protects the identity of the source of information, but is open to objection.

A statement should not contain legal argument (*Dunhill (Alfred) Ltd v Sunoptic SA* [1979] F.S.R. 337), nor quotations from the opinion of counsel or of the author of an article in a learned journal. Such opinions do not constitute evidence (per Megarry VC in *Gleeson v Wippell (J) & Co* [1977] 1 W.L.R. 510). They may also amount to a waiver of legal professional privilege. However, a statement relying on the contents of a report by Department of Trade and Industry investigators is admissible (*Deutsche Ruckversichering AG v Walbrook Insurance Co Ltd* [1995] 1 W.L.R. 1017).

There is power to order oral cross-examination of a witness but it is rare for such **5-17** an order to be made at the interim stage in an injunction case. If an order is made and the witness does not attend, his evidence is not admissible without the leave of the court. In urgent cases, whether the application is to grant or to discharge an injunction, the hearing will not be postponed to allow oral cross-examination to take place.

Two cautionary notes should be sounded with regard to evidence. If the witness subsequently gives oral evidence at trial, it is open to other parties to cross-examine him as to discrepancies between the statement and the oral evidence. Also, where a statement is filed either at the time or subsequently and the solicitor for a party discovers that statements in it are untrue, he is under a duty as an officer of the court to see that the falsity is corrected or alternatively to cease to act for the client concerned (*Myers v Elman* [1940] A.C. 282).

It is "utterly deplorable" for the solicitor to a party who has obtained a without notice injunction to distribute copies of the evidence in support to persons not party to the case (*Patel v Sharaby, The Times,* 29 October 1992, per Millett J).

Draft order (without notice)

The draft order (unless a freezing injunction or search order) should follow the **5-18** form prescribed in the *Practice Direction (Judge in Chambers: Revised Procedure)* [1996] 1 W.L.R. 1432 (Precedents 1 and 2), as updated from time to time. The Chancery Division have published versions of these forms as CH10 and CH11 (Precedents 3 (P3-01) & 4 (P4-01)). It should specify the precise relief sought and also, as a general rule, provide for the defendant to apply on notice for discharge or variation of the order and for costs to be reserved. The claimant will usually be required to give an undertaking in damages (see paras 3-03 to 3-11) and also to undertake to notify the defendant of the terms of the order forthwith. In any case where no claim has been issued, either because of exceptional urgency or because, for example, leave was required to issue a claim for service out of the jurisdiction, the order must record an undertaking by the claimant to issue a claim forthwith.

The general practice in the Queen's Bench Division, Chancery Division and county courts alike is for without notice injunctions to be granted on an interim basis, that is to say only until a specified return date. CPR PD 25A para.5.1 requires a return date to be given unless the court orders otherwise (*Thane Investments Ltd v Tomlinson* [2003] EWCA Civ 1272 at [21]). If the parties come to terms, the order on the return date can be made by consent, whereas if they do not it should be for the claimant to persuade the court that the injunction should continue, not for the defendant to demonstrate that the order should be discharged (see per Munby J in *R. (on the application of Casey) v Restormel BC* [2007] EWHC 2554 (Admin); [2007] N.P.C. 118 at [38]).

5-19   Occasionally, it is not only legitimate, but correct that a without notice injunction should not specify a return date (*East Hampshire DC v Scott, The Independent,* September 6, 1993 CA). In practice this is usually where the defendant is thought to be untraceable and the fixing of a second hearing would simply lead to pointless additional costs. A without notice injunction may be granted until further notice in a restraint of publication case, for example where it appears that there is unlikely to be a dispute as to the sensitive private nature of the information (*G v G and Wikimedia Foundation Inc* [2010] E.M.L.R. 14), but it is an exceptional order.

If a without notice order is made, the procedure in the Queen's Bench Division is for the applicant's solicitor to email the draft order to the court or take the original initialled by the judge, together with two fair copies, to the order room for a service copy to be sealed. In the Chancery Division, the draft order should be emailed to the Judge's clerk or arrangements should be made with the associate for the drawing up and sealing of the order. Certain additional undertakings are required in freezing injunction and search order cases (see Chs 7 and 8 respectively).

For the need for precision in the orders made see paras 5-33 to 5-34.

Notice of application

5-20   An application notice for the return date should then be served: see Precedent 12.

A claimant who has obtained an interim injunction without notice is under an obligation to apply to the court for the earliest appropriate date for the hearing of the application. If he delays to do so and the delay is inordinate and inexcusable, the court will ordinarily dismiss the application and thus discharge the injunction (*Hong Kong Toy Centre Ltd v Tomy UK Ltd, The Times,* 14 January 1994). The current practice is for the judge granting an injunction without notice to specify a return date, thus avoiding this problem.

5   ON NOTICE APPLICATIONS

Procedure

General

5-21   The defendant is now brought into the case, possibly for the first time. He must be given at least three working days' notice of the hearing unless, as sometimes happens, the claimant has been given leave to serve shorter notice. A few injunction applications are made by defendants against claimants, but it is convenient to follow the terminology for the standard case.

The following documents must be served on the defendant: the claim, application notice, copy witness statements or affidavits with exhibits, and the without notice injunction if one was granted. The claimant's solicitors are also under a duty to supply a note of the hearing without notice.

Before the hearing, the defendant will generally need to prepare evidence to answer the claimant's case. The claimant's side, on reading the defence material, may in turn reply, and so on, in theory, *ad infinitum*.

If the defendant fails to attend, service of the documents must be proved. In cases where this may occur, a certificate of service (CPR r.6.10) should be prepared in advance of the return day.

The hearing is normally before a High Court judge, circuit judge or recorder. Until 2015 in non-family proceedings a district judge or master could only grant an injunction with consent of the parties, but PD 2B removed this restriction so that the only limitation on their jurisdiction is that they cannot grant search orders, freezing orders and ancillary orders. The rationale for this extension stemmed from the width of the CPR definition of an injunction as "a court order prohibiting a person from doing something or requiring a person to do something" which could be argued to include all orders, not just injunctions. However it is thought that injunction applications will continue to be generally listed before High Court or circuit judges, particularly where there are penal consequences of a breach. See para.1-10 above, for the guidance given by the Chancellor of the High Court.

Although the duty of full and frank disclosure does not apply at the inter partes stage, the duty not to mislead the court remains. The court operates in large measure by trusting the lawyers and parties who appear in cases before it. There is no general principle that where a breach of the duty not to mislead is the fault of the solicitors, the client will be relieved of the consequences: *Boreh v Republic of Djibouti* [2015] 3 All E.R. 577, Flaux J.

Queen's Bench general list

Interim injunction applications on notice at the Royal Courts of Justice are initially listed before either the Interim Applications Judge in Court 37 or another judge. Up to one hour is allowed for the hearing. If the parties are agreed that this is insufficient, the applicant may, if he chooses, seek on filing the application notice to have the matter placed directly into the Interim Hearings Warned List; alternatively, he must as soon as practicable and at least 24 hours before the hearing transfer the matter into the Interim Hearings List.   **5-22**

In relation to most injunction applications, this is only part of the story. In practice, the applicant for an injunction will generally wish to be heard as soon as possible—delay almost always weakens the case for an injunction. So unless temporary terms can be agreed, the judge at the initial hearing forms a view (if the parties are not agreed) as to how urgent the application is and decides:

(a) how soon the substantive application should be heard (in a very urgent case it may be within days) and what is the likely duration of the hearing;

(b) what, if any, interim relief should be granted until the substantive hearing; and

(c) whether directions should be given for the service of evidence.

The claimant's solicitors should lodge in Room WG08 a bundle (agreed if possible), properly paged in order of date and indexed. The bundle should contain copies of the application notice, statements of case and orders, and of all written evidence upon which any party intends to rely. It is worth referring to the instructions on the composition of bundles given in the Chancery Guide since they represent good practice in any list and any division.   **5-23**

The bundle must be lodged three clear days before the date has been fixed for hearing. If no date has been fixed (which is unusual in an injunction case), the bundle is to be lodged 48 hours after the parties are notified that the case is to appear in the warned list. A skeleton argument and/or chronology should be lodged not later than 24 hours before the hearing. A list of and bundle of authorities should be provided to the usher by 09.00 on the day of the hearing. Where parties obtain evidence after the bundle has been lodged it is advisable to arrange for paginated copies to be delivered to court the day before the hearing, to be added to the bundle.

Chancery Division

5-24   In the Chancery Division, injunction applications estimated to last less than two hours are listed before the Interim Applications Judge. Interim applications are heard on any weekday in the High Court term (except the last day of term); the applicant's solicitor can choose the date. An application likely to last more than two hours is not heard in the ordinary list and is adjourned "to come on as an interim application by order" on a fixed date. This can involve delay, and the urgency of the case will often make it necessary for the claimant to seek interim relief by application to the judge, who may at the same time give directions for evidence.

The hearing of the interim applications list, in which injunction applications figure prominently, is an art form in its own right. The list is "called over" in court at 10.30 and counsel for each applicant is asked to say whether the application is "effective" (i.e. being contested that day) or "ineffective" (i.e. settled, or not ready for hearing, or being stood over to come on as an application by order) and, if the application is effective, to give a time estimate. Ineffective applications are taken first; the applications judge then decides the order in which the effective applications will be heard. Without notice and unlisted applications may be taken at the end of the list or earlier at the judge's discretion, and applications involving the liberty of the subject are by tradition given priority over all other cases. If negotiations to settle an application are in progress on the morning of the hearing, counsel asks for permission to "mention the matter at a convenient moment".

5-25   Two copies of the claim and notice of application, one of these stamped with the appropriate fee, must be lodged at the Chancery Listing Office by noon on the working day before that for which notice of application has been given.

Injunctions may be granted in a consent order on application without the defendant attending or being represented provided that a letter of consent is lodged, signed by his solicitors and counsel. Applications may also be stood over to any day in term except the last two days of a sitting, and undertakings may be continued (but not varied, nor given for the first time) by consent for up to 14 days up to three times successively, without any party's attendance in court, by personal application at the Chancery Listing Office at the Rolls Building, by 16.00 the day before the hearing. If the parties agree that the application will take over two hours they can agree for it to be adjourned to be heard as an Interim Application by Order by lodging an agreed timetable for the filing of evidence.

In the absence of consent, there is no right to have an application stood over; it is a matter for the judge's discretion and the claimant may be required to make the application with such ammunition as he has ready, or to abandon it (*Max Factor & Co v MGMIUA Entertainment Co* [1983] F.S.R. 577).

The need for a prompt decision

5-26   "Applications for interim relief need to be dealt with expeditiously, since delay may frustrate the very purpose for which the application is made. It is often possible, at least in a reasonably straightforward case, for the judge to announce his decision and to give his reasons for it at the conclusion of the hearing or after a short adjournment. If that cannot be done, it is sometimes possible to announce a decision at the conclusion of the hearing but to reserve the reasons for it ... If that is done, the reasons should follow without undue delay, especially if the decision is one that may be subject to appeal. It is sometimes necessary to reserve the decision as well as the reasons, because more time is required for consideration of the evidence and submissions; and the more complex the case, the longer the time that may be required. Again, however, it is important for the decision to follow without undue delay. In that situation one would normally expect the reasons to be given at the same time as the decision; but if there is a good reason to defer the giving of reasons, once more the delay should be kept to a minimum, especially if the decision may be subject to appeal." (Per Richards LJ in *EE and Brian Smith (1928) Ltd v Hodson* [2007] EWCA Civ 1210.)

Order for speedy trial

Where it appears to the court, on the hearing of an interim application for an   **5-27**
injunction, that the matter in dispute can be better dealt with by an early trial than by considering the whole merits for the purpose of the application, the court may make an order accordingly and may also make such order as respects the period before trial as the justice of the case requires. Where the court makes an order for early trial, it shall by the order determine the place and mode of the trial. In deciding whether to order a speedy trial, the judge must weigh the nature of the case against the fact that it will be "jumping the queue" at the expense of other cases waiting for trial. An interim injunction is a factor to be taken into account when deciding whether to order a speedy trial, but such an order does not follow as a matter of course (*Warner-Lambert Co LLC v Teva UK Ltd* [2011] F.S.R. 44). In *W L Gore & Associates GmbH v Geox SpA* [2008] EWCA Civ 622 Lord Neuberger articulated four factors to be considered: (1) good reason – some "real and pressing urgency", (2) the level of interference with the administration of justice, (3) the prejudice to the other side and (4) other special factors.

A claimant who secures an interim injunction on the basis that there will be a speedy trial is at risk of having the injunction discharged if he fails to work diligently towards that objective (*EDO Technology Ltd v Hills* [2006] EWHC 598 (QB), *The Times,* 24 May 2006, Walker J).

Standing over to trial

It sometimes emerges, when both sides have filed or produced their evidence, that   **5-28**
there is a direct conflict of fact so as to make the matter inappropriate for decision on written evidence alone. Faced with this difficulty, the claimant may do one of the following:

(a) abandon the application;
(b) pursue it immediately;
(c) file evidence in reply and then pursue the application;
(d) ask for the application to be "stood over to the trial".

The fourth possibility is the subject of some controversy. Essentially it is a costs device, whereby the claimant avoids abandoning his application and thus incurring an order for the defendant's costs in any event (see para.5-37). It requires the leave of the court which may, if the defendant objects, be refused. The danger of allowing such a procedure is that it enables a claimant to "go fishing" by launching an interim application with no chance of success, examining the affidavits put in by the defence (thus making far easier his task of drafting particulars of a statement of case) and then asking for the matter to be stood over to the trial with costs in the case. The court does have a discretion, however, and where it is necessary to determine issues of fact, but impossible to do so on written evidence alone, the matter may be stood over on appropriate terms (*Société Francaise v Electronic Concepts Ltd* [1976] 1 W.L.R. 51), which may be that costs are reserved (*Simons Records Ltd v WEA Records Ltd* [1980] F.S.R. 35) or that an order is made for the defendant's costs in the case (*Kodak Ltd v Reed International Plc* [1986] F.S.R. 477). It will be obvious that such an application is something of a last resort for the claimant and to be confined to cases where the urgency of obtaining an injunction is outweighed by the consequences in costs of pressing an interim application which is likely to fail. Where costs have been modest and the case is urgent, the claimant will be better advised to continue with his application and do the best he can.

Interim declarations

5-29   CPR r.25.1(1)(b) now expressly confers a power to grant an interim declaration, thus putting an end to a somewhat arid controversy about whether such an order could ever be made. It remains unlikely to become a routine remedy. In *Governor and Company of the Bank of Scotland v A* [2001] 1 W.L.R. 751, the Court of Appeal held that the discretionary power to grant an interim advisory declaration should only be used where there is a real dilemma which requires the court's intervention—in that case, on the application of a financial institution cooperating with law enforcement authorities. Another example of the power being used was to grant a declaration that a particular transaction by which a contemnor was seeking to purge a contempt would not be a further breach of a freezing order (*AB v CDE* [2010] EWCA Civ 533). But in *Bank St Petersburg v Arkhangelsk* [2014] EWHC 574 (Ch) Hildyard J declined to grant an interim declaration that the defendants had dealt with assets in breach of a freezing order, because of the risk that such an order could be used as a stepping stone to a committal for contempt without the breach having been proved to the requisite criminal standard.

An interim declaration is an exceptional remedy even in the public law context (*N v Royal Bank of Scotland* [2017] 1 WLR 3938). It is not appropriate for the court to give an interim answer to substantive legal questions and then only where there is the high degree of assurance generally required of mandatory injunctive relief. To make an interim declaration of private law contractual rights would circumvent the procedural safeguards of an interim injunction (*BALPA v British Airways Cityflyer Ltd* [2018] EWHC 1889 (QB)). It is necessary to consider the balance of justice and what degree of prejudice each side would suffer if the interim remedy turned out to have been wrongly granted (*Secretary of State for Education v National Union of Teachers* [2016] EWHC 812 (QB)).

Discharge of without notice orders

5-30   Any order granted without notice should contain liberty to the defendant to apply to vary or discharge it. Such applications are not always easy to fit into county court lists, but in *G v G, The Times,* 23 November 1989, the Court of Appeal emphasised that the defendant has a right to an expeditious hearing of an application to vary or discharge an order made in his absence. In *R. (on the application of Casey) v Restormel BC* [2007] EWHC 2554 (Admin); [2007] N.P.C. 118, Munby J expressed the view that there is

> "an absolute obligation on the court to list any application for the discharge of an ex parte injunction for hearing before a judge in court as a matter of urgency—and that means within a matter of days at most, not weeks and certainly not months."

When an interim injunction has been granted without notice and the matter comes back before the court on an application to continue the injunction, the court has an inherent discretion to discharge the injunction if it appears right to do so, even though the defendant does not appear or does not apply for the order to be discharged (*Harbottle v National Westminster Bank Ltd* [1978] QB 146 at 157) (as to the discharge of injunctions, see paras 6-13 to 6-14).

Disposing of the claim

It has already been pointed out that the grant or refusal of an interim injunction **5-31** often effectively decides the case. In other cases the application for an interim injunction is compromised on terms which the parties wish to treat as ending the litigation altogether. There are two ways in which this can be formally recognised. The first is for the parties to consent to treat the hearing of the application as the trial; in that event any injunction or undertaking will not contain the words "until judgment or further order" and provision should be made in the order for costs and any other outstanding matters. The second, which is less conclusive but allows time for reflection, is to extend time for whatever pleading is next to be served. If the claimant has not served a statement of case, the defendant can agree to extend time for service of the statement of case generally subject to, say, 14 days' notice. If a statement of case has been served, the claimant can likewise extend time for service of a defence statement. This prevents further costs being incurred to no purpose.

6 INTERIM NON-DISCLOSURE ORDERS

In August 2011 Lord Neuberger MR issued *Practice Guidance: Interim Non-* **5-32** *Disclosure Orders* [2012] 1 WLR 1003; White Book paragraph B13-001 giving guidance on applications for interim injunctive relief to restrain the publication of information: an interim non-disclosure order or privacy injunction. Such applications may be founded on rights guaranteed by the European Convention on Human Rights or on grounds of privacy or confidentiality. They may also be made in respect of a threatened contempt of court, a threatened libel or malicious falsehood, harassment, or a *Norwich Pharmacal* application in support of such actions. All such orders will seek to restrict the exercise of the Article 10 Convention right of freedom of expression through prohibiting the disclosure of information. The applicant must satisfy the court that he is likely to establish, at trial, that publication should not be allowed (*Cream Holdings Ltd v Banerjee* [2005] 1 AC 253).

Interim non-disclosure applications often engage both Articles 8 and 10 ECHR which have equal status (*Re S (a child)* [2005] 1 AC 593). Freedom of expression is particularly important where journalistic, literary or artistic material is involved and the Court must assess the public interest for it to be published taking into account any relevant privacy code (such as the IPSO Editor's Code of Practice). Advance notice must be given to persons against whom the application is made, except in the exceptional circumstances set out in Human Rights Act s.12(2)(a) and (b).

Derogations from the general principle of open justice can only be justified in exceptional circumstances, when they are strictly necessary as measures to secure the proper administration of justice and where the necessity is established by clear and cogent evidence (*Ntuli v Donald* [2010] EWCA Civ 1276, *JIH v News Group Newspapers* [2011] EWCA Civ 42). They cannot be made by consent. It is only in the rarest cases that an interim non-disclosure order containing a prohibition on reporting the fact of proceedings (a super-injunction) will be justified on grounds of strict necessity, i.e., anti-tipping-off situations, where short-term secrecy is required to ensure the applicant can notify the respondent that the order is made: *DFT v TFD* [2010] EWHC 2335. It is then only in truly exceptional circumstances that such an order should be granted for a longer period: *Terry v Persons Unknown* [2010] 1 FCR 659.

Both respondents and any non-parties to be served with the order are entitled to notice of the hearing and should be served with a copy of the Application Notice and any supporting documentation before that hearing as they have an interest in the information which is to be protected (*X & V v Persons Unknown* [2007] EMLR 290). Only where there are "compelling reasons" can notice be dispensed with such as blackmail cases (*ASG v GSA* [2009] EWCA Civ 1574) or where there is a real prospect that were a respondent or non-party to be notified they would take steps to defeat the order's purpose (*RST v UVW* [2009] EWHC 24). Only in "truly exceptional circumstances" should a media organisation (and in particular its legal advisers) not be given advance notice of an application for an interim non-disclosure order. Applicants need to satisfy the court that all reasonable and practical steps have been taken to provide notice of the application so that the court can ensure that the requirements of Human Rights Act s12(2) are fulfilled in respect of all non-parties to be served (whose details must be in the schedule to the order). The applicant should first provide the non-party with the Explanatory Note and seek a written undertaking to the Court that the material will only be used for the purpose of the proceedings (see clause 13 of Precedent 14). If this is given the applicant may then supply the supporting written materials, including names.

An advocate applying for an interim non-disclosure order must comply with the "high duty to make full, fair and accurate disclosure of all material information to the court and to draw the court's attention to significant factual, legal and procedural aspects of the case" (Practice Guidance para 30). Each application will be subject to "intense scrutiny". A full and accurate note of any without-notice hearing must be taken by counsel and solicitors: *G & G v Wikimedia* [2010] EMLR 14. The court should wherever possible give a reasoned, necessarily redacted, judgment, but if this is disproportionate a short note or judgment may be given setting out any points of general interest, the reason why those points were raised and brief reasons for the decision.

Interim injunctions restraining freedom of expression must contain case management provisions to bring the matter to trial or to a final determination by agreement: *AVB v TDD* [2013] EWHC 1705 (QB). Where an interim non-disclosure order contains restrictions on access to documents it must be accompanied by an Explanatory Note when served on any non-party who was not present at the hearing of the application (para 34 of the Practice Guidance).

Applicants must keep non-parties informed of developments (*Hutcheson v Popdog* [2012] 1 W.L.R. 782) and the Court will actively case manage these cases to ensure that a return date is specified and kept and that the applicant has complied with its duties, although the hearing can be dealt with on the papers, provided that sufficient material is before the court (*BCD v Goldsmith* [2011] EWHC 674). All orders must be made in public. If the return date is adjourned, the court may dismiss the substantive action, proceed to summary judgment, enter judgment by consent, substitute or add an alternative defendant, or give directions for a trial (*XJA v News Group Newspapers* [2010] EWHC 3174 (QB); *Gray v UVW* [2010] EWHC 2367 (QB)).

7 FORM OF ORDER

Part D of this book contains forms of injunctions. Precedents 1–7 are adapted **5-33** from High Court forms first promulgated in 1999; Precedents 8–10 are prescribed county court forms for an application for an injunction (N16A) and the injunction itself (N16). During the 1990s, some outdated terminology was abandoned. "Servants or agents", which were a puzzle to respondents who had neither, have disappeared, except when the defendant is a firm or a company. The penal notice is now placed at the beginning of the order. All these changes, which followed a successful experiment on the North Eastern Circuit by Judges Fricker and Forrester-Paton, are designed to make injunctions more intelligible to lay people who are required to obey them.

Since an injunction carries with it the sanction of committal for breach, it is particularly important that the order of the court should be stated with precision. As Lord Deas said in a Scottish case in 1874, cited by Lord Hope in *Attorney General v Punch Ltd* [2003] 1 A.C. 1046, "if an injunction is to be granted at all, it must be in terms so plain that he who runs may read". Lord Upjohn in *Redland Bricks Ltd v Morris* [1970] A.C. 652 at 666 said that "the court must be careful to see that the defendant knows exactly what he has to do, and this means not as a matter of law but as a matter of fact"; the case was one of a quia timet application for a mandatory injunction (see para.2-23 and following), but the dictum is of general application. Similarly, Balcombe LJ in *Lawrence David Ltd v Ashton* [1991] 1 All E.R. 385 said:

"I have always understood it to be a cardinal rule that any injunction must be capable of being framed with sufficient precision to enable a person injuncted [sic] to know what it is he is to be prevented from doing. After all, he is at risk of being committed for contempt if he breaks an order of the court."

However, Staughton LJ said in *Channel Tunnel Group Ltd v Balfour Beatty* **5-34** *Construction Ltd* [1992] QB 656 (reversed on other grounds [1993] A.C. 334):

"It used to be regarded as established law that an injunction, whether interim or final, must state with precision what the defendant must or must not do if he is to avoid the peril of imprisonment for contempt of court. There must not be a need for constant supervision by the court in deciding whether what the defendant proposes to do will be, or what he had done was, a breach of the injunction. These principles were reiterated by Lord Upjohn in *Redland Bricks Ltd v Morris* [1970] A.C. 652, 666.

No doubt the importance of these principles is undiminished in the case of a husband who maltreats his wife or molests her in the former matrimonial home, and in the case of an employee who leaves and proposes to make use of his employer's trade secrets. But it does seem to me that over the last 20 years there has been some relaxation of these rules in practice, at any rate in commercial cases. Injunctions of the [freezing] type are not infrequently framed without any high degree of precision, for example, by allowing money to be spent on living costs or ordinary business expenses. On occasion the courts are asked to vary an injunction so as to clarify what is within that licence. And substantive interim orders of a mandatory nature are sometimes made, for example, in charter party cases.

Commercial concerns have ready access to lawyers, and are well able to apply to the court if they are in doubt as to what they must or must not do."

Even a small error in a freezing injunction could render it unclear and uncertain and a defendant should not find himself at risk of imprisonment in dealing with his assets, when the order was deficient (*Re Vantage Point Europe* [2016] EWHC 1866 (Ch)). In the case of a mandatory injunction, the judgment must specify the date by which, or the period after service of the order within which, the act is to be done. The order may be to do the act "forthwith", which means as soon as is reasonably practicable (*Hillingdon LBC v Cutler* [1968] 1 QB 124). The court has a discretion to extend the time for compliance originally specified in the mandatory order.

8 UNDERTAKINGS

5-35

If a decision is likely to be given in favour of the claimant, the defendant frequently offers undertakings in lieu of an injunction, "not to do X until after final judgment on the claim" (see Precedent 3). This is enforceable in the same way as an injunction would be. Just as an injunction will not be granted unless it makes clear to the party enjoined what he must do or refrain from doing, so the court will not accept an undertaking which is too vague to be enforceable.

In *Zipher Ltd v Markem Systems Ltd* [2009] F.S.R. 14, Lord Neuberger of Abbotsbury considered the proper approach to the recording and interpretation of undertakings in lieu of injunctions:

"An undertaking is a very serious matter with potentially very serious consequences. It is a solemn promise to the court, breach of which can lead to imprisonment or a heavy fine. Accordingly, there should never be room for argument as to whether or not an undertaking has been given. Further, while there is inevitably sometimes room for argument as to the interpretation of an undertaking, the circumstances in which such arguments can be raised should be kept to a minimum. Accordingly, any undertaking should be expressed in full and clear terms and should also be recorded in writing …

It seems to me that it must follow from this that, in a case where there is a bona fide dispute as to whether an undertaking has been given, the fact that neither the existence nor the terms of the undertaking has been recorded in writing militates against an undertaking having been given. All the more so where the court has made an order in which the undertaking, if given, could and should have been recorded. As Neill LJ said in *Hussain v Hussain* [1986] Fam 134, 142B, in a case where an undertaking has been given, even where the court makes no order, that ought itself [to] be recorded in a formal order which should recite in full any undertaking that has been given.

I consider that it must also follow from the above analysis that, where the terms of an undertaking could equally well be interpreted as having a narrow scope or a wide scope, it is the narrower scope which must prevail. An accusation that there has been a breach of an undertaking has similarities with an allegation of criminal behaviour, and it therefore must be right that, where two interpretations of an undertaking are equally convincing, the less stringent one should prevail. (Of course, in some circumstances, the terms of an undertaking may be ambiguous in such a way as to render the undertaking simply unenforceable.) …

The fact that undertakings should be recorded formally in writing in clear terms does not mean that the court is bound to conclude that, where that has not happened, no undertaking has been given. There is no rule that an undertaking given to the court must be recorded in writing before it can be effective. In other words, whether an undertaking has been given is ultimately a question of fact in each case. Equally, the fact that, in cases of doubt, an undertaking should be construed beneficially to the person who gave it, does not mean that the court should search for uncertainties or ambiguities in undertakings. Ultimately, an undertaking is to be interpreted in the same way as any other document (assuming that it is in documentary form, as it ought to be)."

5-36

Undertakings in lieu of injunctions have been placed on a more formal footing by CPR r.81.7, which requires that a copy of the document recording the undertaking shall be delivered by the court to the party giving the undertaking: (a) by handing a copy of that document to him before he leaves the court building; (b) by posting a copy to him at his place of residence; or (c) by posting a copy to his solicitor.

"Where delivery cannot be effected in this way, the proper officer shall deliver a copy of the document to the party for whose benefit the undertaking is given and that party shall cause it to be served personally as soon as it is practicable."

The most satisfactory alternative is for the respondent to sign an undertaking in Form N117 (Precedent 10).

The claimant may be justified in refusing the offer of an undertaking and insisting on an injunction, even though in a case not concerned with domestic violence or anti-social behaviour the sanctions available do not differ. If he does accept an undertaking, he must ensure that it is properly worded (see para.6-02 for the position at trial). He cannot re-open a claim for an interim injunction if it turns out that the defendant's undertaking does not give adequate protection before the trial (*GCT (Management) Ltd v Laurie Marsh Group Ltd* [1973] R.P.C. 432).

Culpable delay by the claimant in pursuing the claim may justify the discharge of the defendant's undertaking (*Greek City Ltd v Demetriou* [1983] 2 All E.R. 921).

The court should not, having accepted an undertaking, add a "declaration" that the claimant is entitled to an injunction in the terms of the undertaking. Such an order is meaningless (*S v S* (1980) 10 Fam. Law 153).

9   COSTS

Costs in injunctions applications are subject to the usual general principles set out in Part 44 of the CPR and the court retains a high level of discretion as to the appropriate order. At a without notice hearing in the absence of the defendant, costs should generally be reserved; the matter is best left to be considered at the on notice stage. Obviously, if the defendant is not present, the only costs will be those incurred by the claimant. If, however, the defendant does attend the without notice hearing and the claimant's application fails, the claimant may be ordered to pay the costs of the defendant, despite the fact that the defendant's attendance is optional.   **5-37**

At the hearing on notice, the following are the main alternative orders as to costs (assuming that it is the claimant who has sought an interim injunction):

(a)   claimant's costs in any event;
(b)   defendant's costs in any event;
(c)   claimant's costs in the case;
(d)   defendant's costs in the case;
(e)   costs in the case;
(f)   costs reserved;
(g)   no order as to costs.

These terms are defined by "PD 44 para.8.5 (the Costs Practice Direction)".

An order for one party's costs in any event is made when the other party has taken unnecessary or improper action, or the hearing is one which should never have had to take place. Where the order is for "claimant's costs in any event", the defendant will be required to pay to the claimant his costs of the hearing even if the defendant is ultimately successful and awarded costs at trial. The same is true with the positions reversed if the order is for "defendant's costs in any event". An order for "claimant's costs in any event" is unusual in injunction cases, being more appropriate to applications where, for example, a defendant seeks an extension of time. An order for "defendant's costs in any event" could be made where a claimant had made a frivolous or clearly unmeritorious application for an injunction, such as where the court has no jurisdiction to grant the injunction asked for.   **5-38**

Alternatively, the judgment at the hearing on notice may contain an order for the successful party's costs in the case. The grant of an interim injunction with "claimant's costs in the case" means that the defendant will have to meet his own costs of the interim proceedings whatever the final outcome, and will also have to pay the claimant's interim costs if, but only if, the claimant succeeds at trial. Conversely, on the refusal of an injunction, the court may make "no order save defendant's costs in the case"; the claimant then pays his own interim costs whatever the final outcome, and also the defendant's if the defendant succeeds at trial. Where the order is simply "costs in the case" (i.e. costs of both parties in the case), the interim costs will follow the outcome of the trial, the successful party being awarded all his costs. This is a common form of order when the merits of the case are not yet clear.

The court may reserve the interim costs to the trial judge. This option may be appropriate where the application is decided on the balance of convenience and the judge is simply 'holding the ring' pending a trial or other determination (*Desquenne et Giral UK Ltd v Richardson* [2001] F.S.R. 1; see also *Picnic at Ascots Inc v Derigs* [2001] F.S.R. 2 where Neuberger J suggested that the usual order where a claimant obtained an interim injunction was for costs to be reserved). The costs in such circumstances could be determined once the true merits of the application were able to be assessed. The effect of this is that such costs will follow the outcome of the trial unless otherwise ordered (or need to be provided for if the claim is compromised before trial).

5-39   The decision to award one or other party his costs in the case may appear academic if the case does not go to trial, since "the case" will then never be finally determined. The claimant who succeeds at the interim stage must, in the absence of express agreement by the defendant, serve a statement of case. In a great many cases, however, the action simply "goes to sleep" or is compromised. The court has a discretion to allow an action which has become dormant after the grant of an interim injunction with costs in the case to be discontinued on terms that each side should pay its own costs (*Stratford & Son Ltd v Lindley (No.2)* [1969] 1 W.L.R. 1547). In an action that is dismissed by consent except for the costs of the interim hearing, the court needs to determine who, in effect, won at the interim stage (*Fox Gregory v Spinks* [2006] EWCA Civ 1544; (2006) 150 S.J.L.B. 1327).

There are judicial indications that the practice of awarding costs in the case or reserving costs on interim applications is giving way to a final costs order. In *Taylor v Burton* [2014] EWCA Civ 21, Rimer LJ said:

"Whereas in times gone by 'costs in cause' orders, or 'claimant's costs in cause' orders were commonly made on interim applications, nowadays they are more rarely made, and the winner of an interim application will commonly be awarded his costs there and then, regardless of what happens at trial."

The same view was taken in *Friendly Pensions Ltd v Austin* (unreported, 10 February 2015), when Mann J considered that earlier authorities no longer represented the 'usual' approach to the approach to costs under the CPR. The 'usual' approach may be an unhelpful principle to apply in the discretionary sphere of costs. As Moore-Bick LJ said in *R. (Hysaj) v Secretary of State for the Home Department* [2015] 1 W.L.R. 2472 "in some cases, of which *Desquenne et Giral UK Ltd v Richardson* is an example, it may be appropriate to defer making an order for costs until the outcome of the substantive proceedings is known, but that will not invariably be the best course". A court may order that the claimant should recover his costs in any event where the merits of the application were so obvious that it should not have been contested or when it is clear that a trial is unlikely to take place. The defendant may get his costs if the injunction application was concluded by undertakings which could have been obtained by pre-action dialogue (*Pathology Group Ltd v Reynolds* [2011] EWHC 3958 (QB)).

The risks with a determinative costs order is that it may later transpire that the injunction was obtained or declined on an incorrect basis rendering it unjust for the party successful at the interim stage to have had his costs paid by the losing party. As Andrew Smith J observed in *Dar Al Arkan Real Estate v Al Refai* [2015] EWHC 1793, there is no straightforward legal mechanism to require a recipient to disgorge costs already paid.

The amount of costs recoverable is the amount allowed after assessment on the standard basis unless the judge considers it appropriate to order assessment on the indemnity basis. In *Fourie v Le Roux* [2007] 1 W.L.R. 320, an injunction had been discharged with indemnity costs on the grounds that a substantive cause of action had not been properly formulated. The House of Lords held that in those circumstances, the judge's award of indemnity costs was difficult to justify, though it was upheld by a majority as a proper exercise of discretion. By way of contrast, in *Bir v Sharma, The Times,* 7 December 1988, a freezing injunction had been obtained without notice by means of fabricated evidence. Although it was not yet clear whether the claimant had been party to the fabrication, Vinelott J discharged the injunction and ordered the claimant to pay the defendant's costs on the indemnity basis, to be assessed and paid forthwith. **5-40**

The effect of the various orders may be illustrated as follows (the orders made are *not* the only possible ones, and the case is hypothetical):

(1) Claimant applies without notice for interim injunction and fails because the case is clearly unsuitable for without notice relief. Defendant has attended and "observed". Defendant's costs in any event.

(2) Claimant succeeds at on notice hearing. Claimant's costs in case.

(3) The injunction is varied slightly by consent. No order as to costs.

(4) Directions given for trial. Costs in case.

If the claimant succeeds at trial he will be awarded his costs of the trial and of applications (2) and (4), but will have to deduct the defendant's costs of application (1).

If the defendant succeeds at trial he will be awarded his costs of the trial and of applications (1) and (4).

10 SUMMARY JUDGMENT AND DEFAULT JUDGMENT

Summary judgment

A claimant may seek summary judgment under CPR Pt 24 for a permanent injunction, or a defendant may seek judgment under the same rule if the claimant's claim for an injunction has no real prospect of success. The application must be made directly to a judge. The claimant cannot make the application unless the defendant has filed an acknowledgment of service or a defence (CPR r.24.4(1)). **5-41**

It must be emphasised that an application under CPR Pt 24 is for final, not interim, relief so that, if it succeeds, it determines the matter. For this reason it will require a strong case to succeed; the claimant's claim must be one to which there is no defence, even when the defendant's evidence is taken into account. For example, in *Cadogan v Muscatt, The Times,* 15 May 1990, a tenant had lowered a parapet wall in flagrant breach of a covenant in her lease. The landlords obtained summary judgment for a mandatory injunction requiring her to reinstate the wall.

Judgment in default

5-42   If the defendant fails to acknowledge service of the claim or, having done so, fails to file a defence, the claimant seeking an injunction is not permitted, as he would be in a simple money claim, to enter judgment in default "over the counter"—an application must be made to a judge (CPR r.12.4(2)(a)).

The court may, on such terms as it thinks just, set aside or vary any judgment in default of defence pursuant to CPR Pt 13.

11   STRIKING OUT A CLAIM FOR AN INJUNCTION

5-43   In each of two reported cases in 1990, the claimant sought a permanent injunction in their pleadings but did not seek an interim injunction. The defendant applied to strike out the claim for a permanent injunction unless the claimant was willing to apply for an interim injunction and to give an undertaking in damages. In *Blue Town Investments Ltd v Higgs & Hill Ltd* [1990] 2 All E.R. 897, Browne-Wilkinson VC held that the case for an injunction being granted at trial was not "wholly unarguable", and consequently refused simply to strike out the claim for an injunction; he held, however, that the claimant's prospects of obtaining an injunction at trial were "minimal" and granted the defendant's application that the claim for an injunction should be struck out unless the claimant was willing to apply for an interim injunction and give a satisfactory undertaking in damages. In *Oxy Electric Ltd v Zainuddin* [1991] 1 W.L.R. 115, however, the claimant had a seriously arguable case for a permanent injunction and Hoffmann J refused the defendant's application altogether. These two cases are considered further at para.3-05.

If an interim injunction has been granted but the whole claim is struck out for non-payment of court fees, the injunction ceases to have effect 14 days after the striking out unless, within that time, the claimant applies to reinstate the injunction (CPR r.25.11).

CHAPTER 6

Other Proceedings

1 THE TRIAL AND JUDGMENT

Once an interim injunction has been granted or refused, the remaining pre-trial procedure follows the same pattern as in a claim for damages and does not call for comment, likewise with the trial itself. **6-01**

If the court finds for the claimant at trial, it may:

(a) give judgment for a permanent injunction;
(b) require an undertaking to the court from the defendant as an alternative to the grant of an injunction; or
(c) grant a declaration.

Undertakings in lieu

The claimant whose case has been contested at trial is entitled to insist on an injunction and refuse to accept an undertaking (*Royal Insurance Co v G & S Assured Investment Co Ltd* [1972] 1 Lloyd's Rep. 267 at 285). If the claimant does accept an undertaking, he must ensure that its wording gives him adequate protection: see, e.g. *Haddonstone Ltd v Sharp* [1996] F.S.R. 767 where a defendant's undertaking not to make and sell a product "of the same design as" the claimant's was held not to be breached by the design and sale of a strikingly similar, but not identical, product. Although an undertaking may be discharged on application to the court in the same way as an injunction may, it cannot be varied if, for example, the claimant discovers that it is not sufficient to prevent the continuation of the activity complained of (*Cutler v Wandsworth Stadium Ltd* [1945] 1 All E.R. 103). **6-02**

An appellate court may accept an undertaking in lieu of an injunction where the acts complained of have ceased between trial and appeal, but no court should accept, in lieu of an injunction restraining a breach of law, an undertaking by a defendant to "do his best" to observe the law (*Attorney General v Birmingham, Tame and Rea District Drainage Board* [1912] A.C. 788). When the court makes "no order" upon undertakings being given, it is still advisable to have an order drawn up, reciting the undertakings in a preamble; this can then be indorsed with a penal notice and served on the defendant: see Precedent 3.

Undertakings in lieu of injunctions must be served in accordance with CPR r.81.7 if committal is to be an option. That rule requires that: **6-03**

"(1) Subject to paragraph (2) and rule 81.8, a copy of any document recording an undertaking will be delivered by the court to the person who gave the undertaking—
   (a) by handing to that person a copy of the document before that person leaves the court building;

(b) by posting a copy to that person at the residence or place of business of that person where this is known; or

(c) by posting a copy to that person's solicitor.

(2) If delivery cannot be effected in accordance with paragraph (1), the court officer will deliver a copy of the document to the party for whose benefit the undertaking was given and that party must serve it personally on the person who gave the undertaking as soon as practicable.

(3) Where the person referred to in paragraph (1) is a company or other corporation, a copy of the judgment or order must also be served on the respondent."

The most satisfactory alternative is for the respondent to sign an undertaking in Form N117 (Precedent 10). There is old authority that because an undertaking to the court is freely and knowingly given, service of the order containing the undertaking is not necessary and notice of it is sufficient (*D v A & Co* [1900] 1 Ch. 484); but it will be seen in Chapter 9 below that contempt applications require strict adherence to procedural rules.

Declarations

6-04   In *Llandudno UDC v Woods* [1899] 2 Ch. 705, the claimants sought a declaration that the defendant was not entitled to hold services or deliver sermons on the seashore without their consent, and an injunction to restrain him from so doing. The judge held that he could not refuse a declaration since the defendant was indeed not entitled in law to act as he did, but he declined to grant an injunction, which was "a formidable legal weapon which ought to be reserved for less trivial occasions". In cases where an immediate injunction would be oppressive, the court may grant a declaration with permission to the claimant to apply for an injunction after a specified time (*St Mary, Islington, Vestry v Hornsey UDC* [1900] 1 Ch. 695); this is an alternative, though an unusual one, to granting an injunction while suspending its commencement.

2 INQUIRY AS TO DAMAGES

6-05   Where an interim injunction is granted, but is subsequently discharged, the defendant may well have suffered damage by reason of having had to comply with the injunction in the meantime. He may then seek to enforce the undertaking as to damages which the claimant will have been required to give at the earlier hearing (see paras 3-03 to 3-11). In order to enforce the undertaking, the damage sustained must be assessed by means of an *inquiry as to damages*, generally before a master or district judge:

"Two questions arise whenever there is an application by a defendant to enforce the cross undertaking in damages. The first question is whether the undertaking ought to be enforced at all. This depends on the circumstances in which the injunction was obtained, the success or otherwise of the plaintiff the trial, the subsequent conduct of the defendant and all the other circumstances of the case. It is essentially a question of discretion. Discretion is usually exercised by the trial judge since he was bound to know more of the facts of the case than anyone else. If the first question is answered in favour of the defendant, the second question is whether the defendant suffered any damage by reason of the granting of the injunction." (Per Lloyd LJ in *Financiera Avenida SA v Shiblaq, The Times*, 14 January 1991, cited in *Dadourian Group International Inc v Simms* [2009] 1 Lloyd's Rep. 601 at [184].)"

At the inquiry the onus is on the defendant to prove both the fact of damage and its causation (*Tharros Shipping Co Ltd v Bias Shipping Ltd* [1994] 1 Lloyd's Rep. 577). The assessment is made on the same basis as that on which damages for breach of contract would be assessed if the undertaking had been a contract between the claimant and the defendant that the claimant would not prevent the defendant from doing the act prohibited by the injunction (*F Hoffman-La Roche & Co AG v Secretary of State for Trade and Industry* [1975] A.C. 295 at 361, per Lord Diplock). The defendant must show that both the type of loss and any links in the chain of causation can reasonably be regarded as having been in the contemplation of the parties when the injunction was granted (*Tharros Shipping* case, above, per Waller J). A claimant giving the undertaking must have reasonably foreseen at the time of the order loss of the type which was suffered but not the particular loss (unless it has special knowledge). The correct approach is that the remote consequences of obtaining an injunction are not to be taken into account. Logical and sensible adjustments may sometimes be needed, because in truth the court is awarding compensation for loss rather than damages for breach of contract (*Abbey Forwarding Ltd v Hone (No.3)* [2015] Ch. 309, CA).

The general principles for assessing damages payable under an undertaking or cross-undertaking in damages were outlined by Norris J in *Les Laboratoires Servier v Apotex Inc* [2009] F.S.R. 3. He said:

"(a)   The undertaking is to be enforced according to its terms. In the instant case (as in many others) it is that [the claimant] will comply with any order the court may make 'if the court…finds that this Order has caused loss to the defendants.' The question for me is therefore: what loss did the making of the Order and its continuation until discharge cause to [the defendant]?

(b)   The approach is therefore essentially compensatory and not punitive;

(c)   The approach to assessment is generally regarded as that set out in the *obiter* observation of Lord Diplock in *Hoffmann-La Roche v Secretary of State for Trade* [1975] AC 295 at 361E namely:-

'The assessment is made upon the same basis as that upon which damages for breach of contract would be assessed if the undertaking had been a contract between the plaintiff and the defendant that the plaintiff would *not* prevent the defendant from doing that which he was restrained from doing by the terms of the injunction: see *Smith v Day* (1882) 21 Ch D 421 per Brett LJ at p 427.'

(d)   What [the defendant] was trying to do (and what the Order restrained it from doing) was to enter a new market…. It was denied exploitation of this opportunity. The outcome of such exploitation is attended by many contingencies but *Chaplin v Hicks* [1911] 2 KB 786 establishes (per Vaughan Williams LJ at p.791) that whilst 'the presence of all the contingencies on which the gaining of the prize might depend makes the calculation not only difficult but incapable of being carried out with certainty or precision' damages for the lost opportunity are assessable.

(e)   The fact that certainty or precision is not possible does not mean that a principled approach cannot be attempted…. A principled approach in such circumstances requires [the defendant] first to establish on the balance of probabilities that the chance of making a profit was real and not fanciful: if that threshold is crossed then the second stage of the inquiry is to evaluate that substantial chance (see *Allied Maples v Simmons & Simmons* [1995] 1 WLR 1602). As Lord Diplock explained in *Mallett v McMonagle* [1970] AC 166 at 176E-G

'…. in assessing damages which depend on its view as to what…. would have happened in the future if something had not happened in the past, the Court must make an estimate as to what are the chances that a particular thing…. would have happened and reflect those chances, whether they are more or less than even, in the amount of damages it awards…'

(f)   The conventional method of undertaking this exercise is to assess damages on a particular hypothesis and then to adjust the award by reference to the percentage chance of the hypothesis occurring. In many cases it is sufficient to postulate one hypothesis and make one discount: but there is no reason in principle why one should not say that either Scenario 1 or Scenario 2 would have occurred and to discount them by different percentages."

Approving Norris J's principles the Court of Appeal endorsed an award of £27 million in damages under a cross-undertaking in *AstraZeneca AB v KRKA dd Novo Mesto* (2015) 145 B.M.L.R. 188. Kitchin LJ also made some further observations on the calculation in this context of damages for loss of a chance.

6-06   In an appropriate case, general damages can be awarded for upset, stress, loss of reputation or general loss of business opportunities so long as such damages are realistic compensation. Damages may include unusual loss where a defendant cannot reasonably be expected to apply for a variation to the injunction to avoid such a loss. Damages for emotional distress are only recoverable in exceptional circumstances. Aggravated damages are justified where an order has been obtained by means of deliberate concealment of a material fact. Exemplary damages are not available in respect of the cross-undertaking in a freezing order, and may be awarded in respect of a search order only where the order has been carried out in breach of its terms or the applicant's solicitors have acted in breach of their duty to the court (*Al-Rawas v Pegasus Energy Ltd* [2009] 1 All E.R. 346, per Jack J).

An inquiry as to damages may be refused if it is likely to prove fruitless (*McDonald's Hamburgers Ltd v Burgerking (UK) Ltd* [1987] F.S.R. 112) or if there has been great delay in making the application (*Smith v Day* (1882) 21 Ch. 421). However it is not refused merely on the ground that there was no impropriety at the interim stage. An undertaking as to damages is enforced in order to compensate the party suffering damage, not as a penal sanction, and where the claimant obtains an interim injunction but ultimately fails on the merits, an inquiry as to damages will be granted save in exceptional circumstances (*Bowring (CT) & Co (Insurance) Ltd v Corsi Partners Ltd* [1994] 2 Lloyd's Rep. 567).

6-07   The most obviously suitable time for the defendant to apply for an inquiry as to damages is at the trial. However the case may never come to trial. Nonetheless, the defendant is not entitled as of right to an inquiry whenever an interim injunction is discharged prior to trial. The court has a number of options open to it, as set out by the Court of Appeal in *Cheltenham and Gloucester Building Society v Ricketts* [1993] 1 W.L.R. 1545. It can:

(1)   grant the application and determine the amount of damages there and then, but this is likely to be appropriate only in the most straightforward of cases where all the relevant facts are known;

(2)   grant the application, and order an inquiry at a specified time without waiting for a trial;

(3)   stand the application over to the trial;

(4)   order an inquiry but direct that the question of liability be determined at the hearing of the inquiry; however this, it is submitted, achieves nothing, and was disapproved by the Court of Appeal in *Norwest Holst Civil Engineering Ltd v Polysius Ltd, The Times,* 23 July 1987;

(5)   refuse the application; however, as with (1), this will only be appropriate in a straightforward case, such as where it is clear that the defendant has suffered no loss by reason of the order.

The two options most used in practice are (2) ordering an inquiry when discharging the injunction, and (3) standing the application over to trial. The Court of Appeal in *Cheltenham and Gloucester Building Society v Ricketts,* above, indicated that (3) should be the more usual course, though it is a matter for the discretion of the judge hearing the interim application.

Examples of (2) include where the claimant's case was undermined before trial **6-08** by a decision of the House of Lords in another case (*Novello v James* (1864) 5 De G.M. & G. 876), and where the claimant obtained a freezing injunction and served it on the defendant's bank despite a lack of any evidence that the defendant was likely to dissipate his assets (*Barclays Bank Plc v Rosenberg* (1985) 135 N.L.J. 633).

An inquiry will not be ordered prior to trial where the injunction is discharged owing to a change of circumstances since it was granted, as it does not follow from this that the injunction should not have been granted in the first place. In such a case the application for an inquiry may be stood over to the trial (*Ushers Brewery Ltd v King (PS) & Co Ltd* [1972] Ch. 148).

Where a freezing injunction is discharged, an inquiry as to damages may be sought at any time. In *Yukong Line Ltd of Korea v Rendsburg Investments Corp* [2001] 2 Lloyd's Rep. 113, Potter LJ said:

"Whereas the usual practice in respect of interlocutory injunctions is not to order an inquiry into damages on the cross-undertaking until the merits of the action have been finally decided at trial, in cases where a *Mareva* injunction is involved, a defendant or other party bound in respect of whom the injunction is discharged at any stage may seek, and be granted, an inquiry into damages on the basis that, regardless of the ultimate merits of the action, the injunction was wrongly granted."

On the other hand, in *Fourie v Le Roux* [2007] 1 W.L.R. 320, where a freezing injunction had been discharged but the claimants still had a reasonably arguable case of fraud against the defendants, the House of Lords regarded it as "plainly wrong in principle" that an order had been made for the immediate enforcement of the cross-undertaking (per Lord Scott of Foscote at [41]).

A defendant who has been subject to a freezing injunction on cogent grounds has **6-09** no automatic right to an inquiry as to damages if the claimant seeks leave to discontinue on the basis that the defendant is not worth pursuing; it remains a matter of discretion (*Goldman Sachs International Ltd v Lyons, The Times*, 28 February 1995). Similarly, a defendant against whom a meritorious claimant seeks no injunction at trial is not entitled as of right to an inquiry as to damages (*Waterlow Publishers Ltd v Rose* [1995] F.S.R. 207). However an inquiry as to damages remains the normal course if a freezing injunction is discharged, and an order for an inquiry should not readily be refused or discharged (*FSL Services Ltd v Macdonald* [2001] EWCA Civ 1008).

A claim in respect of an undertaking in damages should not be pleaded by way of counterclaim. It cannot be dealt with before the court has decided whether or not the interim injunction should continue permanently and before the court has exercised its discretion as to whether or not to order the payment of damages on the undertaking. There is no tort in respect of which the defendant can sue independently of seeking the aid of the court to enforce the undertaking (*Fletcher Sutcliffe Wild Ltd v Burch* [1982] F.S.R. 64; *Digital Equipment Corp v Darkcrest Ltd* [1984] Ch. 512).

There is no jurisdiction to order a defendant enforcing an undertaking as to damages to give security for costs (*Bowring (CT) v Corsi Partners*, above). When an inquiry as to the damages the claimant "ought to pay" has been ordered, all questions of liability, causation and quantum, including discretion as to the enforcement of liability, remain matters for the judge or master conducting the inquiry (*Balkanbank v Taher* [1995] 2 All E.R. 904).

3 SUSPENSION OF INJUNCTIONS

6-10   Where the claimant has proved his right to an injunction against a nuisance or other injury but the difficulty of removing the problem is great, the court may suspend the operation of the injunction for a period (*Attorney General v Colney Hatch Lunatic Asylum* (1868-69) 4 Ch. App. 146). In a case where the loss to the defendants from the grant of an immediate injunction (against pollution of a stream) would have been out of all proportion to the gain to the claimant, and the defendants undertook to pay for any damage caused in the interim, an injunction was granted but suspended for two years, with liberty to the defendants to apply for a further suspension if special grounds could be shown (*Stollmeyer v Petroleum Development Co Ltd* [1918] A.C. 498n). The public interest may also be taken into account. In *Frost v King Edward VII Memorial Association* [1918] 2 Ch. 180, heard during the First World War, the injunction sought was to close down a hospital; the court granted an injunction but suspended it for six months with liberty to the defendants to apply for an extension of the suspension if the war was still in progress.

In *Trenberth v National Westminster Bank Ltd* (1979) 123 S.J. 388, where the claimants had refused permission but the defendants had nonetheless entered their land to erect scaffolding necessary for repairs which the defendants were under a statutory duty to carry out, an injunction was granted to restrain the trespass and Walton J refused to suspend it. The judge held that, as the claimants would have succeeded in obtaining a quia timet injunction on prior notice of the trespass, they should not be put in a worse position by the actual commission of the trespass. This is the usual approach in "crane" cases (*Anchor Brewhouse Developments Ltd v Berkley House (Docklands) Development* (1987) 38 B.L.R. 82); see also *Patel v WH Smith (Eziot) Ltd* [1987] 1 W.L.R. 853 as to injunctions against trespass generally. In *Charrington v Simons & Co Ltd* [1971] 1 W.L.R. 598, it was held not to be a proper exercise of judicial discretion to suspend an injunction for three years to enable the defendant to carry out ameliorative works requiring the claimant's consent and, at the same time, to suggest that if such consent were not forthcoming, an application by the defendants to discharge the injunction would be likely to succeed.

A short period of suspension (for example 14 or 28 days) may be appropriate in order to give the defendant the opportunity to close down his activities in such a way as to prevent deterioration of his plant and equipment (*Lotus Ltd v British Soda Co Ltd* [1972] Ch. 123).

In quia timet proceedings to restrain a nuisance, an injunction should not be granted with suspended any more than with immediate effect if the defendant has not yet been shown to be in the wrong (*Bridlington Relay Ltd v Yorkshire Electricity Board* [1965] Ch. 436).

6-11   There have been a number of recent cases in which local authorities have obtained injunctions against gypsies prohibiting them from using land for residential purposes, and the defendants have made a planning application and sought suspension of the injunction until it is determined. In *Mid-Bedfordshire DC v Brown* [2005] J.P.L. 1060, a judge's decision to grant such a suspension was reversed by the Court of Appeal, where Mummery LJ said:

"The practical effect of suspending the injunction has been to allow the defendants to change the use of the land and to retain the benefit of occupation of the land with caravans for residential purposes. This was in defiance of a court order properly served on them and correctly explained to them. In those circumstances there is a real risk that the suspension of the injunction would be perceived as condoning the breach. This would send out the wrong signal, both to others tempted to do the same and to law-abiding members of the public. The message would be that the court is prepared to tolerate contempt of its orders and to permit those who break them to profit from their contempt.

The effect of that message would be to diminish respect for court orders, to undermine the authority of the court and to subvert the rule of law. In our judgment, those overarching public interest considerations far outweigh the factors which favour a suspension of the injunction so as to allow the defendants to keep their caravans on the land and to continue to reside there in breach of planning control."

A similar approach was taken in *Coates v South Bucks DC* [2004] EWCA Civ 1378 and *South Bedfordshire DC v Price* [2006] EWCA Civ 493; [2006] J.P.L. 1805.

In *Newham LBC v Ali* [2014] 1 W.L.R. 2743 the Court of Appeal held that where there has been a substantial breach of a planning obligation entered into under s.106 of the Town and Country Planning Act 1990, an injunction should normally be granted. An outstanding planning appeal will usually be irrelevant to this decision, but the court has power to suspend the injunction pending the planning appeal where it is fair, just and reasonable to do so. In the case before them the Court of Appeal did so on the grounds that the planning appeal was imminent, and the appellants would suffer considerable harm if they had to carry out the removal works the subject of the injunction and were then successful on the planning appeal, whereas little countervailing harm would be caused by the suspension of the injunction. Lord Dyson MR said that the power to suspend an injunction under s.106(5) of the Act should be exercised sparingly.

An alternative to granting an injunction and suspending its operation is to make **6-12** no order but to grant the claimant liberty to apply for an injunction after a specified period, particularly if the court expects that the problem may by that time have disappeared (*Stollmeyer v Trinidad Lake Petroleum Co Ltd* [1918] A.C. 485). The defendant may still be required to pay the costs of the application even though no immediate injunction is granted. However, such an order is not always suitable since, on the later application, the claimant may have to establish as a matter of fact that circumstances have arisen justifying the grant of an injunction which was not granted at trial (*Pride of Derby and Derbyshire Angling Association Ltd v British Celanese Ltd* [1953] Ch. 149).

Suspension of an injunction is also possible after it has been granted. The defendant should apply by notice of application, and must support the application with evidence indicating why it is essential that the injunction be suspended. The application should be made, if possible, to the judge who tried the case (or heard the interim application on notice, if the case has not yet come to trial); this may properly be done even if he refused an injunction and it was granted by the Court of Appeal (*Shelfer v City of London Electric Lighting Co* [1895] 2 Ch. 388).

For suspension of an injunction pending appeal see para.6-21.

4 DISCHARGE OF INJUNCTIONS

An interim injunction may be discharged at any time on the application of the **6-13** party enjoined or, in the case of a without notice order obtained improperly, by the court of its own application at the hearing on notice (*Harbottle Ltd v National Westminster Bank Ltd* [1978] QB 146 at 157). In particular, a claimant is obliged to give full and frank disclosure on an application without notice; the affidavit in support must give a "reasonably detached appreciation of the case" (per Potter J in *Sumitomo Heavy Industries Ltd v Oil and Gas Natural Commission* [1994] 1 Lloyd's Rep. 45 at 62). This is of great importance in freezing order cases, as to which see para.7-04. On an application to discharge an injunction, the court should have regard to the evidence as at the date of the hearing of the application (*The Niedersachsen* [1983] 2 Lloyd's Rep 600 at 619).

Discharge of injunctions for such a failure is to act as a deterrent to ensure that persons who make ex parte applications realise that they have this duty of disclosure and of the consequences if they fail in that duty (*State Bank of India v Mallya* [2018] 1 W.L.R. 3865). Christopher Clarke J put it like this:

"The obligation of full disclosure, an obligation owed to the court itself, exists in order to secure the integrity of the court's process and to protect the interests of those potentially affected by whatever order the court is invited to make. The court's ability to set its order aside, and to refuse to renew it, is the sanction by which that obligation is enforced and others are deterred from breaking it. Such is the importance of the duty that, in the event of any substantial breach, the court strongly inclines towards setting its order aside and not renewing it, so as to deprive the defaulting party of any advantage that the order may have given him. This is particularly so in the case of freezing and seizure orders" (*In re OJSC Ank Yugraneft* [2009] 1 BCLC 298).

Interim injunctions on notice are usually granted until trial "or further order", and one kind of further order is an order discharging the injunction. Except where an urgent application is made pursuant to liberty to apply, the defendant should proceed by application notice. If the court (as it usually does) makes time for the expeditious hearing of an application for an injunction without notice, it should likewise grant a speedy hearing of an application to discharge the injunction (per Millett J in *Re Capital Expansion and Development Corp Ltd, The Times,* 30 November 1992; see also *G v G, The Times,* 23 November 1989).

6-14   One obvious ground for discharge is where the injunction was granted on terms and those terms have not been fulfilled. Another is where the continuing effect of the injunction has become oppressive or there has been inordinate delay by the claimant, who is under a duty to proceed with diligence (*News Group Newspapers Ltd v Mirror Group Newspapers Ltd* [1991] F.S.R. 487; *Richardson (John) Computers Ltd v Flanders* [1992] F.S.R. 391). A third is that the law has been changed or clarified by the decision of an appellate court since the injunction was granted (*Regent Oil Co v Leavesley (JT) Ltd* [1966] 1 W.L.R. 1210).

The defendant may also mount an attack on an interim injunction by applying to have the injunction discharged or the claim dismissed if the claimant, having obtained relief until trial or further order, fails to press on expeditiously with the substantive case (for example, by failing to serve particulars of claim): see *Greek City Ltd v Demetriou* [1983] 2 All E.R. 921; *Lloyds Bowmaker Ltd v Britannia Arrow Holdings Ltd* [1988] 1 W.L.R. 1337.

However, a claimant granted a without notice injunction with no return date can continue to rely on that injunction even though there has been no trial because of the defendant's default in serving pleadings. It is for the defendant to apply to discharge such an injunction, if appropriate, on the merits (*East Hampshire DC v Scott, The Independent,* September 6, 1993 CA).

5   RELEASE FROM UNDERTAKINGS

6-15   Care must be taken if a defendant consents to give undertakings but wishes to preserve his right to apply to be released from them at a later date. Where a defendant chooses not to seek an adjournment of an application for an interim injunction, but instead accepts that it should be dealt with there and then by his offering undertakings until trial or further order, there must be good grounds before he can apply to modify or discharge them. Good grounds can consist of a significant change of circumstances or the defendant becoming aware of new facts which could not reasonably have been known or found out before the undertakings were given (*Chanel Ltd v FW Woolworth & Co Ltd* [1981] 1 W.L.R. 485). If it is agreed that the defendant should have the right to apply without being limited to *Chanel* grounds, the form of order should be to adjourn the application on the defendant's undertakings, with liberty to the defendant to apply to vary or discharge the undertakings (*Butt v Butt* [1987] 1 W.L.R. 1351); an application may then be made if reason for doing so is shown (*Lonrho Plc v Fayed (No.4)* [1994] QB 775). As a matter of general approach, the court will allow a defendant to give an undertaking while reserving the possibility of a later application to discharge and will not compel him to contest the application instead, though in special circumstances the continuing uncertainty generated by this approach may be unacceptable (*Gantenbrink v BBC* [1995] F.S.R. 162). Otherwise, an undertaking given in lieu of an injunction may only be varied or discharged (save by consent) by the court which accepted it if there has been a significant change of circumstances (*Mid-Suffolk DC v Clarke* [2007] 1 W.L.R. 980): see also *Emailgen Systems Corp v Exclaimer Ltd* [2013] 1 W.L.R. 2132.

There are also difficulties in appealing against an undertaking:

"In general, if a party gives an undertaking to the court, he is not entitled to appeal against the undertaking. As in the case of a consent order, an undertaking is a voluntary litigation act analogous to entering into an agreement with the other party. It is a voluntary promise made to the court, not a coercive order made by the court. A typical case is an undertaking to the court by a defendant on an application for an interim injunction, in order to avoid the making of an injunction or other order against him. An undertaking is voluntary, even when it is given under the threat of an order in the same terms or of a more drastic order. If the party subsequently wishes to be released from the undertaking or to have it varied, an appeal does not usually lie against the undertaking, for the defendant would be appealing against a litigation decision that he, and not the judge, had made. The normal procedure would be for the party, who had given the undertaking, to apply to the court, to which he had given the undertaking, on a specific ground, usually changed circumstances making the continuation of the undertaking unnecessary, oppressive or unjust." (Per Mummery LJ in *Bell Davies Trading Ltd v Secretary of State for Trade and Industry* [2005] 1 All E.R. 324 at [104].)"

6   PART 36 PAYMENTS

An injunction is not a separate cause of action (see para.1-03). Where a claimant is claiming damages and an injunction, and the defendant makes a Pt 36 payment "in satisfaction of the claimant's cause of action", the claimant cannot accept the payment into court and press on with the injunction claim—acceptance of the money puts an end to the action (*Hargreaves Construction (Lineside) Ltd v Williams, The Times,* 3 July 1982; see also *Wiltshire Bacon Co Ltd v Associated Cinema Properties Ltd* [1936] 3 All E.R. 1044).

6-16

7   DISCONTINUANCE

CPR r.38.2(2)(a) requires a claimant who wishes to discontinue all or part of a claim in relation to which the court has granted an interim injunction to obtain

6-17

permission before doing so. In *Osuji v Holmes* [2011] EWCA Civ 476, an appeal rightly described by Ward LJ as "extraordinary", a claimant had obtained an injunction from the duty High Court judge on the usual undertaking to issue proceedings but had then (wrongly) brought his claim in a county court. He later served notice of discontinuance of the county court claim but, when the defendants sought to enforce an order for costs against him, argued that the discontinuance was a nullity because of the existence of the injunction. He failed. The Court of Appeal held that since the county court had not granted the injunction, permission to discontinue had not been required.

In the Australian case of *Apple Computer Inc v Popiolek* [1984] C.L.Y. 2643, the parties had settled the action on terms that the defendant would consent to a permanent injunction and the claimant would then discontinue. It was held that in these circumstances, the injunction survived the discontinuance, which was intended to affect only the claimant's claims for damages.

8   APPEALS

6-18   Permission is required to appeal from the grant or refusal of an interim injunction. The only exception relevant to injunction cases is that an appeal lies as of right from the grant (not the refusal) of an order for committal (CPR r.52.3(1)(a)(i)). If the decision below was in the High Court or was made by a circuit judge sitting on an appeal, the appeal is to the Court of Appeal. In a case heard by a circuit judge or recorder in the county court, appeal is to a single High Court judge unless otherwise ordered; and if it was by a district judge, appeal is to a circuit judge unless otherwise ordered.

A defendant should not appeal against a without notice injunction without first applying to the judge (or, if he is not available, another judge) for its discharge; the appeal is then from the refusal to discharge. To appeal against the without notice order direct is an abuse of process (*WEA Records Ltd v Visions Channel 4 Ltd* [1983] 1 W.L.R. 721). It is similarly inappropriate to appeal against an "opposed without notice" order when only one side's evidence was before the court. The party aggrieved by such an order should file his evidence, if any, and apply to the judge on notice for the discharge of the injunction before going to the appeal court (*Hunter and Partners v Welling and Partners* [1987] F.S.R. 83). However where the judge in the first instance did have affidavit evidence from both sides, even though the defendants had been compelled to attend a hearing at short notice, and the judge had granted an injunction, the defendants' only recourse was to appeal (*London Underground Ltd v National Union of Railwaymen (No.2)* [1989] I.R.L.R. 343).

Where a without notice injunction has been granted by the Court of Appeal (the judge having refused it), application to discharge it is nevertheless to be made to a judge of first instance, not to the Court of Appeal (*Ocean Software Ltd v Kay* [1992] QB 583).

For consideration of whether it is possible to appeal against an undertaking, see para.6-15.

6-19   An appeal is instituted by filing an appellant's notice under CPR r.52.4 and serving the notice on the other parties directly affected by the appeal within 14 days of the decision of the court below. In cases of great urgency, the Court of Appeal will sometimes begin hearing an appeal from the grant or refusal of an interim injunction within hours of the judge giving his decision. For example, in *McWhirter v Independent Broadcasting Authority* [1973] QB 629 the judge refused an injunction; the Court of Appeal sat at 17.00 the same evening and granted an interim injunction restraining the screening of a television programme due to be shown at 22.30. In *C v S* [1988] QB 135, an injunction to prevent an abortion was refused by Heilbron J on Monday morning and by the Court of Appeal on Tuesday morning; the Appeal Committee of the House of Lords dismissed a petition for leave to appeal on the Tuesday afternoon. The ability of the courts to hear swift appeals in order to ensure justice is best summed up by the memorable opening words of the judgment of the Court of Appeal in *Araci v Fallon* [2011] L.L.R. 440:

"The issue in this appeal is whether Mr Kieren Fallon, the well-known jockey, should ride in the Epsom Derby today. This appeal was issued at 3.00 pm yesterday afternoon. The court sat from about 4.00 pm to 6.30 pm yesterday evening, in order to hear argument. It is now 9.00 am on Derby Day and we are giving judgment at the first practical opportunity."

The appeal, whether from an interim or a final judgment, is by way of a review of the decision of the lower court unless the court considers that in the circumstances of a particular case the appeal should be by way of rehearing (CPR r.52.11(1)). The appeal court is not required to consider whether it would have granted an injunction, but whether the judge had been wrong to do so., respecting the judge's findings where the remedy was a discretionary one (*Frank Industries Pty UK v Nike Retail BV* [2018] EWCA Civ 497 applying *DB's Application for Judicial Review, Re* [2017] UKSC 7, [2017] N.I. 301). Fresh evidence will not be admitted unless the court so orders. The classic case for the exercise of these discretions is where the facts have changed between the first instance hearing and the appeal. It was held under the old rules that it is quite proper for the Court of Appeal to discharge an injunction if the nuisance complained of has abated between the trial and the appeal (*Attorney General v Birmingham, Tame and Rea District Drainage Board* [1912] A.C. 788); it is submitted that the same approach would be followed under the CPR.

It is rare for the Court of Appeal to sit in camera; it has no general jurisdiction **6-20** to sit in chambers and is therefore covered by the rule in *Scott v Scott* [1913] A.C. 417, reinforced by art.6 of the EHCR, that every court hearing shall be open to the public unless justice cannot thereby be done. Appeals may, however, be heard in camera where secrecy is of the essence, as for example in appeals without notice from a judge's refusal to grant a search order or in a freezing application against a bank, which depends on public confidence for the continuation of its business (*Polly Peck International Plc v Nadir, The Times,* 11 November 1991 CA). Enquiry should be made of the Civil Appeals Office.

It is not the function of an appellate court in an injunction case to substitute its own discretion for that of the judge (*Hadmor Productions Ltd v Hamilton* [1983] 1 A.C. 191). It may do so, however, where the judge has misdirected himself on the law (*Mercury Communications Ltd v Scott-Garner* [1984] Ch. 37).

9   INJUNCTIONS PENDING APPEAL

The court has jurisdiction to grant interim protection to a party who has been **6-21** unsuccessful at first instance pending an appeal. Such interim protection can arise in two ways. An unsuccessful defendant may be granted a stay of an injunction to be granted against him pending the appeal. Such stays are not granted automatically, but may be granted where solid grounds are shown and subject in appropriate cases to conditions. Similarly an unsuccessful claimant may be granted interim protection if he is seeking to restrain some irreparable harm pending appeal, notwithstanding that he has been unsuccessful in asserting his right at trial.

In *Minnesota Mining v Johnson and Johnson* [1976] R.P.C. 671 the Court of Appeal set out the principles which are to apply where the claim succeeds and the grant or stay of an injunction pending appeal is being considered. At page 676 Buckley LJ said:

> "It is not in dispute that where a plaintiff has at first instance established a right to a perpetual injunction, the court has a discretion to stay the operation of that injunction pending an appeal by the defendant against the judgment. On what principles ought such a discretion to be exercised? The object, where it can be fairly achieved, must surely be so to arrange matters that, when the appeal comes to be heard, the appellate court may be able to do justice between the parties.."

Buckley LJ went on to discuss the various measures open to the court in the case of a successful claimant:

> "Where an injunction is an appropriate form of remedy for a successful plaintiff, the plaintiff, if he succeeds at first instance in establishing his right to relief, is entitled to that remedy upon the basis of the trial judge's findings of fact and his application of the law. This is, however, subject to the defendant's right of appeal. If the defendant in good faith proposes to appeal, challenging either the trial judge's findings or his law, and has a genuine chance of success on his appeal, the plaintiff's entitlement to his remedy cannot be regarded as certain until the appeal has been disposed of. In some cases the putting of an injunction into effect pending appeal may very severely damage the defendant in such a way that he will have no remedy against the plaintiff if he, the defendant, succeeds on his appeal. On the other hand, the postponement of putting an injunction into effect pending appeal may severely damage the plaintiff. In such a case a plaintiff may be able to recover some remedy against the defendant in the appellate court in respect of his damage in the event of the appeal failing, but the amount of this damage may be difficult to assess and the remedy available to the appellate court may not amount to a complete indemnity. It may be possible to do justice by staying the injunction pending the appeal, the plaintiff's position being suitably safeguarded. On the other hand it may, in some circumstances, be fair to allow the injunction to operate on conditions that the plaintiff gives an undertaking in damages or otherwise protects the defendant's rights, should he succeed in his appeal. In some cases it may be impossible to devise any method of ensuring perfect justice in any event, but the court may nevertheless be able to devise an interlocutory remedy pending the decision of the appeal which will achieve the highest available measure of fairness. The appropriate course must depend on the particular facts of each case."

If a claimant has succeeded at trial in establishing an entitlement to a permanent injunction to restrain infringement of intellectual property rights, an injunction should only be withheld pending appeal if enforcement would be grossly disproportionate to the right protected (*Virgin Atlantic v Premium Aircraft* [2010] F.S.R. 15).

6-22   In *Novartis AG v Hospira (UK) Ltd* [2014] 1 W.L.R. 1264 Floyd LJ summarised the principles which apply to the grant of an interim injunction pending appeal where the claimant has lost at first instance as follows:

(i)   The court must be satisfied that the appeal has a real prospect of success.

(ii)   If the court is satisfied that there is a real prospect of success on appeal, it will not usually be useful to attempt to form a view as to how much stronger the prospects of appeal are, or to attempt to give weight to that view in assessing the balance of convenience.

(iii)   It does not follow automatically from the fact that an interim injunction has or would have been granted pre-trial that an injunction pending appeal should be granted. The court must assess all the relevant circumstances following judgment, including the period of time before any appeal is likely to be heard and the balance of hardship to each party if an injunction is refused or granted.

(iv)   The grant of an injunction is not limited to the case where its refusal would render an appeal nugatory. Such a case merely represents the extreme end of a spectrum of possible factual situations in which the injustice to one side is balanced against the injustice to the other.

(v)   As in the case of the stay of a permanent injunction which would otherwise be granted to a successful claimant, the court should endeavour to arrange matters so that the Court of Appeal is best able to do justice between the parties once the appeal has been heard.

As to whether a planning injunction should be suspended pending the hearing of an appeal to the Secretary of State, see 6-11.

If a *mandatory* injunction refused at first instance is to be granted pending appeal, a strong prima facie case must be shown that the appeal will succeed (*R. v Westminster City Council Ex p. Augustin* [1993] 1 W.L.R. 730).

An appellate court has jurisdiction to grant an interim injunction to preserve the subject matter of a pending appeal and to ensure that any order which it makes on the eventual hearing of the appeal will not be rendered nugatory (*Belize Alliance of Non-Governmental Organisations v Department of the Environment* [2003] 1 W.L.R. 2839 PC). Thus, the Court of Appeal may restrain a defendant from disposing of assets pending an appeal by a claimant who was unsuccessful at first instance provided that the claimant has a good arguable appeal (*Ketchum International Plc v Group Public Relations Holdings Ltd* [1997] 1 W.L.R. 4).   **6-23**

The Court of Appeal has power to grant or continue an injunction pending appeal to the Supreme Court (*Sturla v Freccia* (1879) 12 Ch. D. 438).

Ketchum International was a case about freezing injunctions where the claimant at first instance must show among other things a "good arguable case" rather than merely a serious question to be tried. Stuart-Smith LJ said at 10 G-H: **6-24**

"I cannot see any reason in principle why the considerations which are applicable when the court is considering the grant of a Mareva injunction should not be applied in favour of a plaintiff, even if he has lost in the court below, though the question will not be 'Does he have a good arguable case?' but 'Does he have a good arguable appeal?' This is likely to be a more difficult test to satisfy, and, if the case turns upon questions of fact which the judge has resolved against the plaintiff, may well be insuperable. This threshold must be at least as high as that which has to be satisfied when the court considers whether or not to grant leave to appeal where that is required."

A claimant who is successful in obtaining a *perpetual* injunction is not usually required to give an undertaking in damages, even pending an appeal by the defendant, but there is discretion to require such an undertaking if the Court of Appeal might well take a different view from the judge on the substantive issue (*Gwembe Valley Development Co Ltd v Koshy (No.4)*, *The Times,* 28 February 2002, Rimer J). At the end of the trial in *American Cyanamid Co v Ethicon Ltd* [1979] R.P.C. 215 at 275, Graham J, having found in favour of the claimants, declined to grant an immediate perpetual injunction but instead continued the pre-trial interim injunction pending appeal, with the claimants renewing their undertaking in damages. This is an unusual form of order, even if it did do justice between the parties in that action. In both *Minnesota Mining Co v Johnson Ltd* [1976] R.P.C. 671 and *Chiron v Organon (No.10)* [1995] F.S.R. 325, the successful claimants at trial offered an undertaking in damages pending appeal; this assisted them in persuading the court not to suspend the injunctions pending appeal instead.

CHAPTER 7

Freezing Orders

1   JURISDICTION

Until 1975, it was a long-established rule of English law that "you cannot get an injunction to restrain a man who is alleged to be a debtor from parting with his property" (per James LJ in *Robinson v Pickering* (1881) 16 Ch. D. 660). The claimant had to obtain summary judgment or judgment after a trial and then levy execution or issue bankruptcy or winding-up proceedings. This was of little comfort if, by the time judgment was given, the defendant had transferred all his assets abroad. The Court of Appeal, in a series of decisions beginning with two in 1975 (*Nippon Yusen Kaisha v Karageorgis* [1975] 1 W.L.R. 1093; *Mareva Compania Naviera SA v International Bulk Carriers SA* [1980] 1 All E.R. 213; [1975] 2 Lloyd's Rep. 509), developed a major exception to the traditional rule. The principle may be stated as follows: where a claimant can show a good arguable claim to be entitled to money from a defendant and there is a real risk that the defendant will remove assets from the jurisdiction or deal with them so as to render them unavailable or untraceable, the court may grant an injunction to restrain the defendant from removing them from the jurisdiction or from dealing with assets (whether located within the jurisdiction or not). Until the advent of the CPR, such an order was known as a *Mareva* injunction but it is now generally referred to as a freezing order or freezing injunction. It was described by Lord Donaldson MR as "one of the law's two nuclear weapons", the other being the search order (see Ch.8).

The jurisdiction was derived from the discretionary power, now contained in s.37(1) of the Senior Courts Act 1981 but originating far earlier, to grant an interim injunction in all cases in which it appears just and convenient. In the early years after 1975 there was some controversy about whether the power could be used against defendants in England and Wales, but s.37(3) of the same Act stated:

7-01

"The power of the High Court under subsection (1) to grant an interlocutory injunction restraining a party to any proceedings from removing from the jurisdiction of the High Court, or otherwise dealing with, assets located within that jurisdiction shall be exercisable in cases where that party is, as well as cases where he is not, domiciled, resident or present within that jurisdiction."

CPR r.25.1(1)(f) now gives the court power to grant:

"[A]n order (referred to as a 'freezing injunction')—

(a)   restraining a party from removing from the jurisdiction assets located there; or
(b)   restraining a party from dealing with any assets whether located within the jurisdiction or not."

Freezing injunctions originated in the Commercial Court, but they are also granted regularly in the Queen's Bench general list and in the Chancery and Family

Divisions. An early example was a Fatal Accidents Act claim (*Allen v Jambo Holdings Ltd* [1980] 1 W.L.R. 1252). A freezing order may only be made by a judge and not by a master or district judge (PD 2B para 2). Applications can now be made in the county court (having been removed from the prescribed list in the County Court Remedies Regulations 2014) and will be allocated to a circuit judge authorised for the purpose by the Master of the Rolls or the Deputy Head of Civil Justice (PD 2B para 8).

7-02   The jurisdiction to make a freezing order should be exercised in a flexible and adaptable manner so as to be able to deal with new situations and new ways used by sophisticated and wily operators to make themselves immune to the courts' orders or deliberately to thwart the effective enforcement of those orders (*JSC BTA Bank v Ablyazov* [2014] 1 W.L.R. 1414). In *Derby & Co Ltd v Weldon (Nos 3 and 4)* [1990] Ch. 65 Lord Donaldson MR stated that the court should not permit the defendant artificially to create a situation where "come the day of judgment", it is not possible for the claimant to obtain satisfaction of that judgment fully or at all. The court will, on appropriate occasions, take drastic action and will not allow its orders to be evaded by manipulation of shadowy offshore trusts and companies formed in jurisdictions where secrecy is highly prized and official regulation is at a low level (*International Credit & Investment Co (Overseas) Ltd v Adham* [1998] B.C.C. 134). However, once made, a freezing order must be construed strictly because of its potentially draconian effect on the commercial and economic freedom of an individual against whom no substantive judgment has yet been granted (*Federal Bank of the Middle East Ltd v Hadkinson* [2000] 1 W.L.R. 1695).

The European Commission of Human Rights held in *APIS v Slovakia* (2000) 29 E.H.R.R. CD105 that art.6(1) of the ECHR is inapplicable to proceedings for injunctions of this kind since the proceedings do not involve the determination of a civil right.

A freezing injunction may be granted in relation to an arbitration in the same way as in relation to litigation in court (*The Rena K* [1979] QB 377); this power derives from s.37(1) of the Senior Courts Act 1981 or s.44(2)(e) of the Arbitration Act 1996, or both (but see *AES Ust-Kamenogorsk Hydropower Plant LLP v Ust-Kamenogorsk Hydropower Plant JSC* [2012] 1 W.L.R. 920 for discussion of the overlapping powers). A disclosure order, worldwide in appropriate cases, may also be made (*Gidrxslme Shipping Co v Tantomar* [1995] 1 W.L.R. 299).

A freezing injunction may be granted in the High Court to prevent the dissipation of assets by the respondent to a claim in an employment tribunal (*Amicus v Dynamex Friction Ltd* [2005] I.R.L.R. 724, Royce J).

7-03   The granting of a freezing injunction does not have the effect of prohibiting payments by third parties *into* the defendant's frozen account (*Law Society v Shanks* [1988] 1 F.L.R. 504; *Bank Mellat v Kazmi* [1989] QB 541).

A freezing injunction may be granted pending the hearing of an application under s.423 of the Insolvency Act 1986 (transactions at an undervalue prejudicing creditors) (*Aiglon Ltd v Gau Shan Co Ltd* [1993] 1 Lloyd's Rep. 164). A freezing injunction may be granted in support of a statutory adjudication in a building dispute (*Pynes Three Ltd v Transco Ltd* [2005] EWHC 2445 (TCC)).

An injunction may be granted to restrain a defendant from exercising his voting rights as a shareholder in such a way as to dissipate his assets (*Standard Chartered Bank v Walker* [1992] 1 W.L.R. 561).

A freezing injunction does not give the claimant any preference in the event of the defendant's insolvency: see paras 7-39 to 7-40.

2 PROCEDURE

The basic rules of procedure set out in Ch.5 apply to freezing orders as they do   **7-04**
to other types of injunction, but a few distinctive features are to be noted. The initial
application is almost invariably made without notice and in private; if it were
otherwise, the defendant would be able to dispose of the assets before an order was
made. The documents required are a claim form or draft claim form, an affidavit
and a draft of the injunction which is being sought. Precedent 6, which is the
standard form approved by the senior judiciary, should be followed, subject to any
changes made in recent case law, and proposed departures from it drawn to the
judge's attention. For the dangers of failing to do this, see *Memory Corp Plc v Sidhu*
[2000] 1 W.L.R. 1443 (see para.5-12 where counsel's personal duty to check the
form and detail of the order is explained). It should be noted that, contrary to the
earlier Queen's Bench practice, freezing injunctions without notice in all divisions
are now granted until a return date.

In making the application, the claimant is under an important duty of frankness:
giving full and frank disclosure of any adverse matters of which he is aware. The
affidavit(s) in support must set out the facts on which the applicant relies for the
claim being made against the respondent, including any material facts of which the
court should be aware (PD 25A para.3.3); in other words, there is a duty to state
fairly any arguments expected to be advanced by the defendant *against* the grant
of an injunction (*Third Chandris Shipping Corp v Unimarine SA* [1979] QB 645).
If this is not done, the injunction may be discharged for non-disclosure (see paras
7-34 to 7-36). For example, if the claimant is in financial difficulties, this must be
made clear (*Manor Electronics Ltd v Dickson* [1988] R.P.C. 618); likewise if the
claimant is a purchaser and plans to use the injunction to prevent the seller from
dealing with money about to be handed over on a completion (*Negocios del Mar
SA v Doric Shipping Corp SA, The Assios* [1979] 1 Lloyd's Rep. 331; *The P* [1992]
1 Lloyd's Rep. 470). Advocates applying for freezing orders without notice to the
other party should draw the court's attention to any departures from the standard
form of order and ensure that there is a note on the court file that they made the
court aware of any such departures (*Finurba Corporate Finance Ltd v Sipp SA*
[2011] EWCA Civ 465, *The Times,* 22 April 2011). If that is not done, it is proper
for the court at a subsequent hearing to take the omission into account as a factor
against continuing the injunction.

Even serious and well-founded criticisms of a defendant's character do not mean
that claimants can be less scrupulous in complying with their duties to the court
when applying for a freezing order (*Fiona Trust and Holding Corporation v
Privakov (No. 2)* [2017] 2 All E.R. 570, per Males J).

The duty not to mislead the court continues at hearings on notice: *Boreh v
Republic of Djibouti* [2015] 3 All E.R. 577, discussed at para.5-21 above.

The claimant must give an undertaking in damages. In a proper case, a freezing   **7-05**
injunction may be granted even though a claimant has civil legal aid funding or is
of limited means (*Allen v Jambo Holdings Ltd* [1980] 1 W.L.R. 1252). However in
most cases it is essential to satisfy the court that the claimant is "good for the
undertaking". If the claimant is a company other than a well-known and publicly
quoted one, it is advisable to exhibit accounts evidencing the company's assets
(*Intercontex v Schmidt* [1988] F.S.R. 575). The court has a discretion to require the
undertaking in damages to be fortified by a bond or other security and the amount
of fortification should be an intelligent estimate of the likely loss which may be suf-

fered due to the freezing order (*Energy Venture Partners Ltd v Malabu Oil and Gas Ltd* [2015] 1 W.L.R. 2309) see para.3-07.

The claimant will be required to undertake to serve upon the defendant as soon as practicable the order, the claim form, an application notice for the continuation of the order and the affidavit(s) and exhibits in support. So far as third parties (such as banks) affected by the order are concerned, the order should expressly inform them of their right to apply to the court for a variation of the order or for directions. Anyone notified of the order must be given a copy of it by the applicant's legal representatives. They may also request a copy of any material read by the judge, including material prepared after the hearing at the direction of the judge or in compliance with the order, or a note of the hearing (Practice Direction 25A para 9.2).

7-06   The need to protect innocent third parties requires that, save in exceptional circumstances such as where the third party is not innocent, an applicant for a freezing order must undertake to abide by orders of the court in respect of third party losses caused by the order (*Banco Nacional de Comercio Exterior SNC v Empresa de Telecommunicaciones de Cuba SA* [2008] 1 W.L.R. 1936).

The order should always specify a maximum amount of assets to which the injunction is to apply. In a matrimonial case this should never be the whole of the respondent's assets (*Ghoth v Ghoth* [1992] 2 All E.R. 920). Where an individual defendant is resident within the jurisdiction, it should be stipulated that particular amounts may be withdrawn from an account to meet normal living expenses, business debts or the costs of defending the claim. There should also be provision for withdrawals from an account with the prior written consent of the claimant's solicitors.

7-07   Amounts specified for living expenses should have regard to the defendant's usual standard of living, and the claimant has no right to exert pressure on the defendant by having too small a figure specified (*PCW (Underwriting Agencies) Ltd v Dixon* [1983] 2 All E.R. 158 and 697); nevertheless, the usual practice is for a "modest" weekly figure to be stipulated on the without notice application, leaving the defendant to apply for more if necessary (*House of Spring Gardens Ltd v Waite* [1984] F.S.R. 277). An ordinary living expenses proviso does not cover extraordinary items, and to use enjoined funds to meet such items without specific leave is a contempt of court (*TDK Tape Distributors (UK) Ltd v Videochoice Ltd* [1986] 1 W.L.R. 141). There is much to be said for parties agreeing what is a reasonable sum for the ordinary living expenses of a respondent to a freezing injunction and a reasonable sum for legal advice and representation. If the parties can agree, that avoids the risk of subsequent allegations of breach of the order on the part of the respondent. If the parties cannot agree, the decision is one which the court may be asked to determine. In default of an agreement or an application to the court, it is for the respondent to a freezing injunction to make at his own risk decisions as to what is the reasonable expenditure which the injunction cannot preclude him from making (per Tugendhat J in *O'Farrell v O'Farrell* [2012] EWHC 123 (QB)).

If, following a hearing on notice, an injunction is confirmed "until judgment or further order", care should be taken not to enter, for example, a default judgment in the action without further application to a judge; the effect of doing so would be to discharge the injunction automatically and thus enable the defendant to escape enforcement of the judgment. The proper course, once the claimant is entitled to a judgment, is to apply without notice to a judge for leave to enter judgment and for the freezing injunction to be continued in aid of execution (*Stewart Chartering Ltd v C & O Managements SA* [1980] 1 W.L.R. 460). This is unnecessary if the injunction is expressed to run simply "until further order", as was the case in *Cantor Index Ltd v Lister* [2002] C.P. Rep 25.

An injunction may also be granted after judgment to restrain the disposal of as- **7-08** sets pending execution of the judgment (CPR r.25.1(1)(b) and see *Orwell Steel Ltd v Asphalt and Tarmac (UK) Ltd* [1984] 1 W.L.R. 1097), and such an injunction may be worldwide (*Banco Nacional de Comercio Exterior SNC v Empresa de Telecommunicaciones de Cuba SA* [2008] 1 W.L.R. 936), or pending assessment of the costs to be paid by the defendant or in support of any other order for the payment of money where the exact sum has not yet been quantified (*Jet West Ltd v Haddicam* [1992] 1 W.L.R. 487).

An appeal lies with permission to the Court of Appeal from the grant or refusal of a freezing injunction. The Court of Appeal has expressed the view, perhaps more in hope than expectation, that such appeals should be rare and confined to points of principle (*Derby v Weldon* [1990] Ch. 48, per Parker LJ).

It is occasionally necessary to seek a freezing injunction during a trial or other on notice hearing, but it is wholly wrong to do so to the trial judge on a without notice basis since it allows allegations to be made against the defendant in the absence of his counsel or solicitor (*Re All Starr Video Ltd, The Times,* 25 March 1993 CA).

3   WHAT THE CLAIMANT MUST SHOW

A cause of action justiciable in England and Wales

A freezing injunction, like any other injunction, can only be granted if it is ancil- **7-09** lary to a substantive claim. In *Fourie v Le Roux* [2007] 1 W.L.R. 320, Lord Bingham of Cornhill said:

> "*Mareva* (or freezing) injunctions were from the beginning, and continue to be, granted for an important but limited purpose: to prevent a defendant dissipating his assets with the intention or effect of frustrating enforcement of a prospective judgment. They are not a proprietary remedy. They are not granted to give a claimant advance security for his claim, although they may have that effect. They are not an end in themselves. They are a supplementary remedy, granted to protect the efficacy of court proceedings, domestic or foreign ... In recognition of the severe effect which such an injunction may have on a defendant, the procedure for seeking and making *Mareva* injunctions has over the last three decades become closely regulated. I regard that regulation as beneficial and would not wish to weaken it in any way. The procedure incorporates important safeguards for the defendant. One of those safeguards, by no means the least important, is that the claimant should identify the prospective judgment whose enforcement the defendant is not to be permitted, by dissipating his assets, to frustrate. The claimant cannot of course guarantee that he will recover judgment, nor what the terms of the judgment will be. But he must at least point to proceedings already brought, or proceedings about to be brought, so as to show where and on what basis he expects to recover judgment against the defendant."

A possible future cause of action is not enough (*Steamship Mutual v Thakur Shipping Co Ltd* [1986] 2 Lloyd's Rep. 439). Thus, there is no jurisdiction to grant an injunction to freeze all or part of the purchase price payable on delivery of a ship or other goods against any feared defects (*Veracruz Transportation Inc v VC Shipping Co Inc* [1992] 1 Lloyd's Rep. 353), nor in a case where the defendants are contractually obliged to deliver shares in three months' time (*Zucker v Tyndall*

Holdings Plc [1993] 1 All E.R. 124). In *HM Revenue and Customs Commissioners v Ali* [2012] S.T.C. 42, however, Warren J granted an interim freezing injunction against a taxpayer on whom the Revenue had served a direction for payment and issued an assessment, even though the tax was not payable until 30 days after the assessment. Pitchers J had done the same in *Director of the Assets Recovery Agency v McCormack* [2007] EWHC 908 (QB).

An injunction can be granted even if a cause of action (in its strict sense) does not yet exist, if it is possible to issue a contribution notice. If a co-defendant is entitled to issue and serve a contribution notice, he has a cause of action for so doing and a freezing order can be issued in support of a valid contribution notice (*Kazakhstan Kagazy plc v Zhunus* [2017] 1 W.L.R. 1360).

7-10   In some cases it may be possible to confer jurisdiction by claiming a substantive quia timet injunction: see *Rowland v Gulfpac Ltd* [1999] Lloyd's Rep. Bank. 86 and *Papamichael v National Westminster Bank Plc* [2002] 2 All E.R. (Comm) 60. In *Jones v Goldsack* [1994] C.L.Y. 3733, it was held that a freezing injunction cannot be granted in support of an order against a legally aided party for "costs not to be enforced without leave", since until an assessment under s.17 of the Legal Aid Act 1988 had been made there was no substantive claim.

The Department of Social Security could not obtain an injunction in the High Court freezing the assets of a father against whom the Child Support Agency had made a maintenance assessment, since enforcement of such assessments was reserved exclusively to county courts and magistrates' courts (*DSS v Butler* [1995] 4 All E.R. 193).

7-11   A foreign defendant who consents to a renewal of a freezing injunction will, unless the contrary is made clear in the order, be taken to have submitted to the jurisdiction of the English courts (*Esal (Commodities) Ltd v Pujara* [1989] 2 Lloyd's Rep. 479).

A problem which occurs regularly is that the claimant has a cause of action against the defendant and obtains a freezing injunction against him, but the defendant's affidavit sworn in answer to a disclosure order (see paras 7-20 to 7-26) suggests that while he personally has very limited assets (or so he says), his wife, or a company controlled by him, has substantial assets. The claimant has no cause of action against the spouse or the company, yet if an injunction could not be granted against her/it as well, the freezing jurisdiction would be easily frustrated. In practice such injunctions are granted. Four methods of doing so have been devised:

(1)   The claimant joined as second defendant the company (*TSB Private Bank International SA v Chabra* [1992] 1 W.L.R. 231; *Yukong Line Ltd of Korea v Rendsburg Investments Corp* [2001] 2 Lloyd's Rep. 113) or the defendant's husband (*C Inc v L* [2001] 2 Lloyd's Rep. 459, a post-judgment case). Banks are occasionally joined as defendants for the same purpose: see *Commissioners of Customs and Excise v Barclays Bank* [2007] 1 A.C. 181 at [108]. The *Chabra* jurisdiction is not, however, unlimited: see per Flaux J in *Linsen International Ltd v Humpuss Sea Transport Pte Ltd*) [2011] 2 Lloyd's Rep. 663. It arises when a third party against whom there is no cause of action is in possession of assets beneficially owned by the defendant, where that defendant has control or a power of disposition over the third party's assets and there is some legal process available to require the defendant to transfer those assets held by the third party.

(2)   A defendant's wife had not been joined as a second defendant, but an injunction was granted against her anyway on the grounds that there was a good

arguable case that the assets in her name were in truth the defendant's (*SCF Finance Co Ltd v Masri* [1985] 1 W.L.R. 876).

(3) A company was not joined as a second defendant but was enjoined from aiding and abetting a breach by the defendant of an injunction against him (*Hubbard v Woodfield* (1913) 57 S.J. 729, a case which, of course, long antedates the freezing injunction).

(4) A company was not joined but the defendant was enjoined from directing or procuring the disposal or charging of assets by the company (*Re A Company* [1985] B.C.L.C. 333).

See the summary by Christopher Clarke LJ in *JSC BTA Bank v Ablyazor (No. 11)* [2015] 1 W.L.R. 1287 at [82].

Where an accused person has money in a bank account which the police reasonably believe to have been stolen or fraudulently obtained, it has been held that the police may apply for an interim injunction restraining the removal of the money from the account (*Chief Constable of Kent v V* [1983] QB 34). The cause of action in such a case appears to be the common law right of the police to seize property which they believe to have been stolen. The decision has always been controversial. It is now more satisfactory for the Crown Prosecution Service, Serious Fraud Office or the Serious Organised Crime Agency to apply for a restraint order (see para.7-56).

7-12

The presentation of a winding-up petition by a minority shareholder under s.994 of the Companies Act 2006 does not give the court jurisdiction to grant a freezing jurisdiction unless the petition contains allegations which could be said to amount to a cause of action against the directors (*Re Premier Electronics GB Ltd, The Times,* 27 February 2001 decided under s.459 of the Companies Act 1985).

The Secretary of State or the appropriate regulator may apply for a freezing injunction under s.380(3) of the Financial Services and Markets Act 2000 against persons contravening certain provisions of the Act (see para.4-59).

A good arguable case

The claimant's case need not be so strong as to warrant summary judgment under CPR Pt 24; however, a case which is no more than arguable is not enough. The claimant's evidence must show that he has a good arguable case (*Rasu Maritima SA v Pertamina* [1978] QB 644): this means a case which is more than barely capable of serious argument, and yet not necessarily one which the judge believes to have a better than 50 per cent chance of success (*The Niedersachsen* [1983] 1 W.L.R. 1412). "That said", David Steel J observed in *Fiona Trust Holding Corp v Privalov* [2007] EWHC 1217 (Comm) that:

7-13

"it must be accepted that the margin between a serious issue to be tried and a good arguable case is a narrow piece of territory, and it may not always be easy to identify which side of the central reservation a particular claim which is legitimately pleaded falls."

A court should not attempt to resolve disputed issues of fact or difficult points of law on an application for a freezing injunction (*Sukhoruchkin v Van Bekestein* [2014] EWCA Civ 399 applying *Derby & Co Ltd v Weldon (No.1)* [1990] Ch. 48) but focus on the good arguable case test and a proportionate exercise of judicial discretion. As Lord Neuberger MR said in *Finurba Corporate Finance Ltd v Sipp SA* [2011] EWCA Civ 465, *The Times,* 22 April 2011:

"In the light of the increasing sophistication of fraudsters, and their extensive use of companies and other entities to mask their activities and assets, the courts should adopt a robust and realistic approach to technical points of substantive law or evidence raised against the grant of a freezing order, in cases where there is good reason to believe that fraud has occurred. Having said that, a freezing order can have very serious adverse effect often over a long period, sometimes even financial ruin, for the individual or company against whom it is made. The court should be satisfied not only that there is a properly arguable case against the defendant and a risk of dissipation or hiding of assets, but also as to the proportionality of the order, and it should be especially concerned about making the order when there seems to be little real value in the cross-undertaking."

Assets of the defendant within the jurisdiction

7-14   There must be prima facie evidence from which it may be inferred that the defendant has assets within the jurisdiction, although (per Mustill J in the *Pertamina* case, above) "since the defendant is *ex hypothesi* a somewhat elusive character it will usually be impracticable to establish exactly what assets he has available". There must be grounds for believing that the respondent is in possession of assets which can be caught by the order. It is not enough for an applicant to assert that the respondent is an apparently wealthy person who must have assets somewhere (*Ras Al Khaimah Investment Authority v Bestfort Development LLP* [2018] 1 W.L.R. 1099). To the extent to which the assets are known or suspected to exist, these should be identified even if their value is unknown, and if it is known or suspected that they are in the hands of third parties, in particular of banks, everything should be done to define their location to the greatest possible extent. In the case of bank accounts, the claimant should make every effort to try to indicate: (a) which bank or banks hold the accounts in question; (b) at which branches the accounts are held; and (c) if possible, under what numbers (*Z Ltd v A-Z* [1982] QB 558 at 588G). Once an order is made it applies not only to assets in the defendant's hands at the time it was granted, but also to those which he acquires subsequently (*TDK Tape Distributors (UK) Ltd v Videochoice Ltd* [1986] 1 W.L.R. 141).

The jurisdiction applies to goods as well as money (per Lord Denning MR in the *Pertamina* case); in *Allen v Jambo Holdings Ltd* [1980] 1 W.L.R. 1252, the asset whose removal was restrained was an aircraft. An injunction may be granted to restrain the sale of a company's goodwill (*Darashah v UFAC (UK) Ltd* (1982) 79 L.S.G. 678; *Templeton Insurance v Thomas* [2013] EWCA Civ 35—goodwill is no less valuable an asset than other intangibles). Injunctions are also regularly granted to prevent dealing in real property, on the grounds that an interest in land may be mortgaged or charged and the proceeds removed or concealed, thus depriving the claimant of an effective remedy. When a freezing injunction is obtained in respect of registered land, a restriction should be entered under the Land Registration Act 2002 (previously an inhibition). It should not be protected by a land charge: *Stockler v Fourways Estates Ltd* [1984] 1 W.L.R. 25). Indeed any person who has applied for a freezing order may apply for the entry of a restriction by lodging a certified copy of the court application for the freezing order. In this context, it should be remembered that the register is open to inspection. In the case of unregistered land, the claimant has to rely on less scientific methods such as notification to estate agents and solicitors. Although the contractual right to draw down under a loan facility agreement is not an asset for the purposes of a freezing injunction (applying the usual restrictive interpretation), the proceeds of such an agreement could be assets under the extended definition in the recent standard form (*JSC BTA Bank v Ablyazov* [2015] 1 W.L.R. 4754).

7-15   The beneficiary of a bank guarantee or a documentary credit may be enjoined from removing the proceeds from the jurisdiction. However payment by a bank under an irrevocable letter of credit or performance bond or guarantee will not be interfered with unless there is a substantial challenge to the validity of the document itself or it is proved to be seriously arguable that any demand for payment will clearly be fraudulent (*Bolivinter Oil SA v Chase Manhattan Bank* [1984] 1 W.L.R. 392; *Themehelp Ltd v West* [1996] QB 84).

If the freezing order is worded so as to cover assets, "whether the respondent was interested in them legally, beneficially or otherwise", that includes assets held by the defendant as a trustee or nominee for a third party (*JSC BTA Bank v Solodchenko* [2011] 1 W.L.R. 888). Wide wording may be justified where there is strong evidence that the defendant against whom a freezing order is sought has or is likely to have assets in a company which he wholly owns and controls (*Group Seven Ltd v Allied Investment Corpn Ltd* [2014] 1 W.L.R. 735). The standard wording of Commercial Court freezing orders does not extend to assets of a company entirely owned by a defendant, however it does restrain a defendant from diminishing the value of any of his assets and so could restrain him from procuring the company to dispose of its assets in a way which was likely to result in such a diminution (*Lakatamia Shipping v Su* [2015] 1 W.L.R. 291).

In exceptional cases where worldwide freezing relief is warranted (see paras 7-44 to 7-45), an injunction may be granted even though the defendant may have no assets within the jurisdiction (*Derby v Weldon (Nos 3 and 4)* [1990] Ch. 65). Lord Donaldson MR said in that case that

"the existence of sufficient assets within the jurisdiction is an excellent reason for confining the jurisdiction to such assets, but, other considerations apart, the fewer the assets within the jurisdiction, the greater the necessity for taking protective measures in relation to those outside it."

A real risk of removal or disposal of the assets

It is important that there be solid evidence adduced to the court of a real risk of dissipation (*Thane Investments Ltd v Tomlinson* [2003] EWCA Civ 1272). Objective facts are required, not mere expressions of anxiety or suspicion (*Third Chandris Shipping Corpn v Unimarine SA* [1979] QB 645; *CEF Holdings Ltd v Mundey* [2012] F.S.R 929).

7-16

Until 1981, evidence of a risk of assets being removed from the jurisdiction was essential for the grant of a freezing injunction, although if there was such evidence, the form of order commonly made prohibited the defendant not only from transferring the assets abroad but also from dealing with or disposing of them within the jurisdiction. In *Z Ltd v A-Z* [1982] QB 558, the availability of the remedy was substantially widened by including cases where assets may be "spirited away" within the jurisdiction (per Kerr LJ at 585F):

"The danger of assets being removed from the jurisdiction is only one facet of the 'ploy' of a defendant to make himself 'judgment-proof' by taking steps to ensure that there are no available or traceable assets on the day of judgment; not as the result of his using his assets in the ordinary course of his business or for living expenses, but to avoid execution by spiriting his assets away in the interim ... It is, therefore, logical to extend the scope of this jurisdiction whenever there is a risk of a judgment which a claimant seems likely to obtain being defeated in this way."

However Kerr LJ went on to emphasise that the injunction should be refused if there is no real danger of the defendant dissipating his assets to make himself "judgment-proof":

"[The jurisdiction] would not be properly exercisable against the majority of defendants who are sued in our courts. In non-international cases, and also in many international cases, the defendants are generally persons or concerns who are established within the jurisdiction in the sense of having assets here which they could not, or would not wish to, dissipate merely in order to avoid some judgment which seems likely to be given against them; either because they have property here, such as a house or a flat on which their ordinary way of life depends, or because they have an established business or other assets which they would be unlikely to liquidate simply in order to avoid a judgment … the great value of this jurisdiction must not be debased by allowing it to become something which is invoked simply to obtain security for a judgment in advance, and still less as a means of pressurising defendants into settlements."

This remains good law nearly 40 years later (see the review of the authorities in *JSC BTA Bank v Ablyazov* [2015] 1 W.L.R. 4754). Indeed, as Peter Gibson LJ said in *Thane Investments Ltd v Tomlinson* [2003] EWCA Civ 1272 at [26]–[28]:

"It is important on applications for so seriously intrusive an order as a freezing order that great care should be taken in the presentation of the evidence to the court, so that the court can see not only whether the applicant has a good arguable case but also whether there is a real risk of dissipation of assets … [Counsel] submitted that it has now become the practice for parties to bring ex parte applications seeking a freezing order by pointing to some dishonesty [and saying that this] is sufficient to enable this court to make a freezing order. I have to say that if that has become the practice, then the practice should be reconsidered. It is appropriate in each case for the court to scrutinise with care whether what is alleged to have been the dishonesty of the person against whom the order is sought really justifies the inference that that person has assets which he is likely to dissipate unless restricted."

7-17   The mere fact that the defendant's actual or feared conduct would risk impairing the claimant's ability to enforce a judgment or award does not in every case mean that a freezing order should be granted. The conduct in question must be unjustifiable (*Ketchum International Plc v Group Public Relations Ltd* [1997] 1 W.L.R. 4; *Mobil Cerro Negro v Petroleos de Venezuela* [2008] 1 Lloyd's Rep. 684). *Alternative Investment Solutions (General) Ltd v Valle de Uco Resort and Spa SA* [2013] EWHC 333 (QB) doubted the need for a claimant to show an intention to dissipate assets, dishonesty or fraud, but there certainly needs to be evidence of unjustified conduct in relation to the assets (*L v K* [2014] Fam. 35).

In *ABC v P* [2011] EWHC 1953 (QB), a 17-year-old girl sought a freezing injunction in a claim against her stepfather for damages for alleged indecent assault and rape. It was held that the fact that the defendant had been convicted of voyeurism, although that involved deceit and breach of trust, did not demonstrate a real risk of dissipation of the defendant's assets. General dishonesty is not enough by itself to show a risk of dissipation (*UCB Home Loans Corp Ltd v Grace* [2011] EWHC 851 (Ch)).

7-18   There is power to grant a freezing injunction directly against a bank, although given the relationship of a bank with its depositors and the need for public confidence if its business is to continue, the circumstances must be unusual for such an injunction to be granted. However, an injunction may be granted requiring the bank to preserve a specified sum subject to a tracing claim pending trial (*Polly Peck International Plc v Nadir (No.2)* [1992] 4 All E.R. 769, where the bank in question was based in North Cyprus). In *Etablissement Esefka v Central Bank of Nigeria* [1979] 1 Lloyd's Rep. 445, the defendant bank was controlled by the Nigerian Government. The Court of Appeal discharged a freezing injunction on the ground that it was inconceivable that the bank would fail to honour any judgment given against it in the English courts. A similar course was taken in *Montecchi v Shimco (UK) Ltd* [1979] 1 W.L.R. 1180: the parties whom it was sought to enjoin were Italian residents of good financial standing and any English judgment against them would be enforceable in Italy.

The order should be framed so as to result in the minimum interference with the respondent's rights; its purpose is not to punish the respondent but to protect the applicant (*Gill v Flightwise Travel Service Ltd* [2003] EWHC 3082 (Ch), Neuberger J). In any event the remedy is always discretionary and the courts should not be treated as rubber stamps. The remarks of Lord Denning MR in *Negocios del Mar SA v Doric Shipping Corp SA* [1979] 1 Lloyd's Rep. 331 at 334 should be borne in mind:

> "The judge said that caution should be used in granting *Mareva* injunctions. I agree with him. The *Mareva* injunction has proved most valuable in practice to the City of London and to all those who operate in the shipping world and elsewhere. But we must be careful that it is not stretched too far, else we should be endangering it. It must be kept for proper circumstances and not extended so far as to be a danger to the proper conduct of business."

The defendant may apply to exclude from the freezing order funds for its legal costs or pre-existing contractual obligations. The court must assess whether the claimant has an arguable claim to the money and if so, whether the defendant has grounds for denying that claim. If there is a defence, then the defendant must show that it needs the release of the funds to defend effectively (*Independent Trustee Services Ltd v GP Noble Trustees Ltd* [2009] EWHC 161 (Ch)).

The relevance of delay

There is no rule that delay is fatal to an application for a freezing injunction. The **7-19** applicant is entitled to take up time in making reasonable enquiries prior to launching an application, the more so where the nature of his case is based on fraudulent activity (*Fiona Trust v Privalov* [2007] EWHC 1217 (Comm), David Steel J). It is no answer for a defendant to come to the court to say that his horse may have bolted before the gate is shut and then put that forward as a reason for not shutting the gate (*Antonio Gramsci Shipping Corporation v Recoletos Ltd* [2011] EWHC 2242 (Comm), Cooke J). In *Madoff Securities International Ltd v Raven* [2011] EWHC 3102 (Comm) Flaux J gave a summary of the law which was approved by the Court of Appeal in *JSC Mezhdunarodny Promyshlenniy Bank v Pugachev (No. 3)* [2015] W.T.L.R. 1759:

(1) The mere fact of delay in bringing an application for a freezing injunction or that it has first been heard inter partes, does not, without more, mean there is no risk of dissipation. If the court is satisfied on other evidence that there is a risk of dissipation, the court should grant the order, despite the delay, even if only limited assets are ultimately frozen by it;

(2) The rationale for a freezing injunction is the risk that a judgment will remain unsatisfied or be difficult to enforce by virtue of dissipation or disposal of assets ... In that context, the order for disclosure of assets normally made as an adjunct to a freezing injunction is an important aspect of the relief sought, in determining whether assets have been dissipated, and, if so, what has become of them, aiding subsequent enforcement of any judgment;

(3) Even if delay in bringing the application demonstrates that the claimant does not consider there is a risk of dissipation, that is only one factor to be weighed in the balance in considering whether or not to grant the injunction sought."

Delay may be excusable or even necessary. A claimant may need time to investigate the alleged wrongdoing, to take advice and prepare for litigation. A claimant may take time to ensure compliance with the obligation of full and frank disclosure before making a without notice application (*Sukhoruchkin v Van Bekestein* [2013] EWHC 1993 (Ch)).

4   NOTIFICATION INJUNCTIONS

7-20   In *Holyoake v Candy* [2016] 3 W.L.R. 357 the applicants applied for a notification injunction—an order requiring the defendants to notify them before disposing or dealing with their assets—rather than a freezing order. This was on the basis that under s.37(1) of the Senior Courts Act 1981 the categories of injunction that the High Court may order (whether interlocutory or final) are not closed so long it appears to the court to be just and convenient to make such an order. Nugee J granted the order saying that it was a "plainly less invasive interference with the defendant's rights than a simple injunction restraining all disposal".

The Court of Appeal, while agreeing that s.37(1) gave jurisdiction to make such an order, did not agree that it was substantially different from a freezing order. A notification injunction in wide terms is a modified version of a freezing order, rather than a distinct type of injunction (*Holyoake v Candy* [2018] Ch. 297):

> "Both are concerned with protecting the applicant against a risk that the other party will dissipate their assets so as to defeat enforcement of a possible future judgment. Both operate by prohibiting the affected party from dealing with or disposing of all their assets, subject to certain exceptions. In both cases this prohibition is supported by the threat of contempt proceedings for breach of the order, including against third parties who knowingly assist the affected party in breaching the order."

Both forms of injunction involve a draconian interference with rights to deal with personal or business assets and carry a reputational stigma. From the perspective of third parties dealing with the affected party, a notification injunction is indistinguishable from a freezing order as they will need evidence that the proposed transaction complies with an exception to the prohibition. The Court of Appeal rejected the contention that a notification injunction is less onerous and that therefore the threshold of likelihood of dissipation is less than that required for a freezing order.

The Court of Appeal did not approve the notion that a diluted or less intrusive version of a conventional freezing order could be obtained more easily with a lower threshold commenting that such orders would then become the ubiquitous alternative which would undermine the close regulation of potent injunctions of this kind. There is a "binary threshold, not a sliding scale" (*Holyoake v Candy* [2018] Ch. 297 at [41]).

However the Court of Appeal accepted that a simple order requiring notification to be given of a proposed disposition of a specific property would be judged on a lower threshold than a freezing order. But where a wide notification order was sought, the applicant must show a good arguable case on the underlying merits. There must be a real risk, judged objectively, that a future judgment would not be met because of unjustifiable dissipation of assets.

5   ANCILLARY REMEDIES

Disclosure of documents or information

7-21   The court may make an order directing a party to provide information about the location of relevant property or assets, or to provide information about relevant property or assets which are or may be the subject of an application for a freezing injunction (CPR r.25.1(1)(g)). Such an order will be made to assist in locating and "freezing" the defendant's assets, but not merely to establish the extent of breaches of an injunction or undertaking by the defendant. It may be sought when an application for a freezing injunction is on foot or where it is at least likely that there will be such an application; in the latter event a reasonable possibility, based on credible evidence, should be sufficient to satisfy the jurisdictional requirement (per Henderson J in *Lichter and Schwarz v Rubin, The Times,* 18 April 2008). Like the freezing injunction itself, a disclosure order may in appropriate cases extend to overseas assets, though in such a case the claimant is required to undertake not to use the information disclosed without the leave of the court (*Derby v Weldon* [1990] Ch. 48). However a company ordered to give information as to its assets does not need to give details of the assets of its subsidiaries: *Linsen International Ltd v Humpuss Sea Transport Pte Ltd* [2010] EWHC 303 (Comm). The disclosure order is an interim mandatory injunction carrying the contempt sanction for non-compliance and it should be noted that only the court, not the claimant's solicitors, can properly extend time for compliance with such an order (though a consent order to this effect will readily be granted).

In swearing an affidavit in accordance with a disclosure order, a defendant is under a duty not only to give a truthful account but to take reasonable steps to investigate its truth (*Bird v Hadkinson, The Times,* 7 April 1999).

Disclosure may be resisted on the grounds of self-incrimination if it would expose the defendant to a real risk of prosecution under English law (*AT & T Istel Ltd v Tully* [1993] A.C. 45). There are statutory exceptions in intellectual property cases (Senior Courts Act 1981 s.72) and for offences under the Theft Act 1968 (s.31 of that Act) and the Fraud Act 2006, including conspiracy to defraud and a further exception, derived from the law of trusts, in favour of a claimant seeking to recover documents which are his own property. In *AT & T Istel Ltd v Tully* itself, disclosure in aid of the freezing injunction was ordered despite the real possibility of a criminal fraud trial (which, prior to the 2006 Act, would have entitled the defendant to assert the privilege against self-incrimination), since the Crown Prosecution Service had stated in writing that it would not make use of material disclosed pursuant to the order. A risk of self-incrimination under foreign law does not confer privilege from disclosure, but the court has a discretion to refuse or limit disclosure if there is such a risk (*Arab Monetary Fund v Hashim* [1989] 1 W.L.R. 565). **7-22**

In some cases disclosure may be appropriate to elicit the true beneficial ownership of assets ostensibly held by third parties. In *X Bank Ltd v G* (1985) 82 L.S.G. 2016 (reported as *Re A Company* [1985] B.C.L.C. 333), the Court of Appeal upheld an order for disclosure of information in respect of a network of foreign companies and trusts over which the defendant exercised substantial or effective control and which appeared to be "vehicles" entitled directly or indirectly to assets in England. The court has jurisdiction to order disclosure relating to discretionary trusts against one of the discretionary beneficiaries in order to identify the true extent of his control of assets held within the trust structures (*JSC Mezhdunarodniy Promyshlenniy Bank v Pugachev* [2016] 1 W.L.R. 160. In the latter case it was held that the threshold for such an application is "some credible material"; it is not necessary to show that a freezing order would be granted against the assets held by the trusts.

Disclosure may be ordered against a bank or other innocent third party in order to assist in tracing assets; the banker's duty of confidence may be overridden for this purpose (*Norwich Pharmacal Co v Customs and Excise Commissioners* [1974] A.C. 133; *Bankers Trust Co v Shapira* [1980] 1 W.L.R. 1274): for an order see Precedent 19. A bank may be joined as a defendant if the claimant needs informa- **7-23** tion about money in accounts held at the bank (*Mirchandani v Bannerjee*, unreported, December 19, 2000), but generally they are just given notice of the order as an interested third party.

There is also a long standing statutory power under s.7 of the Bankers' Books Evidence Act 1879 to grant an order permitting any party to an action to inspect and copy bank records for the purposes of the action. The order may be made without notice and, unless the judge otherwise directs, the bank must be served with the order three clear days before the time for compliance. An order under s.7 in aid of a freezing injunction was granted in *A v C (No.2)* [1981] QB 956. For guidance as to what a third party should do in cases where the "tipping-off" legislation applies, see *C v S (Money Laundering: Discovery of Documents)* [1999] 1 W.L.R. 1551.

7-24   In exceptionally complex cases it may be appropriate for a firm of chartered accountants to be appointed, at the claimant's expense, to assist in preparing a schedule of the defendant's assets (see *PCW (Underwriting Agencies) Ltd v Dixon* [1983] 2 All E.R. 697).

If opposition to the freezing injunction is abandoned, an order for disclosure may no longer be appropriate (*Bank of Crete SA v Koskotas* [1991] 2 Lloyd's Rep. 587).

There is no entitlement to a stay on a disclosure order pending the determination of an application to set aside, or an appeal from, a freezing order (*Motorola Credit Corporation v Uzan (No.1)* [2002] EWCA Civ 989; [2002] 2 All E.R. (Comm) 945); it is a question for the discretion of the judge (*VTA Capital Plc v Malofeev* [2011] EWCA Civ 1252).

A worldwide disclosure order may be made in support of an injunction ancillary to an English arbitration claim (*Gidrxslme Shipping Co v Tantomar* [1995] 1 W.L.R. 299).

Cross-examination

7-25   If a defendant has filed an evasive affidavit, an order may be made for him to be cross-examined on it (*Bekhor (AJ) & Co v Bilton* [1981] QB 923). The cross-examination is in private and tape recorded; no transcript or other record may be used for any purpose other than the action in question except by the witness, with his consent or by leave of the court. It is conducted before a master or district judge unless a judge orders otherwise; the master or district judge may refer the matter to an examiner of the court (PD 2B para.7). The purpose of such cross-examination is to establish whether or not the defendant has given proper disclosure and, in so far as he has not, to elicit any necessary information as to the extent and whereabouts of the assets (*House of Spring Gardens Ltd v Waite* [1985] F.S.R. 173). However it is an exceptional measure, which should not become a routine feature of freezing cases (*Yukong Line of Korea v Rendsburg Investments*, *The Times*, 22 October 1996). Phillips LJ said in the *Yukong* case:

"In my judgment it is undesirable that a plaintiff should be able in Mareva proceedings to extract, by cross-examination under order of the court, material upon which to build his case for the substantive hearing. I envisage circumstances where, if this were the price that had to be paid for an effective Mareva injunction, it would, nonetheless, be a price worth paying in the interests of justice. But the court must be astute to guard against abuse of the Mareva process by plaintiffs who are using it in an attempt to discover facts that will assist them in the action. The fact that cross-examination on a Mareva discovery affidavit will relate to matters which are relevant to the substantive issues, is a matter to which the judge should have regard when considering whether to permit this process."

The legal principles that apply to an application to cross-examine have been summarised in a number of cases (see per Field J in *Otkritie Investment Management Limited v Urumov* [2012] EWHC 3106 (Comm)):

"(i) The statutory jurisdiction discretion to order cross-examination is broad and unfettered. It may be ordered whenever the court considers it just and convenient to do so.

(ii) Generally, an order for cross-examination in aid of asset disclosure will be very much the exception rather than the rule.

(iii) It will normally only be ordered where it is likely to further a proper purpose of the order by, for example, revealing further assets that might otherwise be dissipated so as to prevent an eventual judgment against the defendants going unsatisfied.

(iv) It must be proportionate and just, in the sense that it must not be undertaken oppressively or for an ulterior purpose. Thus, it will not normally be ordered unless there are significant or serious deficiencies in the existing disclosure.

(v) Cross-examination can, in an appropriate case, be ordered where assets have already been disclosed in excess of the value of the claim against the defendants."

The defendant has a right to invoke the privilege against self-incrimination, not merely on the grounds that an answer might increase the risk of prosecution but in respect of any piece of information or evidence on which a prosecuting authority might wish to rely in establishing guilt or in determining whether to prosecute, and the court should uphold the privilege even if the defendant is acting from mixed motives or in bad faith. Ordering information to be passed to a supervising solicitor does not afford adequate protection (*Den Norske Bank v Antonatos* [1999] QB 271).

7-26

The privilege applies in respect of the risk not only of prosecution but also of proceedings for contempt of court (*Memory Corp Plc v Sidhu* [2000] Ch. 645). The applicant may therefore be required, as a condition of the order for cross-examination, to undertake not to use transcripts of evidence in any way without the permission of the court. The court should not, however, shrink from granting such permission in contempt proceedings if that is necessary to protect the applicant's position (*Dadourian Group International Inc v Simms (No.2)* [2007] 1 W.L.R. 2967).

An applicant may obtain an order for cross examination before the court on any affidavit of assets required to be sworn by a defendant as part of the freezing injunction. Information obtained on the cross-examination is covered by an undertaking given by the applicant to the court as part of the freezing injunction and limiting the use of "information obtained". The cross-examination must be confined to the purpose for which the affidavit was required: to establish the relevant assets of a defendant, and must not be undertaken for an ulterior purpose (*Jenington International Inc v Assaubayev* [2010] EWHC 2351 (Ch)). The cross-examination exists to supplement or correct the information given by the affidavit, so that the relevant assets of the defendant are known. The claimant is not entitled to use such information for the purpose of any other proceedings, including contempt proceedings, without the express permission of the court (*British Sky Broadcasting Group v Digital Satellite Warranty Cover* [2012] 1 W.L.R. 219). For the court's approach to a respondent to a $133m freezing order who was putting forward a range of reasons why the cross-examination should not proceed, see *Access Bank Plc v Rofos Navigation Ltd* [2013] EWHC 441 (Comm).

Appointment of a receiver

7-27   Section 37(1) of the Senior Courts Act 1981 allows the court not only to grant an injunction but also to appoint a receiver in any case where it is just and convenient to do so. The appointment of a receiver may be a desirable adjunct to a freezing injunction, or a substitute for it, in cases where some independent control of the assets is desirable. It is not a routine feature of freezing cases. In *Derby v Weldon (Nos 3 and 4)* [1990] Ch. 65, a receiver was appointed over the assets of a foreign company which had not been shown to have any assets within the jurisdiction.

6   THIRD PARTIES

7-28   A third party who, knowing of the terms of a freezing injunction, wilfully assists in a breach of it, is liable for contempt of court. This is so whether or not the defendant himself has had notice of the injunction (per Eveleigh LJ in *Z Ltd v A-Z* [1982] QB 558 at 581). Solicitors and banks must exercise particular care. In *Re Hurst* [1989] L.S.G. November 1, 1989, p.48, a solicitor had permitted a sum to be paid from an account subject to a freezing injunction. He was penalised for contempt by the court and then suspended from practice by the Solicitors' Disciplinary Tribunal. In *Z Bank v D1* [1994] 1 Lloyd's Rep. 656, a bank which had through gross negligence permitted repeated breaches of a freezing injunction had its assets sequestrated (though the order was suspended on terms that the bank paid the amount lost by the claimant into court). However the House of Lords held in Commissioners of *Customs and Excise v Barclays Bank* [2007] 1 A.C. 181 that a bank notified of a freezing injunction does not owe a duty of care in tort to the claimant to prevent payment out of the account subject to the injunction. Any sanction, therefore, is under the contempt jurisdiction, not in damages.

Practice Direction 25A para 9.2 provides that, where a third party requests a copy of any material read by the judge, including material prepared after the hearing at the direction of the judge or in compliance with the order, or a note of the hearing, the applicant (or their legal representative) must comply promptly with the request, unless the court orders otherwise.

Banks are very frequently affected as third parties by the grant of freezing injunctions, and it is essential to notify the defendant's bank of a without notice order concerning a specified account before notifying the defendant himself. When the injunction identifies a particular account, there is no real difficulty for the bank, but if the account is unspecified and the bank is to be put to trouble and cost in locating it, the claimant must undertake to pay the reasonable costs incurred by the bank (*Searose Ltd v Seatrain UK Ltd* [1981] 1 W.L.R. 894), hence the desirability of the claimant identifying so far as possible the account, the branch at which it is held and the account number.

7-29   It has already been noted in the previous section that in the exercise of the freezing order jurisdiction, the court gives priority to the protection of third party rights. A third party may intervene in the action and apply for a variation of the injunction, for example to obtain payment of money due from the defendant (see *The Angel Bell* at paras 7-39 to 7-40). However, if the "third party" is the defendant's wife or a company controlled by the defendant, the court does not have to take assertions about ownership of assets at face value. It may order a preliminary issue to be tried or may direct that the question should await the outcome of the main action if there is good reason to suppose that the assets are in fact those of the defendant (*SCF Finance Co Ltd v Masri* [1985] 1 W.L.R. 876).

The defendant's bank will be allowed to exercise its usual contractual rights of set-off in respect of facilities granted prior to the injunction, and use the defendant's funds to reduce an overdraft or repay a loan (*Oceanica Castellana Armadora SA v Mineralimportexport* [1983] 1 W.L.R. 1294) or to exercise any rights of security it has over the frozen assets (*Gangway Ltd v Caledonian Park Investments (Jersey) Ltd* [2001] 2 Lloyd's Rep. 715). The bank does not need to obtain permission from the court to exercise that security (*Taylor v Van Dutch Marine Holding Ltd* [2017] 1 W.L.R. 2571).

Where a third party intervenes successfully in the action, its costs should generally be ordered to be paid by the claimant (*Project Development Co Ltd SA v KMK Securities Ltd* [1982] 1 W.L.R. 1470).

The financial undertaking required of the claimant may extend beyond the payment of administrative expenses. In *Clipper Maritime Co Ltd v Mineralimportexport* [1981] 1 W.L.R. 1262, the claimants sought an injunction restraining the removal from the jurisdiction of cargo on board a ship in the port of Barry. The application was granted on the condition that the claimants undertook to reimburse the port authority for loss of income (as well as costs) incurred as a consequence of the grant of the injunction; Robert Goff J also stated that the port authority should have the discretion to move the ship within the jurisdiction or, in the event of danger, outside the jurisdiction. The judge invited third parties with representations to make as to the effect of freezing injunctions to direct them to the secretary of the Commercial Court Committee.

7-30

Where the effect of granting a freezing injunction would be to interfere substantially with an innocent third party's business, for example by interfering with his performance of a contract made with the defendant, the third party's rights should prevail over the claimant's wish to secure the ultimate recovery of debts or damages from the defendant with which the third party is in no way concerned. The fact that the claimant offers an indemnity does not entitle him to an injunction; he has no right to effect a "compulsory purchase" of the third party's rights (*Galaxia Maritime SA v Mineralimportexport* [1982] 1 All E.R. 796).

7 VARIATION AND DISCHARGE

Applications by the defendant

A freezing injunction may be varied or discharged on the defendant's application. As with other injunctions, the application may in theory be made without notice, but it would be exceptional for a freezing injunction to be discharged this way. The form of order for an injunction commonly granted states expressly that the defendant shall have liberty to apply for a variation or discharge on notice to the claimant. In some cases the defendant puts up security to the value of the claim and the freezing injunction is then discharged by consent (a parent company guarantee from a Nigerian company removed the risk of dissipation and frustration of enforcement: *IOT Engineering Projects Ltd v Dangote Fertilizer Ltd* [2014] EWCA Civ 1348). However applications to discharge freezing applications on their merits should not be permitted to turn into mini-trials: *Kazakhstan Kagazy plc v Arip* [2014] 1 C.L.C. 451 in which dicta of Toulson J in *Crown Resources AG v Vinogradsky* (Unreported, 15 June 2001) were approved by the Court of Appeal:

7-31

"… issues of non-disclosure or abuse of process in relation to the operation of a freezing order ought to be capable of being dealt with quite concisely. Speaking in general terms, it is inappropriate to seek to set aside a freezing order for non-disclosure where proof of non-disclosure depends on proof of facts which are themselves in issue in the action, unless the facts are truly so plain that they can be readily and summarily established, otherwise the application to set aside the freezing order is liable to become a form of preliminary trial in which the judge is asked to make findings (albeit provisionally) on issues which should be more properly reserved for the trial itself."

It is an abuse of process to obtain a freezing order and then not to proceed with the claim (*Comdel Commodities Ltd v Siporex Trade SA* [1997] 1 Lloyd's Rep. 424). Failure to progress the action gives grounds for an application to discharge the order, in particular if the claimant "warehouses" the proceedings and chooses not to progress them (*Société Générale v Goldas Kuyumculuk Sanayi Ithalat Ihracat AS* [2017] EWHC 667 (Comm)). A claimant should promptly apply to the court for the discharge of a freezing order if it is no longer needed or to reduce the amount if it is set too high (*Willetts v Alvey* [2010] EWHC 155 (Ch)).

An order restraining a defendant from disposing of or dealing with assets within the jurisdiction will be varied on the defendant's application if he swears an affidavit showing to the court's satisfaction that he needs money (apart from any sums specified in a proviso to the without notice order) to meet bona fide living or business expenses or to pay the costs of contesting the litigation itself. The order may then be varied to allow the defendant to draw specified sums from an account subject to the injunction (*Cantor Index Ltd v Lister* [2002] C.P. Rep 25). In the *Cantor* case the defendant, subject to a freezing injunction with a living expenses proviso of £500 per week, used his credit card or other sources of borrowing to incur expenditure well above that level. Neuberger J held that this was not a breach of the order, but others may take a different view.

7-32
The courts have taken a firm line in upholding the rights of defendants, as illustrated by remarks of Lloyd J in *PCW (Underwriting Agencies) Ltd v Dixon* [1983] 2 All E.R. 158 at 164g:

"All injunctions are, of course, in the end, discretionary. I would regard it as unjust in the present case if the defendant were compelled to reduce his standard of living, to give up his flat or to take his children away from school, in order to secure what is as yet only a claim by the claimants. I would regard it as even more unjust that he should be prevented from defending himself properly (for that is what it would amount to), merely because the claimants say that in doing so he is using someone else's money."

In *Halifax Plc v Chandler* [2001] EWCA Civ 1750, Clarke LJ approved the following passage as good law:

"The court will always be concerned to see that a [freezing] injunction does not operate oppressively and that a defendant will not be hampered in his ordinary business dealings any more than is absolutely necessary to protect the [claimant] from the risk of improper dissipation of assets. Since the [claimant] is not in the position of a secured creditor, and has no proprietary claim to the assets subject to the injunction, there can be no objection in principle to the defendant's dealing in the ordinary way with his business and with his other creditors, even if the effect of such dealings is to render the injunction of no practical value."

However, the ordinary course of business exception may be omitted from an immediately enforceable post judgment asset freezing order (*Mobile Telesystems Finance SA v Nomihold Securities Inc* [2011] EWCA Civ 1040), but not where enforcement is not presently available because of a stay of execution or similar.

The defendant will usually be permitted to meet reasonable legal expenses in the action from enjoined funds; such expenditure is prima facie not dissipation of assets (*Cala Cristal SA v Emran Al-Borno, The Times,* 6 May 1994). This applies even though the enjoined funds are small and the defendant has substantial assets abroad (*Southern Cross Commodities v Martin* [1986] C.A.T. 128; *Kea Corp v Parrot Corp Ltd* [1986] C.A.T. 808), unless the defendant is in contempt (*National Bank of Greece v Dimitriou, The Times,* 16 November 1987).

If the assets which it is sought to use for this purpose are arguably the claimant's, however, the court will not allow them to be used for legal costs unless the defendant has shown that he has no other assets available for the purpose (*Fitzgerald v Williams* [1996] QB 657 at 669, per Sir Thomas Bingham MR; *Ostrich Farming Corpn v Ketchell* [1997] EWCA Civ 2953). A respondent with non-proprietary assets which could be realised in the future had to explain why he could not use them to fund his expenses (*Marino v FM Capital Partners Ltd* [2016] EWCA Civ 1301). In *Sundt Wrigley & Co Ltd v AC Wrigley* (1993) C.A.T. 685, June 23, 1993, an action by companies against a former director alleging a secret profit, the defendant was refused leave to withdraw £500,000 for legal expenses from a frozen fund of £1.4 million. The Court of Appeal drew a distinction between "ordinary" cases, where there is a risk of dissipation of the *defendant's* assets, and tracing actions, where the claimant claims that the fund at risk is his money and that he will be prejudiced, if successful in the action, by having financed the defence.

Restraint orders made under the Proceeds of Crime Act 2002 (see paras 7-56 to7-59), though not under earlier statutes, operate a different regime. Withdrawals from the frozen funds to meet legal expenses are not permitted.

In considering what assets are available to meet legal and other expenses, the court is not limited to funds to which the enjoined defendant has a legal right if there are reasonable grounds for believing that he/she/it could obtain money otherwise. The corporate veil may be lifted, for example, to take into account the resources of the parent company to which the defendant has transferred most of its assets (*Atlas Maritime Co SA v Avalon Maritime Ltd (No.3)* [1991] 4 All E.R. 783). In the same litigation the court refused to vary an injunction to allow the defendant to repay a "loan" from its ultimate parent company (*Atlas Maritime Co SA v Avalon Maritime Ltd (No.1)* [1991] 4 All E.R. 769).

Where withdrawals are to be permitted, the defendant must satisfy the court that it is right for the payments to be made from the account in question (*A v C (No.2)* [1981] QB 956). In many, if not most cases, he will have to show that he has no other free assets which can be used to make the relevant payments, but this is not an inflexible rule; in some cases it can be demonstrated that certain debts are in the ordinary course discharged out of a particular fund, and in such circumstances the bona fides of the payments may be established without a full disclosure of assets (*Avant Petroleum Inc v Gatoil Overseas Inc* [1986] 2 Lloyd's Rep. 236). Retrospective permission may well be given for legal expenses, but a retrospective application for 20 weeks' ordinary living expenses was refused in *Cantor Index Ltd v Lister* [2002] C.P. Rep. 25.

Non-disclosure

A freezing injunction, like any other order obtained without notice, is liable to be discharged for material non-disclosure (see *R. v Kensington Income Tax Commissioners Ex p. Princess Edmond de Polignac* [1917] 1 K.B. 486). The principles applicable were summarised by Ralph Gibson LJ in *Brink's-MAT Ltd v Elcombe* [1988] 3 All E.R. 188:

7-33

7-34

7-35

(a) the claimant must make a full and fair disclosure of all material facts;
(b) materiality is to be decided by the court, not by the claimant or his legal advisers;
(c) proper inquiries must be made before making the application, and the duty of disclosure applies not only to facts known to the claimant but to those which he would have known if he had made proper inquiries;
(d) the extent of the inquiries which are necessary must depend on the nature of the case, the probable effect of the order on the defendant, the degree of legitimate urgency and the time available for making inquiries;
(e) the court will be astute to ensure the claimant is deprived of any advantage he may have derived by his breach of duty;
(f) whether the undisclosed fact is sufficiently material to justify immediate discharge of the order without examination of the merits depends on its importance; the fact that nondisclosure was innocent, in the sense that the fact was not known to the claimant or not perceived to be relevant, is an important consideration, but not decisive, because of the need to make proper inquiries;
(g) there is a discretion to continue the order, or to grant a new one on terms, notwithstanding proof of material non-disclosure. The discretion is to be "exercised sparingly" (per Balcombe LJ at 194), but the application of the principle should not be "carried to extreme lengths" (per Slade LJ at 194). Slade LJ continued:

> "I have suspected signs of a growing tendency on the part of some litigants against whom without notice injunctions have been granted, or of their legal advisers, to rush to the *R. v Kensington Income Tax Comrs* principle as a *tabula in naufragio* [literally 'a plank in a shipwreck'], alleging material nondisclosure on sometimes rather slender grounds, as representing substantially the only hope of obtaining the discharge of injunctions in cases where there is little hope of doing so on the substantial merits of the case or on the balance of convenience."

7-36   The fact that the judge might well have made the same order even if the full facts had been disclosed is beside the point (*Behbehani v Salem* [1989] 1 W.L.R. 723; in that case it was also held that any existing or contemplated proceedings against the defendant in another jurisdiction must be disclosed on the without notice application). See also per Potter J in *Sumitomo Heavy Industries Ltd v Oil and Gas Natural Commission* [1994] 1 Lloyd's Rep. 45 at 62.

The place to disclose the relevant facts, both favourable and unfavourable, is in the affidavit, not the exhibits (*National Bank of Sharjah v Dellborg* [1993] 2 Bank. L.R. 109): see para.5-16.

If non-disclosure was entirely the fault of the claimant's solicitor, that may be a ground for refusing to discharge the injunction (*Eastglen International Corp v Monpare SA* (1987) 137 N.L.J. 56). But if the non-disclosure was not innocent in the sense used by Ralph Gibson LJ in the *Brink's-MAT* case (fact not known to the claimant or not perceived to be relevant), an outright discharge of the order is almost inevitable.

7-37   The injunction is unlikely to be continued or replaced if the claimant has delayed unreasonably in pursuing the claim (*Lloyds Bowmaker Ltd v Britannia Arrow Holdings Ltd* [1988] 1 W.L.R. 1337).

Where a freezing injunction has been granted on one basis and the claimant ultimately fails on that claim but succeeds on a related one, it is a matter of discretion whether the injunction should be discharged and an inquiry as to damages ordered on the cross-undertaking (*Dadourian v Simms* [2009] 1 Lloyd's Rep. 601). Damages under a cross-undertaking in a freezing order are assessed on the same basis as damages for breach of contract with logical and sensible adjustments as an applicant should not be saddled with losses that no reasonable person would have foreseen (*Abbey Forwarding Ltd v Hone* [2015] Ch. 309 applying *F Hoffmann La Roche & Co AG v Secretary of State for Trade and Industry* [1975] A.C. 295). However if a defendant suffers an unusual loss due to the claimant's unreasonable response to a request to vary the order, a court may order him to pay for it.

Applications by the claimant

If there is a material change of circumstances after the grant of the without notice order, it is the duty of the claimant to return to the court and disclose it (*Commercial Bank of the Near East v ABC and D* [1989] 2 Lloyd's Rep. 319). It is also the duty of a claimant who has the benefit of a freezing injunction to pursue the action diligently (*Lloyds Bowmaker* case), or to have the injunction discharged (*Town and Country Building Society v Daisystar Ltd* (1989) 139 N.L.J. 1563). It is submitted, however, that the *Daisystar* case is distinguishable in a claim where the parties have agreed to keep the proceedings "on ice", for example while the claimant is attempting to execute judgment obtained against another defendant. If it appears that the injunction was too wide and a lower amount is sufficient, then the claimant should take steps to reduce the amount: *Willetts v Alvey* [2010] EWHC 155 (Ch).

7-38

Stay or strike-out

As with other interim injunctions, a freezing order is automatically discharged after 14 days in the event of a claim being struck out for non-payment of court fees (CPR r.25.11). However freezing orders are specifically excluded from the operation of CPR r.25.10, which provides for automatic discharge if the claim (save by agreement) is stayed.

7-39

8 COMPETING CREDITORS

The freezing jurisdiction was not intended to rewrite the law of insolvency. The claimant who obtains a freezing injunction does not thereby acquire a proprietary interest in the assets enjoined, nor is he given preference over other creditors in the event of the defendant's insolvency (*Iraqi Ministry of Defence v Arcepey Shipping Co SA (The Angel Bell)* [1981] QB 65). Neither a freezing injunction nor a consent order embodying a similar undertaking imposes an obligation to satisfy any judgment debt out of the frozen assets (*Flightline Ltd v Edwards* [2003] 3 All E.R. 1200). An injunction does not defeat the claim of a debenture holder whose fixed charge on an asset crystallises after the grant of an injunction (*Cretanor Maritime Co Ltd v Irish Maritime Management Ltd* [1978] 1 W.L.R. 966).

7-40

The claimant has no right to be joined as a party in an action between the defendant and another creditor (*Sanders Lead Co Inc v Entores Metal Brokers Ltd* [1984] 1 W.L.R. 452). If the defendant has genuine trade debts awaiting payment, he will be allowed to pay them, even if there will then be little or nothing left to meet the claimant's unsecured and disputed claim (*Admiral Shipping v Portlink Ferries Ltd* [1984] 2 Lloyd's Rep. 166).

In the *Angel Bell* case, the claimants claimed damages for loss of their cargo aboard the defendant's ship which sank in February 1976. They were granted a freezing injunction against the prospective proceeds of an insurance policy on the

7-41

ship. Another company was owed £200,000 by the defendants as the outstanding balance of a loan made by it to the defendants in 1974; it intervened as a third party and applied for the injunction to be varied so as to allow (but not compel) the defendants to repay the loan out of enjoined assets. The application was granted: per Robert Goff J [1981] QB 65 at 73B:

> "For a defendant to be free to repay a loan in such circumstances is not inconsistent with the policy underlying the *Mareva* injunction. He is not in such circumstances seeking to avoid his responsibilities to the claimant if the latter should ultimately obtain a judgment; on the contrary, he is seeking in good faith to make payments which he considers he should make in the ordinary course of business. I cannot see that the *Mareva* jurisdiction should be allowed to prevent such a payment. To allow it to do so would be to stretch it beyond its original purpose so that instead of preventing abuse it would rather prevent businessmen conducting their business as they are entitled to do."

Even if the payment is in respect of a "debt of honour" or is the purchase price of (say) a picture rather than a business obligation, this does not preclude a variation of the order provided that the court is satisfied by evidence that the defendant's desire to use assets caught by the injunction is not merely to evade its underlying purpose, and that the payment would normally have been made out of such assets had there been no injunction (*A v B (X intervening)* [1983] 2 Lloyd's Rep. 532). A bona fide settlement of a dispute is a transaction in the ordinary course of business, and a proposed settlement will not be restrained by a freezing injunction unless there is clear prima facie evidence of bad faith or collusion (*Normid Housing Association Ltd v Ralphs & Mansell* [1989] 1 Lloyd's Rep. 274).

9   ORDERS NOT TO LEAVE THE COUNTRY

7-42

In order to prevent a defendant leaving England and Wales with assets and thereby prejudicing a claimant's valid claim, the traditional remedy was the High Court prerogative writ *ne exeat regno* (*Al Nahkel v Lowe* [1986] QB 235). This ancient remedy, dating from the thirteenth century, had been thought obsolete, there being no reported case between 1893 and 1985 of the writ being issued. It may be doubted whether it is still appropriate for the writ to be issued.

The requirements for the grant of the writ are as follows (see per Megarry J in *Felton v Callis* [1969] 1 QB 200, a judgment which reviews the history of the remedy in detail):

(1) The action must be one in which the defendant would, before the passing of the Debtors Act 1869, have been liable to arrest at law. This appears to mean that the action is in debt, or for the recovery of money had and received by the defendant. A claim for damages, even for fraudulent conspiracy, does not qualify (*Allied Arab Bank v Hajjar* [1988] QB 787). In *Thaha v Thaha* [1987] 2 F.L.R. 142, Wood J granted leave to issue the claim form against the respondent husband in an ancillary relief application in matrimonial proceedings (sed quaere).

(2) A good cause of action for at least £50 is established.

(3) There is "probable cause" for believing that the defendant is about to leave England and Wales unless he is arrested. Such evidence must be clear and direct (*Re Underwood* (1903) 51 W.R. 335).

(4) The absence of the defendant from England will materially prejudice the claimant in the prosecution of the action. The reference to "the prosecution of the action" means that the writ is available only before judgment is

entered, not after judgment as an aid to execution (*Lipkin Gorman v Cass, The Times,* 29 May 1985), and as an aid to the substantive action, not to the enforcement of a disclosure order ancillary to a freezing injunction (*Allied Arab Bank Ltd v Hajjar,* above).

These four requirements are satisfied in a significant proportion of cases where freezing injunctions are granted against individual defendants, and in theory the writ could be granted as a matter of routine. However, this does not occur in practice. In both *Lipkin Gorman v Cass* and *Al Nahkel v Lowe,* the defendant had apparently been guilty of theft. It is submitted that the writ is only likely to be granted when not only the above requirements are fulfilled, but the defendant has behaved dishonestly. In *Ali v Naseem, The Times,* 3 October 2003, it was held that the writ can only be issued if the remedy is proportionate and necessary to secure the ends of justice. The authors are not aware of any recent example of the writ being issued. A precedent for it can be found in earlier editions of this book.   **7-43**

In some cases there is no jurisdiction to grant a writ ne exeat regno, for example because the action is for damages for breach of copyright and not for the recovery of a debt or money had and received.

The modern equivalent of the writ ne exeat regno is an order (precedent 17) restraining the defendant from leaving the country and requiring him to deliver up his passport (*Bayer AG v Winter* [1986] 1 W.L.R. 497; *Re Oriental Credit Ltd* [1988] Ch. 204; *Young v Young* [2012] Fam 198; *Re B (A Child)* [2015] Fam. 209). The jurisdiction to do so derives from the court's discretion under s.37(1) of the Senior Courts Act 1981 to grant an injunction in all cases in which it appears just and convenient to do so.   **7-44**

If the evidence, viewed objectively, demonstrates a real risk that the defendant will leave the country in order to frustrate the court's processes, that is sufficient to give the court jurisdiction provided that the restriction is proportionate in all the circumstances of the case (*JSC Mezhdunarodniy Promyshlenniy Bank v Pugachev (No.2),* CA, 29 May 2015, unreported).

The Court of Appeal in the *Bayer* case held that such an injunction, being an interference with the liberty of the subject, should run only for so long as was necessary to give effect to other search orders and orders for disclosure made on the claimants' without notice application. The claimants, having executed the search orders and obtained disclosure from the defendant which they claimed to be inadequate, then sought an extension of the order preventing the defendant's departure from the jurisdiction in order that he should be required to submit to cross-examination. Scott J refused the application (*Bayer AG v Winter (No.2)* [1986] 1 W.L.R. 540).

The defendant in *Zakaharov v White* (2003) 153 N.L.J. 1669 had failed to comply with an order, ancillary to a freezing injunction, ordering him to deliver up his passport. Roderick Evans J issued a bench warrant. The old methods are sometimes the best.

10   EXTRA-TERRITORIAL FREEZING INJUNCTIONS

Until 1988 it was the settled practice of the courts to confine the operation of freezing injunctions to assets of the defendant within the jurisdiction. There was then a change of policy by the Court of Appeal, which held in a series of cases that a worldwide order could be granted, either after judgment (*Babanaft International SA v Bassatne* [1990] Ch. 13) or before judgment (*Republic of Haiti v Duvalier*   **7-45**

[1990] QB 202; *Derby v Weldon* [1990] Ch. 48; *Derby v Weldon (Nos 3 & 4)* [1990] Ch. 65). In the first three cases, there were dicta to the effect that worldwide orders should be granted only in "extreme situations", "very rare cases indeed", or "exceptional cases", but in the last-named case Lord Donaldson MR said that "once the court is concerned with an international operator, the position may well be different". When the order is granted it will contain an undertaking by the claimant (see Precedent 6 Sch.B para.10) not to seek to enforce it outside England and Wales without the permission of the court granted at a subsequent hearing.

In *Dadourian Group International Inc v Simms (No.1)* [2006] 1 W.L.R. 2499, the Court of Appeal set out guidelines for the exercise of the court's discretion when an application is made for permission to enforce the worldwide freezing order ("WFO") abroad:

(1) The principle applying to the grant of permission to enforce a WFO abroad is that the grant of that permission should be just and convenient for the purpose of ensuring the effectiveness of the WFO and, in addition, that it is not oppressive to the parties to the English proceedings or to third parties who may be joined to the foreign proceedings.

(2) All the relevant circumstances and options need to be considered. In particular, consideration should be given to granting relief on terms, for example terms as to the extension to third parties of the undertaking to compensate for costs incurred as a result of the WFO and as to the type of proceedings that may be commenced abroad. Consideration should also be given to the proportionality of the steps proposed to be taken abroad, and in addition to the form of any order.

(3) The interests of the applicant should be balanced against the interests of the other parties to the proceedings and any new party likely to be joined to the foreign proceedings.

(4) Permission should not normally be given in terms that would enable the applicant to obtain relief in the foreign proceedings which is superior to the relief given by the WFO.

(5) The evidence in support of the application for permission should contain all the information (so far as it can reasonably be obtained in the time available) necessary for the judge to reach an informed decision, including evidence as to the applicable law and practice in the foreign court, evidence as to the nature of the proposed proceedings to be commenced and evidence as to the assets believed to be located in the jurisdiction of the foreign court and the names of the parties by whom such assets are held.

(6) The standard of proof as to the existence of assets that are both within the WFO and within the jurisdiction of the foreign court is a real prospect, that is the applicant must show that there is a real prospect that such assets are located within the jurisdiction of the foreign court in question.

(7) There must be evidence of a risk of dissipation of the assets in question.

(8) Normally the application should be made on notice to the respondent, but in cases of urgency, where it is just to do so, the permission may be given without notice to the party against whom relief will be sought in the foreign proceedings but that party should have the earliest practicable opportunity of having the matter reconsidered by the court at a hearing of which he is given notice.

7-46 The same principles apply in an application to continue a worldwide post-judgment freezing order where there was solid evidence of a real risk of dissipation of assets (*SPL Private Finance v Arch Financial Products LLP* [2015] EWHC

1124 (Comm)). Some limit on the extra-territorial effect of the injunction is necessary to avoid conflict with the jurisdiction of foreign courts. A bank should be protected by a suitable proviso permitting it to comply with what it reasonably believes to be its obligations, contractual or otherwise, under the law of a foreign country where assets subject to a worldwide freezing injunction are located, unless in a particular case the court considers such a proviso inappropriate; a claimant wishing to have more stringent protection must apply to the foreign court (*Bank of China v NBM LLC* [2002] 1 W.L.R. 844). However, if the case is strong enough for a worldwide freezing injunction, a disclosure order is appropriate even where the defendant is contesting the court's jurisdiction (*Grupo Torras SA v Al Sabah* [1995] 1 Lloyd's Rep. 374).

The standard form of order allows the defendant to deal with or dispose of assets outside the jurisdiction so long as the total unencumbered value of his assets, whether inside or outside the jurisdiction, exceeds the maximum sum. In *JSC BTA Bank v Ablyazov* [2009] EWHC 3267 (Comm), where the maximum sum was £175 million, the claimants sought an order which only allowed dealing with overseas assets if assets *within* England and Wales exceeded £175 million; this would have indirectly compelled the defendant to move assets into the jurisdiction. Teare J refused to make such an order, although he did include a clause requiring the defendant to disclose his dealings with his overseas assets.

11   FREEZING INJUNCTIONS IN AID OF FOREIGN CLAIMS

Foreign judgments

A claimant who has obtained a money judgment in his favour in a country to   **7-47**
which either Pt II of the Administration of Justice Act 1920 or Pt I of the Foreign Judgments (Reciprocal Enforcement) Act 1933 applies can seek leave to register it in the High Court for enforcement in England (CPR r.74.3). While registration and enforcement proceedings are underway a freezing injunction can be granted to prevent the dissipation of assets in England and Wales. An injunction may also be granted in aid of a foreign judgment or arbitration award where, because the Acts of 1920 and 1933 do not apply, the claimant has to bring an action on the judgment in England. A freezing injunction in support of a foreign judgment or award registered in England should not be granted with worldwide effect (*Banco Nacional de Comercio Exterior SNC v Empresa de Telecommunicaciones de Cuba SA* [2008] 1 W.L.R. 1936). For an authoritative discussion of the effect of registering a worldwide freezing order granted by a foreign court as a judgment of the High Court of England and Wales, see *Cyprus Popular Bank Public Co Ltd v Vgenopoulos* [2018] 2 WLR 1330, CA.

Foreign litigation

In *The Siskina* [1979] A.C. 210, the claimants, cargo owners in Saudi Arabia,   **7-48**
sued the defendant shipowners, a Panamanian company. The bills of lading issued on shipment of the cargo in Italy conferred exclusive jurisdiction on the courts of Genoa; the ship was registered in Panama and the claim was in respect of discharge of the cargo in Cyprus. The dispute thus had no connection with England, but the Siskina, the defendants' sole asset, had subsequently sunk and the insurance money was payable in London. The House of Lords held that there was no cause of action triable in the English courts and that the claimants were accordingly not entitled

to an injunction restraining the removal of the insurance money from the jurisdiction. However the result in *The Siskina* has been effectively reversed by statute: first, as regards proceedings pending in other Judgments Regulation or Brussels Convention territories, by s.25 of the Civil Jurisdiction and Judgments Act 1982 (as amended by the Civil Jurisdiction and Judgments Order 2001 (SI 2001/3929)); then as regards Lugano Convention countries by the Civil Jurisdiction and Judgments Act 1991; and finally, by the Civil Jurisdiction and Judgments Act 1982 (Interim Relief) Order 1997 (as amended by the Civil Jurisdiction and Judgments Regulations 2009 (SI 2009/3131), which extends s.25 to any proceedings regardless of where they are commenced or whether their subject matter falls within the Judgments Regulation. Section 24 of the Act provides for the grant of interim relief pending the trial (in England) of an issue relating to the court's jurisdiction to entertain the proceedings.

These statutory changes allow the English court to grant interim relief where proceedings between the same parties are pending in the courts of another country, for example where a defendant to a civil claim in Germany has assets in England against which a freezing injunction could be granted (see Precedent 20). In cases where jurisdiction depends on s.25 of the 1982 Act and it is thought inexpedient to make an order, the court may refuse to do so. This is a two-stage process according to Morritt LJ in *Refco Inc v Eastern Trading Co* [1999] 1 Lloyd's Rep. 159. The first question is whether the interim relief sought would be warranted if the substantive proceedings were being brought in England. If the answer is yes, the second question is whether the fact that jurisdiction is dependent on s.25 makes it inexpedient to grant the relief. The same judge (by then Morritt VC) said in *Fourie v Le Roux* [2005] EWCA Civ 204; [2006] 2 B.C.L.C. 531 at [32] that "the foreign claim must be such that the relief sought in England can be identified as interim relief in relation to the final order sought abroad in the proceedings relied on".

7-49   The judgment of the Court of Appeal in *Motorola Credit Corp v Uzan (No.2)* [2004] 1 W.L.R. 113 contains a useful review of the principles on which the High Court should deal with applications for worldwide freezing orders in support of foreign litigation. McCombe J has emphasised "the extreme caution required on the part of members of the legal profession in this country when invited to prepare and present applications in aid of foreign proceedings under the 1982 Act" (see *Eliades v Lewis* [2005] EWHC 2966 (QB) [14]).

In *Credit Suisse v Cuoghi* [1998] QB 818, the Court of Appeal decided that a worldwide freezing injunction (and worldwide disclosure order) could be made against a defendant resident within the jurisdiction in support of litigation in Switzerland, even though a Swiss court would not have had jurisdiction to make an equivalent worldwide order.

7-50   For consideration of injunctions in support of confiscation proceedings overseas, see para.7-58 below, and *USA v Abacha* [2015] 1 W.L.R. 1917.

The High Court may grant a freezing injunction under the International Criminal Court Act 2001 if it is satisfied that a forfeiture order has been made or there are reasonable grounds for thinking that such an order may be made in proceedings before the ICC.

12   ORDERS IN CONFISCATION PROCEEDINGS

Before the Proceeds of Crime Act 2002

7-51   By the Criminal Justice Act 1988, the Drug Trafficking Act 1994 and the Terrorism Act 2000 the Crown Court is given power to make a confiscation order if it is satisfied that the defendant has benefited by at least £10,000 from an indictable offence (and certain others) committed wholly or partly before March 24, 2003, of which he has been convicted or which is taken into consideration in sentencing. The Acts have stringent provisions requiring assets to be preserved with a view to satisfying a possible compensation order. Although the pre-2003 regime is of diminishing importance, it is not yet obsolete; some offences of fraud are committed over a long period or take many years to come to light.

If a prosecution for a relevant offence has been or is about to be instituted, the High Court may make a restraint order under RSC Ord.115 prohibiting dealings with the defendant's realisable property pending the conclusion of the Crown Court trial. This is similar, though not identical, to a freezing injunction. The application is made without notice on affidavit by the prosecution to a judge in the Administrative Court list. The court may also make a charging order without notice over land or securities held beneficially by the defendant or by a person to whom he has directly or indirectly made a gift caught by the Acts. A recommended form of order is set out at Precedent 8. The prosecutor is *not* required to give an undertaking in damages in favour of the defendant (RSC Ord.115 r.4(1)) or third parties (*Re R* [1990] QB 307).

The duty to make full and frank disclosure applies to applicants for restraint orders as much as to applicants for freezing injunctions. Where there has been a failure in discharging that duty, however, the fact that the Crown acts in the public interest militates against the sanction of discharging a restraint order if, after consideration of all the evidence, the court thinks that an order remains appropriate (*Jennings v Crown Prosecution Service* [2006] 1 W.L.R. 182). Hughes LJ said in In *Re Stanford International Ltd* [2011] Ch. 33:

> "In effect a prosecutor seeking an ex parte order must put on his defence hat and ask himself what, if he were representing the defendant or a third party with a relevant interest, he would be saying to the judge, and, having answered that question, that is precisely what he must tell."

In some cases the extent of the defendant's alleged criminality will be such that the risk of dissipation of assets will be self-evident. In any other case, the evidence adduced by the prosecutor should deal with the point and, if there has been a delay in bringing the proceedings during which no dissipation has occurred, should explain why there is thought to be a risk now (*Jennings v CPS*, above).

A restraint order may be made subject to conditions and exceptions, including, but not limited to, conditions relating to the indemnifying of third parties against costs incurred in complying with the order, and exceptions relating to the living expenses, legitimate trading expenses and legal expenses of the defendant (see *Customs and Excise Commissioners v Norris* [1991] 2 QB 293). The order need not stipulate a maximum sum for legal expenses (*Re P and Re W, The Times*, 11 April 1990 CA).

An application for variation or discharge of a restraint order or charging order may be made by any person affected by it, supported by an affidavit giving grounds and specifying the property in respect of which the application is made. The initial order may be, and regularly is, varied to permit the payment of legal expenses, but the court is not bound to accede to such a request if there are other sources of funds available (*Serious Fraud Office v X* [2005] EWCA Civ 1564).

There is a discretion to vary the order to enable a third party judgment creditor to be paid (*Re X* [2005] QB 133, Davis J; contrast with *Re W, The Times*, 15 November 1990). A defendant will generally be permitted to meet ordinary outgoings as they fall due, but not to pay out a capital sum, for example to secure the payment of future school fees (*Re Peters* [1988] QB 871).

7-52

7-53

7-54

The without notice restraint order has effect (unless the court otherwise directs) until a date fixed for the hearing of an on notice application. The prosecutor is required to serve copies of the order and the affidavit on the defendant and other named persons restrained by the order and to notify the terms of the order to all other persons or bodies affected by its terms (RSC Ord.115 r.4(2)–(3)). The order can be the subject of an appeal to the Civil Division of the Court of Appeal (*Re O*, below). It does not prevent a bank from carrying out a set-off between accounts (*Re K (Restraint Order)* [1990] 2 QB 298), though a variation order should be applied for as a matter of prudence.

7-55   It was held in *Re O (Disclosure Order)* [1991] 2 QB 520 that there is an inherent power in the High Court to require a defendant to disclose his assets and income so as to render a restraint order effective; however, in order to preserve a defendant's right against self-incrimination, a condition should be attached to the order that no disclosure made in compliance with it may be used as evidence in the prosecution of an offence by the person making the disclosure or that person's spouse.

The court can pierce the corporate veil and grant a restraint order over the assets of a company which the defendant has used as a device or facade to conceal criminal activities (*Re H (Restraint Order: Realisable Property)* [1996] 2 All E.R. 391).

The High Court has power pursuant to a statutory instrument made under the 1994 Act to make a restraint order in support of an "external confiscation order", that is to say one made by the courts of a foreign state designated under the order (see *Re J-L (Restraint Order: External Confiscation Order)* [1996] QB 272).

7-56   The prosecution, but not the defendant (*Re M (Restraint Order)* [1992] QB 377), may apply for a receiver of the defendant's assets to be appointed. The receiver may recover his remuneration and expenses from the restrained assets (*Hughes v Customs and Excise Commissioners* [2003] 1 W.L.R. 177). In the latter case, though, Simon Brown LJ, with whom Laws and Arden LJJ agreed, said:

> "Given that restraint and receivership orders can, as perhaps these very cases show, bear heavily upon the individuals involved and may leave acquitted defendants with substantially depleted assets, the court should, in deciding whether initially to make, and whether thereafter to vary or discharge, such orders, weigh up the balance of competing interests with the greatest care. The Crown's concern to safeguard an accused's property against dissipation or removal abroad must always be weighed against the possibility that the price to be paid will fall upon an innocent man. It is important that this legislation continues to be operated to strip criminals of their ill-gotten gains. But it is important too that the court keeps a close control over those it appoints to act as receivers on its behalf and that costs are not too readily incurred, particularly before any confiscation order is made."

Proceeds of Crime Act 2002

7-57   The Proceeds of Crime Act 2002 made substantial changes in the regime of restraint orders. The power to make a restraint order in respect of offences occurring entirely after 24 March 2003 (the commencement date of s.41) has been transferred to the Crown Court and is not covered in detail in this book. RSC Ord.115 continues to apply to cases where any of the alleged offences occurred before 24 March 2003.

The essential features of the 2002 Act regime are as follow:

(1)   an order prohibits the specified person from dealing with any realisable property held by him;

(2)   an order gives the prosecutor priority over other creditors;

(3) no undertaking in damages is required;

(4) no maximum sum is specified;

(5) debts to unsecured creditors cannot be paid from the defendant's assets unless there is no conflict with the statutory objective of satisfying any confiscation order that had been or might be made (*Director of the Serious Fraud Office v Lexi Holdings Plc* [2009] QB 376);

(6) the burden of proof is on the defendant to prove that assets are of legitimate origin if they are not to be confiscated in the event of conviction;

(7) the prosecutor applying without notice is under the usual obligation of full and frank disclosure (*Director of the Serious Fraud Office v A* [2007] EWCA Crim 1927; for subsequent proceedings see *Re Al-Zayyat* [2008] EW Misc 3).

However, the transfer of the power to make restraint orders to the Crown Court **7-58** does not mean that the High Court has ceased to be involved with the recovery of the proceeds of crime. Part 5 of the 2002 Act enabled the National Crime Agency (formerly the Serious Organised Crime Agency, and before that the Assets Recovery Agency) to bring civil proceedings in the High Court for a "recovery order" against anyone who the agency thinks holds property which is the proceeds of unlawful conduct. The civil standard of proof applies (*Serious Organised Crime Agency v Gale* [2011] 1 W.L.R. 2760, but the court should not proceed on the basis that there were other assets the applicant was concealing (*Serious Organised Crime Agency v Azam* [2013] 1 W.L.R. 3800). There is power under the Act to appoint an interim receiver, and under s.245A, introduced by amendment in 2005, an interim property freezing order may also be sought in the Administrative Court: see *Director of the Assets Recovery Agency v Creaven* [2006] 1 W.L.R. 622. The *Practice Direction: Civil Recovery Proceedings* contains detailed guidance.

Recovery orders and property freezing orders may only be made in respect of property in England and Wales (*Serious Organised Crime Agency v Perry* [2012] 3 W.L.R. 379). A recovery order is appropriate where property was obtained through unlawful conduct and it would be just or equitable to make a recovery order having regard to any ECHR rights: *National Crime Agency v Khan* [2017] Lloyd's Rep. F.C. 153.

Proceedings under Part 5 of the 2002 Act are properly characterised as civil proceedings for Article 6 purposes (*Gale v SOCA* [2011] 1 W.L.R. 2760) and in domestic law (s.240(1)(a) of the 2002 Act). The overriding objective and the usual wide discretionary case management powers under the Civil Procedure Rules apply (*National Crime Agency v Robb* [2015] Ch. 520). Section 58(5) of the Act provides that if a court in which proceedings are pending in respect of any property is satisfied that a restraint order has been applied for or made in respect of the property, the court may either stay the proceedings or allow them to continue on any terms it thinks fit. The court must give an opportunity to be heard to the applicant for the restraint order and to any receiver appointed in respect of the property.

Section I of CPR Pt 25 and PD 25A do not apply to applications for property freezing orders. The court has power under s.245C(5) of the 2002 Act to make an exclusion from a property freezing order to enable a person to meet legal expenses that he has incurred, or might incur, in respect of proceedings under Part 5 of the 2002 Act (*National Crime Agency v Robb* [2015] Ch. 520 at [88], Sir Terence Etherton C).

When application is made in the Crown Court under the 2002 Act, the realis- **7-59** able property of the defendant is subject to restraint wherever it is situated (s.84). The High Court may also make a restraint order on the application of a foreign prosecutor under the Proceeds of Crime Act 2002 (External Requests and Orders) Order 2005 (SI 2005/3181), but in such a case the restraint order can only apply to property within the jurisdiction (*King v Serious Fraud Office* [2009] 1 W.L.R. 718).

An interim freezing injunction which had been granted to the United States in respect of some assets of two companies was discharged because it had not been expedient to grant the injunction under the Civil Jurisdiction and Judgments Act 1982 s.25. The Proceeds of Crime Act 2002 and the Proceeds of Crime Act 2002 (External Requests and Orders) Order 2005 provide a comprehensive regime for English enforcement authorities to apply for prohibition and recovery orders in respect of assets located in England which have been the subject of orders in foreign proceedings to recover proceeds of crime (*USA v Abacha* [2015] 1 W.L.R. 1917).

7-60   Where a defendant has breached a restraint order made in the Crown Court, that court has power to deal with the contempt—it is not necessary to apply to the High Court (*R v M* [2009] 1 W.L.R. 1179). The breach is properly classified as a civil, rather than criminal, contempt (*OB v Director of the Serious Fraud Office* [2012] EWCA Crim 67).

CHAPTER 8

Search Orders

This chapter groups together three types of mandatory order: search orders, orders for the interim preservation of property, and orders for the delivery up of goods. They are not usually described as injunctions, but in practice the effect is the same. The most important is the search order.

8-01

1 SEARCH ORDERS

Entry on premises and removal of material

The court has power (see para.8-18) to authorise one party to enter upon premises owned by another party and inspect or detain and preserve property being kept there. If an application of this kind is made on notice, there is a danger that the defendant may dispose of or destroy the property before the application is heard. The problem became particularly acute with the appearance of pirates (who make unauthorised copies of copyright recordings) and bootleggers (who make unauthorised recordings of live performances). The need arose for claimants to be able to obtain something in the nature of a search warrant—a without notice mandatory injunction requiring the defendant to permit the claimant to enter his premises and remove the offending items.

8-02

It was held in *EMI Ltd v Pandit* [1975] 1 W.L.R. 302 that there is jurisdiction to grant such an order without notice, in "exceptional and emergency cases". The first case to go to the Court of Appeal was *Anton Piller KG v Manufacturing Processes Ltd* [1976] Ch. 55, which led to the order being described as an Anton Piller order—in CPR terminology, a search order. The jurisdiction was given statutory force by s.7 of the Civil Procedure Act 1997, which provides:

"(1) The court may make an order under this section for the purpose of securing, in the case of any existing or proposed proceedings in the court—(a) the preservation of evidence which is or may be relevant, or (b) the preservation of property which is or may be the subject-matter of the proceedings or as to which any question arises or may arise in the proceedings.

(2) A person who is, or appears to the court likely to be, a party to proceedings in the court may make an application for such an order.

(3) Such an order may direct any person to permit any person described in the order, or secure that any person so described is permitted—(a) to enter premises in England and Wales, and (b) while on the premises, to take in accordance with the terms of the order any of the following steps.

(4) Those steps are—(a) to carry out a search for or inspection of anything described in the order, and (b) to make or obtain a copy, photograph, sample or other record of anything so described.

(5) The order may also direct the person concerned—(a) to provide any person described in the order, or secure that any person so described is provided, with any

information or article described in the order, and (b) to allow any person described in the order, or secure that any person so described is allowed, to retain for safe keeping anything described in the order.

(6)   An order under this section is to have effect subject to such conditions as are specified in the order.

(7)   This section does not affect any right of a person to refuse to do anything on the ground that to do so might tend to expose him or his spouse or civil partner to proceedings for an offence or for the recovery of a penalty.

(8)   In this section—

"court" means the High Court, and "premises" includes any vehicle;
and an order under this section may describe anything generally, whether by reference to a class or otherwise."

Grounds for a Search Order

8-03   In *Anton Piller KG v Manufacturing Processes*, the Court of Appeal laid down the following requirements:

(1)   The applicant must have an extremely strong prima facie case. Suspicion is not enough; an assessment of the merits of the claimant is necessary as it is not sufficient for the applicant to show merely a serious question to be tried (*Indicii Salus Ltd v Chandrasekaran* [2006] EWHC 521 (Ch)).

(2)   The potential or actual damage to his interests must be very serious. If an order is sought in order to forestall the destruction of evidence, that evidence must be of major importance.

(3)   There must be clear evidence that the defendant has in his possession incriminating documents or things and that there is a real possibility that he may dispose of or destroy such material before any application on notice can be made. The risk of destruction must be more than merely possible and not just extravagant fears because a respondent has behaved improperly (*Booker McConnell v Plascow Plc* [1985] R.P.C. 425).

The harm to the respondent's business or affairs from the search order (normally involving seizure of stock or confidential commercial documents) must not be excessive or out of proportion to its legitimate object. The court must apply proportionality when exercising its discretion whether to grant a order.

In *MXI Ltd v SES SA* [2018] EWHC 717 (Ch) Sir Geoffrey Vos C said that there are five main elements required for the grant of a search order: first that there is a strong prima facie case of a civil cause of action; secondly, that serious damage to the claimants will be avoided by the grant of a search order; thirdly, that there is clear evidence that the defendant has in his possession incriminating documents or things; fourthly, that the risk of destruction or removal of evidence is a good deal more than merely possible; and fifthly, that the harm likely to be caused to the defendant and to his business affairs by the execution of a search order is not excessive or out of proportion to the legitimate objects of the order. In that case the Chancellor held that the grant of a search order would be disproportionate, but he did make an order requiring the preservation of digital material which the claimants had sought to obtain by means of a search order. This list of five conditions may be taken as an authoritative statement of the current law: see eg *Bayerische Motoren Werke AG v Premier Alloy Wheels (UK) Ltd* [2018] EWHC 1713 (Ch).

The form of order is set out at Precedent 7.

Search orders raise obvious issues under ECHR art.8, whether the search is of a defendant's home or his office (as to which see *Niemietz v Germany* (1993) 16 E.H.R.R. 97); however, invasions of a claimant's private and family life may be justified under art.8(2) as necessary to protect the rights of others, and a challenge to search orders in principle was rejected by the European Court of Human Rights in *Chappell v United Kingdom* (1990) 12 E.H.R.R. 1.

The claimant must give an undertaking as to damages and the court must be satis-   **8-04**
fied that the claimant is good for such damages. It is prudent for the claimant, when making his application, to produce specific evidence to that effect (*Vapormatic Co Ltd v Sparex Ltd* [1976] 1 W.L.R. 939). As in freezing cases, any potential difficulty in meeting the undertaking must be disclosed (*Swedac Ltd v Magnet & Southerns Plc* [1989] F.S.R. 243). The claimant must also undertake not to allow any person (even the Customs authorities) to have access to the goods or documents seized without leave of the court, which will only exceptionally be granted (*Customs and Excise Commissioners v Hamlin (AE) & Co* [1984] 1 W.L.R. 509). The case should be heard in private, since the whole point of the procedure is lost if the defendant learns that the without notice application is being made. A claim form or draft claim form, affidavit, draft order and draft notice of application are required. A county court has no jurisdiction to grant a search order, except for the Patents County Court, per Judge Birss QC in *Suh v Ryu* [2012] EWPCC 20.

The order should require the defendants to deliver any offending articles into the custody of the claimant's solicitors (*Universal City Studios Inc v Mukhtar & Sons Ltd* [1976] 1 W.L.R. 568); exceptions are sometimes made for particularly bulky items. An order will usually be made only in respect of specified premises and not of "any other premises under the control of the defendant" (*Protector Alarms v Maxim Alarms Ltd* [1978] F.S.R. 442). The prohibitory elements of the order are usually expressed to continue only until the date fixed for an application to be heard on notice.

In appropriate cases the court may allow the removal not only of material infring-   **8-05**
ing the claimant's copyright (or evidence of such infringement) but of chattels such as motor vehicles or *objets d'art* bought from the proceeds of sale of articles in breach of the copyright. The following guidelines were given by the Court of Appeal in *CBS United Kingdom Ltd v Lambert* [1983] Ch. 37:

(1) There must be evidence or inference that the defendant had acquired the property as a result of his alleged wrongdoing, and clear evidence that he is likely, unless restrained by order, to dispose of it in order to deprive the claimant of the fruits of any judgment he might obtain.

(2) No order should be made for delivery up of a defendant's clothes, bedding, furnishings, materials or stock-in-trade likely to be used in a lawful business—except that furnishings of great value bought with the purpose of frustrating judgment creditors may be included in an order.

(3) The order must specify clearly what chattels or classes of chattel are to be delivered up. If the claimant cannot identify the chattels, no order should be made.

(4) The claimant cannot be authorised to enter upon or seize the defendant's property without the defendant's permission. The order should be in the form requiring the defendant to give permission.

(5) No order should be made for delivery up to anyone other than a solicitor or a receiver appointed by the High Court. The court should appoint a receiver to take possession of the chattels if it is not satisfied that the solicitor has suitable safe custody for what is delivered to him.

(6) So far as chattels in the custody of third parties are concerned, the court should follow the guidelines on the rights of third parties set out in the context of freezing cases in *Z Ltd v A-Z* [1982] QB 558 (see Ch.7).

(7) Provision should always be made for liberty to apply to stay, vary or discharge the order.

8-06 Where infringing material is stored on a computer, the defendant may be ordered to print out the material in readable form (*Gates v Swift* [1982] R.P.C. 339). On a less technological note, if it is suspected that locked cabinets at the defendant's premises may contain offending material, the defendant may be ordered to hand over the key or allow the removal of the cabinet (*Hazel Grove Music Co v Elster Enterprises* [1983] F.S.R. 379). The evidence adduced in support of the application, including any exhibits which can be copied, should be served on the defendant together with the order (*International Electronics Ltd v Weigh Data Ltd* [1980] F.S.R. 423).

A solicitor independent of the firm acting for the claimant and with experience of search orders must be appointed at the claimant's expense as "supervising solicitor" (see below). A list of suitable persons can be obtained from the Law Society or the London Solicitors' Litigation Association. He must offer to explain the effect of the order to the defendant fairly in everyday language and to inform him of his right to seek legal advice before complying with the order; failure by the solicitor to do so is a contempt (*VDU Installations v Integrated Computer Systems* [1989] 1 F.S.R. 378).

The claimant is not entitled to effect entry by force. If the defendant refuses to obey the court's order and permit inspection, the claimant should bring this contempt to the notice of the court and apply if necessary for committal. The powers given to the claimant are thus less than those given to police officers executing a search warrant, and the execution of a search order should be kept quite separate from a search by the police (*ITC Film Distributors Ltd v Video Exchange Ltd (No.2)* (1982) 126 S.J. 672). A police officer may, however, be asked to accompany the solicitor serving the order if there is a risk of violence.

8-07 In appropriate cases an order may be granted against defendants representing a group (*EMI Records Ltd v Kudhail* [1985] F.S.R. 36) but, as in all injunction cases, this can only be done if there is a cause of action against all the members of the group (see paras 1-12 to 1-13). No order can be made against a person against whom the claimant has no cause of action, such as the defendant's employer in a case where the employer has no connection with the activities complained of (*AB v CDE* [1982] R.P.C. 509). If several defendants are to be involved, it may be advisable to issue separate proceedings against them to reduce the risk of collaboration in the early stages. Certainly execution at more than one location should be simultaneous.

A search order should not be executed on the foreign premises of a foreign defendant until the defendant has been given the opportunity to challenge the order (*Altertext Inc v Advanced Data Communications Ltd* [1985] 1 W.L.R. 457). The position may be different, however, if the defendant who occupies the foreign premises has been validly served *within* the jurisdiction (*Cook Industries Inc v Galliher* [1979] Ch. 439).

Information obtained pursuant to a search order may not be used for any purpose other than the claim itself without permission (as to which see *Crest Homes Plc v Marks* [1987] A.C. 829). A claimant will generally be allowed to inform the police of what property of his has been recovered from the defendant, but the supervising solicitor's report should not, on the whole, be disclosed to the police (*Process Developments Ltd v Hogg* [1996] F.S.R. 45).

8-08 Provided that full disclosure is made of how the material was discovered, permission may be granted to a new claimant who was not involved in the original case (*Piver (LT) Sarl v S & J Perfume Co Ltd* [1987] F.S.R 159; *Twentieth Century Fox*

Film Corp v Trycare Ltd [1991] F.S.R. 58). Leave may also be given for the information to be used in overseas proceedings between the same parties, where such proceedings are for the purpose of obtaining protective measures to preserve assets rather than to litigate the substantive merits of the dispute (*Bayer AG v Winter (No.3)* [1986] F.S.R. 357). In *Garvin v Domus Publishing Ltd* [1989] Ch. 335, permission was given to use the information on a contempt application.

Where the dominant purpose of seeking a search order was to use its fruits in committal proceedings in an existing action, the order is liable to be set aside (*Cobra Golf Inc v Rata* [1998] Ch. 109). If a search order has been improperly obtained, the court has jurisdiction not merely to order the claimant to return to the defendant evidence resulting from it, but to prohibit the claimant from making use of such evidence (*NAF NAF SA v Dickens (London) Ltd* [1993] F.S.R. 424).

A search order may be granted to assist in the execution of a judgment (*Distributori Automatici Italia SpA v Holford General Trading Co Ltd* [1985] 1 W.L.R. 1066, Leggatt J). In *Abela v Baadarani (No.2)* [2018] 1 WLR 89 Nugee J held that post-judgment steps against a judgment debtor are "proceedings" for the purposes of section 7 of the 1997 Act; and that a search order can be made under section 7 against persons who are not defendants, and against whom there is no cause of action, if they hold evidence which may be relevant to proceedings and an order is necessary for the purposes of securing that evidence, whether or not a third party disclosure order has been made.

Safeguards

By the mid-1980s, search orders, despite being described in several cases as   **8-09**
"extreme", "draconian" and so forth, had become relatively easy to obtain. One firm of solicitors acting for the entertainment industry had obtained about 300 in 10 years, their applications invariably being granted. In *Dunlop Holdings Ltd v Staravia Ltd* [1982] Com. L.R. 3 Oliver LJ noted:

> "It has certainly become customary to infer the probability of disappearance or destruction of evidence where it is clearly established on the evidence before the court that the defendant is engaged in a nefarious activity which renders it likely that he is an untrustworthy person. It is seldom that one can get cogent or actual evidence of a threat to destroy materials or documents. So it is necessary for it to be inferred from the material which is before the court."

This more relaxed attitude led to miscarriages of justice: in the *Piver* case, above, Walton J stated that in the hands of some solicitors, search orders had become "oppressive to the point of shutting down genuine businesses because they have in fact erred and strayed in minor ways". Dillon LJ in *Booker McConnell Plc v Plascow* [1985] R.P.C. 425 emphasised the stringent requirements originally laid down in the search case itself, in particular the need to show the real possibility of documents being destroyed:

> "The phrase 'a real possibility' is to be contrasted with the extravagant fears which seem to afflict all plaintiffs who have complaints of breach of confidence, breach of copyright or passing off. Where the production and delivery up of documents is in question, the courts have always proceeded, justifiably, on the basis that the overwhelming majority of people in this country will comply with the court's order, and that defendants will therefore comply with orders to, for example, produce and deliver up documents without it being necessary to empower the plaintiff's solicitors to search the defendant's premises.
>
> It follows that the making of an *Anton Piller* order against a trading company may well be regarded as a serious stigma on that company's commercial reputation. Even more importantly for present purposes, it follows that there is a responsibility in each case on

the plaintiff's advisers to consider seriously whether it is justifiable to seek an search order against the particular defendant, or whether it would be enough to obtain negative injunctions with, if appropriate, an order to deliver up documents or material, for example, where, as here, the documents sought are the property of the plaintiff.''

In *Lock International Plc v Beswick* [1989] 1 W.L.R. 1268 at 1280, Hoffmann J, discharging a search order and granting an inquiry as to damages, said:

"*Anton Piller* orders are frequently sought in actions against former employees who have joined competitors or started competing businesses of their own. I have learned to approach such applications with a certain initial scepticism ... Some employers seem to regard competition from former employees as presumptive evidence of dishonesty. Many have great difficulty in understanding the distinction between genuine trade secrets and skill and knowledge which the employee may take away with him. In cases in which the plaintiff alleges misuse of trade secrets or confidential information concerning a manufacturing process, a lack of particularity about the precise nature of the trade secrets is usually a symptom of an attempt to prevent the employee from making legitimate use of the knowledge and skills gained in the plaintiff's service ... Even in cases in which the plaintiff has strong evidence that an employee has taken what is undoubtedly specific confidential information, such as a list of customers, the court must employ a graduated response. To borrow a useful phrase from the jurisprudence of the European Communities, there must be proportionality between the perceived threat to the plaintiff's rights and the remedy granted. The fact that there is overwhelming evidence that the defendant has behaved wrongfully in his commercial relationships does not necessarily justify a search order. People whose commercial morality allows them to take a list of the customers with whom they were in contact while employed will not necessarily disobey an order of the court requiring them to deliver it up. Not everyone who is misusing confidential information will destroy documents in the face of a court order requiring him to preserve them.
    In many cases it will be sufficient to make an order for delivery up of the plaintiff's documents to his solicitor or, in cases in which the documents belong to the defendant but may provide evidence against him, an order that he preserve the documents pending further order, or allow the claimant's solicitor to make copies. The more intrusive orders allowing searches of premises or vehicles require a careful balancing of, on the one hand, the plaintiff's right to recover his property or to preserve important evidence against, on the other hand, violation of the privacy of the defendant who has had no opportunity to put his side of the case. It is not merely that the defendant may be innocent. The making of an intrusive order ex parte even against a guilty defendant is contrary to normal principles of justice and can only be done where there is a paramount need to prevent a denial of justice to the claimant. The absolute extremity of the court's powers is to permit a search of a defendant's dwelling house, with the humiliation and family distress which that frequently involves.''

8-10   *Columbia Picture Industries Inc v Robinson* [1987] Ch. 38 was the first action to go to a full trial after the grant and execution of a search order. At the end of the hearing lasting 41 days, Scott J held that there had been a "serious failure" by the claimants' solicitors on the without notice application to disclose material facts within their knowledge, and that the execution of the order had been "oppressive" and in "flagrant disregard of the defendant's rights". He expressed "very grave disquiet" at the operation of the search procedure, which he described as "Draconian and essentially unfair", adding that "a common, perhaps the usual, effect of the service and execution of an search order is to close down [the defendant's] business" (at 73F). He considered that

"the practice of the court has allowed the balance to swing much too far in favour of claimants and that *Anton Piller* orders have been too readily granted and with insufficient safeguards for respondents.''

The following safeguards (see Precedent 7) were to be observed (at 76E):

"(1)   Search orders should be so drawn as to extend no further than the minimum extent necessary to achieve the purpose for which they are granted, namely the preservation of documents or articles which might otherwise be destroyed or concealed.

(2)   Once the claimants' solicitor [now the 'supervising solicitor'—see below] has satisfied himself what material exists and has had an opportunity to take copies, the defendant's property should be returned to its owner; material whose ownership is in dispute and which cannot safely be returned to the defendant should be handed over to the defendant's solicitors, as soon as any are on the record, on their undertaking as to its safe custody and production. (In cases concerning confidential information they may be required to undertake further not to allow their client access to the documents containing the information.)

(3)   A detailed record must be made of the material taken before it is removed from the defendant's premises, so as to avoid disputes at a later stage as to what was taken.

(4)   Only material clearly covered by the terms of the order may be taken. The practice whereby defendants are persuaded to 'consent' to the removal of additional material is unacceptable.

(5)   The affidavit in support of the application must err on the side of excessive disclosure. The court, not the claimants or their solicitors, should be the judge of relevance.

(6)   Where a search order is executed in an improper and oppressive manner the defendant may be awarded aggravated damages on the claimants' undertaking in damages."

But even after the warnings given in *Columbia Picture v Robinson and Lock International v Beswick*, abuses continued. In *Universal Thermosensors v Hibben* [1992] 1 W.L.R. 840, Nicholls VC laid down additional requirements, now incorporated in CPR PD 25A, paras 7 and 8. Various provisions apply to search orders in addition to those listed in the remainder of PD 25A. The Supervising Solicitor must be experienced in the operation of search orders and may be contacted either through the Law Society or, for the London area, through the London Solicitors Litigation Association. As regards the evidence, the affidavit must state the name, firm and its address, and experience of the Supervising Solicitor, also the address of the premises and whether it is a private or business address, and must disclose very fully the reason the order is sought, including the probability that relevant material would disappear if the order were not made. **8-11**

The order must be served personally by the Supervising Solicitor, unless the court otherwise orders, and must be accompanied by the evidence in support and any documents capable of being copied. Confidential exhibits need not be served but they must be made available for inspection by the respondent in the presence of the applicant's solicitors while the order is carried out and afterwards be retained by the respondent's solicitors on their undertaking not to permit the respondent to see them or copies of them except in their presence and to make or take away any note or record of them.

The Supervising Solicitor may be accompanied only by the persons mentioned in the order, must explain the terms and effect of the order to the respondent in everyday language and advise him of his right to take legal advice, and to apply to vary or discharge the order; and that he may be entitled to avail himself of legal professional privilege and the privilege against self-incrimination.

The search order may only be served between 9.30 a.m. and 5.30 p.m. on Monday to Friday unless the court orders otherwise. Where the Supervising Solicitor is a man and the respondent is likely to be an unaccompanied woman, at least one other person named in the order must be a woman and must accompany the Supervising Solicitor.

The premises must not be searched and no items shall be removed from them **8-12** except in the presence of the respondent or a person who appears to be a responsible employee of the respondent. No material shall be removed unless clearly covered by the terms of the order. Where copies of documents are sought, the documents should be retained for no more than 2 days before being returned to the owner. Where material in dispute is removed pending trial, the applicant's solicitors should place it in the custody of the respondent's solicitors on their undertaking to retain it in safekeeping (and insured where appropriate) and to produce it to the court when required. The Supervising Solicitor must make a list of all material removed from the premises and supply a copy of the list to the respondent who must check it before material is removed.

The respondent must immediately give the applicant's solicitors effective access to the computers, with all necessary passwords, to enable them to be searched for document in computer data form, and cause the listed items to be printed out. Often an image is taken of the relevant hard disk of the computer. The applicant must take all reasonable steps to ensure that no damage is done to any computer or data. The applicant and his representatives may not themselves search the respondent's computers unless they have sufficient expertise to do so without damaging the respondent's system. Forensic computer experts are now commonly used.

The Supervising Solicitor shall provide a report on the carrying out of the order to the applicant's solicitors, who must serve a copy of it on the respondent and file a copy of it with the court.

Where the Supervising Solicitor is satisfied that full compliance with list checking or printing out of data is impracticable, he may permit the search to proceed and items to be removed without compliance with the impracticable requirements.

The Supervising Solicitor must not be an employee or member of the applicant's firm of solicitors. If the court orders that the order need not be served by the Supervising Solicitor, the reason for so ordering must be set out in the order. The search order must not be carried out at the same time as a police search warrant. There is no privilege against self-incrimination in:

(1) intellectual property cases in respect of a 'related offence' or for the recovery of a 'related penalty' as defined in section 72 of the Senior Courts Act 1981;

(2) proceedings for the recovery or administration of any property, for the execution of a trust or for an account of any property or dealings with property, in relation to—

    (a) an offence under the Theft Act 1968 (see section 31 of the Theft Act 1968); or

    (b) an offence under the Fraud Act 2006 (see section 13 of the Fraud Act 2006) or a related offence within the meaning given by section 13(4) of that Act —that is, conspiracy to defraud or any other offence involving any form of fraudulent conduct or purpose; or

(3) proceedings in which a court is hearing an application for an order under Part IV or Part V of the Children Act 1989 (see section 98 of the Children Act 1989).

However, the privilege may still be claimed in relation to material or information required to be disclosed by an order, as regards potential criminal proceedings outside those statutory provisions.

Applications in intellectual property cases should be made in the Chancery Division. Further requirements are laid down in footnotes to the Practice Direction. None of the persons included in the search party should be people who could gain personally or commercially from anything they might read or see on the premises, unless their presence is essential. If it is envisaged that the respondent's computers are to be imaged (i.e. the hard drives are to be copied wholesale, thereby reproducing listed items and other items indiscriminately), special provision needs to be made and independent computer specialists need to be appointed who should be required to give undertakings to the court. As the order must be served in the morning after 9.30 am on a weekday this enables the respondent more readily to obtain legal advice.

Applying to discharge

The defendant is, of course, entitled to apply to the court to discharge the injunction; such an application should be made on notice to the claimant. This requires access to immediate legal advice and the negotiation of some kind of temporary truce by which the representatives of the claimants' solicitors can watch over the premises while an application is being made. Provided that the application is made promptly, the documents are protected meanwhile and there is no subterfuge or impropriety, the defendant will not be held to be in contempt (*Bhimji v Chatwani* [1991] 1 All E.R. 705). However, the Court of Appeal has emphasised that defendants who refuse to comply with injunctions do so at their peril if their application to discharge fails, and if they use the interval to destroy evidence the consequences will be extremely grave (*WEA Records Ltd v Visions Channel 4 Ltd* [1983] 1 W.L.R. 721). The practicalities of such applications are now provided for in the recommended form of order: see Precedent 7.

In *Systematica Ltd v London Computer Centre Ltd* [1983] F.S.R. 313, Whitford J noted that it was unnecessary to use the procedure where an alleged infringer was operating perfectly openly; in *NAF NAF SA v Dickens (London) Ltd* [1993] F.S.R. 424, Hoffmann J treated the failure to state that the defendant was openly dealing in the claimant's goods as justifying the discharge of the order for material non-disclosure. Lawton LJ in *Hytrac Conveyors Ltd v Conveyors International Ltd* [1983] 1 W.L.R. 44 deplored the practice of claimants using search orders as a means of finding out what charges they could make (in other words, fishing for evidence). He stated that "those who make charges must state right at the beginning what they are and what facts they are based upon". The claimants' failure to serve a statement of claim in accordance with rules of court led to the action being dismissed for want of prosecution.

The duty of full and frank disclosure is especially important in search cases (*Thermax v Schott Industrial Glass Ltd* [1981] F.S.R. 289; *Jeffrey Rogers Knitwear Production Ltd v Vinola (Knitwear) Manufacturing Co* [1985] F.S.R. 184).

Even a fully executed order can be discharged if it is established that it should never have been made (*Booker McConnell Plc v Plascow* [1985] R.P.C. 425; *Lock International Plc v Beswick* [1989] 1 W.L.R. 1268). If the application to discharge involves a detailed examination of the merits, the courts prefer to leave it to the trial. As Scott J pointed out in the *Columbia Pictures* case, the discharge itself is a somewhat academic exercise. In most cases the real sanction lies in the enforcement of the claimant's undertaking in damages. This liability arises out of the undertaking itself and should not be the subject of a counterclaim in the action (*Digital Equipment Corp v Darkcrest Ltd* [1984] Ch. 512).

Material departure from the recommended form of order (Precedent 7) and the requirements of the Practice Direction is likely to lead to the discharge of the order (*Gadget Shop Ltd v Bug.Com Ltd* [2001] F.S.R. 26).

8-13

8-14

Disclosure orders in intellectual property cases

8-15　　　It is a legitimate extension of the search order principle to order a defendant to disclose forthwith the names and addresses of suppliers of offending material and surrender documents such as order books. The safeguards laid down in the *Anton Piller* case remain applicable (*EMI Ltd v Sarwar* [1977] F.S.R. 146). The effect of the procedure was for a time largely undermined by *Rank Film Distributors Ltd v Video Information Centre* [1982] A.C. 380, in which the House of Lords held reluctantly that a defendant who might be liable to prosecution was, to that extent, protected from giving discovery or answering interrogatories (though not from allowing access to his premises and the removal of material belonging to the claimant or infringing the claimant's copyright) by the privilege against self-incrimination. In its application to cases involving passing off or rights in intellectual property (defined as including not only copyright, patents, trademarks and registered designs but also any "technical or commercial information"), however, this decision was immediately reversed by statute. Section 72 of the Senior Courts Act 1981 provides that a defendant in such (civil) proceedings shall not be excused, by the privilege against self-incrimination, from answering questions put to him or complying with any order of the court, but that any statement or admission made by him when answering the questions or complying with the order shall be inadmissible in criminal proceedings for any related offence. If the civil action is brought to prevent future infringement of copyright, the withdrawal of privilege applies even where the offence which might be revealed by the defendant having to comply with the order is unconnected with the question of copyright (for example, the manufacture of pornographic films) (*Universal City Studios Inc v Hubbard* [1984] Ch. 225).

8-16　　　As in freezing cases, the court may even go a stage further and order the cross-examination of the defendant. However such an order should not be made unless there is a reasonable likelihood that the defendant has information which should have been disclosed and which would lead to the disclosure of sources or the location of illicit goods. The claimants cannot be allowed a "roving cross-examination" merely because they harbour suspicions that the defendant has not been entirely open in his disclosure; all defendants in search cases are the subject of suspicions, and cross-examination should not become the norm (*RAC Ltd v Allsop* Unreported October 3, 1984, followed in *CBS UK Ltd v Perry* [1985] F.S.R. 421). See paras 7-24 to 7-25 for cases on the cross-examination of defendants on their affidavits in freezing injunction cases, which are generally applicable to search order cases as well.

　　　In appropriate cases a defendant may be ordered to reveal the names of his customers as well as his suppliers, but such an order is highly disruptive and will rarely be made on a without notice application.

　　　It should be noted that s 10 of the Contempt of Court 1981 provides that "no court may require a person to disclose ... the source of information contained in a publication for which he is responsible unless it be established to the satisfaction of the court that disclosure is necessary in the interests of justice: see *MXI Ltd v SES SA* [2018] EWHC 717 (Ch) at [63].

　　　In *Coca-Cola v Gilbey* [1995] 4 All E.R. 711; [1996] FSR 23 the defendant sought to discharge a disclosure order on the grounds that complying with it would put him at risk of reprisals. The Court of Appeal, refusing to set aside the order, held that because of the public interest in upholding the rule of law it would only be in the most exceptional circumstances, if ever, that such an argument could succeed.

Cases not involving intellectual property

The search jurisdiction was developed in intellectual property cases in the   **8-17**
Chancery Division; in such cases the "search and seizure" order generally related
to articles which were the subject matter of the action in that they had been made
allegedly in breach of the claimant's copyright, patent or similar rights. In *Yousif v
Salama* [1980] 1 W.L.R. 1540, a Queen's Bench claim for money due under an
agency agreement, the claimant sought a search order in respect of documents—
namely an office file and a desk diary—which he claimed were essential evidence
in support of his case and which he feared the defendant might destroy. The Court
of Appeal (by a majority) granted the application on that basis, even though the
documents were not the subject matter of the action. This is a decision of potentially
very wide application (see per Donaldson LJ, dissenting).

In *Emanuel v Emanuel* [1982] 1 W.L.R. 669 a similar order was made in a Family Division application for ancillary relief following divorce. The husband had
ignored orders for discovery and had disposed of property in breach of undertakings not to do so. On the wife's without notice application an order was made
permitting her solicitor to enter premises occupied by the husband, and also
premises which he had "sold" to his sister (who was made the second respondent
to the interim application), for the purpose of inspection and removal for copying
of documents relating to the husband's income and capital over the previous five
years and the sale by him of two properties in contempt of court.

It is to be noted that s.72 of the Senior Courts Act 1981 applies only to intellectual property and passing off actions and others involving technical or commercial information. Section 31(1) of the Theft Act 1968 and s.13 of the Fraud Act
2006 make similar provisions where the possible offence of which the defendant's
answers might incriminate him are substantive offences under those Acts; the
defendant may be compelled to comply with an order made in the civil claim, but
his statements or admissions made in compliance with it are inadmissible in the
criminal courts against the defendant or the defendant's spouse. There is no longer
a privilege against self-incrimination where the potential criminal charge is
conspiracy to defraud or any other offence involving any form of fraudulent conduct
or purpose as defined by the 2006 Act. Moreover, it was held in *C Plc v P (A-G
intervening)* [2008] Ch. 1 that the privilege, where it still exists, does not extend
to material (such as indecent images of children) found in the course of executing
the search order but which came into existence independently of, and usually prior
to, any compulsory questioning or any application of the court's compulsory
discovery process.

2   INTERIM PRESERVATION OF PROPERTY

The court—either a judge or a master or district judge—may make an order under   **8-18**
CPR r.25.1(1)(c) for the detention, inspection, custody or preservation of any
property, the taking of a sample, the carrying out of an experiment, or the sale of
property which is the subject of a claim or as to which a question may arise in a
claim and which is perishable or ought to for good reason be sold quickly; the latter category includes land (CPR r.25.1(2)). To enable the order to be carried out,
the court may authorise any person to enter upon any land or building in the possession of one of the parties (CPR r.25.1(1)(d)), but this authorisation may only be
given by a judge.

"Property" in this rule includes money. In *West Mercia Constabulary v Wagener*

[1982] 1 W.L.R. 127, an order was made without notice under the old RSC Ord.29 r.2 (the equivalent of CPR r.25.1(1)(c)) on the application of the police to preserve money in a bank account, the money having allegedly been obtained by fraud. This use of the rule was criticised by Donaldson and Slade LJJ in *Chief Constable of Kent v V* [1983] QB 34, since there was no substantive civil action between the police and the defendant. Prosecutors can now apply under statutory powers for restraint orders prohibiting dealings with funds identified as the proceeds of crime (see paras 7-56–7-59 and following and Precedent 6).

8-19
Where an order for delivery up is to be executed at the premises of the respondent or a third party, similar provisions for their benefit should be included as those included in a search order: see "para.8.1 of CPR PD 25A (Interim Injunctions)".

Section 44(3) of the Arbitration Act 1996 empowers the court, on the application of a party or proposed party to arbitration proceedings, to make orders in cases of urgency for the purpose of preserving evidence or assets, but not on a wider basis: *Cetelem SA v Roust Holdings Ltd* [2005] 1 W.L.R. 3555 (the limitations of s.44 cannot be circumvented by s.37 of the Senior Courts Act 1981: *AES Ust-Kamenogorsk Hydropower Plant LLP v Ust-Kamenogorsk Hydropower Plant JSC* [2012] 1 W.L.R. 920).

3   DELIVERY UP OF GOODS

8-20
The Torts (Interference with Goods) Act 1977 s.1 gave the old torts of conversion, trover, trespass to goods and other damages to goods, the generic title of "wrongful interference". Section 4 provides for interim relief in proceedings for wrongful interference, whether in the High Court or the county court. The court is empowered to order the delivery up of goods which are (or which may become) the subject matter of subsequent proceedings for wrongful interference and such order may provide for delivery up to the claimant or to a person appointed by the court for the purpose (s.4(2)–(3); CPR r.25.1(1)(e)). The application may be made before a claim is issued and may be made to a master or district judge. However if it is desired to seek an order in the form of a mandatory injunction carrying the contempt sanction, the application should be made to a judge.

The claimant may apply before issue of the proceedings if the urgency of the case warrants it. Interim preservation is more readily granted without notice than is delivery up, particularly to the claimant.

8-21
The jurisdiction may be exercised in any case where goods are being detained, whether or not there is a risk of their being disposed of, lost or destroyed (*Perry (Howard E) & Co Ltd v British Railways Board* [1980] 1 W.L.R. 1375).

An undertaking in damages is required and, also where appropriate, an understanding to indemnify third parties against the cost of complying with the order (*Guinness Peat Aviation (Belgium) NV v Hispania Lineas Aereas SA* [1992] 1 Lloyd's Rep. 190).

CPR r.25.1(1)(m) confers a similar power to order the delivery up of personal property on terms that the applicant pays money into court pending the outcome of the proceedings. The jurisdiction may be exercised by a master or district judge. The old RSC Ord.29 r.6 which this rule replaces only allowed an order to be made in cases where the respondent was claiming a lien, and only if the whole sum claimed by the respondent was paid into court. The CPR confers a broader discretion.

CHAPTER 9

Contempt of Court

1 JURISDICTION

"[If an] injunction is to be effective the law must be able to prescribe effective penalties **9-01** where a person deliberately sets the injunction at nought. Without sanctions an injunction would be a paper tiger. Sanctions are necessary to maintain the rule of law; in the language of the convention [the ECHR], to maintain the authority of the judiciary. If the rule of law is to be meaningful, the decision of the court on how, and to what extent, the status quo should be maintained pending the trial must be respected. It must be respected by third parties as well as the parties to the proceedings." (Per Lord Nicholls in *Attorney General v Punch Ltd* [2003] 1 A.C. 1046 at [32].)

Accordingly, when a defendant disobeys a prohibitory injunction or fails to comply with a mandatory injunction within the time specified in the order, the judgment of the court may be enforced by an order of committal against him (CPR r.81.4(1)). An undertaking given to the court is equivalent to an injunction and its breach may be punished in the same way (CPR r.81.4(4)). In the case of a prohibitory injunction, the prohibition is absolute and is not to be related to intent unless so stated in the order (*Knight v Clifton* [1971] Ch. 700). The breach of an injunction or an undertaking constitutes contempt even though it was committed on the basis of legal advice that the acts comprising the breach were lawful (*Re Mileage Conference Group's Agreement* [1966] 1 W.L.R. 1137).

The party in whose favour an order has been made is entitled to have it enforced, and the effective administration of justice normally requires some penalty for disobedience to an order of a court if the disobedience is more than casual or accidental and unintentional (*Heaton's Transport Ltd v Transport and General Workers' Union* [1973] A.C. 15 at 109).

It used to be held that there was jurisdiction to commit or sequestrate assets **9-02** whenever contempt involved a degree of fault or misconduct, including negligent failure to comply with an injunction; however committal for negligence has always been rare (*Guildford BC v Valler, The Times,* 15 October 1993 CA), and the modern law is stated in the case of *In re A (A Child) (Removal from Jurisdiction: Contempt of Court)* [2009] 1 W.L.R. 1482. Hughes LJ said that contempt of court "involves a contumelious, that is to say a deliberate, disobedience to the order". He also emphasised that contempt must be proved to the criminal standard, that is to say so that the judge is sure and that the burden or proof lies at all times on the applicant. "Nor is it enough to suspect recalcitrance; it has to be proved." The court must be sure that unlawful breach of an order has been committed (*South Cambridgeshire DC v Thomas Buckley* [2012] EWHC 1669 (QB)).

Where the defendant is in technical breach of a complex order in circumstances where the breach is trivial and not blameworthy, an application to commit may be dismissed with costs on the grounds that it is a disproportionate response to the breach (*Adam Phones Ltd v Goldschmidt* [1999] 4 All E.R. 486).

9-03   If the defendant is a body corporate, the order of committal may issue against any director or officer of the company who is responsible for the breach (CPR r.81.4(3)). A company director who is aware of an injunction or undertaking binding the company is under a duty to take reasonable steps to see that the order or undertaking is complied with; if he wilfully fails to do so he is liable to committal unless he reasonably believed that another director or employee of the company was taking such steps (*Attorney General for Tuvalu v Philatelic Distribution Corp Ltd* [1990] 2 All E.R. 216).

A corporate employer itself is liable in contempt (whether or not it would be vicariously liable in tort) for the activity of an employee who does an act in breach of an injunction against the company, even if he does so contrary to the company's express prohibition and its taking all reasonable steps to prevent him, and without the company's knowledge (*Re Supply of Ready Mixed Concrete (No.2), Director General of Fair Trading v Pioneer Concrete (UK) Ltd* [1995] 1 A.C. 456).

9-04   An injunction restraining the defendant organisation from using the initials WWF, "whether directly or indirectly by its officers, servants, agents, subsidiaries and licensees", obliged it to take all reasonable steps within its power to prevent its licensees from doing the prohibited acts but did not make the defendants absolutely responsible for the acts of licensees pursuing their own commercial interests under agreements antedating the injunction. The licensees, who were able to show that eliminating the use of the initials was genuinely impracticable, were accordingly granted a declaration that their actions did not constitute a contempt (*World Wide Fund for Nature v World Wrestling Federation Entertainment Inc* [2004] F.S.R. 10).

The court has "undoubted jurisdiction" to commit for contempt a person, not included in an injunction nor a party to the action, who, knowing of the injunction, aids and abets a defendant in committing a breach of it (*Seaward v Paterson* [1897] 1 Ch. 545; *Acrow (Automation) Ltd v Rex Chainbelt Inc* [1971] 1 W.L.R. 1676). When an injunction had been granted against two newspapers prohibiting publication of extracts from the book *Spycatcher*, and three other newspapers, not parties to the action, published the same material themselves, they were held liable for criminal contempt on the grounds that their action was intended to impede the administration of justice by destroying the confidentiality which the court was seeking to protect (*Attorney General v Times Newspapers Ltd* [1992] 1 A.C. 191). In relation to breach of an interim injunction restraining the publication of confidential material by the MI5 dissident David Shayler, the actus reus of contempt was held to lie in the destruction of the confidentiality of the material which it was the purpose of the injunction to preserve pending the trial. Whether publication of the material was intended to, or whether it did in fact, damage national security was irrelevant; the prejudice to the administration of justice was sufficient to establish contempt (*Attorney General v Punch Ltd* [2003] 1 A.C. 1046).

9-05   Gray J held in *Jockey Club v Buffham* [2003] QB 462 that the principle that a person commits a contempt of court by doing an act which has the effect of undermining a court order of which he has knowledge but to which he was not a party applies only to interim orders, not to final ones, since the essence of the contempt is interference with the course of justice: so that where a final injunction had been granted against a former employee of the Jockey Club restraining him from divulging confidential information, it would not be a contempt of court on the part of the BBC to broadcast that information, the publication of which was in the public interest. This decision was queried in *Hutcheson v Popdog Ltd* [2012] 1 W.L.R. 782 at [26]: Lord Neuberger MR said that it "cannot be safely assumed" that it would be approved by the Court of Appeal.

Committal may be ordered even though the injunction has ceased to be effective between the breach and the court hearing (*Jennison v Baker* [1972] 2 QB 52).

The party in whose favour an injunction has been granted may waive, or consent to, non-compliance (*Home Office v Harman* [1983] A.C. 280 at 310).

Where an injunction has been granted in respect of the occupation of land in breach of planning control against "persons unknown", anyone who moves onto the land or remains there after being told of the terms of the injunction is in breach of it and thus in contempt of court (*South Cambridgeshire DC v Gammell* [2006] 1 W.L.R. 658). **9-06**

A county court has no power to deal with a contempt of court which is neither contempt in the face of the court nor disobedience of an order made by, or undertaking given to, a county court. Thus, when a parent applying for contact in the county court published details sufficient to identify volunteers at the contact centre by name, only the Queen's Bench Division of the High Court had jurisdiction (*Re G (A Child) (Contempt: Committal)* [2003] 1 W.L.R. 2051).

The Law Officers have *locus* to apply for the committal of an alleged contemnor even if the contempt consists of the breach of an injunction, granted in proceedings between private individuals (*Re Jones* [2014] 1 F.L.R. 852, per Sir James Munby P).

Alleged breaches of anti-social behaviour injunctions under the Anti-Social Behaviour, Crime and Policing Act 2014 or gang-related injunctions under the Policing and Crime Act 2009 may be the subject of an application to commit for contempt if the respondent is an adult; but where the respondent is under 18 the proper course is an application for a supervision or detention order under the procedures set out in Sch.2 to the 2014 Act and Sch.5A to the 2009 Act respectively (*Practice Guidance: Committal for Contempt of Court—Open Court*, 24 June 2015).

2 NOTICE OF THE INJUNCTION

It is a prerequisite for enforcement of an injunction by way of committal that the defendant has been served personally with a copy of the injunction (CPR rr.81.5 and 81.6). There is, however, a discretion under CPR r.81.8 to dispense with personal service, either: **9-07**

(a) in the case of a prohibitory injunction, if the respondent has had notice by being present when the order was granted, or has been notified by telephone or email; or

(b) in any case, if the court considers it just to do so. An alternative method of service may be provided for in the order dispensing with personal service.

The option of notification without service is important—it enables an injunction to take effect immediately without the necessity for personal service. However, it is for the claimant to prove beyond reasonable doubt, by affidavit evidence from a process server or solicitor or otherwise, that the defendant had notice of the injunction. Even where notice has been given in writing, the defendant will not be committed for contempt if he swears positively that he acted in the bona fide belief that the communication was a hoax and that no injunction had in fact been granted, provided that the circumstances show such belief to be reasonable (*Ex p. Langley* (1879) 13 Ch. D. 110, where the means of communication was a telegram). The opportunity for such a defence may be averted if the claimant's solicitor communicates with the defendant's solicitor so that the latter can give notice of the order to the defendant.

In the case of a mandatory injunction, the requirement of personal service is not satisfied unless the copy order has been served before the expiration of the time within which the defendant was required to do the act (CPR r.81.5(1)(a)).

Penal notice

9-08   There must be prominently displayed on the front of the copy of an order served under this rule a warning to the person required to do or not do the act in question that disobedience to the order would be a contempt of court punishable by imprisonment, a fine or sequestration of his assets (CPR r.81.9(1)). Forms of penal notice are given in Precedent 2.

In the county court, the injunction order is drawn up by the court office in Form N16 (Precedent 9-01), indorsed with a penal notice. This copy is served on the respondent personally.

There is a discretion to enforce an order notwithstanding a failure to indorse it with a penal notice (*Sofroniou v Szigetti* [1991] F.C.R. 332). However where an injunction had not been served and there was no evidence that the defendant, though present in court, had been told what the consequences of breach would be (as he would have been by a penal notice), a sentence of imprisonment for contempt could not stand (*Cleveland CC v L, The Times,* 8 April 1996).

Where a defendant has given an undertaking to the court in lieu of an injunction, a penal notice is not required (CPR 81.9(2)).

A declaratory order cannot be enforced by committal and should not have a penal notice indorsed on it (*D v D (Access: Contempt: Committal)* [1991] 2 F.L.R. 34).

3   NOTICE OF THE APPLICATION TO COMMIT

9-09   An application for an order of committal for breach of a High Court injunction or undertaking must be made by filing an application notice under CPR r.81.10. The application notice must set out in full the grounds on which the application for committal is made and must identify, separately and numerically, each alleged act of contempt, including (if known) the date of each of the alleged acts.

Evidence in support must be in an affidavit. Both the notice and a copy of the affidavit must be served personally on the person sought to be committed (CPR r.81.10(4)). This is an entirely separate rule from that requiring notice of the original order; the defendant must first have had notice of the injunction, then breached it, and then had notice of the application to commit before a committal order can be made. Mere knowledge on the part of the defendant of the claimant's intention to apply to commit does not dispense with the necessity of endeavouring to effect personal service, and the appearance of the defendant at the hearing does not constitute a waiver of any objection on his part, on the grounds either of lack of personal service or of any irregularity (*Mander v Falcke* [1891] 3 Ch. 488).

The court may dispense with personal service of the application and, in effect, make a committal order without notice if it thinks it just to do so (CPR r.81.10(5)). The question is whether injustice has been caused, not whether the circumstances are exceptional (*Khawaja v Popat* [2016] EWCA Civ 362).

In an exceptional case, service of the injunction or the notice may be dispensed with (*Wright v Jess* [1987] 1 W.L.R. 1076; see, however, *Lewis v Lewis* [1991] 1 W.L.R. 235). An old example of the exercise of this power is *O'Donovan v O'Donovan* [1955] 1 W.L.R. 1086 (against a party, moreover, who was out of the jurisdiction), where a father had detained a child abroad in breach of an undertaking to the court to return him to England by a specific date. The father had not been served with notice of the committal proceedings since his whereabouts were unknown; the court dispensed with service. If the hearing date is adjourned in the defendant's absence, notice of the new date must be served on him personally (*Chiltern DC v Keane* [1985] 1 W.L.R. 619).

The above procedure, subsequent to service of the application to commit, is not **9-10** applicable where the respondent is brought before a judge by the police pursuant to a power of arrest for breach of injunction granted under the Family Law Act 1996 (see para.10-29 and following for the procedure in such cases).

In *Zakaharov v White* (2003) 153 New L.J. 1669, Roderick Evans J held that a judge has inherent jurisdiction to issue a bench warrant for the arrest of an individual to whom an injunction was addressed with which he has not complied, even where no finding has been made that the respondent is in contempt. The respondent's solicitors can be ordered to provide his contact details to facilitate service of the notice of application (*JSC BTA Bank v Solodchenko (No.3)* [2013] Ch 1).

4   PROCEDURE AT THE HEARING

For a committal application, the following documents must be lodged together **9-11** with a copy of each of:

(a) the application notice, signed by the applicant's solicitor with address, telephone number, document exchange number and reference;
(b) the affidavit in support and exhibits;
(c) the claim form;
(d) particulars of claim and any other pleadings—a generally indorsed claim form is regarded as inadequate;
(e) the order breached, with a penal notice prominently indorsed or attached;
(f) an affidavit of service of the order breached; and
(g) a time estimate signed by counsel.

In addition, proof of service of the notice of application to commit will be required at the hearing.

The Lord Chief Justice's *Practice Guidance: Committal for Contempt of Court— Open Court* [2015] 1 W.L.R. 2195 issued on 26 March 2015 emphasises that the fundamental principle of open justice applies to all committal hearings for contempt of court irrespective of the court in which they are being heard. Derogations from the general principle can only be justified in exceptional circumstances, and only to the extent that they are strictly necessary to secure the proper administration of justice. In all cases in which a court finds that a contempt of court has been committed, even if the hearing has been conducted in private, the court must sit in public to announce the name of the contemnor, the nature of the contempt and the penalty imposed, and details must be provided both to the national media via the CopyDirect service and to the Judicial Office for publication on the Judiciary website.

The applicant may not, except with leave of the court, rely at the hearing upon **9-12** any grounds for committal except those set out in the notice of application (CPR r.81.28(1)). If the judge considers that other alleged contempts require consideration, the correct course is to invite amendment of the application notice and then provide any necessary adjournment so that the respondent can prepare to deal with those new matters (*Hewlett Packard Enterprise Co v Sage* [2017] 1 W.L.R. 4599).

The court may, contrary to the usual rules of procedure, call evidence itself to find out whether the defendant is in contempt of court (*Yianni v Yianni* [1966] 1 W.L.R. 120).

The standard of proof is proof beyond reasonable doubt (*Re Bramblevale Ltd* [1970] Ch. 128; *In re A (A Child) (Removal from Jurisdiction: Contempt of Court)* [2009] 1 W.L.R. 1482; "SCPD 52 para.1.4"). The evidence must be such as to prove a breach of the court's order by the defendant "with all the strictness that is necessary in such a proceeding as this, when you are going to deprive people of their liberty" (*Churchman v Joint Shop Stewards' Committee* [1972] 1 W.L.R. 1094), although hearsay evidence is admissible (*Daltel Europe Ltd v Makki* [2006] 1 W.L.R. 2704). Moreover, as Jenkins J put it in *Redwing Ltd v Redwing Forest Products Ltd* (1947) 64 R.P.C. 67 (in words plainly applicable to injunctions as much as to undertakings: see *Commission for Equality & Human Rights v Nicholas John Griffin* [2010] EWHC 3343 (Admin)):

> "[A] defendant cannot be committed for contempt on the ground that upon one of two possible constructions of an undertaking being given he has broken that undertaking. For the purpose of relief of this character [i.e. committal] I think the undertaking must be clear and the breach must be clear beyond all question."

In *Re L-W (Enforcement and Committal: Contact) CPL v CH-W and Others* [2011] 1 F.L.R. 1095 Munby LJ said:

> "(1) The first task for the judge hearing an application for committal for alleged breach of a mandatory (positive) order is to identify, by reference to the express language of the order, precisely what it is that the order required the defendant to do. That is a question of construction and, thus, a question of law. (2) The next task for the judge is to determine whether the defendant has done what he was required to do and, if he has not, whether it was within his power to do it. To adopt Hughes LJ's language, Could he do it? Was he able to do it? These are questions of fact. (3) The burden of proof lies throughout on the applicant: it is for the applicant to establish that it was within the power of the defendant to do what the order required, not for the defendant to establish that it was not within his power to do it. (4) The standard of proof is the criminal standard, so that before finding the defendant guilty of contempt the judge must be sure (a) that the defendant has not done what he was required to do and (b) that it was within the power of the defendant to do it. (5) If the judge finds the defendant guilty the judgment must set out plainly and clearly (a) the judge's finding of what it is that the defendant has failed to do and (b) the judge's finding that he had the ability to do it."
>
> (2) Bearing in mind that a defendant is not in breach of a mandatory order, even if he has not done what the order required, if it was not within his power to do it, issues of force majeure are properly to be considered as going to questions of breach rather than reasonable excuse. So, for example, if a parent taking a child for contact is prevented from going or is delayed by unforeseen and insuperable transport or weather problems – one thinks of the sudden and unexpected grounding of the nation's airlines by volcanic ash – then there will be no breach. Reasonable excuse, in contrast, arises where, although it was within the power of the defendant to comply, he has some good reason, specifically, a "reasonable excuse", for not doing so. A typical case might be where a child suddenly falls ill and the defendant, reasonably in the circumstances, takes the child to the doctor rather than going to contact.'"

9-13   Both the rules of natural justice and the provisions of CPR r.81.10(3) make it clear that the respondent must have details of the alleged acts of contempt, information about how and from whom to obtain legal aid, the opportunity to take legal advice, and a reasonable time in which to respond to the application and if necessary prepare a defence: see *James v James* [2018] EWCA Civ 1982. If he is unable to understand English, the court should assist in arranging for an interpreter to attend the hearing.

The respondent is entitled to give oral evidence on his own behalf if he wishes to do so, whether or not he has filed written evidence. He cannot be compelled. If he does, he may be cross-examined. Alternatively, he may give evidence by affidavit although, if he does this, the judge may as a matter of discretion allow cross-examination of him (*Comet Products UK Ltd v Hawkex Plastics Ltd* [1971] 2 QB 67). The court will generally exercise its discretion in favour of cross-examination if it can be limited to the alleged contempt (*Great Future International Ltd v Sealand Housing Corporation, The Times,* 1 March 2004, Lewison J).

The respondent has no right to make a submission of "no case to answer", as in a criminal court, before deciding whether to adduce evidence (*BZW Securities Ltd v Nadir, The Times,* 25 March 1992).

Allegations of contempt often occur at an interlocutory stage. Whether they should be determined before, during or after a main trial is a case management decision for the judge on the facts of the individual case. Where the alleged contempt is said to relate to the breach of a freezing order, the public interest in ensuring the efficacy of such orders is likely to weigh heavily in the balance. Accordingly, overlap, of itself and without more, does not necessitate postponing the determination of a contempt application until after the trial (*Ablyazov v JSC BTA Bank* [2012] 1 W.L.R. 1988).

9-14

On a contempt application for breach of a freezing injunction, there is an evidential burden of proof on the defendant who has disposed of assets to establish, where it is in issue, that the value of his other assets within the jurisdiction exceeds the maximum sum in the injunction (*Canadian Imperial Bank of Commerce v Bhattessa, The Times,* 10 September 1991; affirmed by CA, unreported, 21 April 1993; *Great Future International Ltd v Sealand Housing Corp, The Times,* 1 March 2004, Lewison J).

Committal proceedings should not be conducted simultaneously with other applications, such as for contact with a child (*Hammerton v Hammerton* [2007] 2 F.L.R. 1133; see para.10-42).

In *Hewlett Packard Enterprise Co v Sage* [2017] 1 WLR 4599 Henderson LJ observed that "it is a salutary discipline for any judge who is delivering or writing a judgment on a committal application to set out each relevant ground of committal before proceeding to consider whether it is made out on the evidence to the criminal standard of proof".

5   PARALLEL CIVIL AND CRIMINAL PROCEEDINGS

Where a contempt (such as an assault in breach of a non-molestation order) is also the subject of a pending criminal trial, the civil court is placed in some difficulty. In *Keeber v Keeber* [1995] 2 F.L.R. 748, the Court of Appeal held that breaches of a non-molestation order should be listed before a circuit judge, dealt with "swiftly and decisively", and only adjourned to await the outcome of a prosecution if there was a real risk of serious prejudice which might lead to injustice: see also *R v AA and SA* [2010] EWCA Crim 2805, per Aikens LJ at [41]-[42].. In *M v M (Contempt: Committal)* [1997] 3 F.C.R. 288, Lord Bingham of Cornhill CJ, while upholding a stay of the contempt application on the facts of that case, emphasised the need to ensure that orders of the court are not flouted with impunity and that the party for whose protection they are made does receive effec-

9-15

tive protection. Similarly in *Lomas v Parle* [2004] 1 W.L.R. 1642 (see para.10-48), an important case on the interrelationship between contempt applications and criminal prosecutions, the Court of Appeal held that the application to commit should be listed and heard without delay.

The principle is that the contemnor should not be punished twice for the same events (*Hale v Tanner* [2000] 1 W.L.R. 2377). A transcript of the judgment should be made available to the court which passes sentence in the subsequent criminal case if that results in a conviction; the second court must take account of the first court's penalty. The civil court is sentencing for the fact of the contempt rather than its content, but sentences for contempt must not be manifestly discrepant with those passed in criminal proceedings for comparable offences (*Slade v Slade* [2010] 1 W.L.R. 1262).

9-16 In domestic violence cases, which are the most common type in which the problem arises, Parliament has resolved it by enacting s.42A of the Family Law Act 1996. This section makes it a criminal offence punishable with up to five years' imprisonment to breach without reasonable excuse a non-molestation order of which the defendant was aware. If a prosecution is brought and the defendant is convicted, he cannot be punished for contempt of court, and vice versa. See the extended discussion at para.10-37.

In civil cases where the party initiating contempt proceedings has also brought a substantive claim against the same defendant, it should only be in exceptional cases that the court should allow the contempt application to be heard ahead of the trial, particularly where resolution of the contempt charge depends on evidence which can be more appropriately assessed in the light of full disclosure at trial (per Elias LJ in *JSC BTA Bank v Ereshchenko* [2013] 1 Lloyd's Rep. 561).

6 THE PENALTY FOR CONTEMPT

9-17 "The sentence for contempt in the form of non-compliance with a court order performs a number of functions. First, it upholds the authority of the court by punishing the contemnor and deterring others. Such punishment has nothing to do with the dignity of the court and everything to do with the public interest that court orders should be obeyed. Secondly, in some instances, it provides an incentive for belated compliance, because the contemnor may seek a reduction or discharge of sentence if he subsequently purges his contempt by complying with the court order in question." (Per Jackson LJ in *JSC BTA Bank v Solodchenko* [2012] 1 W.L.R. 350.)

Committal must be for a fixed term of not more than two years (Contempt of Court Act 1981 s.14(1)); therefore a case such as *Re Lusty* [1967] C.A.T. 33, in which a contemnor was released after serving over three years of an indefinite sentence, could no longer occur. A committal order may be immediate or suspended. Consecutive sentences may be imposed for separate breaches but the total must not exceed two years (*Re R* [1994] 1 W.L.R. 487), even when a suspended sentence is being activated (*Villiers v Villiers* [1994] 1 W.L.R. 493). After finding the respondent to be in contempt, the judge must hear mitigation before passing a custodial sentence (*Goldsmith v Goldsmith* [2006] EWCA Civ 1670, *The Times,* November 22, 2006).

9-18 A defendant cannot be committed "until further order" (*Linnett v Coles* [1987] QB 555), nor remanded in custody for preparation of reports (*Delaney v Delaney* [1996] QB 387). If the sentencing judge is uncertain as to the appropriate sentence, he could impose a sentence "at the top end of the bracket" and have the case relisted for further argument later. Whatever the period specified, the court retains jurisdiction to order the defendant's earlier discharge on his or the Official Solicitor's application. In *Burton v Winters* [1993] 1 W.L.R. 1077, the Court of Appeal upheld a committal for two years but suggested that the Official Solicitor should keep the case under review.

If a person is committed to prison for breach of a mandatory order requiring him to do a certain act by a certain date, he cannot be made subject to a further committal for a continuing breach of the same order; it is necessary to return to court and seek a further order first (*Kumari v Jalal* [1996] 4 All E.R. 65; *Re Jones* [2014] 1 F.L.R. 852). However if a further order is made and that too is flouted, another term of imprisonment may be imposed: as in *Re W (a child: abduction: contempt)* [2011] EWCA Civ 1196 and *Williamson v Anjum* [2012] 1 W.L.R. 1036. In the latter case, the first sentence had been the maximum of two years, but that did not prevent a further term from being imposed.

Where an application to commit has been dismissed on the merits, a second application cannot be made, but it is otherwise if the first application failed on a technicality such as a defect in the notice (*Jelson (Estates) v Harvey* [1983] 1 W.L.R. 1401; *Harmsworth v Harmsworth* [1987] 1 W.L.R. 1676). **9-19**

The court has no power, having made a committal order without notice, to increase the penalty at the hearing on notice (*Lamb v Lamb* (1984) 14 Fam. Law 60).

There are many cases in the family jurisdiction discussing the appropriate penalties for contempt, notably *Hale v Tanner* [2000] 2 F.L.R. 879: see para.10-46. In *Murray v Robinson* [2006] 1 F.L.R. 365, Lord Woolf CJ noted that the Protection from Harassment Act 1997 (see para.4-62) carries a maximum penalty in both civil and criminal jurisdictions of five years' imprisonment, and suggested that where a case may warrant a sentence near the top of the Contempt of Court Act range, the appropriate course is to bring proceedings under the 1997 Act.

JSC BTA Bank v Solodchenko (No.2) [2012] 1 W.L.R. 350 contains a useful review by Jackson LJ of the principles of sentencing for a contempt which consists of non-compliance with the disclosure provisions of a freezing order: **9-20**

> "Freezing orders are made for good reason and in order to prevent the dissipation or spiriting away of assets. Any substantial breach of such an order is a serious matter, which merits condign punishment. Condign punishment for such contempt normally means a prison sentence. However, there may be circumstances in which a substantial fine is sufficient: for example, if the contempt has been purged and the relevant assets recovered.
>
> Where there is a continuing failure to disclose relevant information, the court should consider imposing a long sentence, possibly even the maximum of two years, in order to encourage future co-operation by the contemnor. In the case of continuing breach, out of fairness to the contemnor, the court may see fit to indicate (a) what portion of the sentence should be served in any event as punishment for past breaches and (b) what portion of the sentence the court might consider remitting in the event of prompt and full compliance thereafter. Any such indication would be persuasive, but not binding upon a future court. It should also be noted that what the court is passing is a nominal sentence. The actual time spent in prison will be less, because of remission, possible release on tagging and so forth. The court does not have regard to those factors in determining the proper sentence in any case."

In *Universal Business Team Pty Ltd v Moffitt* [2017] EWHC 3251 (Ch) a defendant who admitted numerous contempts of court in breach of a search order, including deliberately erasing data from his electronic devices and transferring them to another person, was sentenced by Marcus Smith J to 14 months' imprisonment. The judge observed that imprisonment was an option of last resort, but in the instant case it was the only option. In *Billington v Davies* [2017] EWHC 3725 Barling J imposed a sentence of 12 months' imprisonment for flagrant disregard of several court orders, and dispensed with personal service since he was satisfied that the respondent had had notice of the proceedings and had repeatedly and deliberately chosen to take no part in them.

While it is desirable so far as possible to consider on a single occasion all extant allegations of contempt of court, there is no fixed rule to such effect. The aim is desirable because the Contempt of Court Act 1981 limits the sentence for contempt of court which can be imposed on any occasion to a maximum term of two years' imprisonment. That timetable should not be manipulated by multiple applications in an attempt to procure a term of imprisonment in excess of two years; efforts to do so are overwhelmingly likely to fail. However, there is no invariable rule. A decision whether or not to leave over for future consideration extant allegations of contempt is a case management decision for the judge with which the Court of Appeal will be slow to interfere. Where alleged contempts arose in the context of a worldwide freezing order, coupled with a variety of ancillary and related provisions, there is likely to be a strong public interest in ensuring that the freezing order is appropriately policed, enforced and thus made effective; in that regard, the bringing of contempt proceedings may encourage improved compliance with its terms (*Ablyazov v JSC BTA Bank* [2012] 1 W.L.R. 1988).

Suspended committal orders

9-21   The court may suspend the operation of a committal order (*Lee v Walker* [1985] QB 1191). This may be either on specified terms (to give the respondent a last chance to comply) or for a fixed period (as in *Churchman v Joint Shop Stewards' Committee* [1972] 1 W.L.R. 1094, where the committal order granted at first instance was suspended for a short period in order to enable the individual defendants to appear before the court to explain their conduct). It may even be appropriate to suspend a committal order for so long as the contemnor complies with another order which is itself expressed to run "until further order", i.e. of indefinite duration, although this has the effect of suspending the prison sentence indefinitely (*Griffin v Griffin* [2000] 2 F.L.R. 44). However, although the practice of making suspended committal orders may be effective in some cases, careful consideration must be given to the question of how and in what circumstances the suspension is to be removed and the committal order activated (*Ansah v Ansah* [1977] Fam. 138).

Activation is not an inevitable consequence of a further breach during the period of suspension. There has to be a further application to the court, when the judge has to take a view on the merits in the round (*Re AB* [2010] EWCA Civ 533 at [37]). There is power to impose consecutive suspended sentences (*McCann v Wright* [1995] 1 W.L.R. 1556). Where a comprehensive application to commit has been made and a substantial term of imprisonment imposed, it is normally wrong to leave over for possible future activation any suspended sentence or consideration of other alleged contempts (*Phillips v Symes (No.3)* [2005] 1 W.L.R. 2986).

9-22   Breach of the conditions of a suspended committal order must be proved to the criminal standard if it is sought to impose a new sentence, but only to the civil standard if some other course is to be followed such as the making of an order for further affidavits (*Phillips v Symes* [2003] EWCA Civ 1769; *Alfa Laval Tumba AB v Separator Spares International Ltd* [2010] EWHC 674 (Ch)).

Alternatives to committal

As an alternative to committal, CPR r.81.20 enables the claimant to apply for   **9-23**
leave to issue a writ of sequestration. This is available against any defendant,
whether corporate or not. It gives an effective remedy against, for example, a
company incorporated abroad but with assets within the jurisdiction (*Hospital for
Sick Children v Walt Disney Productions Inc* [1968] Ch. 52), or a parent who has
taken a child abroad in breach of a court order (*Richardson v Richardson* [1989]
Fam. 95). It has also been at times a remedy sought against trade unions since it
avoids the threat of imprisonment. Third parties, including the contemnor's audi-
tors, are under a duty to co-operate with the sequestrators (*Messenger Newspapers
Group Ltd v National Graphical Association* [1984] 1 All E.R. 293). Sequestrated
property, including a freehold, may be sold by order of the court (*Mir v Mir* [1992]
Fam. 79). It may be an appropriate remedy for breach of a disclosure order in a post-
judgment freezing injunction (*Trafigura Ltd v Emirates General Petroleum Corp*
[2010] EWHC 3007 (Comm), where the sum covered by the injunction was £90
million). For an example of an order for sequestration against a bank for persistent
breaches of a freezing injunction involving a "high degree of negligence", see *Z
Bank v D1* [1994] 1 Lloyd's Rep. 656. A county court may enforce an injunction
by sequestration of the defendant's assets, whether the defendant is an individual
or a company (*Rose v Laskington Ltd* [1990] QB 562).

The fact that a company does not have assets within the jurisdiction of the court
does not always mean that a writ of sequestration would be futile: *Touton Far East
Pte Ltd v Shri Lal Mahal Ltd* [2017] EWHC 621, and see *VIS Trading Co v Nazarov*
[2016] 4 W.L.R. 1.

The court may impose a fine in lieu of committal or sequestration (*Phonographic
Performance Ltd v Amusement Caterers Ltd* [1964] Ch. 195). This may be enforced
by the Queen's Remembrancer as if it were a judgment debt due to her (Senior
Courts Act 1981 s.140; Contempt of Court Act 1981 s.16). There is also jurisdiction to make an award of damages to the applicant (*Midland Marts Ltd v Hobday*
[1989] 1 W.L.R. 1143). Fines should not be imposed on defendants jointly (*McMillan Graham Printers Ltd v RR (UK) Ltd, The Times*, March 19, 1993).

A county court may take judicial notice of previous breaches of undertakings to   **9-24**
it by a local authority when imposing a fine for such a breach (*Mullen v Hackney
LBC* [1997] 2 All E.R. 906).

Counsel for an applicant should always be in a position to advise the judge as to
the extent of his powers, any sentencing guidelines and provisions for the remis-
sion of prison sentences; however, as sentence is a matter between the court and the
contemnor, the applicant's counsel should not be invited to make submissions on
sentence (*Rehbeim v Isufai* [2005] EWCA Civ 1046).

7   DEFECTS IN THE COMMITTAL ORDER OR THE NOTICE OF APPLICATION

Committal orders must be in the prescribed form and must state (as must the   **9-25**
judge in giving his decision) with sufficient particularity what contempt has been
found proved and which injunction or undertaking has been breached (*Chiltern DC
v Keane* [1985] 1 W.L.R. 619). An order which does not do so is irregular, and a
long line of cases laid down that this was fatal. However in *Linnett v Coles* [1987]
QB 555 the Court of Appeal, overruling the previous authorities, held that it had

the power to rectify a defective committal order and thus enable the committal to stand.

Not all defects will be corrected. The Court of Appeal stated in 1992 that its power to rectify defective committal orders is only to be used in the contempt jurisdiction in exceptional cases (*M v P (Contempt of Court: Committal Order)* [1993] Fam. 167). In *M v P* the court went on, however, to say that it has a complete discretion to exercise the power. It held that the fundamental requirements are that the alleged contemnor: is informed of the charges he had to meet; is advised and represented (or, presumably, is given the opportunity to be advised and represented); is given the opportunity to answer those charges; and, if found guilty, is informed in sufficiently clear terms of what has been found against him.

There has been a marked trend away from allowing technical objections to succeed. In *Nicholls v Nicholls* [1997] 1 W.L.R. 314, Sir Thomas Bingham MR observed that

> "the court must not only take into account the interests of the contemnor but also the interests of the other parties and the interests of upholding the reputation of civil justice in general. Today it is no longer appropriate to regard an order for committal as being no more than a form of execution available to another party against an alleged contemnor. The court itself has a very substantial interest in seeing that its orders are upheld. If committal orders are to be set aside on purely technical grounds which have nothing to do with the justice of the case, then this has the effect of undermining the system of justice and the credibility of court orders. While the procedural requirements in relation to applications to commit and committal orders are there to be obeyed and to protect the contemnor, if there is non-compliance with the requirements which does not prejudice the contemnor, to set aside the order purely on the grounds of technicality is contrary to the interests of justice. As long as the order made by the judge was a valid order, the approach of [the Court of Appeal] will be to uphold the order in the absence of any prejudice or injustice to the contemnor as a consequence of doing so."

9-26   The reported cases give some guidance as to which defects will be rectified and which will not. In *Linnett v Coles* [1987] QB 555, the defect which the Court of Appeal was prepared to correct was that the committal order was expressed to be "until further order". In *M v P*, an appeal from the High Court, the contemnor was present in court to hear the judge's decision and a copy of the committal order was served on his solicitors but not on him; the order was allowed to stand. In *Butler v Butler*, an appeal from the county court heard and reported together with *M v P*, the contemnor was not served with the order but had been present in court when it was made; he had a long record of breaching injunctions and the sentence was fully justified (so that an early application to purge his contempt would have failed). Again, the order was allowed to stand.

The general rule has been that where the defect is a failure to specify in the order for committal the breaches of injunction for which it is being imposed, the Court of Appeal will not rectify the order; people have a right to know why they are being sent to prison (*Linkleter v Linkleter* [1988] 1 F.L.R. 360; *Clarke v Clarke* [1990] 2 F.L.R. 115; *Smith v Smith (Contempt: Committal)* [1992] 2 F.L.R. 40). It is desirable that the order should specify the date on which the breach took place, but the omission of the date does not necessarily invalidate the order (*Burrows v Iqbal* (1985) 15 Fam. Law 188).

If justice requires the quashing of the committal order, one option available is to order a retrial (see *Duo v Osborne (formerly Duo)* [1992] 1 W.L.R. 611).

8 APPLICATIONS BY A PARTY IN CONTEMPT

A person committed to prison for contempt of court may apply to be discharged. **9-27** The procedure is set out in CPR r.81.31. There is no power to prohibit an application for discharge being made until a specified period has elapsed (*Vaughan v Vaughan* [1973] 1 W.L.R. 1159), nor to override the early release provisions contained in ss.33 and 45 of the Criminal Justice Act 1991 (*Thompson v Mitchell* [2004] EWCA Civ 1271, *The Times,* September 13, 2004). On the contemnor's application for discharge, the court must say either "yes" or "no"—it cannot suspend the unserved part of the sentence (*Harris v Harris* [2002] Fam. 253). *CJ v Flintshire CC* [2010] EWCA Civ 393 (see para.10-45) contains a useful summary of the questions which a court should ask when a contemnor applies for early release.

In *Smith v Doncaster MBC* [2014] EWCA Civ 16 Sir Stanley Burnton noted that an order for committal includes both a punitive and a coercive element, and that:

"Persistent failure to comply with an injunction after imposition of a sentence of committal aggravates the gravity of the defendant's conduct, and therefore will increase the weight to be given to the punitive element of the sentence."

The courts traditionally took the line that they would not hear an application to vary or discharge an injunction by a party in contempt of it until and unless he had purged his contempt (*Fakih Brothers v Moller (AP) (Copenhagen) Ltd* [1994] 1 Lloyd's Rep. 103; see also *Hadkinson v Hadkinson* [1952] P. 285; *X v Morgan-Grampian Publishers Ltd* 1 [1991] A.C. 1 at 46). However in *Pyke v National Westminster Bank, The Times,* December 10, 1977, Megarry VC said that:

"it was neither the law, nor ought it to be, that a person in contempt was an outlaw, unable to take proceedings in the courts until has purged his contempt, and liable until then to have any proceedings that he brought struck out."

In *Arab Monetary Fund v Hashim* [1997] EWCA Civ 1298, Lord Bingham of Cornhill CJ said:

"[It] is wrong to take as a starting point the proposition that the court will not hear a party in contempt and then to ask if the instant case falls within an exception to that general rule. It is preferable to ask whether, in the circumstances of an individual case, the interests of justice are best served by hearing a party in contempt or by refusing to do so, always bearing in mind the paramount importance which the court must attach to the prompt and unquestioning observance of court orders."

In *Motorola Credit Corp v Uzan* [2004] 1 W.L.R. 113, for example, the Court of Appeal heard an appeal by defendants who had been imprisoned for contempt in failing to comply with an order for disclosure ancillary to a freezing injunction. The court held that "the circumstances will be rare indeed" in which a contemnor can properly be shut out from appealing or seeking to appeal in due time. A similar approach was taken in *Raja v van Hoogstraten* [2004] 4 All E.R. 793 and in *JSC BTA Bank v Ablyazov* [2012] EWCA Civ 639, in which Moore-Bick LJ held that it is not ordinarily appropriate to require security for the costs of an appeal or impose other conditions on an appeal when the liberty of the subject is in issue. The current attitude of the courts is clearly in favour of allowing contemnors to be heard. As Laddie J asked, rhetorically but pertinently, in *Re Swaptronics Ltd, The Times,* August 17, 1998: "[I]f a persistent and serious criminal is allowed to litigate, why should a party in contempt of court be prevented from doing so?"

9   DECLARATION THAT ACT WOULD NOT BREACH INJUNCTION

9-28   The rule (see para.9-01) that having acted on legal advice is not a defence to a committal application causes problems in practice. Suppose that a defendant against whom an injunction has been granted believes, and is advised, that a particular course would be lawful; the claimant, however, claims that it would be unlawful and threatens contempt proceedings. In *R. v British Coal Corp Ex p. Price (No.3)*, *The Times*, May 28, 1993, an injunction had been granted prohibiting British Coal from reaching a final decision to close any of 10 named pits until a particular procedure had been followed. On a subsequent application by British Coal, the court granted a declaration that the procedure had been followed and that the company would not be in breach of the earlier injunction by proceeding to close the pits. This is a sensible form of remedy in appropriate cases and is in keeping with the observation by Staughton LJ in *Channel Tunnel Group Ltd v Balfour Beatty Construction Ltd* [1992] QB 656 (cited at para.5-34) that "commercial concerns have ready access to lawyers, and are well able to apply to the court if they are in doubt as to what they must or must not do". Another example of the power being used was to grant a declaration that a particular transaction by which a contemnor was seeking to purge a contempt would not be a further breach of a freezing order (*Re AB* [2010] EWCA Civ 533). The courts are not legal advice bureaux, however, and retain the discretion to refuse to decide such applications.

10   APPEALS

9-29   In contempt cases where an order for committal has been made, there is one appeal from that order as of right pursuant to the Administration of Justice Act 1960 s.13(2)(a) and CPR r.53.2(1)(a)(i). For these purposes, a suspended committal order is treated as an order for committal (*Wilkinson v S* [2003] 1 W.L.R. 1254). Either party may appeal as of right against an order or suspended order for committal; the right of appeal is not limited to the contemnor (*Lomas v Parle* [2004] 1 WLR 1642; *Wood v Collins* [2006] EWCA Civ 743, *The Times*, June 26, 2006). However on an appeal by the complainant, the Court of Appeal will only interfere in exceptional cases, where the decision below was plainly wrong (*Wilson v Webster* [1998] 1 F.L.R. 1097); there is an analogy with the approach of the Criminal Division of the Court of Appeal in cases of "unduly lenient" sentences (*Neil v Ryan* [1998] 2 F.L.R. 1068; see para.10-46). Ward LJ has expressed the view that such appeals should be exceptional and are to be discouraged (*M v M (Breaches of Orders: Committals)* [2006] 1 F.L.R. 1154).

In the civil case of *JSC BTA Bank v Ereshchenko* [2013] EWCA Civ 829 Lloyd LJ noted at [38] that an appeal against a judge's refusal to commit for contempt is legally possible, with permission, but that reported examples of such appeals are rare.

9-30   The circumstances would be rare where it would be right to prevent a contemnor from arguing an appeal against an order for committal (*Motorola Credit Corpn v Uzan (No.2)* [2004] 1 W.L.R. 113. However, a court might be justified in declining to hear a contemnor who not only wilfully refused to comply with an order but also made it clear that he would continue to defy the court's authority if the order was affirmed on appeal (*JSC BTA Bank v Ablyazov* [2012] EWCA Civ 639).

An appeal against any order other than for immediate or suspended committal requires permission, including an appeal by a corporate defendant against a financial penalty for contempt (*Masri v Consolidated Contractors International Co SARL* [2012] 1 W.L.R. 223).

The Court of Appeal held in *Barnet LBC v Hurst* [2003] 1 W.L.R. 722 that if a district judge has made an order for committal and the circuit judge has affirmed it, a further appeal requires permission, but if committal was ordered for the first time by a circuit judge, even on appeal, an appeal to the Court of Appeal lies as of right. The case is a good illustration of the complexities of the rules about permission to appeal.

There is a broad discretion to admit fresh evidence from the contemnor on an appeal, even where the usual criteria for the admission of such evidence are not satisfied (*Iretlli v Squatriti* [1993] QB 83, CA).

PART C: MATRIMONIAL AND DOMESTIC PROCEEDINGS

CHAPTER 10

Family Injunctions and Protective Orders

1 INTRODUCTION

The injunction is a particularly important remedy in the area of family and **10-01** domestic relations. The urgent nature of a crisis in a family dispute often requires an immediate decision of the court without a substantive trial on the merits. In the two instances of domestic violence and issues concerning the welfare of children, the criteria for the grant of interim injunctions described in Ch.3 (preservation of the status quo, adequacy of damages, balance of convenience) will be inapplicable. In violence cases, the court will be concerned to prevent a recurrence of the violence; in cases involving children, their welfare will be the principal concern.

Part IV of the Family Law Act 1996 (the 1996 Act) governs all applications made for protective orders against domestic violence and provides a single comprehensive code applicable in all courts dealing with work of this type. It was extended to include civil partners by amendments under the Civil Partnership Act 2004. Where the 1996 Act does not apply, the Protection from Harassment Act 1997 may well provide remedies for those cases that cannot be brought within the 1996 Act.

On 22 April 2014, the single Family Court came into existence. Apart from those aspects of family jurisdiction reserved to the Family Division of the High Court, all family work is heard in the Family Court. The judiciary within the Family Court comprises judges of the High Court, circuit judges, district judges and district judges (Magistrates Court) and lay judges (the justices of the former Family Proceedings Court). The reform has become a reality 40 years after the idea was put forward in the report of the Finer Commission. There are new Allocation Rules and separate guidance on the exercise of allocation powers as between levels of judiciary within the Family Court.

The relevant legislation does not contain a definition of the term "domestic **10-02** violence". In *Yemshaw v Hounslow LBC* [2011] UKSC 3, Baroness Hale discussed the scope of the term in the context of the homelessness legislation and commented that "the understanding of domestic violence has moved on from a narrow focus upon battered wives and physical contact". She referred to the Home Office document *Domestic Violence: A National Report*, which defined the term in the following way:

> "Any incident of threatening behaviour, violence or abuse (psychological, physical, sexual, financial or emotional) between adults who are or have been intimate partners or family members regardless of gender or sexuality,"

and to the definition in the *President's Practice Direction: Residence and Contact Orders: Domestic Violence and Harm* [2009] 2 F.L.R. 1400:

""Domestic violence" includes physical violence, threatening or intimidating behaviour and any other form of abuse which, directly or indirectly, may have given rise to the risk of harm."

The Legal Aid, Sentencing and Punishment of Offenders Act 2012 (LASPO) has its own definition of domestic violence to identify eligibility for legal aid in family cases at para.12(9) Sch.1:

"...any incident of threatening behaviour, violence of abuse (whether psychological, physical, sexual financial or emotional) between individuals who are associated with each other."

The Family Procedure Rules 2010 Practice Directions 12B and 12J paragraph 3 contain a comprehensive definition of domestic abuse which has been expanded in the revised Practice Direction 12J effective from 2 October 2017. The scope of the conduct with which the court deals in applications for protective orders is very wide and concerns all aspects of the personal relationship between the parties to the application. The restrictions in eligibility for the grant of legal aid had an effect on the number of cases issued since the purpose was to limit public funding to those cases that could not be dealt with by any other means than an application to the court and genuinely required the intervention of the court.

Under s.5 of the Protection from Harassment Act 1997 the criminal courts can make a restraining order on a conviction or an acquittal of any offence on or after September 30, 2009 and the power is no longer limited to offences under the 1997 Act itself. This offers another source of protective orders in cases of domestic violence.

10-03   Although changes to the law relating to bad character and hearsay in criminal proceedings allow a wider range of evidence to be considered in a criminal prosecution for domestic violence, there are likely to continue to be cases in which evidence which would be considered by a civil court in a 1996 Act application would be inadmissible in a criminal prosecution.

The Forced Marriage (Civil Protection) Act 2007 came into force on November 25, 2008 and introduced Pt IVA and ss.63A–63S into the 1996 Act. This permits the nominated Family Courts and in cases with an international element, the High Court, to make a forced marriage protection order for the purpose of protecting a person from being forced into a marriage against their will, or from any attempt to do so or for the protection of a person who has been forced into such a marriage. The court is given wide powers against third parties and in respect of acts out of the jurisdiction.

The Female Genital Mutilation Act 2003 was amended by s.73 of the Serious Crime Act 2015 to create a new protective remedy called a Female Genital Mutilation Protection Order which can be made by a court to protect a girl who has either been a victim of female genital mutilation or is at risk of it. The provisions came into force on 17 July 2015. The jurisdiction is limited to nominated courts and the Act and schedule confer wide powers to make orders against third parties.

The Court of Appeal indicated in two decisions in 2009, *Re P-B (Contact: Committal)* [2009] EWCA Civ 143 and *Re S (Eligible Child)* [2008] EWCA Civ 1140, that the committal jurisdiction may be available against a local authority which breaches orders of the court made in public law proceedings under the Children Act 1989.

10-04   Over the last 15 years, the courts have developed an increased awareness of the relevance of domestic violence to other issues arising within the family, including in particular disputed issues of contact between parent (usually the father) and child where there are allegations of domestic violence between the parents. These issues were considered at length in the judgment of the Court of Appeal in *Re L, V, M and H (Domestic Violence)* [2000] 2 F.L.R. 334, and guidance was given as to how cases involving such allegations ought to be dealt with by the court, including the requirement that allegations of domestic violence which might have an effect on the outcome of the application for contact must be adjudicated on and found proved or not proved. In *Re H (Contact: Domestic Violence)* [2005] EWCA Civ 1404; [2005] 1 F.L.R. 943, the court emphasised the importance of findings of domestic violence in the context of parental contact to children. The revised Practice Direction 12J Family Procedure Rules 2010 is the most recent guidance in this area and provides guidance on the need for a fact-finding hearing in child arrangement order applications under s.8 Children Act 1989 (previously contact and residence orders) where it is likely to be relevant to the court's decision. The term "domestic violence" is replaced by "domestic abuse" and culturally specific forms of domestic abuse form part of the definition.

Practice Direction 12L makes clear the need for safeguarding checks and a risk assessment under s.16A of the 1989 Act to be carried by CAFCASS and CAFCASS CYMRU prior to the court considering the application. One of the purposes is to identify if there is any information of concern known to the police or the local authority about the parents of the children. This would include any reported history of domestic abuse. Where present, this would make a case unsuitable for mediation or a MIAM (Mediation Information and Assessment Meeting) which is otherwise a compulsory first step before a Child Arrangement Order application can be made.

Section 31(9) of the Children Act 1989 includes as part of the definition of harm "impairment suffered from seeing or hearing the ill-treatment of another". This wording will cover cases in which it is alleged that there has been violence within the family home to a parent or carer or any other member of the household, including a child. It is now part of paragraph 3 of the revised Practice Direction 12J and adds emphasis to the need to evaluate the overall impact of domestic abuse on the welfare and well-being of the children in a family. Therefore, when dealing with an application for a domestic injunction, it will be important to consider the impact of decisions made at that stage in any further proceedings involving children which will include possible future care proceedings. In *Re J-C (Committal Proceedings)* [2007] EWCA Civ 896, the court held that the fact that the findings of the judge in a committal hearing might be ventilated in later care proceedings relating to the parties' daughter was irrelevant to the course of the committal hearing or its outcome.

Part 3A Family Procedure Rules 2010 gives specific guidance on the participation by vulnerable parties and witnesses in family proceedings. The guidance applies also to protected parties. It is relevant to all applications for protective orders in family proceedings and is not confined to issues of domestic abuse only. The court is under a duty to consider the vulnerability of a party or witness and how the witness's participation or the quality of their evidence may be diminished by reason of their vulnerability. There is a positive duty to consider whether to make one or more participation directions and to consider the wishes of the party or witness about their participation in the proceedings.

10-05

Rule 3A.7 sets out the factors which the court must consider when deciding whether to make one or more participation directions:

- The impact of any actual or perceived intimidation including any behaviour towards the party or witness by any other party, witness or family members

or associates of the other party or witness or on the part of any members of
the family of the party or witness.

- Any mental or physical disorder or physical disability or any significant
  impairment of intelligence or social functioning or any medical treatment
  that the individual might be receiving.
- The nature and extent of the information before the court which could
  include an assessment of the party or witness and their ability to give
  evidence.
- The issues in the proceedings including but not limited to any concerns aris-
  ing in relation to abuse.
- Whether a matter is contentious.
- The age, maturity and understanding of the party or witness.
- The social and cultural background and ethnic origin of the party or witness.
- The domestic circumstances and religious beliefs of the party or witness.
- Whether questioning will be undertaken by the court under s.31G(6) of the
  Matrimonial and Family Proceedings Act 1984.
- Any characteristic of the party or witness which may be relevant.
- The measures available to the court and their cost.

Rule 3A.8 sets out the measures available which in practice will mean a remote
live link, the use of screens in the courtroom, an intermediary to assist with
participation and questioning, and a communication device. However, the court cannot use public funds to provide a measure, save possibly the costs of the intermediary to assist with questioning which can be funded by HMCTS. If a necessary
measure is not available the court must set out the reasons for it in the order.

Practice Direction 3AA provides additional information in the application of the
rule. Paragraph 2.1 gives an extended definition of abuse to be used in applying
Rule 3.7(d). It includes domestic, sexual physical and emotional abuse; racial and
/or cultural abuse or discrimination; forced marriage and so called honour-based
violence; female genital or other physical mutilation; abuse based on gender or
sexual orientation; and human trafficking. Paragraph 3.1 requires the court to
consider with the assistance of the relevant parties the ability of the party or witness to understand the proceedings and their role in them when in court; to put their
view to the court; to instruct their representative/s before during and after the hearing; and to attend the hearing without significant distress.

The court's powers include giving directions about the scheduling of the party's
or witness's evidence; holding a grounds rules hearing about the extent and nature
of the questioning including the questions that will be asked and by whom; and the
use of any evidence given in criminal proceedings about the same subject matter
which will cover any pre-recorded cross examination and unused recorded evidence
from family and criminal proceedings.

Where public funding is not available to the party against whom the allegations
are made, it is inappropriate for that party to cross examine the alleged victim in
person. In *K and H (Private Law: Funding)* [2015] EWCA Civ 543 the Court of
Appeal decided that the court had to respect the boundaries drawn by Parliament
for public funding of legal representation and it was not possible for an order to be
made that HMCTS should fund legal representation for the purposes of cross
examination. The court should use the extent of its case management powers which
included questioning by the judge in a simple straightforward case. The judge would
know what the party's case was and the unrepresented party could be asked to
prepare questions for the court to consider in advance.

However, it was recognised that there would be cases where questioning by the
judge would not be appropriate. This included complicated oral evidence or

complex medical or other expert evidence. A further category could be complex and/or confused evidence from a vulnerable witness. It was possible that in the above instances that no steps could be taken by the court to make up for the absence of legal representation in which case the conclusion could be that the lack of legal representation resulted in the proceedings not being conducted in compliance with Article 6 and Article 8 of the European Convention. Lord Dyson MR giving the judgment of the court suggested that consideration should be given to a statutory provision allowing for the use of public funds where reasonably necessary to cover the cost of a legal representative to conduct the cross examination to avoid breaches of the European Convention. Such a provision would be analogous to s.38(4) of the Youth Justice and Criminal Evidence Act 1999 and s.19(3) of the Prosecution of Offences Act 1985 in relation to sexual offences in criminal proceedings.

The issue of how a vulnerable party will be cross examined by an alleged abuser is a matter within the scope of Part 3A Family Procedure Rules 2010 and the above guidance will need to be carefully considered. Although there has been general acceptance of the need for a statutory provision as outlined by Lord Dyson MR it has not yet made its way to the statute book for implementation in the foreseeable future.

In addition to the precedents provided in this book, Standard Family Orders which were approved by the President of the Family Division Sir James Munby in June 2018 are available in hard copy and electronically from Class Legal. The range of orders available covers Forced Marriage and Female Genital Mutilations Orders. Where amendments have been made to existing precedents the guidance from Standard Family Orders Handbook and the work of its authors is acknowledged.

Legal aid

The legal aid scheme is administered by the Legal Aid Agency under the overall **10-06** responsibility of the Ministry of Justice. The scope of legal aid has been reduced in private family law cases following the Legal Aid, Sentencing and Punishment of Offenders Act 2012 (LASPO) coming into force on 1 April 2013 and is limited to those cases in which there is evidence of domestic violence and in children cases where there is evidence of child protection risks. It is also preserved in domestic violence injunction cases.

Section 9 and Schedule 1 of LASPO define the scope of eligilibty for legal aid. There are three principal sets of Regulations which should be referred to for detailed guidance: the Civil Legal Aid (Procedure) Regulations 2012, the Civil Legal Aid (Merits Criteria) Regulations 2013 and the Civil Legal Aid (Financial Resources and Payment for Services) Regulations 2013.

The Civil Legal Aid (Procedure)(Amendment)(No 2) Regulations 2017 introduced important changes to the previous limitations on the type of supporting evidence and the age of the allegations that would be accepted as part of an application for civil legal aid. In response to the decision of the Court of Appeal in The *Queen (on the Application of Rights of Women) v The Lord Chancellor and Secretary of State for Justice* [2016] EWCA Civ 91 that the scope of acceptable evidence was too restricted and the requirement that the events relied upon must have happened within two years of the date of the application for legal aid excluded many potential applicants who could be at risk, the Regulations were amended to enlarge the scope of acceptable supporting evidence and the period of two years was extended to five years under the Civil Legal Aid (Procedure)(Amendment) Regulations 2016.

In 2017 the Ministry of Justice undertook research investigating the domestic violence evidential requirements for legal aid in private family disputes. The result of the Research Paper finding was the 2017 Regulations which came into effect on 8 January 2018. The important changes are the broadening of existing categories of evidence; new forms of evidence; the time limit of five years is removed altogether; and evidence relating to abuse of previous partners or other family members is accepted. Further, the list of protective injunctions is replaced by a definition which refers to their purpose or effect. Regulation 42 allows legal aid to be withdrawn if a without notice order is later set aside by the court or if a public authority has written to confirm that the applicant was neither at risk nor a victim of domestic violence.

The Lord Chancellor has provided Written Guidance dated June 2014 on the exercise of powers under the Act and Regulations. The Written Guidance has been updated to reflect the changes introduced under the 2017 Regulations. In the first quarter of 2018 applications for civil representation supported by evidence of domestic or child abuse had risen by 21% and there had been a 14% increase in those granted compared with the same period last year. Unsurprisingly the Legal Aid Agency consider this is as a result of the changes.

There are four types of legal assistance which are available in domestic violence and private law family cases:

(i)   family help (lower) which can be utilised for negotiation prior to the issue of proceedings and for the issue of proceedings to obtain a consent order following settlement;

(ii)   family help (higher) which includes those services available under legal representation other than preparation for and representation at a final hearing;

(iii)   family mediation and help with family mediation;

(iv)   full representation which is available to a party to proceedings, someone who wishes to apply to become a party or is thinking about the issue of proceedings; it is not available to a potential respondent.

Full representation includes advocacy and representation at court. Family help does not permit assistance to obtain any of the forms of evidence set out in regs 33 and 34 of the Civil Legal Aid (Procedure) Regulations 2012 which are the requirements for eligibility for civil legal aid under LASPO Schedule 1. Templates of draft letters to obtain evidence requirements from third party professionals and agencies which have been designed by MoJ are available on the LAA website.

10-07   The merits criteria for the determination for full representation in cases of domestic violence are set out in reg.64 and 67 of the 2013 Regulations. The prospects of success must be very good, good, moderate or borderline and the proportionality test must be met. Regulation 5(1) (a)-(d) defines each of the terms: "very good" means an 80 per cent chance of achieving a successful outcome ; "good" means between a 60-79 per cent chance of a successful outcome; "moderate" means a 50-59 per cent chance; "borderline" means that it is not possible to categorise the chance of a successful outcome as 50 per cent or more or as poor (i.e. a successful outcome is unlikely) because of disputed law, fact or expert evidence. The proportionality test is defined in reg.8 and the likely benefits to the individual and others should justify the likely costs having regard to the prospects of success and all the other circumstances of the case. "Likely costs" is further defined under reg.10.

The Lord Chancellor's Guidance explains at para.10.27 that the prospects of success are likely to be poor if the incidents complained of are of a trivial nature unless there is a history of incidents in which case the cumulative effect of the incidents may be taken into account. A further illustration is that the conduct complained of is not likely to be repeated and there is a suggested more than three week cut off point before the application for legal aid unless there is a history of violent conduct.

Further guidance appears at para.10.29 that conduct amounting to a criminal offence should be notified to the police for possible charges and a grant of legal representation may only be appropriate if there is good reason not to pursue criminal proceedings because of its financial or other impact on the family or there is reason to believe the police will not be able assist or provide adequate assistance.

A respondent is required to demonstrate that the allegations are very serious, or plausibly denied wholly or substantially if funding is to be granted. If an undertaking is likely to be the outcome because the allegations are not serious or are substantially admitted, funding will be refused and legal help under reg.20 will be more appropriate. There is an exception in cases of mental incapacity or age on the part of the respondent. In relation to the proportionality test the impact on the client of the order sought will be taken into account including any impact on contact or other related family proceedings: Lord Chancellor's Guidance at paras 10.31 and 10.32.

In the case of an application for an occupation order, if the respondent has left **10-08** the property voluntarily and is unlikely to return, funding is likely to be refused. The clearest case will be where the applicant is in a refuge or other temporary accommodation having been recently excluded from the property or where there is a significant risk if the applicant were to return without an order. A respondent who is out of the property and has no good reason to return is unlikely to be funded unless there are other relevant issues in the proceedings which will have a significant impact on child arrangement order proceedings.

In relation to enforcement proceedings, the existence or availability of criminal proceedings is a factor in the grant of legal aid, as is the seriousness of the allegations of breach and the likelihood of obtaining a further order. It may be necessary to justify why a warning letter will not be sufficient to deter further breaches and to provide the reasons why the police have declined to become involved.

In committal proceedings the likelihood of loss of liberty is relevant and would usually be sufficient to meet the proportionality test: Lord Chancellor's Guidance para.10.36. However, in *Brown v London Borough of Haringey* [2017] 1 WLR 542 the court considered the availability of legal aid in committal proceedings and reached the conclusion that the Court of Appeal, the High Court and the Crown Court had powers which enabled a judge to grant legal aid but the powers did not extend to the Family Court. In cases before the Family Court the grant of legal aid for committal proceedings was the exclusive preserve of the Legal Aid Agency. A detailed analysis of the scheme is to be found in *Kings Lynn and West Norfolk Council v Bunning (Legal Aid Agency: Interested Party)* [2015] 1 WLR 531.

Regulation 2 of the Civil Legal Aid (Merits Criteria) Regulations 2013 defines the term "family dispute" by reference to specified paragraphs of Pt 1 of Sch.1 of LASPO.

Financial eligibility also affects the grant of legal aid. The Regulations identify certain income based benefits which will satisfy the means criteria. There is no entitlement if gross monthly income exceeds £2657. An income contribution will be expected if the applicant has £316 per month or more disposable income. A sum in excess of £8000 disposable capital is a bar to funding and a contribution is required if capital is between £3000 and £8000. The capital test applies to all applications whether or not the applicant is in receipt of income based benefits. The

Regulations permit a waiver of eligibility in the case of injunction or committal proceedings where it is equitable to do so.

2   JURISDICTION UNDER THE FAMILY LAW ACT 1996

Jurisdiction

10-09   This jurisdiction is part of the single Family Court since 22 April 2014. The 1996 Act gives all courts the power to make non-molestation and occupation orders. Allocation between the tiers of judiciary in the Family Court is governed by the Family Court (Composition and Distribution of Business) Rules 2014. Schedule 2 of the Rules identifies the remedies which may not be granted by lay judges.

The Act permits non-molestation orders and occupation orders to be granted on free-standing applications as well as in other family proceedings: see s.42(2). In *Re T (A Child)* [2017] EWCA Civ 1889 it was held that a non-molestation order could be made in proceedings under the inherent jurisdiction concerning a child who was subject already to a a care order even though a power of arrest could not be attached to an injunction under the inherent jurisdiction. The court was not persuaded that the criminal sanction under section 42A(1) made it inappropriate to use the jurisdiction under the 1996 Act.

The prescribed forms of application and for orders granted are unchanged under the FPR 2010—Forms FL401–417. Separate orders must be issued for non-molestation orders and occupation orders. The forms are Forms FL404a and FL404 respectively.

The hearing will usually take place in private but if the court grants a non-molestation order or an occupation order with a power of arrest attached and the person to whom it is addressed was not present and was not given notice of the hearing (a without notice application) the terms of the order and the name of the person to whom it is addressed shall be announced in open court at the earliest opportunity which may be on the next day that the court is hearing cases in open court if there is no further open court business on the day on which the order is made: Practice Direction 10A Family Procedure Rules 2010.

The earlier legislation which was repealed by the 1996 Act included the Domestic Violence and Matrimonial Proceedings Act 1976, the Matrimonial Homes Act 1983 and ss.16–18 of the Domestic Proceedings and Magistrates' Courts Act 1978.

Immediate and short-term protection from domestic abuse can be obtained under the Crime and Security Act 2010 other than through an application for an injunction. A Domestic Violence Protection Notice (DVPN) can be issued to an individual aged 18 years or older where an authorising police officer not below the rank of superintendent has reasonable grounds for believing that they have been violent or have threatened violence to an associated person and the issue of a DVPN is necessary to protect that associated person from violence or the threat of violence from that individual. "Associated person" has the same definition as in s.62 of the Family Law Act 1996: see para.10-10, below. The officer must consider the welfare of any person under the age of 18 whose interests may be relevant; the opinion of the person for whose benefit the notice is being issued; and any representations made by the person against whom the notice is issued. The DVPN must contain a provision prohibiting molestation and, where the parties live in the same address exclusion from the property, a distance restriction and a prohibition from entering the property. It must be in writing and personally served by an officer on the person the subject of the notice. Breach of the notice is an arrestable matter which is dealt with by the magistrates within 24 hours of the arrest.

If a DVPN is issued, an application by complaint for a Domestic Violence Protection Order must be made to the magistrates' court and should be heard not less than 48 hours after the DVPN was issued. The grounds for granting an order are the same as for a DPVN and include the opinion of any other associated person who lives in the premises to which the order would relate. The standard of proof is the balance of probabilities. A DVPO must last for at least 14 days and not more than 28 days from the date on which the order was made.

Injunctions against molestation

A person may apply for a non-molestation injunction if he or she is included in the category of "associated persons" established by s.62(3). Amendments were made to this category by s.82 of the Civil Partnership Act 2004 and by s.4 of the Domestic Violence, Crime and Victims Act 2004. This category includes:

10-10

(a)   a spouse or ex-spouse; a civil partner or former civil partner;
(b)   cohabitants or former cohabitants; the definition is extended to include two persons who are living together as if they were civil partners;
(c)   those who live or have lived in the same household otherwise than by reason of being an employee, tenant, lodger or boarder; relatives (limited by s.63(1)); those who have agreed to marry or have entered into a civil partnership agreement (see ss.33, 42 and 44);
(d)   in relation to a child, a parent or a person who has parental responsibility for the child;
(e)   those who are parties to the same family proceedings (other than under Pt IV of the Act);
(f)   persons connected through adoption proceedings (s.62(5)) where the child has been adopted, can be placed under s.19 of the Adoption and Children Act 2002 or is the subject of a placement order application;
(g)   persons who have or have had an intimate personal relationship which is or was of significant duration (amendment by the Domestic Violence, Crime and Victims Act 2004).

Historically, the courts have adopted a purposive approach to the construction of the Act in the interpretation of the provisions conferring jurisdiction so that borderline cases where there is a need for protection are not excluded: see for example *G v G (Non-Molestation Order: Jurisdiction)* [2000] 2 F.L.R. 533, in which a man and woman were held to be "associated" persons within the meaning of s.62 as former cohabitants where the evidence from the woman was that they used to spend four to five nights per week together, were engaged in a sexual relationship and operated a joint bank account.

The amendment to include as "associated persons" those who have or have had an intimate personal relationship of significant duration removed the need to overinterpret the definition of cohabitant, and will reduce the number of cases not covered by the Act to those in which there is no intimate relationship or one brief in nature. Such cases will continue to fall outside the scope of the Act and will still be governed by an action for an injunction in a tort claim or under the Protection from Harassment Act 1997.

Under s.62(6) a body corporate and another person cannot be regarded as associated with each other for the purposes of subs.3(f) and (g). This excludes a local authority from applying for a non-molestation order under the Act even though it may hold parental responsibility under either an interim or final care order or is a party to proceedings involving the other person. This does not prevent the court using its powers under s.42(2) to make an order in care proceedings for the protec-

10-11

tion of another party to those proceedings other than the local authority or a relevant child. However the local authority cannot apply to extend the order on behalf of the party who is intended to be protected. An application for a non-molestation order can be made either as a free-standing application or in family proceedings (s.42), which are defined in s.63. The court has the power to act of its own motion. A child under 16 can apply with leave of the court if the child has sufficient understanding. Family Court (Composition and Distribution of Business) Rules 2014, rules 16(3)(xii) and (5), provide that a without notice application made by an applicant under 18 years shall not be heard by lay justices. An order can be made for the benefit of any party to the proceedings or any relevant child. A relevant child is defined by s.62(2) of the Act as a child living with or who might reasonably be expected to live with either party, whose welfare is being considered in Children Act or Adoption Act proceedings or whose interests the court considers relevant.

In deciding to make an order, the court must consider all the circumstances, including the need to secure the health, safety and well-being of the applicant and any relevant child. The categories of applicants and criteria mean that for instance in the case of former cohabitants,there is no requirement for the incident giving rise to the application to have occurred before cohabitation ceased.

10-12   The order may be expressed in terms of molestation in general or by reference to particular acts or both. The Act does not contain a definition of molestation, but the old law is likely to be a reliable guide where a definition is needed; *Vaughan v Vaughan* [1973] 1 W.L.R. 1159 established that whether communication amounts to molestation is a question of fact and degree, and that a good synonym for "molest" is "pester". The Law Commission expressed the following view in its report *Domestic Violence and Occupation of the Family Home*:

> "Molestation includes, but is wider than, violence. It encompasses any form of serious pestering or harassment and applies to any conduct which could properly be regarded as such a degree of harassment as to call for the intervention of the court."

It includes handing menacing letters to the applicant and intercepting her on her way to work (*Horner v Horner* [1982] Fam. 90) and sending partially nude photographs to a national newspaper for publication with the intent of causing the victim distress (*Johnson v Walton* [1990] 1 F.L.R. 350). However, in *C v C* [1998] 1 F.L.R. 554, an application on behalf of a husband for an injunction restraining his wife from publishing any account of the personal or financial side of the marriage failed because such conduct was held not to be within the concept of molestation covered by s.42 of the Act. Threatening or abusive material posted on social networking sites is likely to be a fertile area for applications

In *Re T* (above) the Court of Appeal advised that the Family Court had to apply "good sense and judgement" in determining whether or not particular conduct amounts to molestation and declined to offer any further precision in the definition. However, McFarlane LJ accepted that intention was not a necessary element in molestation. It was sufficient if the conduct was deliberate and it had the consequence of causing or being likely to cause distress or harassment to the child.

It was made clear in *R v R* [2014] EWFC 48 [2015] 1 W.L.R. 2743 that an order to vacate a property is properly an occupation order and thus a provision that the Respondent is excluded from the road in which he lives cannot be included in a non-molestation order. However, if a party has already left the property an order to stay away, with or without an exclusion area, can be included in a non-molestation order and does not require an occupation order. Exclusion areas and orders prohibiting any direct communication between the parties should only be included where there is specific evidence to justify them and not routinely. The case is an interesting narrative of how things can go badly wrong if the correct procedures are not followed by the court.

The practice under the 1996 Act has been to set out the types of behaviour prohibited under the order. In the interests of clarity, this is the preferred course and would be consistent with guidance from the Court of Appeal in relation to "ASBOs": *R. v Shane Tony P* [2004] EWCA Crim 287; *R. v Boness* [2005] EWCA Crim 2395. This may be of particular benefit if the issue of prosecution for the offence of breach is being considered, as it is easier to prove a specific act than to ask a jury to decide whether certain conduct was molestation. In a prosecution under the Protection from Harassment Act 1997, a jury would have to decide what constituted "harassment" for the purposes of an offence under s.4 of that Act.

The order can be made for a specified period or until further order. Research findings from a joint Home Office and Scottish Office study suggested that there was a high proportion of male respondents who were the subject of court sanction and who committed a further violent act within three months of the first incident. This suggests that an initial period of six months may provide better protection for the applicant and should be the normal duration of the order. Permanent orders can be made and are not to be confined to "exceptional" or "unusual" cases but should be determined by the needs of the individual case. If an order is made in family proceedings, it will cease to have effect if those proceedings are withdrawn or dismissed.

The general practice in applications for a non-molestation order without notice **10-13** was to make an order for a period appropriate to a "final" order and fixing a return date when the question of discharge and/or variation could be argued by the respondent; however, the applicant remained protected by the order throughout the proceedings without the need to renew it if the return day hearing had to be adjourned because the application was contested. If there was a short return period for a without notice order, the first order made should have been to a date beyond the date fixed for the on notice hearing to prevent the order lapsing before the court was in a position to extend or renew it. This ensured the protection of the applicant during the hearing process.

The President's Practice Guidance dated 13 October 2014 has been superseded by revised Practice Guidance dated 18 January 2017 which fixes the parameters for the duration of without notice orders.

- Unlimited time orders should never be made in the Family Court or in the Family Division in any type of proceedings although the Guidance does not affect the principles and safeguards to be observed in without notice freezing or search orders.
- The order must specify when it is to expire and it is not sufficient to provide a return day only.
- A return day must be specified not more than 14 days after the date on which the without notice order was made. The time estimate for the return day is in the discretion of the judge and can be for a short hearing if the nature of the case justifies it.
- A non-molestation order can be made for longer than 14 days and for a period of 6 or up to 12 months when needed for the personal protection of the Applicant.
- The duration of the order should be relevant to the nature of the harm and should be for such time as will allow the problem to be addressed. Long term abuse or particular circumstances may justify longer than 6 months.
- The order must specify if it was made in the absence of the Respondent and should record if it was made only on the evidence of the Applicant and that

no findings of fact were made. Any written evidence considered must be identified in the order and whether any oral or photographic evidence was taken into account in making the order should be recorded on the face of the order or reduced to writing and served on the Respondent with the order.

- In a Part IV 1996 Act order the court must recite that the criteria for making a without notice order has been considered i.e. sections 45(1) and (2) of the Act.

- The order must spell out the entitlement of the Respondent to apply to set aside or to vary the order before the return day. The inclusion of "Liberty to Apply" is not enough and is specifically disapproved. Any application to set aside or vary should be listed within a few days of being made.

- If the Respondent does not attend on the return day and the original without notice order has specified a duration beyond the return day and has been served on the Respondent re-service of the order is not necessary, but the order from the return day hearing should record that the Respondent did not attend despite having had the opportunity to do so.

- Any variation in the terms of the order to be applied for at the return day hearing must be notified before this hearing in the application or in the order and if this is not done there must be a new return day and the new order must be served on the Respondent.

- Without notice orders are only appropriate if there is great urgency or an emergency so that short or informal notice is not possible or that the purpose of the order will be defeated if notice is given.

Undertakings can be accepted from any party to proceedings where the court has the power to make a non-molestation order, but the court shall not accept an undertaking in any case where the respondent has used or threatened violence against the applicant or a relevant child and it is necessary to make a non-molestation order for the protection of the applicant or child so that any breach may be punishable under s.42A: s.46(3A). The undertaking is enforceable as if the court had made an order in the same terms as the undertaking: s.46(4).

In the 1980s and 1990s, undertakings were accepted in a high proportion of domestic violence cases, but the prevailing view has changed. If there is a prima facie case of significant violence, an injunction is generally considered preferable. However, if the case is not serious and the applicant is content to accept an undertaking, the court is likely to be guided by what the applicant wants and the parties have agreed. The undertaking must be recorded in full in Form N117; it must be signed by the party who is to be bound by the undertaking; the terms of the undertaking and the consequences of breaching the undertaking must be explained to that party.

10-14   The making of a non-molestation order is a discretionary remedy under s.42. The court is required to have regard to all the circumstances of the case including the need to secure the health, safety and well-being of the applicant and of any relevant child: s.42(5). There must be evidence which amounts to molestation; a need for continuing protection; and a need for judicial intervention through the making of an order.

A non-molestation order may be made (s.42(3)) in proceedings for an emergency protection order where the court has included an exclusion requirement under s.44A of the Children Act 1989. In these circumstances, a suspected abuser can be excluded from the home and a non-molestation order granted to protect the child concerned and/or any individuals who are parties to the proceedings.

The court is placed under a mandatory obligation to consider the making of a non-molestation order when considering whether to make an occupation order:

s.42(4A), an amendment introduced by the Domestic Violence, Crime and Victims Act 2004.

Section 45 allows orders to be made without notice to the respondent. In deciding whether to make such an order, the court takes into account all the circumstances including: **10-15**

(a) whether there is any risk of significant harm to the applicant or a relevant child if the order is not made;

(b) whether the applicant will be deterred or prevented from pursuing the application if the order is not made immediately;

(c) whether there is reason to believe that the respondent is aware of the proceedings but is evading service;

(d) whether the applicant or relevant child will be seriously prejudiced by the delay involved.

Rule 10.2(4) of the FPR 2010 requires the applicant for a "without notice" order to state the reasons for no notice having been given in the sworn statement which must accompany the application.

In *FZ v SZ* [2011] 1 F.L.R. 64, Mostyn J said:

> "It is worth my expressing the view that in the short term that I have been sitting as a full time judge I have been shocked at the volume of spurious ex parte applications that are made in the urgent applications list. It is an absolutely elementary tenet of English law that save in an emergency a court should hear both sides before giving a ruling. The only recognised exception to this rule (apart from those instances where an ex parte procedure is specifically authorised by statute) is where there is a well founded belief that the giving of notice would lead to irretrievable prejudice being caused to the applicant for relief. I have the distinct impression that a sort of lazy, laissez-faire practice or syndrome has grown up which says that provided the return date is soon, and provided that the court is satisfied that no material prejudice will be caused to the respondent, then there is no harm in making the order ex parte. In my opinion this is absolutely wrong and turns principle on its head."

The Family Justice Council has issued a protocol for process servers in respect of non-molestation orders through its Domestic Abuse Committee to be found at [2012] Fam. Law 338. Guidance has also been issued by a working party of the Family Justice Council dealing with the disclosure of information from multi agency risk assessment conferences ("MARAC") into court proceedings. These "MARAC"s deal with the highest risk cases of domestic abuse. The information shared at such meetings and the safety plan which is created as a result may be of interest to the court dealing with an injunction application. The guidance sets out the structure of the conference and how information may be obtained by way of a third party disclosure order and is reproduced at [2012] Fam. Law 202. **10-16**

3 OCCUPATION ORDERS

The types of order

The 1996 Act introduced a new system to regulate the occupation of the family home. The Matrimonial Homes Act 1983 and the Domestic Violence and Matrimonial Proceedings Act 1976, which previously dealt with occupation of the home and exclusion from the home or from a specified area in which it is included, are repealed in full. The Act introduced a new code governing the right to occupy the matrimonial home and how it may be restricted. "Matrimonial home rights" ap- **10-17** ply to a dwelling house which is either the matrimonial home or a property which the parties *intended* to be a matrimonial home. Where parties enjoy matrimonial home rights, the court can regulate the exercise of those rights. A spouse with such rights (if in occupation) has a right not to be evicted or excluded from the house or any part of it by the other spouse except with leave of the court given by an order under s.33 of the Act. If not in occupation, the spouse has a right *with the leave of the court* to enter and occupy the home. These rights are extended to persons who are civil partners or former civil partners.

Section 42(4A) requires a court considering whether to make an occupation order to consider whether to exercise the power to make a non-molestation order. This expands the court's powers to make non-molestation orders of its own motion which had previously been confined to family proceedings—s.42(2)(b)—and places a specific and mandatory obligation on the court to consider the making of a non-molestation order.

10-18   An occupation order is not an application for maintenance or a related proceeding within the meaning of art.27 of Brussels 1: *Re T v T (Occupation Orders, Brussels 1 and Protective Measures)* [2010] EWHC 3776 (Fam). Moylan J held that it was within art.31 and the definition "provisional, including protective measures", and therefore the court retained jurisdiction to make an occupation order in respect of an English property owned by the husband who was a French national at a time when the wife was appealing the outcome of the French divorce proceedings.

There are five situations in which occupation orders are available:

(1)   where a person has an estate or interest or contract giving the right to remain in occupation or has matrimonial home rights (s.33);
(2)   where a person is a former spouse or former civil partner with no existing right to occupy (s.35);
(3)   where a person is a cohabitant or former cohabitant with no existing right to occupy (s.36);
(4)   where neither spouse is entitled to occupy (s.37);
(5)   where neither cohabitant nor former cohabitant is entitled to occupy (s.38).

In all five cases the property which will be the subject of the order must be a dwelling house (which includes a caravan or house boat: s.63(1)). Where the parties are spouses or former spouses, civil partners or former civil partners, the property will be the matrimonial home or a property intended to be the matrimonial home.

(1)   A person entitled by law or matrimonial home rights (includes spouses) (s.33)

10-19   The dwelling house referred to "is or at any time has been" the home of the person entitled and of another with whom he is associated, or was intended to be their home.

The range of orders is as follows:

(a)   to enforce the applicant's right to occupy;
(b)   to require the respondent to allow the applicant to enter and remain in the house or any part of it;
(c)   to regulate the occupation of the home by the parties;
(d)   to prohibit, suspend or restrict occupation by a respondent;
(e)   where the court is considering matrimonial home rights, to restrict or terminate those rights;
(f)   to require the respondent to leave the home or part of the home;

(g) to exclude the respondent from a defined area in which the home is included.

The court can also make a declaration as to the applicant's rights in respect of **10-20** the home. Matrimonial home rights lapse on the death of a spouse or civil partner or the termination of the marriage by decree absolute or the civil partnership. In the absence of a declaration by the court that the rights are not brought to an end at death or on the termination of the marriage or civil partnership, an occupation order ends on the happening of any of those events: s.33(9).

The criteria to be applied by the court in deciding whether an order should be made are set out in s.33. The court is to have regard to all the circumstances of the case including:

(a) the housing needs and resources of the parties and any relevant child;
(b) the financial resources of the parties;
(c) the effect of any order or of not making an order on the health and safety or well-being of the parties and of any relevant child;
(d) the conduct of the parties in relation to each other and otherwise;
(e) further, if it appears to the court that the applicant or a relevant child is likely to suffer significant harm if an order is not made, the court *shall* make the order unless it appears to the court that the respondent and any relevant child will suffer significant harm if the order is made and such harm will be as great or greater than the harm likely to be suffered by the applicant or the child if the order is not made—a "balance of harm" test.

The order can be made for a specified time, until a specified event or until further order.

(2) A former spouse or civil partner with no existing right to occupy (s.35)

This section applies to a former spouse or civil partner where the Respondent had **10-21** a right to occupy a dwelling house and the Applicant was not so entitled, and the property was at any time or was intended to be their matrimonial or civil partnership home. The former spouse or civil partner can apply for a similar range of orders as listed in (1) above. The test is also similar and the balance of harm test is applied. However, there are three specific criteria the court must consider under this section concerning ex-spouses or civil partners. These are:

(a) the length of time since the parties ceased to live together;
(b) the existence of any pending financial proceedings between the parties;
(c) the time lapse since the marriage or civil partnership was dissolved or annulled.

Importantly, the duration of an order under this section must be limited to a specific period of up to six months, and it may be extended on one or more occasions but for no more than a further six months.

(3) Cohabitants or former cohabitants without an existing right to occupy (s.36)

This section applies where the Respondent is entitled to occupy a dwelling house **10-22** in which the parties cohabit, have cohabited at any time or intended to cohabit by general law, and the Applicant is not so entitled. The menu of orders is as considered in the other categories but important differences exist in the test to be applied by the court. Although the court is obliged to consider the balance of harm test, it is not obliged, as it would be under ss.33 and 35, to make an order if the test is satisfied. The court will also consider the nature of the parties' relationship, whether children are involved (either children of the parties or those for whom they have parental responsibility), the length of time the parties lived together and the time elapsed since ceasing to live together, and whether there are any other pending financial proceedings under the Children Act 1989 or in relation to the home between the parties. The requirement under s.41 that in the case of cohabitants or former cohabitants, the court should also have regard to the fact that the parties have not given each other the commitment involved in marriage, was repealed and replaced by the obligation on the court to consider "the nature of the parties' relationship", *in particular the level of commitment involved in it*: s.36(6)(e). Any order can be made for up to six months and extended once only for up to six months.

(4)   Neither spouse/former spouse nor civil partner/former civil partner has a right to occupy (s.37)

10-23   Either can apply for an order against the other notwithstanding that neither has a right to occupy by way of general law. This applies to a dwelling house which is or was the matrimonial or civil partnership home and covers occupation under a bare licence or where the property is owned by trustees. It does not affect third parties. The test to be applied by the court includes the balance of harm test but without the duty to make an order. The orders that the court can make regulate entry and occupation of the house and can require a party to leave the house and not enter a defined area in which the house is included. The order can be made for up to six months and is renewable for up to six months.

(5)   Neither cohabitant/former cohabitant has a right to occupy (s.38)

10-24   The balance of harm test is applied but without an obligation on the court to make an order. Third parties are not affected. The requirement under s.41(2) that the court should consider the fact that the parties have not given each other the commitment involved in marriage has been repealed, but there is no new provision corresponding to that under s.36(6)(e). Any order may be made for up to six months and is renewable for up to six months but only on one further occasion: s.38(6).

When an occupation order will be made

10-25   An occupation order is regarded as a "draconian" order, justified only in exceptional circumstances and not appropriate for cases of more conventional domestic disharmony: *Chalmers v Johns* [1999] 1 F.L.R. 392. This was a case in which the applicant did not satisfy the "significant harm" test. The court therefore had a discretion under s.33(6) which should not have been exercised in favour of exclusion in what was a "very slight case" and where there were cross applications for residence of the child. The court emphasised that each of the relevant sections of the Act must be considered and findings made under each of them.

The same approach was followed in *G v G (Occupation Order: Conduct)* [2000] 2 F.L.R. 36, in another discretionary case under s.33(6) where there was no evidence of actual violence to the mother and applications by the mother for residence and financial relief would be determined shortly. The court was more concerned with the effect of behaviour rather than the intent behind it (although lack of intent could be a relevant factor in some cases) and it was possible to regulate the shared occupancy of the home.

In *Re Y (Children) (Occupation Order)* [2000] 2 F.C.R. 470, the Court of Appeal disapproved the pragmatic approach that the "situation had to end sooner rather than later and better sooner than later", in favour of a systematic approach to the statutory tests and the need for an evidential basis for findings of significant harm. Sedley LJ observed:

"The purpose of an occupation order, however large its grounds may potentially be, is not to break matrimonial deadlocks by evicting one of the parties, much less to do so at the expense of a dependent and in this case a heavily pregnant child. Nor is it to use publicly funded emergency housing as a solution for domestic strife."

The court again favoured the use of neutral undertakings and regulation of separate occupation of different parts of the home.

In *Re L (Children)* [2012] EWCA Civ 721, Black LJ confirmed that the discretion to make an occupation order under s.33(6) is not limited to cases where there has been actual physical violence and neither would it be required to establish significant harm under s.33(7). There was no principle that a spouse could only be excluded if he or she was guilty of reprehensible conduct. As the trial judge had found that the children were suffering significant harm to the extent that would justify intervention by a local authority, the harm went beyond that which may usually be expected in the breakup of a marriage. The judge was also entitled to decide which parent should be the primary carer. Black LJ considered that the judge could have considered alternatives to a full exclusion order, but it appeared that none had been put to him and therefore he was not to be criticised on that ground. *Grubb v Grubb* [2009] EWCA Civ 976 is a further example of a case in which actual violence was not essential to justify making an occupation order and excluding a spouse from his long time family home. However, there was appropriate alternative accommodation for him to move to whilst the divorce proceedings were worked through and the court had been entitled to accept the evidence of the applicant's moderately severe depressive illness.

In *Dolan v Corby* [2011] EWCA Civ 1664, the Court of Appeal emphasised that s.33(6) and (7) should be considered separately and not conflated as the recorder had done, but as s.33(6) required the exercise of a judicial discretion, it was not vitiated by the conflation of the two provisions. Further exceptional circumstances were not to be found only in violent behaviour or the threat of violence. The recorder had the benefit of seeing the parties and assessing them.

An example of the court's approach to the balance of harm test is to be found in *B v B* [1999] 1 F.L.R. 715. It was held that the risk of significant harm to the husband's child from a previous relationship who was living with the parties outweighed the risk of harm to the wife and the baby child of the marriage, who could soon be re-housed in permanent accommodation, and the occupation order was set aside. However, the court regarded the facts as unusual and sent a clear message that fathers who treat their partners with domestic violence and cause them to leave the home cannot expect to remain in occupation themselves of the previously shared accommodation, and an application for a residence order in relation to a child of the relationship would not prevent an occupation order being made. The county court also resolved the balance of harm test in favour of an elderly wife with mental health difficulties whose doctors wished to discharge her back into the community, and considered that occupation of the matrimonial home should be resolved in the divorce proceedings that had been issued by the husband: *Banks v Banks* [1999] 1 F.L.R. 726.

S v F (Occupation Order) [2000] 1 F.L.R. 255 is another first instance decision which concerned the balancing exercise under s.35(6) and in which the availability of financial provision proceedings to resolve issues of long-term occupation of the home was a relevant factor. The father, who had been out of occupation

10-26

10-27

for seven years, was given leave to return to the home for six months to provide for a 17-year-old child who wished to remain in the house to pursue his education; the wife had the ability to rent alternative accommodation in the short term until the issue of sale could be decided, although the father was required to undertake to be responsible for the mortgage repayments.

To exclude a respondent without notice is an extreme step which requires clear evidence not likely to be susceptible to challenge.

Where a court makes an occupation order under ss.33, 35 or 36, it may also make an ancillary order (s.40) in respect of matters such as the discharge of rent or mortgage payments, bills, repairs, use of furniture and other effects and house contents. Occupation rent after a party has been ousted may also be provided for. However, it is doubtful whether these provisions have any "teeth", and an application to commit a party for failure to pay outgoings which are the subject of an order under s.40 will fail, as will any application for an attachment of earnings order or any action to treat the respondent as a judgment debtor: *Nwogbe v Nwogbe* [2000] 2 F.L.R. 744. The court tentatively suggested the use of "other" statutory powers which may be available to married parties but are not available to cohabitees, and urged the inclusion of s.40 as an exception to the Debtors Act 1869, which would then permit enforcement.

Matrimonial home rights continue as long as the marriage subsists unless otherwise ordered by the court under s.33(5). The court can extend rights beyond the death of the other spouse or the termination of the marriage if an application is brought during the currency of the marriage.

An Applicant will lose the right to apply to re-enter a property if a tenancy is terminated by the Respondent giving a notice to quit or surrendering the tenancy. The occupation order would need to be made before the act which brings the tenancy to an end. An application to prevent such a step being by the proposed Respondent should be considered.

10-28   Applications can either be free-standing or made as part of other family proceedings. There is no provision for the court to make an order of its own motion as with non-molestation orders.

Where the court is making both a non-molestation order and an occupation order, separate orders should be issued.Orders can be made without notice where it is just and convenient to do so (s.45(1)). The court will consider all the circumstances including those set out in s.45(2), essentially the risk of significant harm, whether the applicant will otherwise be deterred from pursuing the application or where service has been evaded.

4   POWER OF ARREST AND OTHER ENFORCEMENT PROCEDURES UNDER THE FAMILY LAW ACT 1996

10-29   There are three methods of dealing with an alleged breach of the order presently in force:

(a)   power of arrest;

(b)   application for a warrant of arrest;

(c)   application for committal by way of the Part 18 procedure using Form FP 2 in the proceedings in which the judgement or order was made or the undertaking was given: Rule 37.10 Family Procedure Rules 2010. This method is more likely to be used where there have been a series of breaches or where the situation is not urgent.

Under s.42A of the 1996 Act (inserted by s.1 of the Domestic Violence, Crime and Victims Act 2004), it is a criminal offence to breach a non-molestation order provided the conduct engaged in took place at a time when the defendant was aware of the existence of the order and the conduct alleged to amount to the breach was without reasonable excuse. The offence is punishable by up to five years' imprisonment and/or an unlimited fine on conviction on indictment, and on summary conviction by up to 12 months' imprisonment and/or a fine not exceeding the statutory maximum. "Double jeopardy" is avoided by the provision that if the breach of the non-molestation order is dealt with as a criminal offence, it cannot be dealt with as a contempt of court subsequently and if the matter has been punished as a contempt of court, there can be no criminal conviction: section 42A(3) and (4). In the absence of any provision in the section itself, it appears to be for the applicant to decide which route to use.

The offence is an arrestable offence in itself and therefore the intention and the   **10-30**
expectation appears to be that breaches in which the assistance of the police is required will be dealt with under the criminal law. The only other possible indicator is the difference between the maximum penalty on conviction on indictment, which is five years' imprisonment, rather than the maximum of two years' imprisonment available under the Contempt of Court Act 1981. The five-year maximum sentence is the same as under the Protection from Harassment Act 1997 for breach of a restraining order. It appears that this provision allows serious breaches of non-molestation orders to be punished as breaches of the order without the need for separate specific criminal charges to be brought, save in the most serious of offences, for example allegations of rape, wounding or causing grievous bodily harm with intent. However, it is likely to take longer to achieve a trial for the offence of breach of a non-molestation order than it would to achieve a hearing in the county court for breach consequent upon arrest under a power of arrest. The Sentencing Council's *Overarching Principles Domestic Abuse: Definitive Guidelines* came into force on 24 May 2018.

Power of arrest

Section 47(2) allows a power of arrest to be attached to one or more provisions   **10-31**
of an occupation order. The test to be applied by the court in reaching the decision on whether to attach a power of arrest is set out in s.47(2) and is whether "the respondent has used or threatened violence against the applicant or a relevant child". If the court makes such a finding, the Act provides that a power of arrest *shall* attach unless satisfied that in all the circumstances the applicant or the child will be adequately protected without the provision of a power of arrest. The fact that the respondent who is to be subject to the power of arrest is under 18 and cannot be committed to prison for breach of the order will not prevent a power of arrest being attached to the order, since one purpose of the power of arrest is to remove the troublemaker from the scene; the age of the respondent and the relationship of the parties are relevant considerations in the decision whether to attach the power of arrest.

Practice Direction 10A Family Procedure Rules paragraph 3.1 requires the court to announce publicly the terms of a non-molestation order and/or an occupation order to which a power of arrest has been attached which has been made in private on the same day as the order is made when the court hears cases in open court, or on the next day when open court business is listed.

The presumption of attaching a power of arrest has consequences for the acceptance of undertakings because a power of arrest cannot be attached to an undertaking; s.46(3) provides that an undertaking shall not be accepted by the court instead of making an occupation order "where apart from this section a power of arrest would be attached to the order".

If an order is made without notice, the presumption does not operate, but the court may attach a power of arrest if violence has been used or threatened and there is a risk of significant harm to the applicant or a relevant child if the power of arrest is not immediately attached to the order. A power of arrest may be attached to an exclusion order made in conjunction with an emergency protection order or interim care order.

10-32   In respect of an order made without notice, the power of arrest may be attached for a period of time that is shorter than the main order. The power of arrest may be extended on an application to vary or discharge the relevant order. Orders made on notice will usually have a power of arrest of the same duration as the main order. Although there appears to be no comparative provision for different duration as provided for in orders made without notice, it is possible to construe s.47(2) as permitting this but the court would have to be satisfied that the victim would be adequately protected with only a shorter power of arrest: see *Re B-J (Power of Arrest)* [2000] 2 F.L.R. 443, in which the non-molestation order was made for an indefinite period but the power of arrest was for a period of two years.

In *Re H (Respondent under 18: Power of Arrest)* [2001] 1 F.L.R. 641, the Court of Appeal held that an occupation order can be made against a respondent aged under 18 and may have a power of arrest attached to it.

The police should be notified of the making of a non-molestation order and/or an occupation order to which a power of arrest has been attached after the Respondent has been notified of the order. The court may specify the police station or the order is sent to the police station relevant for the address of the applicant. The order on the prescribed form/s should be sent together with a statement showing that the order has been served on the Respondent or the Respondent has been made aware of the terms of the order by presence when the order was made: Part 10 Family Procedure Rules 2010 Rule 10.10.

A constable may arrest without warrant a person he has reasonable cause for suspecting to be in breach of a relevant provision of an occupation order. If arrested, the respondent must be brought before the relevant judicial authority within 24 hours. "Relevant judicial authority" means the court in which the original order was made. If a courtroom is not available it can be at any convenient place: Practice Direction 10A 3.3. The press and public should be permitted to be present unless security needs make it impracticable.The court also has power to remand if the matter is not dealt with at that hearing. A person brought before the court may be remanded in custody or on bail or for a medical examination and report: Practice Direction 10A paras 6 and 7.

"Practice Direction 10A" paras 5.2 and 5.3 provide that the arresting officer does not have to be before the court if a written statement setting out the circumstances of the arrest is available and the circumstances of the arrest are not in dispute. If the officer is a witness of fact to the allegations and his or her attendance is required, arrangements should be made for him to attend a subsequent hearing. The Practice Direction also sets out the process for an application for bail.

Warrant of arrest

10-33   Where the court has made an order but has not attached a power of arrest, or has only attached a power to certain provisions of the order, the applicant can apply to the court that made the original order for the issue of a warrant for the arrest of the respondent. The provisions appear to create the situation that where a power of arrest is attached to all provisions, no application can be made for a warrant of arrest. If there is an allegation of breach of a relevant provision of the order but the police do not arrest the respondent, the applicant will have to proceed by way of an application for committal. An arrest warrant *cannot* be issued in support of an exclusion requirement or undertaking given under ss.38B or 44B of the Children Act 1989. However it will apply to an undertaking given in 1996 Act proceedings: s.46(4).

The right to apply to the court for the issue of a warrant of arrest where an allegation of breach of a non-molestation order is made is preserved under the amended s.47(8), although the court cannot attach a power of arrest to such an order.

Any application for a warrant of arrest must be substantiated on oath and the court must have reasonable grounds to believe that the respondent has failed to comply with the order. The Pt 18 procedures should be used and "PD 10A" applies. The court has a discretion whether to issue the warrant and can alternatively invite the applicant to issue committal proceedings. The prescribed Form FL408 allows the warrant to be backed for bail, although the Act is silent as to this.   **10-34**

Schedule 5 to the Act defines the powers to remand a person which apply in the family court and the High Court. The powers of the magistrates' court to remand are contained in ss.128 and 129 of the Magistrates' Courts Act 1980.   **10-35**

Under the 1996 Act, the court may exercise the power to remand in the following way:

(a) remand the respondent in custody to be brought before the court at the end of the period of remand or at such earlier time as the court may require;

(b) remand the respondent on bail by taking a recognisance or by fixing the recognisances with a view to them being taken subsequently and in the meantime remanding him in custody. Bail conditions can be imposed to prevent a person interfering with witnesses or obstructing the course of justice.

The court can remand a person who has been brought before the court previously and been remanded.

If a court is of the view that a medical report is necessary, the power to remand can be exercised for the purpose of enabling an examination and a report. Where a remand is made for such a report the court may remand for no more than four weeks on bail or three weeks in custody. Subject to the above (and certain other exceptions), Sch.5 provides that the court shall not remand a person for a period exceeding eight days. A person can be committed to the custody of a constable if remanded for a period not exceeding three days. Schedule 5 also provides for "further remands": the court may remand in a person's absence if he is unable to attend through illness or accident, and the time limits in the Schedule do not then apply. The court also has the power to enlarge the recognisance on further remand.   **10-36**

Three particular provisions with respect to the powers of the magistrates should be noted:

(1) The magistrates may (s.50) order that a committal order be suspended upon conditions as to duration and terms as the court may specify if, under s.63(3) of the Magistrates' Courts Act 1980, the court has power to commit for breach of a "relevant requirement", defined as an occupation or non-molestation order, or an exclusion requirement by virtue of s.38A of the Children Act 1989 in interim care proceedings or s.44A of the Children Act 1989 in respect of an emergency protection order.

(2) The magistrates can also (s.51), where a person may otherwise be committed for a breach of a "relevant requirement", make a hospital order or guardianship order under s.37 of the Mental Health Act 1983 (or an interim order under s.38 of that Act) in the case of a person suffering from mental

illness or severe mental impairment. This is, as the Act states, the same power as the magistrates would have in the case of a person convicted of an offence punishable on summary conviction with imprisonment.

(3) The magistrates' jurisdiction is restricted (s.59) where a determination has to be made on entitlement to occupy with reference to interests in a property, unless it is not necessary to resolve the dispute to deal with the application before the court. The magistrates can also decline jurisdiction if the matter would be more conveniently dealt with by another court. This is also recorded in The Family Court (Composition and Distribution of Business) Rules 2014 rule 16(5). The magistrates can also decline jurisdiction if the matter would be more conveniently dealt with by another tier of judiciary within the family court.

Application to commit (see also Ch.9)

10-37   The relevant rule for proceedings in the Family Court is Part 37 of the Family Procedure Rules which is modelled on the Civil Procedure Rules Part 81. It came into effect on 22 April 2014. Part 81 is the applicable rule for proceedings in the High Court.

Rule 37.4 defines the circumstances in which an application for committal can be made, which is either where an act which was required to be done by a judgment or order has not been done in the time fixed by the judgment or order, or where a person has disobeyed a judgment or order not to do an act.

The order must be served personally on the person to whom it is directed before the application to commit can be made: r.37.5. If the order is mandatory, it must be served on the person to whom it is directed before the time for doing the act expires: r.37.5(1)(a). A copy of any document recording an undertaking will be delivered by the court to the person who gave the undertaking by one of the following means:

(i)   handing a copy of the document to the person before that person leaves the court building;

(ii)   posting a copy to that person at the last known address;

(iii)   posting a copy to that person's solicitor; or

(iv)   in default of (i)–(iii), personal service as soon as practicable on the person for whose benefit the undertaking was given: r.37.7.

10-38   Where the order or undertaking requires a person not to do an act, the court has power to dispense with service if it is satisfied that the person affected by the order has had notice by being present when the order was made or given or has been notified of its terms by telephone, email or otherwise: r.37.8(1). The court may dispense with service also in the case of a judgment or order if it thinks it just to do so, or alternatively may make an order for service by an alternative method at an alternative place: r.37.8(2).

The application is made in the family court using the Part 18 procedure in the proceedings in which the order was made supported by an affidavit: r.37.10 (1) and (3)(b). Each alleged act of contempt must be identified separately and numerically: r.37.10(3)(a), and the affidavit, where required by the rules, should set out all the facts relied upon: r.37.10(3)(b).

10-39   The application with the affidavit in support must be personally served. Practice Direction 37A para.12.2 provides for a period of 14 days' service. In the family court substituted service can be ordered, and there is power to abridge time for service. Paragraph 12 of the Practice Direction provides guidance on the management of the hearing, on the matters to be taken into account in deciding whether the case is ready to proceed and on issues of fairness to the respondent.

In *Chelmsford County Court v Ramet* [2014] EWHC 56 (Fam) the President confirmed the principle that a contempt of court can only be punished once as the contemnor had been sentenced for a criminal offence of assault in relation to an incident that was also a contempt in the face of the court.

Practice Direction 37A para.13 sets out the procedure for striking out and discontinuance. An application may be struck out if it does not disclose any reasonable ground for alleging that the respondent is in contempt of court; it is an abuse of the court or is likely to obstruct the just disposal of the existing proceedings; shows a failure to comply with a rule, practice direction or court order: para.13.1. The application notice can be amended only with the permission of the court: Rule 37.27(1) Family Procedure Rules 2010.

The respondent cannot be compelled to give information: Rule 37.27(3), and the court may direct the attendance of witnesses who have filed written evidence. The respondent is entitled to give evidence and to call witnesses whether or not written evidence has been filed by any of them. The allegations must be proved to the criminal standard of proof—"beyond reasonable doubt". If the hearing has to be adjourned, personal service of notice of the adjourned hearing is required unless the respondent was present in court and was told when and where the adjourned hearing would resume.

Paragraph 13.2 provides that the court may waive any procedural defect in the commencement or conduct of the committal application if satisfied that no injustice has been caused to the respondent by the defect. A committal application may only be withdrawn with the permission of the court.

An example of waiver of procedural irregularities is the decision of the President in *Re An Application by Gloucestershire CC for the Committal to Prison of Matthew John Newman (No. 1)* [2014] EWHC 3136 (Fam). The penal notice on the order did not comply with r.37(9) FPR but the contemnor was in no doubt as the consequences of a breach of the order. The use of standard form orders was emphasised and where conduct was restrained by the order it should be in clear and unambiguous terms.   **10-40**

Exceptionally, the court can dispense with service and proceed to hear the application without notice having been given to the respondent if it is just to do so, or may order service by an alternative method or at an alternative place: r.37.10(5). This is likely to happen only where there is good evidence that the respondent knows that there are to be committal proceedings and is evading service, for example by running away from the process server. If the respondent has been served with notice of the hearing but does not attend, the court may proceed in his absence: *Re M (Breach of Undertakings: Committal)* [2013] EWCA Civ 743.

An example of this is the decision in *Re P (Committal for Breach of Contact Order: Reasons)* [2006] EWCA Civ 1792. The mother, who had failed to comply with the penal notice attached to a child contact order, did not attend at the committal hearing. The judge was held to be entitled to proceed in her absence because there was good evidence that she knew of the hearing date, and was also entitled to take into account the mother's previous failures to attend at hearings during the contact proceedings. The judge was criticised for not giving reasons for his decision to make a suspended committal order. However, there was no injustice to the mother because it was perfectly obvious on the facts why the judge had made the order, which had been effective in ensuring that contact took place since the date of issue.

In *Sanchez v Oboz (Committal Proceedings in the Absence of the Respondents)* [2015] EWHC 235 Fam Cobb J provided a list of considerations for making a decision to proceed in the absence of the Respondent:

- Whether the Respondents had been served with the relevant documents including notice of the hearing.
- Whether the Respondents had had sufficient time to prepare for the hearing.
- Whether any reason had been advanced for the Respondents' non-appearance.
- Was it reasonable to conclude that the Respondents knew of or were indifferent to the consequences of the case proceeding in their absence.
- Whether an adjournment would be likely to secure attendance or facilitate representation.
- The extent of any disadvantage to the Respondents in not being able to present their own account of events.
- Whether undue prejudice would be caused to the Applicant by any delay.
- Whether undue prejudice would be caused to the forensic process if the application was to proceed in the absence of the Respondents.
- The terms of the overriding objective under the Family Procedure Rules 2010.

The court concluded that it could proceed in the absence of the Respondents but would adjourn the issue of sentence to allow the Respondents the opportunity to mitigate either themselves or through a legal representative. The court also proceeded in the absence of personal service of the order on the Respondent because he had been in court when the original order was made and its terms had been explained by the judge. The case involved breach of an order for the return of a child to the jurisdiction and the central facts of the breach could not be in dispute. In the end the father was sentenced in his absence to 12 months' imprisonment.

10-41   There is a presumption that the hearing of a committal application will take place in open court. Rule 37.27(5) sets out the circumstances in which such a hearing may be in private. These are:

(a) publicity would defeat the object of the hearing;
(b) it involves matters of national security;
(c) it involves confidential information including information relating to personal financial matters and publication would damage that confidentiality;
(d) a private hearing is necessary to protect the interest of any child or protected party;
(e) it is a hearing without notice and it would be unjust to any respondent for there to be a public hearing; or
(f) the court considers it to be necessary in the interests of justice.

Where the hearing is in private and a committal order is made the court should state in public the name of the respondent, the nature of the contempt in respect of which the committal order is being made; the length of the period of the committal order: r.37.27(6).

The Practice Direction dated 26 March 2015 made by the Lord Chief Justice sets out further procedural steps applicable to all committal applications. It includes how the application shall appear in the court list, where the list should be displayed, the requirement for notice to the press and broadcast media if the respondent is to appear having been arrested overnight and the entitlement of a non-party to be given a copy of a committal application. If the court is considering hearing the application in private or imposing any reporting restrictions, notice must be given to the media and submissions can be made not only form the parties but also from the media.

It is also clear that the fact that the existing proceedings are about a child or in the Court of Protection does not in itself justify hearing the case in private or imposing reporting restrictions. If there are likely to be matters raised in the hearing of the application that should not be made public, it does not justify hearing the case in private if a restriction on what can be published would be appropriate. Where a decision to sit in private is made by the court, a reasoned public judgement must be given before the hearing in private continues. Where the court finds that there has been a contempt of court, the outcome of the hearing must be stated in public and made known to the national media via the CopyDirect service and to the Judicial Office for publication on the website of the Judiciary and this applies in the case of an immediate and suspended committal order. There must be a written record of the judgment of the court which must be published on BAILII and provided to the parties, the media and to the Judicial Office.

Hammerton v Hammerton [2007] EWCA Civ 248 demonstrates the need to **10-42** separate issues relating to children from issues of breach of court orders justifying committal proceedings. The Court of Appeal held that the respondent should have been afforded the opportunity to be legally represented "in the absence of evidence of intransigence" and should have been granted an adjournment to seek representation. Further, the decision of the judge to hear the contact application at the same time as the application for committal virtually compelled the respondent to give evidence in support of his claim for contact when he was not obliged to give evidence in the committal proceedings. Moses LJ considered that it was difficult to envisage circumstances which would compel the court to hear both applications together. A sentence of three months' imprisonment was quashed on procedural grounds.

Guidance was given by the Court of Appeal on the conduct of a committal application hearing in *Re K (Return Order: Failure to Comply: Committal: Appeal)* [2014] EWCA Civ 905. The case concerned the failure by a father to comply with an order for the return of a child to the jurisdiction. He was found in breach of the order and sentenced to 18 months imprisonment by Russell J. The court accepted that the judge should have recused herself on the ground of apparent bias because she had outlined very forcefully the consequences of non-compliance by the father at a previous hearing although it was recognised that her comments had been designed to secure his compliance with the court's order for return. It was important that the contemnor should be advised that he does not have to give evidence and if he does he should be allowed to give his own account before he is cross examined or questioned by the judge. A failure to comply with the order must be deliberate and must relate to the terms of the order rather than any other deceptive conduct.

In *The Solicitor General v JMJ (Contempt)* [2013] EWHC 2579 (Fam) it was **10-43** confirmed that the Law Officers had locus to apply for the committal of an alleged contemnor even if the contempt was civil and involved breach of an order obtained by a private individual in the course of proceedings between private individuals. The Law Officer acted to safeguard the public interest and the administration of justice. However, on the evidence it was out of mother's power to comply with the order.

In *Re C (Children)* [2011] EWCA Civ 1230 it was observed that, even where the order breached related to children, it would be most unusual to join them as parties to an application to commit; however, the court could take into account the impact on the children and their carers of the application and how they might react to it, as well as, when sentencing for contempt in a domestic situation, the fact that emotions run high and judgement can be clouded by it.

However, in *Cambra v Jones* [2014] EWHC (Fam) 913 the President of the Family Division agreed to join the eldest of 4 children to a committal application against the mother for her failure to return the two eldest children to their father in Spain. It was held that J's right to freedom of expression and participation outweighed any paternalistic welfare judgement. There was discussion about whether J's own Article 8 rights were engaged during the hearing and at the sentencing process and as the mother's case was that J was refusing to return herself, only J could give relevant evidence.

The Family Court (Contempt of Court) Powers Regulations 2014 sets out the powers of the different levels of the Family Court. The maximum sentence that can be imposed by a judge of the High Court, a circuit judge or a District Judge or District Judge (Magistrates' Court) for contempt for disobeying an order made under Pt IV is two years' imprisonment. The maximum sentence available to magistrates is two months. In the High Court the maximum fine is unlimited and this power is preserved for proceedings before a High Court judge sitting in the Family Court. The maximum at all other levels of judiciary including the magistrates is a Level 5 fine (£5000). There is a power to impose a fine, and Mental Health Act powers are also available. FPR 10.14 refers to the power to adjourn the hearing for consideration of the penalty. However, if this option is chosen there is no power to remand in custody in the period of consideration. There is power to detain a respondent aged between 18 and 21 years but no power to detain a respondent aged less than 18 years.

10-44   It is also important that the court is clear about the extent of the court's powers and the statute under which the committal proceedings are brought: *Zuk v Zuk* [2012] EWCA Civ 1871 in which the husband was sentenced to nine months imprisonment in judgement summons proceedings when the maximum penalty under the Debtors Act 1869 was six weeks' imprisonment. The Court of Appeal observed that in a judgement summons the ability to pay of the respondent is established when the original lump sum order is made and the burden of proof on the applicant is "lightly discharged" so that an evidential burden shifts to the respondent. The court noted that the respondent must always be given the opportunity to mitigate before sentence is announced: see *London Borough of Tower Hamlets v Ali* [2014] EWHC 845 for an illustration of the procedure where a father in breach of a disclosure order had failed to disclose information which might have led to the location of the children and was sentenced to four months immediate imprisonment.

A custodial term can be suspended. Where a suspended order is made, the court should fix a definite period for the suspension: *Griffin v Griffin* [2000] 2 F.L.R. 44. The power to suspend execution of a committal order is set out in r.37.28.

In *Re An Application by Gloucestershire CC for the Committal to Prison of Matthew John Newman (No.2)* [2014] EWHC (Fam) 3399 the President deferred sentence for 12 months where the primary objective was to secure compliance but with a stern warning that even a trivial breach in the period of deferment would lead to sentence for the original contempt and the fresh breach.

If the result is a term of immediate imprisonment, the court serves the order; where it is suspended, the applicant serves the order unless the court directs otherwise: r.37.28(2).

Where the contemnor applies to purge his contempt, the application is made on notice and the hearing is in the presence of the contemnor. Rule 37.30 sets out the procedure which allows for the application to be made to a district judge even if the order was made by a circuit judge, where the warrant of committal does not provide for the hearing to be before a circuit judge: r.37.30. The court only has the power to allow the application, dismiss it or indicate that a further application might succeed; there is no power to suspend the balance of the sentence: *Harris v Harris* [2002] 1 F.L.R. 248. However the court may order a release at a date in the future.

In *CJ v Flintshire CC* [2010] EWCA Civ 393, Wilson LJ identified eight ques-   **10-45**
tions to be considered when the court has to deal with an application for early
release:

(a) Could the court conclude that the contemnor had suffered punishment
    proportionate to his contempt?
(b) Would the interest of the state be significantly prejudiced by early
    discharge?
(c) How genuine was any expression of contrition?
(d) Had the contemnor demonstrated a resolve and ability not to commit a
    further breach?
(e) Had he done all that he reasonably could to minimise the risk of his com-
    mitting a further breach?
(f) Had any specific proposal been made to augment the protection of those
    whom the order was designed to protect against any further breach?
(g) How long had been served in prison taking account of the full term imposed
    and the term he would be otherwise required to serve prior to release under
    the provisions of the Criminal Justice Act 2003 s.258(2)?
(h) Were there any special factors impinging on the exercise of the discretion?

The contemnor failed in his attempt to secure his release on an application made
two days into a 21-month immediate sentence for breach of an order preventing him
having contact with his children other than that arranged by a local authority, made
after findings of sexual abuse and incest had been made in relation to an older child.
There had been numerous previous breaches of the order and previous sentences
of imprisonment.

A contemnor sentenced to immediate imprisonment must be released unconditionally once he has served half of his sentence: Criminal Justice Act 2003 s.258.
He may be released before he has served half of it in exceptional circumstances on
compassionate grounds. He will not be eligible for release under Home Detention
Curfew but, if he has been sentenced to at least four weeks' imprisonment, has
served at least seven days and has an address to go to, he can be released up to 18
days before the normal release date. Section 240 of the Criminal Justice Act 2003
does not apply to sentences for contempt, by operation of s.305 of the same Act,
and therefore contempt sentences do not benefit from any statutory provision for
credit to be given for time served on remand. However, in *Kerai v Patel* [2008] 2
F.L.R. 2137 it was held that the period spent on remand should be taken into account in fixing the length of a sentence of immediate imprisonment.

An applicant who is dissatisfied with the penalty imposed for a breach of an order   **10-46**
can appeal to the Court of Appeal to *increase* the sentence: *Wilson v Webster* [1998]
1 F.L.R. 1097, where three months' imprisonment was substituted for 14 days
imposed by the court below. In *Neil v Ryan* [1998] 2 F.L.R. 1068, an immediate
sentence of imprisonment of three months was substituted for a suspended sentence
of one month's imprisonment for a first breach. It should be noted that the applicant in committal proceedings requires permission to appeal to the Court of Appeal, whereas the respondent who has been committed to prison may appeal as of
right: *M v M (Breaches of Orders: Committal)* [2006] 1 F.L.R. 1154; Ward LJ
observed that the role of the applicant in sentencing for contempt was to be discouraged and an appeal to the Court of Appeal by a dissatisfied applicant should be an
exceptional course.

There is no general principle of a "free first breach". In *Hale v Tanner* [2000] 2
F.L.R. 879, the Court of Appeal gave guidance as to the approach to be adopted by
lower courts. They did not lay down "sentencing guidelines" in the absence of a

wide range of comparable cases but made the following general observations:

(a) Imprisonment should not be the automatic response of the court, but there is no principle that imprisonment is not to be imposed on the first breach.

(b) Alternatives to imprisonment are limited: the court can make no order, adjourn the application, impose a fine, make an order for sequestration of assets or make a mental health order. All options need to be considered particularly when the court has not found actual violence to be proved.

(c) The length of any order for imprisonment should be fixed without reference to the possibility of suspending it.

(d) The length of the term of imprisonment should be relevant to the two-fold objectives of disapproving of disobedience of the order and securing compliance with the order in the future.

(e) The sentence should bear a relationship to the maximum available sentence of two years.

(f) Suspending the order can be a first means of securing compliance with the court's order.

(g) The length of the suspension can be linked to continued compliance with the underlying order but it requires separate consideration.

(h) The court must consider the circumstances of the breach—for example when emotions run high, people behave in silly ways. The presence of children can be an aggravating or a mitigating feature.

(i) The court cannot ignore parallel criminal proceedings based on the same facts and, even though the overlap may not be exact and the purpose of the proceedings is different, the contemnor ought not to be punished twice for the same events. (The fact that contempt proceedings in the county court have led to the imprisonment of a defendant in criminal proceedings does not mean that it is an abuse of process to pursue criminal proceedings, although the criminal court should take into account the sentence for contempt when deciding what penalty to impose: *DPP v Tweddell* [2001] EWHC Admin 188; [2002] 2 F.L.R. 400). See paras 9-15 to 9-16 for further discussion of the overlap between criminal prosecutions and contempt applications.

(j) The court should always explain the reasons for its decision.

In *Thurstfield v Thurstfield* [2013] EWCA Civ 840 the court approved a sentence of 24 months for breach of a disclosure order in respect of which the husband was still in breach. The sentence was both punitive and coercive to encourage compliance and in the context of the case the guidance in *Hale v Tanner* (above) was not relevant.

On the facts of the case, the court thought that there was good mitigation in an early admission—the fact that the contemnor had not been at court to receive an oral warning and had not received previous legal advice, that it was a first breach and the contemnor was the mother of a very young child. However, an order for committal can be justified where the conduct complained of was such as to cause terror to the victim even if no actual violence was used: *Rafiq v Muse* [2000] 1 F.L.R. 820.

10-47 In *M v M* the court was dealing with breaches of an order prohibiting contact between father and children. There were more than 60 breaches which the judge at first instance found to be worthy of a substantial prison sentence, but he found also that the effect of such a sentence on the children, who were already distressed by the proceedings about them, would be profound to the point where there was a real risk that they would become beyond parental control and require the involvement of the local authority. The Court of Appeal upheld his order making no order in respect of the breaches, commenting that although the welfare of the children was not the paramount consideration in dealing with breaches of the order, it was a material consideration.

In making the decision whether a sentence of imprisonment should be suspended the court is entitled to take into account the number of previous opportunities provided to the contemnor to comply with the order: *Young v Young* [2013] EWHC 34 (Fam). Moor J imposed six months imprisonment for failing to provide information in a financial remedy application after four opportunities for compliance. He rejected also the husband's application for an adjournment to obtain legal representation because the husband could have been legally represented at the hearing.

In *Re W (A child) (Abduction: Committal)* [2011] EWCA Civ 1196, the father had abducted the child to Pakistan and then moved her to Iran to prevent her recovery from Pakistan. He had also offered the mother a substantial sum of money to relinquish her parental responsibility. At a first contempt hearing for his failure to return her to the jurisdiction and to give details of the child's whereabouts he had received a two-year sentence. Three days before he was due to be released from his sentence, a second application was made and, on a finding of a further contempt, the father received a 12-month sentence. It was upheld in the Court of Appeal on the basis that it was a second contempt of the order to reveal information about the child's whereabouts and not the same contempt for which he was being punished. MacFarlane LJ outlined that the court's task was to look at whether a further term of imprisonment was necessary and proportionate. The court should look at past orders and at the cumulative amount of time already spent in prison as well as the likely sentence for similar conduct in the criminal courts. When dealing with repeated contempts it was plain that a time would come when further punishment would be excessive, but whether that stage had been reached was a matter of fact in each case.

An illustration of the principle that there may come a time when to impose a further term of immediate custody was neither proportionate justifiable or lawful is *Button v Salama (No.3)* [2013] EWHC 4152 (Fam). The father was in breach of an order to disclose the whereabouts of his daughter who had been retained in Egypt and to secure her return to the jurisdiction. He had received and served sentences totalling over 2 years for previous breaches and had served the equivalent of a four year sentence, allowing for early release. The possible coercive effect of a further sentence of imprisonment would be negligible in light of the father's clear determination not to comply with the order.

In a series of cases beginning with *Lomas v Parle* [2004] 1 W.L.R. 1642, the **10-48** Court of Appeal has commented on a perceived discrepancy between sentences for breaches of non-molestation orders in civil proceedings and sentences imposed in criminal proceedings at Crown Court level for the same conduct as a criminal offence, either as a discrete criminal offence or under the Protection from Harassment Act 1997. The same views are echoed in *H v O (Contempt of Court: Sentencing)* [2005] 2 F.L.R. 329, in which May LJ at [40] of the judgment refers to some of the relevant considerations in sentencing for contempt, including the fact that breaches of a non-molestation order in the context of contact between a parent and child may be an aggravating rather than a mitigating factor; in *Murray v Robinson* [2006] 1 F.L.R. 365, in which Lord Woolf CJ pointed out that the purposes of criminal sentencing and s.143 of the Criminal Justice Act 2003 (setting out factors relevant to the seriousness of an offence, including reduction in sentence for a guilty plea) should be highly relevant considerations in sentencing for civil contempt. It was also noted that if a case warranted a sentence at the top of the range, it was desirable to bring proceedings under the Protection from Harassment Act 1997 so that greater powers of punishment are available.

The judgment of the court in *Lomas v Parle* is an illustration of how it exercises the power to increase sentence, reference being made to the unduly lenient principle applied in references by the Attorney General under the Criminal Justice Act 1988. The court also suggested that if there were concurrent proceedings under the Family Law Act 1996 and the Protection from Harassment Act 1997, they should be consolidated and tried by the same judge with both civil and family jurisdiction, and it commented favourably on a future examination of an integrated court to deal with criminal and civil proceedings before the same tribunal. The appropriate course was for any application to commit to be issued promptly, and to proceed first so that the contempt would be punished before any sentence was imposed in parallel proceedings. In this situation the first court should not anticipate the sentence of the second court, but the basis of the sentence should be fully expressed and a transcript of the judgment made available to the second court. Further, sentences imposed for breaches under the Family Law Act 1996 should not be discrepant with those under the Protection from Harassment Act 1997, the principal authority on range of sentence in the criminal courts is *R. v Liddle; R. v Hayes* [2000] 1 Cr.App.R.(S.) 131.

The implementation of s.42A of the 1996 Act gives an opportunity to use the criminal rather than the civil courts for breaches of non-molestation orders. One of the conclusions to be drawn from the observations in these three cases is that more serious breaches should be dealt with in the criminal jurisdiction so that the court has the greater power of sentence. Definitive sentencing guidelines exist for offences of assault in the criminal jurisdiction.

5   THE FORCED MARRIAGE (CIVIL PROTECTION) ACT 2007

10-49   The Forced Marriage (Civil Protection) Act 2007 amended the 1996 Act by the introduction of a new section which gives the court the power to grant a forced marriage protection order: ss.63A–63S. The power may be exercised to protect:

(a)   a person from being forced into a marriage or from any attempt to be forced into a marriage;

(b)   a person who has been forced into a marriage.

The new powers are additional to existing remedies under statute or the inherent jurisdiction of the High Court: s.63R.

Section 121 of the Anti-Social Behaviour Crime and Policing Act 2014 creates a criminal offence if violence, threats or any other form of coercion is used which a person may believe or ought reasonably to believe may cause the other person to enter into a marriage without free or full consent, or deception is used with the intention of causing another person to leave the United Kingdom and with the intention that that person should be subjected out of the jurisdiction to conduct that is an offence under section 121(1) or would be an offence if the victim were in England and Wales.

Forced marriage is defined under s.63A(4) as a marriage entered into or to be entered into without the free and full consent of one party to the marriage or proposed marriage. There is a part definition of "force" as including coercion by threats or other psychological means; s.63A(5) allows for the force to be directed against the party to be forced or who has been forced into the marriage or the perpetrator in relation to that person or another person.

In deciding whether to grant relief, the court must have regard to all the circumstances, including the need to secure the health, safety and well-being of the person to be protected: s.63A(2). "Well-being" includes the reasonably ascertainable wishes and feelings of the person to be protected in the light of their age and understanding: s.63A(3).

Often the information which is needed to support the application will have become available through multi agency information sharing in a forum such as a MARAC. The information is confidential and if there is a request by an alleged perpetrator for disclosure the FJC Guidance referred to in paragraph 10-15 should be followed.

There are additional levels of cultural sensitivity and often increased risk to the individual to be protected if information is disclosed in some circumstances. A disclosure application should usually be heard on notice to all parties. A possible outcome is that the information will be disclosed to the court only in the first instance so that a decision about whether the information should be disclosed to protect the Article 6 rights of the other parties can be made. The power to withhold information exists in exceptional cases but a balance has to be achieved between the right of parties to a fair hearing and the risk to the person to be protected if the material is disclosed. The principles are discussed in the context of forced marriage issues in *A County Council v SB, MA, and AA* [2010] EWHC 2528 (Fam).

The issues raised by an application for a forced marriage protection order may mean that it is necessary to withhold information in the form of submissions or evidence from parties to the proceedings. Rule 11.7(2) empowers the court to do so in order to protect the subject of the proceedings or for any other good reason. The court has to balance the arts 2 and 3 rights of the person to be protected and the arts 6 and 8 rights of the respondents. In *Re A (Forced Marriage: Special Advocates)* [2010] EWHC 2438 (Fam) the court considered the issue of the appointment of a special advocate to deal with any issues of public interest immunity. In the instant case it was not necessary to make the appointment, although there would undoubtedly arise cases in which it would be necessary. Moreover, it was open to the court to proceed to make an order on hearsay evidence and/or on evidence from the police which was not disclosed to the respondents. There was no requirement under the Act that the respondents should have the opportunity to rebut the case against them and were therefore alerted to it. The respondents were entitled to have notice of an order which had been made without notice and to make representations about the order. The judge was able in a protective jurisdiction to decide whether an order should be continued without a detailed investigation of the factual issues, and it was arguable that art.6 did not apply to the rights of the respondents in the litigation since there was no civil right to force a person into a marriage against their will. Further, there was no right to information which, if abused, would lead to serious breaches of the rights of the person to be protected. The outcome of the case was that the order was discharged after appropriate expert evidence confirming that the person who was the subject of the order wished to regularise her marriage. The court emphasised the need for the person who was to be protected to have separate and independent legal representation.

If an issue does arise which justifies the use of a special advocate *Re R (Closed Material Procedure: Special Advocates:Funding)* [2017] EWHC 1793 (Fam) is a decision in which the police were required to fund without a costs cap the funding of a second special advocate for the father; there being one already for the mother. The issue concerned the refusal by the police to disclose some material that would have increased the risks to the family. It was necessary to have the material examined to afford the fullest and fairest opportunity to test the case for non-disclosure.

10-50   The court has a wide discretion as to the terms of a forced marriage protection order: s.63B. It can include such prohibitions, restrictions or requirements and other terms as the court thinks appropriate. It is not limited to conduct within England and Wales and can be directed to third parties as respondents even where those persons are not direct perpetrators of "force" and are or may become involved indirectly. The term used is "involvement in other respects" and includes conspiring to force or attempting to force a person to enter into a marriage as well as the other well-established types of secondary participation in unlawful acts. Third parties less directly involved need not be specifically identified for the purposes of an order.

The order may be applied for by way of a specific application, but the court has jurisdiction to grant the order in family proceedings as defined by s.63C(7) where the court considers that a forced marriage protection order should be made to protect an individual who may or may not be a party to the same proceedings, and where the person against whom the order is directed is a party to the proceedings: s.63C(6). Where the order is made other than on a free-standing application, the court must set out in the order a summary of the reasons for the making of the order and the names and addresses of the persons to be served with the order.

The application may be made by the person to be protected by the order or by a *relevant* third party: s.63C(2). "Relevant third party" may include any person specified by order of the Lord Chancellor and may include the Secretary of State. A local authority can be a relevant third party: Family Law Act 1996 (Forced Marriage) (Relevant Third Party) Order 2009. The police are not entitled to bring an application for committal for breach of a FMPO because they are not nominated as a relevant third party under the Act and may only apply for an order with the leave of the court: *Bedfordshire Police Constabulary v RU* [2013] EWHC 2350 (Fam).

10-51   Other third parties may apply with the leave of the court and the following factors may be considered as part of all the circumstances of the case in deciding whether to grant leave: s.63C(4):

(a)   the applicant's connection with the person to be protected;

(b)   the applicant's knowledge of the circumstances of the person to be protected;

(c)   the wishes and feelings of the person to be protected so far as reasonable and ascertainable and in the light of the age and understanding of that person. The order can be applied for without informing and without the consent of the person to be protected.

The Pt 18 procedure should be used to make an application for leave to apply. There is no reason why a family member with a legitimate interest in the welfare of the person to be protected should not apply for and be granted leave to make an application.

If the applicant is a child, he or she may apply without the leave of the court under the Act but the provisions of FPR 2010 Rule 16.6 will apply. Therefore, a child may only bring proceedings through a litigation friend unless the court grants leave to the child to act in person if he or she has sufficient understanding, or the child may apply through a solicitor who considers that the child is able to give instructions and has accepted those instructions.

10-52   Issues of capacity both to conduct litigation and to enter into a marriage may arise. If so they will be determined under the Mental Capacity Act 2005. Expert evidence may be necessary as to the level of understanding and cognitive ability of the person to be protected. The guidance provided by Munby J in *Re E (An Alleged Patient), Sheffield City Council v E and S* [2004] EWHC 2808 (Fam) may be of assistance (though it should be noted that it was doubted in some respects by Baroness Hale of Richmond in *R. v Cooper* [2009] 1 W.L.R. 1786). Reference should also be made to the *Forced Marriage and Learning Disabilities Multi-Agency Practice Guidelines* at *www.fco.gov.uk*.

The court is concerned with the general capacity to marry of the individual rather than his or her capacity to marry one person rather than another.

Capacity to marry is different from whether the decision is a wise one, either generally or as a specific decision, or whether it is in the best interests of the person concerned.

The person must understand not simply that they are going through a marriage ceremony and understand the words; he or she must understand the duties and responsibilities that normally attach to marriage. These are the status of husband and wife conferred by the contract which is an agreement to live together and to love one another as husband and wife to the exclusion of all others. It involves the sharing of a common home and a common domestic life and the right to enjoy each other's society, comfort and assistance. The contract of marriage is in essence a simple one and can be readily understood by anyone of normal intelligence.

Under s.63D, an order may be made without notice where it is just and convenient to do so. Section 63D(2) sets out the criteria for such an application; the court must consider all the circumstances of the case including: **10-53**

(a) any risk of significant harm to the person to be protected or any other person if the order is not made immediately;

(b) whether it is likely that an applicant will be deterred or prevented from pursuing an application if an order is not made immediately;

(c) whether there is reason to believe that the respondent is aware of the proceedings but is evading service, and the delay involved in effecting service will cause serious prejudice to the person to be protected or the applicant, if a different person.

The procedure to be followed is set out in Pt 11 of the FPR 2010. If an order is made without notice, there must be an on notice hearing as soon as just and convenient to give the respondent the opportunity to be heard. The sworn statement in support must set out why notice has not been given: r.11.2. Personal service should be not less than two days before the hearing unless the court abridges time for service: r.11.4(2) and (3). The applicant may request service of the application by the court. If the applicant is a person other than the individual who is the subject of the proceedings, the court will give directions about who is to be served with the application. This can include, in the exercise of the court's general case management power under FPR 2010 r.4.1(3)(a), making the person's support workers such as a social worker or mental health professional aware of the proceedings so that they can attend to support the person at a future hearing; the court can also use this power to secure the attendance of appropriate professionals to assist a person who has communication difficulties: *Re X (A child)* [2011] EWHC 3401 (Fam).

Rule 11.7 provides that the hearing must be in private unless the court otherwise directs. Rule 11.8 requires the court to set out in the order the reasons in summary for making the order and the names of the persons to be served where the court makes an order of its own motion. Further, the court must give directions as to how the order is to be served: r.11.8(3). The order should be served as a matter of course on the following agencies: **10-54**

(i)   the Forced Marriage Unit/Foreign and Commonwealth Office;
(ii)   the UK Border Agency;
(iii)   the Identity and Passport Service;
(iv)   the children's services/adult services
(v)   the appropriate police authority;
(vi)   the relevant embassy if the facts require it.

The order can contain a wide range of provisions but the terms of the order must be consistent with the purposes of the jurisdiction and not for the ancillary protection of other connected persons who may have their own separate statutory remedy: *Re E (Female Genital Mutilation Protection Order* [2015] EWHC 2275 (Fam). The main provision will be a prohibition against the respondents from arranging or holding a celebration of the any marriage in England and Wales or overseas. It can include non-molestation provisions relating to the person to be protected; passport orders which will prevent any application for a passport, cancels an existing passport,prevents a passport being issued without leave of the court, requires the surrender of a passport; for consular officials to have access to the person if outside of the jurisdiction or for a local authority, the police or legal representatives to do so; and for repatriation with the assistance of the Foreign and Commonwealth Office. The Foreign and Commonwealth Office has a Forced Marriage Unit which can offer assistance and in some instances may help a person overseas to start proceedings in England and Wales for protective orders.

10-55   A power of arrest cannot be attached to a FMPO and s.63CA makes a breach of a FMPO an arrestable offence with a maximum penalty on indictment of five years imprisonment or a fine or both and on summary conviction a maximum sentence of 12 months or a fine or both. The provisions in relation to an application by an interested party for a warrant of arrest are preserved and all the consequential powers for remand on bail or in custody or for medical examination and report: ss.63J (2)-(3) and ss.63K and L. Part 18 should be used to apply for a warrant for arrest.

10-56   The court's power to commit for contempt in respect of an order is preserved under s.63O. If an alleged contemnor is prosecuted for breach of the order there cannot be subsequent committal proceedings if for example he is acquitted: s.63CA(3). If the breach has been punished as a contempt of court, the person in breach cannot be convicted of the criminal offence: s.63CA(4). The FMPO should be endorsed with a clear notice of the consequences of a breach of the order which are either that he can be prosecuted for a breach or be subject to proceedings for contempt of court using the wording of the usual penal notice.

Where the subjects of the proceedings are minors at the time of the application, the court can exercise the wardship jurisdiction and make an order for a report under s.37 of the Children Act 1989 requiring the local authority to consider whether it should issue s.31 care proceedings: *A v SM* [2012] EWHC 435 (Fam).

For the present, the jurisdiction to make a forced marriage protection order can be exercised by the High Court and in the Family Court at certain specified centres: Birmingham, Blackburn, Bradford, Bristol, Cardiff, Derby, Leeds, Leicester, Luton, Manchester, Middlesbrough, Newcastle upon Tyne and the Family Courts for London. It may be necessary to consider transfer for hearing before a Family Division judge if significant overseas consular assistance may be required to achieve enforcement of the order and issues of repatriation arise. If the application is to be dealt with in the Family Court it can be allocated to any full time Circuit or District Judge who has authorisation for public and/or private family law proceedings; to any recorder with similar authorisation and to a District Judge of the PRFD or the Central Family Court.

The President's Practice Guidance April 2016 sets out a protocol and information about how to obtain assistance from the FCO and liaison with a British Embassy or High Commission.

There will often be a need to ensure that the order is translated before service to avoid issues at the stage of enforcement.

6   THE FEMALE GENITAL MUTILATION ACT 2003

Section 73 of the Serious Crime Act 2015 has amended the 2003 Act by insert-   **10-57** ing a new s.5A and Sch.2. This creates a new form of protective order for girls who have been the victims of female genital mutilation (FGM) or who may be at risk of the commission of FGM: Sch.2 Pt 1 para.1. It is an additional protective measure which is made clear under para.6(2) in which all the existing remedies are identified.

The 2003 Act defines the acts that amount to FGM in s.1 which creates the criminal offence of FGM and there are 3 other methods by which an offence can be committed. The s.2 offence is committed by a person who aids abets counsels or procures the girl to do the act(s) against herself. Section 3 is the offence of secondary participation in the main offence when committed by a non-UK national or resident outside of the UK. Section 3A makes it an offence for a person who is responsible for her to fail to protect a girl from FGM and can be committed by a person who has parental responsibility and frequent contact with the girl: s.3A(3). The offence can also be committed by a person aged over the age of 18 years who has assumed responsibility for the girls in the manner of a parent. There are statutory defences to each offence. There is no age limit to the definition of a "girl". The offences can be committed by acts outside of the UK by a UK national or UK resident.

The purpose of the Female Genital Mutilation Protection Order (FGMPO) is to   **10-58** create a provision which is similar in nature to the Forced Marriage Protection Order in that it is an order which is capable of being drafted to meet the particular facts of the case and is likely to be used most to prevent a girl from being removed from the UK or taken to a particular location within the UK for the act of FGM to be done to her. The court must take into account all the circumstances including the need to secure the health, safety and well being of the girl: para.1(2) Sch.2.

The FGMPO may contain such prohibitions, restrictions and requirements and such other terms as the court considers appropriate for the purposes of the order: para.1(3) Sch.2. The order can relate to conduct outside as well as inside England and Wales and can be addressed to any person who may become involved in any way in assisting in or creating the opportunity for FGM to be carried out: paras 1(4) and (5). The order can be made for a specified period or indefinitely until varied or discharged: para.1(6). In *Re X (A Child) (FGM Protection Order)(Restriction on Travel)* [2017] EWHC 2898 (Fam) the court found that there was evidence of a significant risk of FGM in Egypt and within the paternal family who had lied about the family's rejection of FGM as an acceptable practice. The court made an order which prohibited the mother and the child, then aged 15 months, from travelling outside of the UK until the child's 16th birthday and a further order prohibiting any application by either parent for a passport or other travel document for the child.

Not every application for an order succeeds. In *Re F and X (Female Genital Mutilation)* [2015] EWHC 2653 (Fam) the order was refused because the evidence did not establish that there was an appreciable risk of the children being subject to FGM and the practice was not followed in the paternal family and the area where the family lived had been one of the first to campaign against FGM. The children were above the age at which it would be carried out if it was to be. The mother's evidence was not reliable and she had lied to the court. The without notice order had been obtained probably as part of an "immigration scam". The father was given permission to remove the children permanently to Nigeria and the FGM Protection Order was discharged.

10-59   Paragraph 2 of Sch.2 sets out the procedure for an application. The application is made to the family court or the High Court and can be made by the girl herself, a relevant third party (currently limited to a local authority (FGMPO (Relevant Third Party) Regulations 2015), or a person who has obtained the leave of the court. In *Re E* (above) the children's mother was an appropriate person to make an application for them. The criteria for the grant of leave are set out in paragraph 2(4) and the court must have regard to all the circumstances of the case including the applicant's connection with the girl to be protected and the applicant's knowledge of the circumstances of the girl. The application for leave may be made without notice: Family Procedure Rules r.11.3(A1) The application may be made within existing family proceedings where there is a need to protect the girl whether or not a party to the proceedings and the respondent to whom the order is going to be directed is a party to the existing proceedings. Otherwise it is a free standing application.

The criminal court has power to make a FGMPO in pending criminal proceedings before conviction against the defendant and in respect of any girl whether or not she is a victim of the offence in the criminal proceedings. A separate application is not required and the court is in effect exercising its own motion powers. It is a requirement that the court considers that the order should be made to protect the girl.

10-60   An application may be made without notice to the respondent. The court has to have regard to all the circumstances including an evaluation of the risk of the girl or any other girl of becoming a victim of genital mutilation if the order is not made immediately; whether an applicant may be deterred from pursuing an application if an order is not granted immediately; whether the respondent is evading service but is aware of the proceedings and the delay in effecting substituted service will cause prejudice to the girl or the applicant: para.(1) and (2). If an order is made without notice the court must give the respondent the opportunity to make representations at a hearing of which all parties have been given notice and which is as soon as just and convenient: para.5(3) and (4).

Paragraph 6 gives the power to vary or discharge the order on the application of the girl herself, any party to the proceedings, or any person affected by the order. Where the order has been made in criminal proceedings the prosecution and the defendant are to be regarded as parties to the proceeding: para.6(2). The court may vary or discharge the order even without an application where the order is made in existing proceedings or in criminal proceedings: para.6(3).

There are duties placed on identified professionals under s.5B of the Act to notify the chief officer of police for the area in which the girl lives if the person discovers that an act of FGM has been carried out on a girl under the age of 18. The professionals are defined as persons who work in a regulated profession and are a healthcare professional, a teacher or a social care worker in Wales. The duty arises if the person is informed by the girl that an act of FGM has been committed against her and/or the person observes physical signs on the girl appearing to show that an act of FGM has been carried out on her and the person has no reason to believe that the act was or was part of a surgical procedure. The duty does not apply if the person has reason to believe that another member of a regulated profession has made a notification in relation to the same act of FGM.

The notification may be in writing or orally and it must be made before the end of one month from the time when the person first discovers that the act of FGM appears to have been carried out on the girl. Further the girl must be identified and there must be an explanation of why the notification has been made: s.5B(5). Making the notification will not amount to a breach of confidence or any other restriction on the disclosure of information: s.5B(7). Interim guidance was issued to local authorities by the Ministry of Justice Criminal and Civil Legal Policy Unit dated July 2015.

Breach of the FGMPO without reasonable excuse is a criminal offence under **10-61** para.4. Where the order is made without notice the person in breach must have been aware of the existence of the order when the conduct complained of took place. The penalty after conviction on indictment is five years imprisonment or a fine or both and on summary conviction 12 months imprisonment or a fine or both.

If there is a conviction for the offence of breach, there cannot be committal proceedings for the same conduct and the reverse is the case if the conduct has been punished as a contempt of court. Paragraph 7 provides the procedure to apply for a warrant for arrest. The application may be made by the girl, the applicant or any other person with the leave of the court. Where a warrant for arrest has been executed there are remand provisions set out in paras 8–14 which permit remand on bail subject to conditions where appropriate, in custody for a period not exceeding eight days or for medical examination and report in which case the remand can be for up to four weeks unless the respondent is in custody when the period of remand cannot exceed three weeks at a time: paras 9(2) and (3).

The Family Procedure Rules 2010 Pt 11 have been amended to cover FGMPO **10-62** applications. The requirements are the same as for Forced Marriage Protection Orders. The application for leave must be made using the Pt 18 procedure and include a draft of the proposed application: r.11.3. The period of notice for service of the application is not less than two days before the hearing unless time has been abridged: r.11.4. The hearing will be in private unless the court directs otherwise: r.11.7. The order must be sent by the court to the police station for the address of the person who is the subject of the proceedings and to such other police station as the court may specify: r.11.12. The order or undertaking must be endorsed with a penal notice and served on the person to whom the order is directed: r.11.15.

There are 23 family courts designated to deal with applications for FGMPOs: Central Family Court, Birmingham Civil and Family Justice Centre, Bradford Combined Court, Brighton Family Court Hearing Centre, Bristol Civil and Family Justice Centre, Cardiff Civil and Family Justice Centre, Derby Combined Court, East London Family Court, Leeds Combined Court, Leicester Civil and Family Court Hearing Centre, Liverpool Civil and Family Court Hearing Centre, Luton County Court and Family Court, Manchester County Court and Family Court, Newcastle upon Tyne Combined Court Centre, Norwich Combined Court and Family Hearing Centre, Oxford Combined Court and Family Court Hearing Centre, Plymouth Combined Court, Portsmouth Combined Court Centre, Preston Family Court, Reading County Court and Family Court Hearing Centre, Sheffield Combined Court Centre, Teeside Combined Court, West London Family Court. Also any location at which the High Court is sitting.

The jurisdiction can be exercised by judges of the High Court, of the Family Court or by a court in criminal proceedings which includes a justice of the peace in criminal proceedings before a magistrates' court.

7   THE PROTECTION FROM HARASSMENT ACT 1997

10-63   The common law did not recognise a separate tort of harassment. In *Khorasandjian v Bush* [1993] QB 727, the plaintiff was granted an interim injunction restraining the defendant from harassing, pestering or communicating with her in any way in circumstances where they had never been married and had not cohabited. The legal basis used in the Court of Appeal for upholding the form of words was that persistent harassment by unwanted telephone calls was actionable as a private nuisance, although the plaintiff had no proprietary interest in the premises where she received the calls. This was an extension of the approach adopted by the Court of Appeal in *Burnett v George* [1992] 1 F.L.R. 525, in which it was decided that there had to be some evidence that the health of the plaintiff was being impaired by molestation or interference calculated to cause such impairment. However, the *Khorasandjian* decision was overruled in part by the House of Lords in *Hunter v Canary Wharf* [1997] A.C. 655. The ability of the common law to protect from harassment an applicant who was neither spouse nor cohabitee of the respondent was even more restricted and uncertain.

Although originally intended to deal with the form of harassment known as "stalking", the 1997 Act goes some way to redress the absence of a tort of harassment by creating a civil remedy in damages in which an application for an interim or permanent injunction can be made. Section 3 provides that an actual or apprehended breach of s.1 may be the subject of a claim in civil proceedings by the person who is or may be the victim of the course of conduct in question. Damages may be awarded for (among other things) any anxiety caused by the harassment or any financial loss resulting from the harassment. In *Singh v Bhakar and Bhakar* [2007] 1 F.L.R. 880, an award of £35,000 was made at Nottingham County Court to a claimant who had been harassed by her mother-in-law in a campaign spanning four months, which had the effect of bringing her marriage to an end and causing serious health problems for the claimant. Section 6 provides that the usual three-year period of limitation does not apply to an action brought under s.3 of the Act and disapplies s.11 of the Limitation Act 1980 in such actions entirely. See also the discussion at paras 4-62–4-64.

10-64   Section 1(1) of the Act provides the core definition for the criminal offences created under the Act and for the civil remedy by providing that a person must not pursue a course of conduct:

    (a)   which amounts to harassment of another;
    (b)   which he knows or ought to know amounts to harassment of the other.

An objective test applies under s.1(2) and the person whose course of conduct is in question will be taken to know that it amounts to harassment of another if a reasonable person in possession of the same information would think the course of conduct amounted to harassment of the other. Conduct will not amount to harassment if the person who pursued it did so:

    (a)   for the purpose of preventing or detecting crime;
    (b)   under any enactment or rule of law;
    (c)   to comply with any condition or requirement imposed by any person under any enactment; or that the circumstances are
    (d)   such that it was reasonable to do so in the particular circumstances.

10-65   The scope of the Act was widened by amendments introduced under s.125 of the Serious Organised Crime and Police Act 2005. By s.1(1A), a person must not pursue a course of conduct which involves harassment of two or more persons which he knows or ought to know involves harassment of those persons and by which he intends to persuade any person, whether or not one of those mentioned above, not to do something that he is entitled or required to do or to do something that he is not under any obligation to do. The purpose of the new provision appears to be to prohibit harassment of persons which is intended to affect third parties who have the ability to take actions, and to influence them to act in a particular way. This third party has the right to apply for injunctive relief in his own right, independent of the rights of the victim. The protection is available only for individuals: section 7(5).

Such conduct is made a criminal offence under s.2 and injunctive relief is available under s.3A. An extended definition is provided by s.7(3A) of secondary participation, and such a secondary party is made responsible for the course of conduct and fixed with the knowledge and purpose of the other party as it was at the time of the secondary participation. This applies both to civil and criminal liability under the Act.

Harassment is not defined in the Act, although s.7(2) provides that harassing a person will include alarming the person or causing the person distress. The Law Commission Report, *Domestic Violence and Occupation of the Family Home*, included some examples of "non-violent harassment or molestation" such as pestering, shouting, denigration, installing a mistress in the family home, nuisance phone calls, anonymous letters, filling car locks with superglue and, in the era of electronic communication, the inappropriate use of social network sites.   **10-66**

One of the key definitions is the term "course of conduct". This must involve conduct on at least two occasions. "Conduct" includes speech: s.7(3) and (4). In order for the "course of conduct" to amount to harassment, it is not sufficient that there have been two separate and individual incidents without any cogent linking conduct between them: *R. v Hills* [2001] 1 F.L.R. 580, in which it was held that two incidents six months apart could not justify a criminal conviction. Two incidents may be sufficient but the fewer the incidents are and the further apart in time they are, the less likely it will be that they constitute a "course of conduct": *Lau v Director of Public Prosecutions* [2000] 1 F.L.R. 799.

The standard of proof on factual issues is the civil standard of balance of probabilities: *Hipgrave and Hipgrave v Jones* [2005] 2 F.L.R. 174. The reasoning of the court primarily was that proceedings under the 1997 Act were dealing with the rights and protection of individuals, and the fact that a breach was punishable as a criminal offence was not determinative as the defendant had to return to court before any penalty was imposed.

There are no new rules of procedure for applications under s.3 and the general rules for interim and final injunctions apply to such applications. Both the High Court and county court have jurisdiction.   **10-67**

There is no provision for the attachment of a power of arrest; s.3(3)–(6) provides for the claimant to seek a warrant of arrest from the court where there is an allegation of breach of the injunction. The application is made to the court that granted the injunction. A warrant may only be issued if the application is substantiated on oath and the judge or district judge has reasonable grounds for believing that the defendant is in breach of the injunction. The procedure after arrest is set out in CPR r.65 and provides for the court to determine whether the facts and the circumstances which led to the arrest amounted to disobedience of the injunction, or whether to adjourn the proceedings and release the arrested person. If the hearing is adjourned, it must take place within 14 days, on not less than two days' notice to the arrested person. There is no power to release the arrested person on bail. A district judge does not have power to hear committal proceedings under the Act. The claimant can also issue an application for committal.

10-68   Breach of an injunction granted under s.3(3) committed without reasonable excuse is also a criminal offence, punishable on indictment with up to five years' imprisonment or a fine, or both, and on summary conviction with imprisonment up to a maximum of six months, or a fine not exceeding the statutory maximum, or both: s.3(9). A defendant in breach of an order cannot be both convicted of a criminal offence and punished for a contempt of court—these are mutually exclusive options: s.3(7) and (8).

The Act creates two criminal offences—s.2 is a summary-only offence and is committed by a person who "pursues a course of conduct in breach of section 1". It is punishable by up to six months' imprisonment or a fine not exceeding the statutory maximum, or both (s.2(2)). The offence is an arrestable offence (s.2(3)). The more serious offence is under s.4 and is committed by a person whose course of conduct causes another to fear, on at least two occasions, that violence will be used against him and where the person responsible for the course of conduct knows or ought to know that his course of conduct will cause the other to fear violence on each of those occasions. The offence under s.4 is punishable on conviction on indictment with up to five years' imprisonment or a fine, or both, and on summary conviction with up to six months' imprisonment or a fine up to the statutory maximum, or both (s.4(4)).

10-69   Section 7(2) provides an objective test as to knowledge—if a reasonable person in possession of the same information would think the course of conduct would cause the other to fear violence, the person responsible for the course of conduct will be taken to know that it will cause the other to fear violence will be used against him.

If the police become involved it may not be necessary to use the civil remedy, and the court on conviction of a criminal offence has the power to make a restraining order under s.5(1) for a specified period or without limit of time. This power has been extended to permit the court to make a restraining order following an acquittal of either an s.2 or an s.4 offence or any other offence: s.5A, inserted by s.12 of the Domestic Violence, Crime and Victims Act 2004. The prosecution or the defence may lead as further evidence any evidence that would be admissible in proceedings for an injunction: s.5(3A); an application to vary or discharge can be made by the prosecutor, the defendant or any person mentioned in the order: s.5(4) and any person mentioned in the order is entitled to be heard on the hearing of an application for variation or discharge: s.5(4A). Breach of such an order without reasonable excuse is a criminal offence punishable on conviction on indictment or on summary conviction with the same penalties as a s.4 offence.

8   INJUNCTIONS CONCERNING CHILDREN

Prohibited steps order

10-70   The Children Act 1989 s.8 introduced the prohibited steps order, which is the most usual form of injunction concerning children. A prohibited steps order may, for example, restrain the removal of a child from the jurisdiction or from the care of the person with whom the child is living. It may be made against anyone (not just the parent of the child), but the only steps which may be prohibited are those which could be taken by a parent in meeting parental responsibilities (and not, for example, the publication of information concerning the child—see below). It is only enforceable as an injunction if the court gives leave under FPR 2010 r.37.9(3) for a penal notice to be endorsed.

In *Re P-B (Contact: Committal)* [2009] EWCA Civ 143 it was held that an appropriately worded order made in public law proceedings in the county court under s.34 of the Children Act 1989 was enforceable by committal, and a county court judge had power to attach a penal notice to such an order. FPR 1991 r.4.21A applied only to private law orders but CCR Ord.29 could be used to fill the gap. The local authority had the duty to ensure that contact orders under s.34 were enforced. To attach a penal notice to such an order was exceptional and it was unnecessary for the judge to sit as a judge of the High Court to do so. The court did not go so far as to identify which officer of the local authority would be the subject of an order for committal in the event of further breach of the order since the case was "nowhere near committal". The judge was "simply serving forceful notice on the local authority that she expected her order to be obeyed".

In *Re S (Eligible Child)* [2008] EWCA Civ 378, the court observed that it "may be possible to commit the local authority's team manager for his contempt of court" in refusing to comply with undertakings given to the court to provide a pathway plan for an eligible child with severe disabilities together with certain other materials relevant to the provision of services for her, as a result of which proceedings brought by the parents for discharge of the care order were dismissed. Wall LJ expressed sympathy for the unenviable position of the individual social worker and was critical of the managers who needed to understand that orders of the court were to be obeyed. In the event, the court required a written explanation from the relevant director of social services.

Application for a prohibited steps order is made in private and may be made in cases of real urgency out of normal court hours. "The President's Guidance November 18, 2010 [2011] 1 F.L.R. 303", which is to be read alongside the previous Practice Directions and guidance, makes clear that it is for cases that cannot wait until the court can convene formally, and therefore substantial documentation is not appropriate. The gist of the case should be reduced to one sheet of A4 or email equivalent or a short telephone conversation. The judge's decision as to what is urgent is final. Misuse of the procedure will lead to wasted costs and/or reporting to professional bodies for serious professional misconduct. An order prohibiting the removal of a child from England and Wales may be made by a district judge (*Practice Direction (Child: Removal from Jurisdiction)* [1973] 1 W.L.R. 657). **10-71**

The court may grant an application, despite no proceedings having been filed, if the applicant undertakes to institute proceedings within 24 hours: FPR 2010 r.12.16(2). Notice of any injunction prohibiting the removal of a child from the jurisdiction should be given to the passport office. That office should also be notified if the court makes an order (as it has power to do) for the surrender of a passport issued to, or containing particulars of, a child (*Practice Direction (Children: Removal from Jurisdiction)* [1983] 1 W.L.R. 558). For details of the "port alert" procedure where a child may be about to be taken abroad, see *Practice Direction (Minors: Preventing Removal Abroad)* [1986] 1 W.L.R. 475. Failure to renew notices to the passport office and/or the port alert procedure can amount to professional negligence.

Where the court refuses to make an order in an application made without notice, it may direct that the application be made on notice (FPR 2010 r.12.16(6)). There is a prescribed form of application (CHA10) in Appendix 1 to the FPR. A copy of any order made without notice to the respondent must be served within 48 hours on any other party and on whoever has care of the child or had such care immediately before the order was made (FPR 2010 r.12.16(4) and (5)).

In *Re S (Ex Parte Orders)* [2001] 1 F.L.R. 308, it was emphasised that the legal **10-72** advisers of those who apply for relief in respect of children without notice to the other party have a responsibility to comply to the letter with undertakings given to the court, and the court will require the following steps of them:

(a) where proceedings have not been issued, the issue and service of proceedings on the respondent either by some specified time or as soon as practicable;

(b) the filing and service on the respondent of sworn evidence in affidavit form where the application had not been made on the basis of sworn evidence, confirming what had been said to the court to justify the granting of the injunction;

(c) service of the proceedings, a scaled copy of the court order, copies of the affidavit(s) and exhibit(s) containing the evidence relied upon by the applicant and notice of the return day together with details of any application to be made on the return day.

If it is not possible to comply with the timescale given to the court, the task must be passed to someone who can do so or an extension of time sought from the court.

10-73   A prohibited steps order is not to be made:

(a) to exclude a parent from his home (*D v D (Ouster Order)* [1996] 2 F.C.R. 496), even for the protection of a child (*Nottinghamshire County Council v P* [1993] 2 F.L.R. 134, in which the judge, on an application to remove from the family home a father who was alleged to have sexually abused his children, used the jurisdiction of the court under ss.10 and 11 of the Children Act 1989 but was held to have been wrong to do so by the Court of Appeal);

(b) in respect of a child in local authority care (s.9(1) of the Act);

(c) with a view to achieving a result which could be achieved by making a child arrangement order;

(d) where the child has reached the age of 16, or for a period during which the child will reach that age, unless the circumstances are exceptional (s.9(6) and (7) of the Act).

In exceptional circumstances, an injunction may be attached to a child arrangement order under s.11(7) of the Act to remedy or prevent an abduction, directing the immediate return of the child to the parent with whom the child lives under the child arrangement order (*Re B (Minors) (Residence Order)* [1992] 3 All E.R. 867).

10-74   Under ss.38A, 38B, 44A and 44B of the Children Act 1989, the court has the power to allow an exclusion requirement to be made in interim care proceedings or on an application for an emergency protection order. The key words in these provisions are that the court must have "reasonable cause" to believe that, if a person is excluded from the house in which the child lives, the child will cease to suffer or be likely to suffer from significant harm, and that another person living in the house (whether a parent of the child or someone else) is able and willing to give the child the care it would be reasonable to expect a parent to give him or her, and consents to the exclusion requirement. The power allows the court to exclude, prohibit entry and exclude from an area in which the house is situated. A similar provision is provided in relation to emergency protection orders (s.44), though due to the wording of s.44 the provision is slightly different.

Schedule 6 also provides for the attachment of a power of arrest to these orders. All courts can accept an undertaking instead of making an order, but a power of arrest cannot be attached.

If the child is removed for a continuous period of over 24 hours by the local authority from the house to other accommodation, the exclusion requirement will lapse.

There is less need to use the inherent jurisdiction as a result of these provisions.

Recovery orders

Section 50 of the Act provides that where there is reason to believe a child who **10-75** is in care, subject to an emergency protection order or under police protection, has been abducted, run away from the person having the care of him or her or is missing, a recovery order may be made. Such an order is in the nature of an injunction, operating as a direction to comply with any request to produce the child. Applications should be made in the Family Court unless proceedings are pending in another court (including where the application is made as a result of a court-directed investigation) and may be heard by lay justices: Family Court (Composition and Distribution of Business) Rules 2014 rule 16(3)(x).

Section 34 of the Family Law Act 1986 further permits an order to be made for a tipstaff, bailiff or constable to enter premises and take charge of a child where an order to give up the child has been disobeyed. The High Court has the power to direct the tipstaff to take charge of a child even if an order to give up a child has not been disobeyed.

Reference should be made to specialist works on the subject.

Emergency protection orders

Emergency protection orders, governed by s.44 of the Act, may be made if, but **10-76** only if, the court is satisfied that the child is likely to suffer significant harm (or, in the case of an application by a local authority, that its enquiries into whether the child had suffered significant harm are being frustrated by unreasonable refusal of access to the child). As with recovery orders, an order is in the nature of an injunction, operating as a direction to comply with any request to produce the child. Again, reference should be made to specialist works on the subject. The jurisdiction to grant an emergency protection order is no longer limited to the magistrates and can he heard by a any judge of the Family Court.

Injunctions in wardship proceedings

The wardship jurisdiction of the High Court is a possible vehicle for seeking an **10-77** injunction for the welfare of a child where statute does not confer jurisdiction. An example is an order prohibiting identification of a child. Where such an order is made in wardship proceedings, it has effect against the world at large (*Re X (A Minor)* [1984] 1 W.L.R. 1422). Any restraint is intended to protect from harassment the ward and those who care for him or her. It must be in clear terms and no wider than necessary to achieve the purpose for which it was imposed and, save perhaps in an exceptional case, the ward cannot be protected from any distress which may be caused to him by reading the publication himself: *Re W (A Minor) (Wardship: Restrictions on Publication)* [1992] 1 All E.R. 794). In *Re Z (A Minor) (Freedom of Publication)* [1996] 1 F.L.R. 191 at 208 it was said:

"The inherent jurisdiction will be used where the material to be published is directed as the child or is directed to an aspect of the child's upbringing by his parents or others who care for him in circumstances where that publicity is inimical to his welfare ... A separate aspect of the Court's inherent jurisdiction is the power to protect the integrity of its own proceedings, for example by preserving the anonymity of those who come forward to assist the court, so encouraging full and free disclosure of all material facts impinging on the child's well-being."

In *Re Jane* [2010] EWHC 3221 (Fam), a local authority involved in care proceedings concerning *Jane* applied for a reporting restriction order using s.100 of the Children Act 1989 against the media, but had failed to give appropriate notice to those organisations that did not subscribe to CopyDirect. The provisions of s.12 of the Human Rights Act 1998 permitting non-service did not apply; moreover, each individual media organisation would have to be served before the order would be effective. There were already information and photographs of the child in the public domain as a result of media attention focusing on the mother, who had taken part in a television programme not long before. Holman J was not prepared to make an order affecting reporting about the mother or the father, but was concerned with preventing the child's placement being undermined at the time or in the future and preventing media attention at any place where she was having contact with her parents, as well as preventing the fact that she was subject to care proceedings to become public. Those images already in the public domain would not be affected by the order, but any future publication of images was prevented. Practice Direction 12I Family Procedure Rules sets out the procedure where there is an application for a reporting restriction. A standard form of reporting restriction order suitable for cases of this kind has been agreed between representatives of the national media, the Official Solicitor and CAFCASS: see Precedent 28.

10-78   An unusual application was made to the Court of Appeal in *DE v AB (No. 2) (Permission Hearing: Publicity Protection)* [2014] EWCA Civ 1064 that the oral permission hearing should be heard in private because the mother who was subject to an injunction not to report to outside agencies parts of the father's sworn evidence intended to refer to the detail of the prohibited information in her application for permission to appeal. Ryder LJ observed that the mother's motives were not to ensure that secret justice was subject to scrutiny but to exact revenge on the father. The order made was that the appeal would be heard in public but subject to immediate and continuing publicity protections to prevent prohibited and withheld information from being disclosed into the public domain without the permission of the court.

The inherent jurisdiction may be used also where parents or their agents are placing information on the internet about issues connected with care proceedings or private law proceedings. The identification of the child or children as the subject of proceedings is prevented during the proceedings by s.97(2) of the Children Act 1989, and the provisions of s.12 of the Administration of Justice Act 1960 remain. However there may be a need on the facts of the case for wider prohibitions during and after proceedings. Tension arises between the art.8 rights of the child and the art.10 rights of a parent asserting the right to freedom of expression. An example of the issues and how to resolve them is found in the decision of *Clayton v Clayton* [2007] 1 F.L.R. 11.

10-79   In *Re J (A Child)* [2013] EWHC 2694 (Fam) the President explored the limitations on the protection of the identity of children in proceedings about them . After a discussion of the transparency debate about the workings of the family justice system the President granted a contra mundem injunction until the child's 18th birthday which struck a balance between the public interest in the workings of the system and the personal privacy and welfare interests of the child and restrained the naming of the child but not the publication of the images of the child. He repeated comments he made in an earlier decision (*Harris v Harris, Attorney-General v Harris* [2001] 2 F.L.R. 895) about the importance in a free society of parents who feel aggrieved at their experiences of the family justice system being able to express their views publicly about what they conceive to be failings on the part of individual judges or failings in the judicial system and also criticism of local authorities and others.

Other situations include the consent to or refusal of medical treatment. This can be exercised within wardship or, where the child is not a ward, under the court's inherent jurisdiction, e.g. *Re W (A Minor) (Medical Treatment: Court's Jurisdiction)* [1993] 1 F.L.R. 1 and more recently *Portsmouth City Council v King Southhampton Hospital Trust and Aysha King* [2014] EWHC 2964 (Fam). In *Re C (Adult: Refusal of Medical Treatment)* [1994] 1 W.L.R. 290 it was held that an injunction may be granted to restrain medical treatment, and such injunctive relief could extend to future circumstances. The court found that an adult patient's capacity was not so reduced that he did not understand the nature, purpose and effects of the proposed treatment, and the patient's right to self-determination had not been displaced. See also *Airedale NHS Trust v Bland* [1993] A.C. 789. Reference should be made to specialist works on the subject.

In *Re SO (Wardship: Extension of Protective Injunction Orders)* [2015] EWHC 935 (Fam) the court extended an injunction order beyond the eighteenth birthday of the young person involved in the proceedings. The mother and the young person were now living in Australia and the child had been subject to proceedings since 1999. The father presented a very high risk of harm having been convicted on two occasions of inciting the mother's murder. He had discovered where they were living. The young person was a British citizen and both mother and daughter were habitually resident in England and Wales when the original wardship proceedings began. The court as a public authority had to have regard to Articles 2, 6 and 8 when making orders that are needed to protect young people who are within its jurisdiction.

Miscellaneous

An adoption order may not have added to it a final order prohibiting the natural **10-80** parents from having contact with the child (*Re D (A Minor) (Adoption Order: Validity)* [1991] Fam. 137). If the child was a ward and an injunction of this nature existed prior to the adoption order, it ends with the termination of the wardship when the adoption order is made (*Re D (Minors) (Adoption Injunction)* [1993] 2 F.L.R. 737). It may be possible to apply for such an injunction under the inherent jurisdiction of the court after the final order for adoption or under Part IV of the Family Law Act 1996 if the conduct can be construed as non-molestation. It is arguable that as adoption proceedings are family proceedings there is jurisdiction within the adoption proceedings themselves to grant an order under the 1996 Act: *Re T (A Child)* [2017] EWCA Civ 1889.

A local authority can be restrained from placing a child up for adoption, even when authorised to do so by a placement order under the Adoption and Children Act 2002, if an application can be made to the court by either a parent or a foster parent for permission to apply to the court for the forms of relief available under the Act, such as permission to apply to revoke a placement order or permission to apply for an adoption order where a foster parent wishes to adopt the child: *Coventry CC v O* [2012] 3 WLR 208. Lord Wilson observed that the jurisdiction arises under s.37 of the Senior Courts Act 1981 and s.38 of the County Courts Act 1984. Although the foster parents could not issue their application for an adoption order until the period of notice required by the Act had expired, the judge had the power to make an injunction preventing the removal of the child almost 10 weeks before the earliest date on which they could make their application because the giving of notice under the Act had started the process. His Lordship's view was that it was unnecessary to invoke the jurisdiction of the Administrative Court. In the event, the foster parents were unsuccessful and Lord Wilson set out at [37] of the judgment the approach to be taken by the court in reaching its decision on the grant of the injunction:

(a) Do the prospects of the applicants establish that the decision to remove is by reference to public law principles irrational, disproportionate or otherwise unlawful or is in breach of the art.8 rights of the foster parents, adopters, and overarchingly the child?

(b) If the answer to (a) is affirmative, have the foster parents brought the proceedings with reasonable promptness?

(c) Might the injunction last for a substantial period and what might be the consequences?

(d) Might the injunction jeopardise the candidacy of the adopters?

(e) Would the consequence of the refusal of the injunction be to disable the foster parents from adopting the children?

(f) What is the status quo and would the injunction preserve or disrupt the status quo?

(g) Does the issue of whether to grant the injunction bear on any aspect of the child's welfare not addressed in the above questions?

10-81 The inherent jurisdiction in relation to children and young people is not limited to wardship and can be used in respect of adults, for example to prevent an adult of an undesirable character being in contact or associating with a child. Such orders can include power for the tipstaff or the local police on his behalf to search premises for any missing passports that have not been surrendered in accordance with the order and to arrest the party in breach for failure to comply. The contempt route is available and bail and remand provisions apply. It is available as a remedy to protect adolescent girls who are at risk of or are being sexually groomed and/or abused by older males and is an important consideration where there is evidence of sexual exploitation of young people either individually or as part of a group.

The inherent jurisdiction can be used to obtain mandatory orders that a parent must surrender any existing passports and be prohibited from obtaining any other passports. This is an important preventive step in cases of unauthorised removal of children to non-Hague Convention jurisdictions. Such orders can include power for the tipstaff or the local police on his behalf to search premises for any missing passports that have not been surrendered in accordance with the order and to arrest the party in breach for failure to comply. The contempt route is available and bail and remand provisions apply. Some of the cases referred to in the Committals section of this Chapter are examples of this jurisdiction.

10-82 An injunction may be granted in a possession action to compel the claimant's 19-year-old son, who had assaulted her, to leave home (*Egan v Egan* [1975] Ch. 218). In *London Borough of Brent v S* [2009] EWHC 1593 (Fam), the court declined to continue an injunction to prevent a 17-year-old Afghan male who was being accommodated by the local authority as an unaccompanied minor from travelling to Pakistan to search for the surviving members of his family, because the balance of his interests did not justify the remedy.

The media will not be prevented from interviewing a ward and publishing the interview unless it is necessary to do so to protect the child from clear and identifiable harm and the injunction sought was proportionate to that aim and no wider than necessary: *Kelly v BBC* [2001] 1 F.L.R. 197.

10-83 A parent or putative parent may be ordered not to leave the jurisdiction pending the carrying out of blood tests (*Re J (A Minor) (Wardship)* [1988] 1 F.L.R. 65).

In two cases, unsuccessful attempts have been made to obtain an injunction to prevent an abortion: *Paton v BPAS* [1979] QB 276 and *C v S* [1988] QB 135.

The court will not grant an injunction to prevent the disclosure by a party to domestic violence proceedings of documents filed or used in the proceedings, the contents of oral evidence given in the proceedings or the terms of the judgment as a matter of course. The court has to consider in each case whether the proper working of the administration of justice requires there to be confidentiality after the end of the proceedings: *Clibbery v Allen* [2002] Fam. 261.

9   ORDERS TO PRESERVE PROPERTY

The court has extremely wide powers under the Matrimonial Causes Act 1973 **10-84** ss.23–25A, as amended, to make ancillary financial orders at or after the hearing of a petition for divorce, judicial separation or nullity. Pending the determination of the financial application, there is an inherent power to grant an injunction to preserve money (including prospective proceeds of a claim for damages), chattels, the matrimonial home or other property. It is not necessary that there should be evidence of an intention to dispose of the property (*Roche v Roche* (1981) 11 Fam. Law 243; *Shipman v Shipman* [1991] 1 F.L.R. 250).

Section 37 of the 1973 Act provides that a spouse applying for financial relief may, if it appears that the other spouse is about to dispose of (otherwise than by will: s.37(6)), deal with or transfer out of the jurisdiction any property, obtain an order restraining him from doing so until the hearing and determination of the financial issue. This order, which is in effect a freezing injunction, can be served on third parties such as banks. It will only be granted where there is evidence that a transaction, the objective effect of which will be to defeat the financial application, is about to take place (*Smith v Smith* (1973) 4 Fam. Law 80). The charging of the matrimonial home is a disposition which may be restrained under s.37 (*Quartermain v Quartermain* (1974) 4 Fam. Law 156). An order may (and usually is) made by a district judge but he may refer the matter to a circuit judge or High Court judge. Discharge of an injunction does not prevent subsequent dispositions from being reviewed and set aside under s.37 (*Sherry v Sherry* [1991] 1 F.L.R. 307).

In *C v C (Without Notice Orders)* [2006] 1 F.L.R. 936, Munby J held that a third **10-85** party served with or given notice of an injunction such as a bank, should be given on request copies of the material read by the judge and information about what took place at the hearing. However, it was not desirable or necessary that the information should be volunteered, although that obligation applied to disclosure to the other party to the application. A separate affidavit could be prepared if the information to be disclosed would require disclosure of material from the substantive application which was not relevant to the involvement of the third party.

Re M (Freezing Injunction) [2006] 1 F.L.R. 1031 illustrates the limits on the jurisdiction of the court to use a freezing order as a means of providing maintenance pending suit. A distinction was drawn by the deputy High Court judge between the situation in which a husband is permitted to spend specified sums of money as an exception to the freezing order and a positive obligation to pay to the wife maintenance payments. It was suggested that it would only be appropriate in the most urgent of cases where the wife and/or children were without means and for the shortest possible duration pending a properly convened maintenance pending suit hearing.

In *UL v BK* [2013] EWHC 1735 (Fam) Mostyn J discussed the jurisdiction to grant a freezing order and the without notice and short notice application requirements. A draft order is appended to the judgement.

The property whose disposal is restrained may be abroad, although an order will **10-86** not be made in respect of foreign property if it would be unenforceable (*Hamlin v*

Hamlin [1986] Fam. 11). There is also jurisdiction pursuant to ss.23 and 24 of the Matrimonial and Family Proceedings Act 1984 to restrain the disposal of property pending the hearing of an application to the English courts for financial relief following an overseas divorce.

In *N v R (Injunction)* [2008] EWHC 1347 (Fam), Black J refused an injunction under s.25 of the Civil Jurisdiction and Judgments Act 1982 in respect of assets of the parties, jointly owned but situated in a Swiss bank account in the wife's sole name, which were said by the husband to be the subject of a claim between the spouses in Egypt. The order was refused on the individual merits of the application. The international flavour of the case is illustrated by the following summary: the marriage was Egyptian; the husband had Egyptian and Lebanese passports; the wife had Croatian and Italian passports; there had been a divorce in Croatia and nullity proceedings in Egypt; the funds were in Switzerland; and the claimed proceedings for the purpose of s.25 were in Egypt. The link with England was the habitual residence of the wife and the existence of English proceedings in relation to the child of the marriage.

10-87	Where no matrimonial suit is pending, questions between husband and wife as to the ownership of property may be resolved by the High Court or county court on an application under s.17 of the Married Women's Property Act 1882. An injunction may be granted restraining the respondent from dealing with the property pending the hearing. The application may be made to a district judge.

The court may impound the passport of a party who may flee the jurisdiction to avoid the court's processes: see para.7-44 above.

A search order for the inspection and removal of relevant documents may be made against a party to financial proceedings in the Family Division (*Emanuel v Emanuel* [1982] 1 W.L.R. 669).

The issue of the unlawful removal of documents during financial proceedings was dealt with in *Imerman v Tchenguez* [2010] EWCA Civ 908. Lord Neuberger MR confirmed that it was a breach of the husband's rights under art.8 for the wife's brothers to clandestinely and without the husband's permission copy documents which related to his private financial affairs and business dealings. Such conduct was a breach of confidence without any subsequent misuse of the documents. The fact that the parties were married did not in itself destroy the confidence attaching to the documents if, on analysis, they were confidential to one spouse. There were sufficient peremptory orders available in the Family Division by way of search and seizure orders, freezing and preservation orders to protect the rights of the wife. The wife was ordered to deliver up all the papers copied and guidance was given as to the circumstances in which she might be prevented from using information which she had gained from the papers rather than the papers themselves in the financial proceedings, and how the court should manage disclosure by the husband if the wife had retained copies of the wrongfully obtained documents. The court did not uphold the interpretation of the *Hildebrand Rules* (a previously approved practice in Family Division financial relief cases whereby a spouse was permitted to use copies of the other spouse's confidential documents and the information contained in them, usually where serious non-disclosure by the other spouse was suspected) adopted at first instance and went so far as to conclude that they were not good law. *UL v BK* (above) is an illustration of these principles and their effects.

10-88	In *Hemain v Hemain* [1988] 2 F.L.R. 388 the Court of Appeal held that an injunction may be granted restraining a party from pursuing family proceedings in a foreign court until the English court has ruled on jurisdiction: see the discussion of this power by Munby J in *R v R (Divorce: Hemain injunction)* [2005] 1 F.L.R. 386.

In *Aliye Ayten Ahmed and Ilkiz Mehmet v Mehmet Mustafa* [2014] EWCA Civ

277, the Court of Appeal upheld an anti-suit injunction the effect of which was to prevent the wife from re-litigating financial issues in another jurisdiction which had been concluded by a final order in the courts of England and Wales. *T v T (Hemain Injunction)* [2012] EWHC 3462 (Fam) is a further example of a case at first instance in which the relationship between financial remedy proceedings in an overseas jurisdiction which might confer an advantage on the husband and proposed proceedings in England and Wales which may have been more beneficial to the wife. Nicholas Francis QC sitting as a Deputy Judge of the High Court dismissed the wife's application to prevent the husband taking steps to advance the overseas litigation

Family proceedings involving search orders can only be dealt with in the High Court: see Ch.8.

10　THE HUMAN RIGHTS ACT 1998

The jurisdiction under the Family Law Act 1996 engages arts 5, 6, 8 and 14 of the ECHR and art.1 of the First Protocol. However, it is unlikely that a proper application of the statutory principles would result in an infringement of the rights of either party.　　**10-89**

Article 1 of the First Protocol guarantees peaceful enjoyment of possessions of which an individual can only be deprived in the public interest and subject to the conditions provided for by law and the general principles of international law. The state can enforce laws as necessary to control the use of property in accordance with the public interest. An occupation order is not a permanent deprivation where there is property ownership but may involve "an interference with the peaceful enjoyment of possessions". It is submitted that the criteria under ss.33–41 of the 1996 Act enable the court to strike a fair balance between the public interest and the rights of the individual, which is within the spirit of the article.

The same result is likely under art.8 because although the making of an occupation order and/or a non-molestation order will interfere with the respondent's right to family life, the right of the individual is qualified by the exceptions contained in art.8, namely public safety, the prevention of crime or disorder, the protection of health and morals and the protection of the rights and freedom of others. Thus far, interpretation of the Convention has permitted a distinction to be drawn between parties who are spouses and parties who are cohabitants: *Lindsay v UK* (1987) 9 E.H.R.R. 555. On this basis it seems unlikely that the requirement in s.41 of the Family Law Act 1996 that the court should have regard to the fact that the parties "have not given each other the commitment involved in marriage" will amount to a breach of art.14.　　**10-90**

The power of arrest under s.47 and the right of an applicant to apply for a warrant of arrest raise issues under art.5. A person may be arrested or detained for "non-compliance with the lawful order of the court or in order to secure the fulfilment of any obligation prescribed by law", and for the purpose of bringing him before the competent legal authority on reasonable suspicion of having committed an offence or when it is reasonably considered necessary to prevent his committing an offence or fleeing having done so: art.5(1)(b) and (c). He can only be arrested on reasonable suspicion formed on objective grounds; honestly held suspicion will not suffice: *Fox, Campbell and Hartley v UK* (1991) 13 E.H.H.R. 157. He is also entitled to be told promptly of the reasons for his arrest and of any charge against him: art.5(2), and he should be tried within a reasonable time or released pending trial: art.5(3). There is a requirement that a person arrested under a power of arrest should be brought before the court within 24 hours, and the practice for those arrested under a warrant is similar in the absence of a specific provision. Such provision and practice is compliant with judicial interpretation of the Convention so far.

10-91   Although committal proceedings and the enforcement provisions after arrest arise in the context of civil obligations, they are likely to be considered as "criminal" rather than civil proceedings because of the requirement of the criminal standard of proof and the availability of imprisonment as a penalty. It follows that a respondent in such proceedings is guaranteed the following rights:

(a)   the presumption of innocence;
(b)   the right to be informed of the accusation;
(c)   the right to have adequate time and facilities for the defence;
(d)   the right to defend oneself, to have representation and legal aid;
(e)   the right to call and cross-examine witnesses;
(f)   the right to an interpreter.

All these rights are provided for in the procedure for committal and enforcement applications and therefore the domestic law is likely to be held compliant with the Convention.

10-92   Article 4 of the Seventh Protocol prohibits double jeopardy. The practice of a person being the subject of committal proceedings and criminal proceedings for the same set of circumstances would appear to be vulnerable to challenge under this provision. Currently, however, the UK Government has not ratified the Seventh Protocol and it is not part of domestic law through the Human Rights Act 1998. Until it is ratified the problem will not arise directly.

Article 8 has a fundamental role in cases concerning children and is being used increasingly to challenge decisions made in adoption-linked applications where injunctive relief is being claimed and/or in judicial review proceedings where the court may be asked to interfere with the otherwise lawful exercise of powers by a local authority acting as an adoption agency. In *DL v LB of Newham* [2011] EWHC 1127 (Admin), Charles J held that it was possible for an adoption agency to breach art.8 even though it was acting within its statutory powers and that the review jurisdiction would be available in such cases, as would a challenge based on ss.6, 7 and 8 of the Human Rights Act 1998. In such proceedings, the court could grant interim relief by way of a stay of the local authority's exercise of its statutory powers so that the court could grant an effective remedy at the conclusion of the proceedings, if justified on the merits. This case, together with *Coventry CC v O*, demonstrates that the court's existing powers to grant interim relief or an injunction can be used to guarantee art.8 rights for claimants and children.

PART D: PRECEDENTS

Precedents

Precedents 1 to 5 are adapted from the five High Court forms prescribed by the Practice Direction (Interim Injunctions: Forms): **P0-01**

(1) Injunction before the issue of a claim form.
(2) Order for an injunction.
(3) Order containing an undertaking instead of an injunction.
(4) Adjournment of an application for an injunction.
(5) Application for an injunction treated as the trial of the action.

All orders of the above types made by the Chancery or Queen's Bench Interim Applications Judge should follow these forms in the absence of good reason to the contrary. Wherever possible, a draft should be provided to the court by email. This will enable the associate to incorporate any amendments made by the judge and to arrange for the immediate sealing and entry of the order. The parties should check with the court which word processing format should be used, but Microsoft Word is normally used.

Precedents 6 and 7 are the High Court forms for freezing injunctions and search orders prescribed by Practice Direction—Interim Injunctions, CPR PD 25A: **P0-02**

(6) Freezing Injunction (order to restrain disposal of assets worldwide or within England and Wales).
(7) Search Order (order for the preservation of evidence and property).

The examples should be modified as appropriate in any particular case: it is good practice for the draft shown to the judge to have any changes from the standard clauses clearly marked.

Precedents 8–10 are the county court general forms for an application for and the grant of an injunction in non-family cases.

Precedents 11 to 27 are a selection of unofficial precedents for use in injunction claims. Attention has been concentrated on documents which are a special feature of injunction cases. Pleadings such as particulars of claim and defences do not differ significantly from the general pattern. **P0-03**

There is an infinite variety of prohibitory clauses—that is to say, the words in a negative injunction stating what it is that the defendant is to be restrained from doing. There is no set form of words. The defendant is entitled to have the order defined with some precision, but the claimant's advisers should ensure that potential loopholes are closed.

1. INJUNCTION BEFORE ISSUE OF A CLAIM FORM

P1-01 IN THE HIGH COURT OF JUSTICE Claim No:
[DIVISION]
Before the Honourable MR(S) JUSTICE [ ]
[Date]
IN A INTENDED CLAIM BETWEEN

Applicant/Intended Claimant

and

Respondent/Intended Defendant

ORDER FOR AN INJUNCTION

Penal Notice

If you [insert name of Respondent] disobey this order you may be held to be in contempt of court and may be imprisoned, fined or have your assets seized.

Any other person who knows of this order and does anything which helps or permits the Respondent to breach the terms of this order may also be held to be in contempt of court and may be imprisoned, fined or have their assets seized.

Important

Notice to the Respondent

You should read the terms of the Order and the Guidance Notes very carefully. You are advised to consult a Solicitor as soon as possible.

An Application was made on [date] by Counsel for the Applicant to the Judge [and was attended by Counsel for the Respondent]. The Judge heard the Application and read the evidence listed in Schedule 1 and accepted the undertakings in Schedule 2 at the end of this Order.

IT IS ORDERED that:

(1) Until after [date] ("the Return Date") [OR final judgment on this claim] the Respondent must/ must not [body of injunction to go here]

(2) The costs of this Application are reserved to be dealt with by [the judge hearing the Application on the return date] [the trial judge].
[SUBSTITUTED SERVICE/SERVICE OUT OF THE JURISDICTION

(3) The Applicant may issue and serve the Claim Form on the Respondent at [location] by [date].

(4) If the Respondent wishes to defend the Claim he must acknowledge service within [ ] days of being served with the Claim Form.]

Guidance Notes

Effect of this Order

P1-02 **(1)** A Respondent who is an individual who is ordered not to do something must not do it himself or in any other way. He must not do it through others acting on his behalf or on his instructions or with his encouragement.

(2) A Respondent which is a corporation and which is ordered not to do something must not do it itself or by its directors, officers, employees or agents or in any other way.

Parties other than the Applicant and Respondent

It is a Contempt of Court for any person notified of this Order knowingly to assist in or permit a breach of this Order. Any person doing so may be sent to prison, fined or have his assets seized.

Variation or discharge of this Order

The Respondent (or anyone notified of this Order) may apply to the Court at any time to vary or discharge this Order (or so much of it as affects that person), but anyone wishing to do so must first inform the Applicant['s legal representatives].

Interpretation of this Order

(1)   In this Order, where there is more than one Respondent, (unless otherwise stated) references to "the Respondent" means both or all of them.

(2)   A requirement to serve on "the Respondent" means on each of them. However, the Order is effective against any Respondent on whom it is served.

(3)   An Order requiring "the Respondent" to do or not to do anything applies to all Respondents.

Schedule 1

Witness statements

The Applicant relied on the following witness statements: **P1-03**

Schedule 2

Undertakings given to the Court by the Applicant

(1)   If the Court later finds that this Order has caused loss to the Respondent, and   **P1-04**
decides that the Respondent should be compensated for that loss, the Applicant will comply with any Order the Court may make.

(2)   As soon as practicable the Applicant will issue and serve on the Respondent a Claim Form in the form of the draft produced to the Court and initialled by the Judge claiming appropriate relief together with this Order.

(3)   The Applicant will cause written evidence to be filed [substantially in the terms of the draft produced to the Court and initialled by the Judge] [confirming the substance of what was said to the Court by the Applicant's Counsel/Solicitors].

(4) As soon as practicable the Applicant will serve on the Respondent an Application Notice for the Return Date together with a copy of the written evidence relied on by the Applicant.[1]

All communications to the court about this order should be sent to —
    [Insert the address and telephone number of the appropriate Court Office]
    If the order is made at the Royal Courts of Justice, communications should be addressed as follows —
    Where the order is made in the Chancery Division
    7 Rolls Buildings, Fetter Lane, London EC4A 1NL, quoting the case number. The telephone number is 0207 947 6690.
    Where the order is made in the Queen's Bench Division
    Room E07, Royal Courts of Justice, Strand, London WC2A 2LL quoting the case number. The telephone number is 020 7947 6924.
    Where the order is made in the Commercial Court
    7 Rolls Buildings, Fetter Lane, London EC4A 1NL quoting the case number. The telephone number is 0207 947 6826.
    The offices are open between 10 a.m. and 4.30 p.m. Monday to Friday.

2. ORDER FOR INJUNCTION

IN THE HIGH COURT OF JUSTICE Claim No:
[DIVISION]
Before the Honourable MR(S) JUSTICE [ ]
[Date]

Claimant/Applicant

and

Defendant/Respondent

ORDER FOR AN INJUNCTION

Penal Notice

If you [insert name of Respondent] disobey this order you may be held to be in contempt of court and may be imprisoned, fined or have your assets seized.

[Note: if the injunction is granted under the Protection from Harassment Act 1997 the penal notice should read "IF YOU THE WITHIN NAMED [name of respondent] DISOBEY THIS ORDER YOU MAY BE HELD TO BE IN CONTEMPT OF COURT AND MAY BE IMPRISONED OR FINED OR YOU MAY BE FOUND TO BE GUILTY OF A CRIMINAL OFFENCE FOR WHICH YOU MAY BE IMPRISONED OR FINED OR BOTH".]

Any other person who knows of this order and does anything which helps or permits the Respondent to breach the terms of this order may also be held to be in contempt of court and may be imprisoned, fined or have their assets seized.

Important

Notice to the Respondent

You should read the terms of the Order and the Guidance Notes very carefully. You are advised to consult a Solicitor as soon as possible.

An Application was made on [date] by Counsel for the Applicant to the Judge [and was attended by Counsel for the Respondent]. The Judge heard the Application and read the evidence listed in Schedule 1 and accepted the undertakings in Schedule 2 at the end of this Order.

IT IS ORDERED that:
(1)   Until after [date] [final judgment on this claim] the Respondent must/ must not [body of injunction to go here]
(2)   The costs of this Application are [the Claimant's/Defendant's costs in the case/in any event/are reserved to be dealt with by [the judge hearing the Application on the return date][the trial judge].

Guidance Notes

Effect of this Order

(1)   A Respondent who is an individual who is ordered not to do something must not do it himself or in any other way. He must not do it through others acting on his behalf or on his instructions or with his encouragement.

(2)   A Respondent which is a corporation and which is ordered not to do something must not do it itself or by its directors, officers, employees or agents or in any other way. (omit where the Respondent is an individual)

Parties other than the Applicant and Respondent

It is a Contempt of Court for any person notified of this Order knowingly to assist in or permit a breach of this Order. Any person doing so may be sent to prison, fined or have his assets seized.

Variation or discharge of this Order

The Respondent (or anyone notified of this Order) may apply to the Court at any time to vary or discharge this Order (or so much of it as affects that person), but anyone wishing to do so must first inform the Applicant['s legal representatives].

Interpretation of this Order

(1) In this Order, where there is more than one Respondent, (unless otherwise stated) references to "the Respondent" means both or all of them.

(2) A requirement to serve on "the Respondent" means on each of them. However, the Order is effective against any Respondent on whom it is served.

(3) An Order requiring "the Respondent" to do or not to do anything applies to all Respondents.

Communications with the Court

All communications to the court about this order should be sent to —
Where the order is made in the Chancery Division: The Rolls Building, 7 Rolls Buildings, Fetter Lane, London EC4A 1NL, quoting the case number. The telephone number is 020 7947 6733.

Where the order is made in the Queen's Bench Division: Room E07, Royal Courts of Justice, Strand, London WC2A 2LL quoting the case number. The telephone number is 020 7947 6010.

Where the order is made in the Commercial Court: 7 Rolls Buildings, Fetter Lane, London EC4A 1NL quoting the case number. The telephone number is 0207 947 6826.

The offices are open between 10 a.m. and 4.30 p.m. Monday to Friday.

Schedule 1

Witness statements

P2-03   The Applicant relied on the following witness statements:

Schedule 2

Undertakings given to the Court by the Applicant

P2-04   **(1)** If the Court later finds that this Order has caused loss to the Respondent, and decides that the Respondent should be compensated for that loss, the Applicant will comply with any Order the Court may make.

(2) As soon as practicable the Applicant will issue and serve on the Respondent a Claim Form [in the form of the draft produced to the Court] claiming the appropriate relief, together with a copy of this Order.

(3)   As soon as practicable the Applicant will file and serve on the Respondent an Application Notice for the return date together with a copy of the witness statements and exhibits containing the evidence relied on by the Applicant.

(4)   Anyone notified of this Order will be given a copy of it by the Applicant['s legal representatives].
   [Name and address of Applicant's Legal Representatives
   The Applicant's legal representatives are:—

Ref: Tel: Fax:
                                                               or

[Name and Address of Applicant]

3. ORDER CONTAINING AN UNDERTAKING INSTEAD OF AN INJUNCTION

P3-01   IN THE HIGH COURT OF JUSTICE Claim No:
[DIVISION]
Before the Honourable MR(S) JUSTICE [ ]
[Date]

Claimant/Applicant

and

Defendant/Respondent

ORDER CONTAINING UNDERTAKINGS TO THE COURT

IMPORTANT:

Notice to the Respondent

(1)   This Order contains the undertaking you have given to the Court.

(2)   If you fail to comply with your undertaking you may be found guilty of Contempt of Court and you may be [fined or any of your directors may be] sent to prison or fined or your assets may be seized.[1]
An Application was made on [date] by Counsel for the Applicant to the Judge and was attended by Counsel for the Respondent.

The Respondent's Undertaking

The Respondent undertakes to the Court that until [date] [after final judgment in this claim] he will/will not [body of undertaking to go here].

The Applicant's Undertaking

If the Court later finds that the undertaking given by the Respondent has caused loss to the Respondent, and decides that the Respondent should be compensated for that loss, the Applicant will comply with any Order the Court may make.

P3-02   IT IS ORDERED that:

The Application

(1)   [The Application be adjourned to be heard by the Judge who tries this Claim./ There be no further Order on the Application.]

Costs of the Application

(2)   [The costs of this Application are reserved to be dealt with by the Judge who tries this Claim.][the Claimant's/Defendant's costs in the case/in any event].

---

[1]   Include the words in square brackets in the case of a corporate Respondent. This notice is not a substitute for the indorsement of a penal notice.

Variation or Discharge of this Order

(3) The Respondent may apply to the Court at any time to vary or discharge his undertaking but if he wishes to do so he must first inform the Applicant's Solicitors in writing at least 48 hours beforehand.

Interpretation of this Order

(1) In this Order the words "he" "him" or "his" include "she" or "her" and "it" or "its".

P3-03

(2) Where there are two or more Respondents then (unless the contrary appears)
  (a) References to "the Respondent" mean both or all of them;
  (b) An undertaking of "the Respondent" to do or not to do anything requires each Respondent to do or not to do it.

Effect of the Respondent's Undertaking

(1) A Respondent who is an individual who undertakes not to do something must not do it himself or in any other way. He must not do it through others acting on his behalf or on his instructions or with his encouragement.

[**(2)** A Respondent which is a corporation and which undertakes not to do something must not do it itself or by its directors, officers, employees or agents or in any other way.][2]
All communications to the court about this order should be sent to—
Where the order is made in the Chancery Division: 7 Rolls Buildings, Fetter Lane, London EC4A 1NL, quoting the case number. The telephone number is 0207 947 6690.
Where the order is made in the Queen's Bench Division: Room E07, Royal Courts of Justice, Strand, London WC2A 2LL quoting the case number. The telephone number is 020 7947 6924.
Where the order is made in the Commercial Court: 7 Rolls Buildings, Fetter Lane, London EC4A 1NL quoting the case number. The telephone number is 0207 947 6826.
The offices are open between 10 a.m. and 4.30 p.m. Monday to Friday.

---

[2]   Include the words in square brackets in the case of a corporate Respondent. This notice is not a substitute for the indorsement of a penal notice.

4. ADJOURNMENT OF APPLICATION FOR AN INJUNCTION

P4-01   IN THE HIGH COURT OF JUSTICE Claim No:
[DIVISION]
Before the Honourable MR(S) JUSTICE [ ]
[Date]

                                                    Claimant/Applicant
                              and
                                                    Defendant/Respondent

ADJOURNMENT OF APPLICATION FOR AN INJUNCTION

IMPORTANT:

Notice to the Respondent

(1)   This Order contains the undertaking you have given to the Court.

(2)   If you fail to comply with your undertaking you may be found guilty of Contempt of Court and you may be [fined or any of your directors may be] sent to prison or fined or your assets may be seized.[1]
An Application was made on [date] by Counsel for the Applicant to the Judge and was attended by Counsel for the Respondent.

The Respondent's Undertaking

The Respondent undertakes to the Court that until after the full hearing of this Application he will/will not [body of undertaking to go here].

The Applicant's Undertaking

If the Court later finds that the undertaking given by the Respondent has caused loss to the Respondent, and decides that the Respondent should be compensated for that loss, the Applicant will comply with any Order the Court may make.

P4-02   IT IS ORDERED that:

The Application

(1)   The hearing of the Application [be adjourned to] [be heard on a date to be fixed with the Listing Office].

Costs

(2)   The costs of the hearing today be decided on the disposal of the Application.

---

[1]   Include the words in square brackets in the case of a corporate Respondent. This notice is not a substitute for the indorsement of a penal notice.

Evidence

(3) The Applicant must [use his best endeavours to] serve his evidence in the Application on the Respondent on or before/by [date].

(4) The Respondent must [use his best endeavours to] serve his evidence in answer to the Applicant's evidence on the Applicant [on or before [date]] [within [number] days after service of the Applicant's evidence.]

(5) The Applicant must [use his best endeavours to] serve his evidence in reply to the Respondent's evidence on the Respondent [on or before [date]] [within [number] days after service of the Respondent's evidence.]

Variation or Discharge of this Order

The Respondent may apply to the Court at any time to vary or discharge his undertaking but if he wishes to do so he must first inform the Applicant's Solicitors in writing at least 48 hours beforehand.

Interpretation of this Order

(1) In this Order the words "a" "him" or "his" include "she" or "her" and "it" or "its".

P4-03

(2) Where there are two or more Respondents then (unless the contrary appears)
  (a) References to "the Respondent" mean both or all of them;
  (b) An undertaking of "the Respondent" to do or not to do anything requires each Respondent to do or not to do it.

Effect of the Respondent's Undertaking

(1) A Respondent who is an individual who undertakes not to do something must not do it himself or in any other way. He must not do it through others acting on his behalf or on his instructions or with his encouragement.

[(2) A Respondent which is a corporation and which undertakes not to do something must not do it itself or by its directors, officers, employees or agents or in any other way.] [2]

All communications to the court about this order should be sent to —
Where the order is made in the Chancery Division: 7 Rolls Buildings, Fetter Lane, London EC4A 1NL, quoting the case number. The telephone number is 0207 947 6690.
Where the order is made in the Queen's Bench Division: Room E07, Royal Courts of Justice, Strand, London WC2A 2LL quoting the case number. The telephone number is 020 7947 6924.
Where the order is made in the Commercial Court: 7 Rolls Buildings, Fetter Lane, London EC4A 1NL quoting the case number. The telephone number is 0207 947 6826.
The offices are open between 10 a.m. and 4.30 p.m. Monday to Friday.

---

[2] Include the words in square brackets in the case of a corporate Respondent. This notice is not a substitute for the indorsement of a penal notice.

5. APPLICATION FOR AN INJUNCTION TREATED AS THE TRIAL OF THE CLAIM

P5-01 IN THE HIGH COURT OF JUSTICE Claim No:
[DIVISION]
Before the Honourable MR(S) JUSTICE [ ]
[Date]

Claimant/Applicant

and

Defendant/Respondent

APPLICATION FOR AN INJUNCTION TREATED AS TRIAL OF THE CLAIM

IMPORTANT:

Notice to the Respondent

(1) This Order [prohibits you from doing] [obliges you to do] the acts set out in this Order. [You should read it all carefully. You are advised to consult a Solicitor as soon as possible.] You have a right to ask the Court to vary or discharge this Order.

(2) If you disobey this Order you may be found guilty of Contempt of Court and [any of your directors] may be sent to prison or fined [and you may be fined] or your assets may be seized.

An Application was made on the [date] by Counsel for the Applicant to the Judge and was attended by Counsel for the Respondent.

The Agreement

The Applicant and the Respondent through their Counsel told the Judge that:
(1) the hearing of the Application was to be treated as the Trial of this Claim;
[(2) the terms of the Settlement set out in the Schedule to this Order were agreed;]
(3) they consented to the making of this Order.

P5-02 IT IS ORDERED THAT:

Injunction

The Respondent [must not] [must] [set out any terms that are intended to be Orders of the Court]

[Costs]

[set out the terms of any Order for costs]

Staying the Claim

There are to be no further steps taken in this Claim other than Applications necessary to enforce [this Order] [the agreed terms of Settlement.]

Applying to the Court

The Applicant and the Respondent may both apply to the Court to enforce [this Order] [the terms.]

The Schedule

Terms of Settlement

[Here set out the terms agreed by the parties]. All communications to the court about this order should be sent to —[1]   **P5-03**

---

[1]   Where the order is made in the Chancery Division: 7 Rolls Buildings, Fetter Lane, London EC4A
1NL, quoting the case number. The telephone number is 0207 947 6690.
Where the order is made in the Queen's Bench Division: Room E07, Royal Courts of Justice,
Strand, London WC2A 2LL quoting the case number. The telephone number is 020 7947 6924.
Where the order is made in the Commercial Court: 7 Rolls Buildings, Fetter Lane, London EC4A
1NL quoting the case number. The telephone number is 0207 947 6826.
The offices are open between 10 a.m. and 4.30 p.m. Monday to Friday.

6. FREEZING INJUNCTION

P6-01   IN THE HIGH COURT OF JUSTICE Claim No:
[DIVISION]
Before The Honourable MR(S) Justice [ ]
BETWEEN

Applicant

and

Respondent

Penal Notice

If you [insert name of Respondent] disobey this order you may be held to be in contempt of court and may be imprisoned, fined or have your assets seized.

Any other person who knows of this order and does anything which helps or permits the Respondent to breach the terms of this order may also be held to be in contempt of court and may be imprisoned, fined or have their assets seized.

This Order

1.   This is a Freezing Injunction made against [ ] ("the Respondent") on [ ] by Mr Justice [ ] on the application of [ ] ("the Applicant"). The Judge read the Affidavits listed in Schedule A and accepted the undertakings set out in Schedule B at the end of this Order.

2.   This order was made at a hearing without notice to the Respondent. The Respondent has a right to apply to the court to vary or discharge the order—see paragraph 13 below.

3.   There will be a further hearing in respect of this order on [ ] ("the return date").

4.   If there is more than one Respondent—
   (a)   unless otherwise stated, references in this order to "the Respondent" mean both or all of them; and
   (b)   this order is effective against any Respondent on whom it is served or who is given notice of it.

Freezing Injunction

P6-02   [For injunction limited to assets in England and Wales]

5.   Until the return date or further order of the court, the Respondent must not remove from England and Wales or in any way dispose of, deal with or diminish the value of any of his assets which are in England and Wales up to the value of £[ ].

[For worldwide injunction]

5.   Until the return date or further order of the court, the Respondent must not—
   (1)   remove from England and Wales any of his assets which are in England and Wales up to the value of £ [ ]; or
   (2)   in any way dispose of, deal with or diminish the value of any of his assets whether they are in or outside England and Wales up to the same value.

[For either form of injunction]

6. Paragraph 5 applies to all the Respondent's assets whether or not they are in his own name and whether they are solely or jointly owned. For the purpose of this order the Respondent's assets include any asset which he has the power, directly or indirectly, to dispose of or deal with as if it were his own. The Respondent is to be regarded as having such power if a third party holds or controls the asset in accordance with his direct or indirect instructions.

7. This prohibition includes the following assets in particular—
(a) the property known as [title/address] or the net sale money after payment of any mortgages if it has been sold;
(b) the property and assets of the Respondent's business [known as [name]] [carried on at [address]] or the sale money if any of them have been sold; and
(c) any money standing to the credit of any bank account including the amount of any cheque drawn on such account which has not been cleared.

[For injunction limited to assets in England and Wales]

8. If the total value free of charges or other securities ("unencumbered value") of the Respondent's assets in England and Wales exceeds £ [ ], the Respondent may remove any of those assets from England and Wales or may dispose of or deal with them so long as the total unencumbered value of his assets still in England and Wales remains above £ [ ].

[For worldwide injunction]

8.(1) If the total value free of charges or other securities ("unencumbered value") of the Respondent's assets in England and Wales exceeds £ [ ], the Respondent may remove any of those assets from England and Wales or may dispose of or deal with them so long as the total unencumbered value of the Respondent's assets still in England and Wales remains above £ [ ].
(2) If the total unencumbered value of the Respondent's assets in England and Wales does not exceed £ [ ], the Respondent must not remove any of those assets from England and Wales and must not dispose of or deal with any of them. If the Respondent has other assets outside England and Wales, he may dispose of or deal with those assets outside England and Wales so long as the total unencumbered value of all his assets whether in or outside England and Wales remains above £ [ ].

Provision of Information

9.(1) Unless paragraph (2) applies, the Respondent must [immediately] [within [ ] hours of service of this order] and to the best of his ability inform the Applicant's solicitors of all his assets [in England and Wales] [worldwide] [exceeding £ [ ] in value] whether in his own name or not and whether solely or jointly owned, giving the value, location and details of all such assets.
(2) If the provision of any of this information is likely to incriminate the Respondent, he may be entitled to refuse to provide it, but is recommended to take legal advice before refusing to provide the information. Wrongful refusal to provide the information is contempt of court and may render the Respondent liable to be imprisoned, fined or have his assets seized.

P6-03

10. Within [ ] working days after being served with this order, the Respondent must swear and serve on the Applicant's solicitors an affidavit setting out the above information.

Exceptions to this Order

11.(1)   This order does not prohibit the Respondent from spending £ a week towards his ordinary living expenses and also £ [ ] [or a reasonable sum] on legal advice and representation. [But before spending any money the Respondent must tell the Applicant's legal representatives where the money is to come from.]

[(2)   This order does not prohibit the Respondent from dealing with or disposing of any of his assets in the ordinary and proper course of business.]

(3)   The Respondent may agree with the Applicant's legal representatives that the above spending limits should be increased or that this order should be varied in any other respect, but any agreement must be in writing.

(4)   The order will cease to have effect if the Respondent—

(a)   provides security by paying the sum of £ [ ] into court, to be held to the order of the court; or

(b)   makes provision for security in that sum by another method agreed with the Applicant's legal representatives.

Costs

12.   The costs of this application are reserved to the judge hearing the application on the return date.

Variation or Discharge of this Order

13.   Anyone served with or notified of this order may apply to the court at any time to vary or discharge this order (or so much of it as affects that person), but they must first inform the Applicant's solicitors. If any evidence is to be relied upon in support of the application, the substance of it must be communicated in writing to the Applicant's solicitors in advance.

Interpretation of this Order

14.   A Respondent who is an individual who is ordered not to do something must not do it himself or in any other way. He must not do it through others acting on his behalf or on his instructions or with his encouragement.

15.   A Respondent which is not an individual which is ordered not to do something must not do it itself or by its directors, officers, partners, employees or agents or in any other way.

Parties Other than the Applicant and Respondent

16.   Effect of this order

P6-04   It is a contempt of court for any person notified of this order knowingly to assist in or permit a breach of this order. Any person doing so may be imprisoned, fined or have their assets seized.

17. Set off by banks

This injunction does not prevent any bank from exercising any right of set off it may have in respect of any facility which it gave to the respondent before it was notified of this order.

18. Withdrawals by the Respondent

No bank need enquire as to the application or proposed application of any money withdrawn by the Respondent if the withdrawal appears to be permitted by this order.

[For worldwide injunction]

19. Persons outside England and Wales

(1) Except as provided in paragraph (2) below, the terms of this order do not affect or concern anyone outside the jurisdiction of this court.
(2) The terms of this order will affect the following persons in a country or state outside the jurisdiction of this court—
    (a) the Respondent or his officer or agent appointed by power of attorney;
    (b) any person who—
        (i) is subject to the jurisdiction of this court;
        (ii) has been given written notice of this order at his residence or place of business within the jurisdiction of this court; and
        (iii) is able to prevent acts or omissions outside the jurisdiction of this court which constitute or assist in a breach of the terms of this order; and
    (c) any other person, only to the extent that this order is declared enforceable by or is enforced by a court in that country or state.

[For worldwide injunction]

20. Assets located outside England and Wales

Nothing in this order shall, in respect of assets located outside England and Wales, prevent any third party from complying with—
    (1) what it reasonably believes to be its obligations, contractual or otherwise, under the laws and obligations of the country or state in which those assets are situated or under the proper law of any contract between itself and the Respondent; and
    (2) any orders of the courts of that country or state, provided that reasonable notice of any application for such an order is given to the Applicant's solicitors.

Communications with the Court

All communications to the court about this order should be sent to—[Insert the address and telephone number of the appropriate Court Office]

If the order is made at the Royal Courts of Justice, communications should be addressed as follows—

Where the order is made in the Chancery Division

Chancery Associates, Ground Floor, The Rolls Building, 7 Rolls Buildings, Fetter Lane, London EC4A 1NL quoting the case number. The telephone number is 0207 947 6690

Where the order is made in the Queen's Bench Division

Room E078, Royal Courts of Justice, Strand, London WC2A 2LL quoting the case number. The telephone number is 020 7947 6924.

Where the order is made in the Commercial Court

7 Rolls Building, Fetter Lane, London, EC4A 1NL quoting the case number. The telephone number is 0207 947 6826.

The offices are open between 10 a.m. and 4.30 p.m. Monday to Friday.

Schedule A

Affidavits

P6-05
The Applicant relied on the following affidavits—
[name] [number of affidavit] [date sworn] [filed on behalf of]
(1)
(2)

Schedule B

Undertakings Given to the Court by the Applicant

P6-06
(1) If the court later finds that this order has caused loss to the Respondent, and decides that the Respondent should be compensated for that loss, the Applicant will comply with any order the court may make.

[(2) The Applicant will—
(a) on or before [date] cause a written guarantee in the sum of £ to be issued from a bank with a place of business within England or Wales, in respect of any order the court may make pursuant to paragraph (1) above; and
(b) immediately upon issue of the guarantee, cause a copy of it to be served on the Respondent.]

(3) As soon as practicable the Applicant will issue and serve a claim form [in the form of the draft produced to the court] [claiming the appropriate relief].

(4) The Applicant will [swear and file an affidavit] [cause an affidavit to be sworn and filed] [substantially in the terms of the draft affidavit produced to the court] [confirming the substance of what was said to the court by the Applicant's counsel/solicitors].

(5) The Applicant will serve upon the Respondent [together with this order] [as soon as practicable]—
(i) copies of the affidavits and exhibits containing the evidence relied upon by the Applicant, and any other documents provided to the court on the making of the application;
(ii) a note of the hearing of this application and any skeleton argument relied upon by the Applicant; [Note: this is not in the published form, but it ought to be, unless the judge otherwise directs]
(iii) the claim form; and
(iv) an application notice for continuation of the order.

[(6) Anyone notified of this order will be given a copy of it by the Applicant's legal representatives.]

(7) The Applicant will pay the reasonable costs of anyone other than the Respondent which have been incurred as a result of this order including the costs of finding out whether that person holds any of the Respondent's assets and if the court later finds that this order has caused such person loss, and decides that such person should be compensated for that loss, the Applicant will comply with any order the court may make.

(8) If this order ceases to have effect (for example, if the Respondent provides security or the Applicant does not provide a bank guarantee as provided for above) the Applicant will immediately take all reasonable steps to inform in writing anyone to whom he has given notice of this order, or who he has reasonable grounds for supposing may act upon this order, that it has ceased to have effect.

[(9) The Applicant will not without the permission of the court use any information obtained as a result of this order for the purpose of any civil or criminal proceedings, either in England and Wales or in any other jurisdiction, other than this claim.]

[(10) The Applicant will not without the permission of the court seek to enforce this order in any country outside England and Wales [or seek an order of a similar nature including orders conferring a charge or other security against the Respondent or the Respondent's assets].]

Name and Address of Applicant's Legal Representatives

The Applicant's legal representatives are—
[Name, address, reference, fax and telephone numbers both in and out of office hours and email]

7. SEARCH ORDER

P7-01 IN THE HIGH COURT OF JUSTICE Claim
No:
[DIVISION]
Before The Honourable MR(S) Justice [ ]
BETWEEN

Applicant

and

Respondent

Penal Notice

If you [insert name of Respondent] disobey this order you may be held to be in contempt of court and may be imprisoned, fined or have your assets seized.

Any other person who knows of this Order and does anything which helps or permits the Respondent to breach the terms of this Order may also be held to be in contempt of court and may be imprisoned, fined or have their assets seized.

This Order

P7-02 **1.** This is a Search Order made against [ ] ("the Respondent") on [ ] by Mr(s) Justice [ ] on the application of [ ] ("the Applicant"). The Judge read the Affidavits listed in Schedule F and accepted the undertakings set out in Schedules C, D and E at the end of this order.

2. This order was made at a hearing without notice to the Respondent. The Respondent has a right to apply to the court to vary or discharge the order—see paragraph 27 below.

3. There will be a further hearing in respect of this order on [ ] ("the return date").

4. If there is more than one Respondent—
    (a) unless otherwise stated, references in this order to "the Respondent" mean both or all of them; and
    (b) this order is effective against any Respondent on whom it is served or who is given notice of it.

5. This order must be complied with by—
    (a) the Respondent;
    (b) any director, officer, partner or responsible employee of the Respondent; and
    (c) if the Respondent is an individual, any other person having responsible control of the premises to be searched.

The Search

P7-03 **6.** The Respondent must permit the following persons—
    (a) [ ] ("the Supervising Solicitor");
    (b) [ ], a solicitor in the firm of [ ], the Applicant's solicitors; and
    (c) up to [ ] other persons being [their identity or capacity] accompanying them, (together "the search party"), to enter the premises mentioned in Schedule A to this order and any other premises of the Respondent disclosed under paragraph 18 below and any vehicles under the Respondent's control on or around the premises ("the

premises") so that they can search for, inspect, photograph or photocopy, and deliver into the safekeeping of the Applicant's solicitors all the documents and articles which are listed in Schedule B to this order ("the listed items").

7. Having permitted the search party to enter the premises, the Respondent must allow the search party to remain on the premises until the search is complete. In the event that it becomes necessary for any of those persons to leave the premises before the search is complete, the Respondent must allow them to re-enter the premises immediately upon their seeking re-entry on the same or the following day in order to complete the search.

Restrictions on Search

8. This order may not be carried out at the same time as a police search warrant.

9. Before the Respondent allows anybody onto the premises to carry out this order, he is entitled to have the Supervising Solicitor explain to him what it means in everyday language.

10. The Respondent is entitled to seek legal advice and to ask the court to vary or discharge this order. Whilst doing so, he may ask the Supervising Solicitor to delay starting the search for up to 2 hours or such other longer period as the Supervising Solicitor may permit. However, the Respondent must—
    (a) comply with the terms of paragraph 27 below;
    (b) not disturb or remove any listed items; and
    (c) permit the Supervising Solicitor to enter, but not start to search.

11.(1) Before permitting entry to the premises by any person other than the Supervising Solicitor, the Respondent may, for a short time (not to exceed two hours, unless the Supervising Solicitor agrees to a longer period)—
    (a) gather together any documents he believes may be incriminating or privileged; and
    (b) hand them to the Supervising Solicitor for him to assess whether they are incriminating or privileged as claimed.
(2) If the Supervising Solicitor decides that the Respondent is entitled to withhold production of any of the documents on the ground that they are privileged or incriminating, he will exclude them from the search, record them in a list for inclusion in his report and return them to the Respondent.
(3) If the Supervising Solicitor believes that the Respondent may be entitled to withhold production of the whole or any part of a document on the ground that it or part of it may be privileged or incriminating, or if the Respondent claims to be entitled to withhold production on those grounds, the Supervising Solicitor will exclude it from the search and retain it in his possession pending further order of the court.

12. If the Respondent wishes to take legal advice and gather documents as permitted, he must first inform the Supervising Solicitor and keep him informed of the steps being taken.

13. No item may be removed from the premises until a list of the items to be removed has been prepared, and a copy of the list has been supplied to the Respondent, and he has been given a reasonable opportunity to check the list.

14. The premises must not be searched, and items must not be removed from them, except in the presence of the Respondent.

15. If the Supervising Solicitor is satisfied that full compliance with paragraphs 13 or 14 is not practicable, he may permit the search to proceed and items to be removed without fully complying with them.

Delivery up of Articles/documents

P7-04 **16.** The Respondent must immediately hand over to the Applicant's solicitors any of the listed items, which are in his possession or under his control, save for any computer or hard disk integral to any computer. Any items the subject of a dispute as to whether they are listed items must immediately be handed over to the Supervising Solicitor for safe keeping pending resolution of the dispute or further order of the court.

17. The Respondent must immediately give the search party effective access to the computers on the premises, with all necessary passwords, to enable the computers to be searched. If they contain any listed items the Respondent must cause the listed items to be displayed so that they can be read and copied. The Respondent must provide the Applicant's Solicitors with copies of all listed items contained in the computers. All reasonable steps shall be taken by the Applicant and the Applicant's solicitors to ensure that no damage is done to any computer or data. The Applicant and his representatives may not themselves search the Respondent's computers unless they have sufficient expertise to do so without damaging the Respondent's system.

Provision of Information

18. The Respondent must immediately inform the Applicant's Solicitors (in the presence of the Supervising Solicitor) so far as he is aware—
   (a) where all the listed items are;
   (b) the name and address of everyone who has supplied him, or offered to supply him, with listed items;
   (c) the name and address of everyone to whom he has supplied, or offered to supply, listed items; and
   (d) full details of the dates and quantities of every such supply and offer.

19. Within [ ] working days after being served with this order the Respondent must swear and serve an affidavit setting out the above information.

Prohibited Acts

20. Except for the purpose of obtaining legal advice, the Respondent must not directly or indirectly inform anyone of these proceedings or of the contents of this order, or warn anyone that proceedings have been or may be brought against him by the Applicant until 4.30 p.m. on the return date or further order of the court.

21.   Until 4.30 p.m. on the return date the Respondent must not destroy, tamper with, cancel or part with possession, power, custody or control of the listed items otherwise than in accordance with the terms of this order.

22.   [Insert any negative injunctions.]

23.   [Insert any further order]

Costs

24.   The costs of this application are reserved to the judge hearing the application on the return date.

Restrictions on Service

25.   This order may only be served between [ ] a.m./p.m. and [ ] a.m./p.m. [and on a weekday].

26.   This order must be served by the Supervising Solicitor, and paragraph 6 of the order must be carried out in his presence and under his supervision.

Variation and Discharge of this Order

27.   Anyone served with or notified of this order may apply to the court at any time to vary or discharge this order (or so much of it as affects that person), but they must first inform the Applicant's solicitors. If any evidence is to be relied upon in support of the application, the substance of it must be communicated in writing to the Applicant's solicitors in advance.

Interpretation of this Order

28.   Any requirement that something shall be done to or in the presence of the Respondent means—   **P7-05**
   (a)   if there is more than one Respondent, to or in the presence of any one of them; and
   (b)   if a Respondent is not an individual, to or in the presence of a director, officer, partner or responsible employee.

29.   A Respondent who is an individual who is ordered not to do something must not do it himself or in any other way. He must not do it through others acting on his behalf or on his instructions or with his encouragement.

30.   A Respondent which is not an individual which is ordered not to do something must not do it itself or by its directors, officers, partners, employees or agents or in any other way.

Communications with the Court

All communications to the court about this order should be sent to—
[Insert the address and telephone number of the appropriate Court Office]
If the order is made at the Royal Courts of Justice, communications should be addressed as follows—
Where the order is made in the Chancery Division
Chancery Associates, Ground Floor, The Rolls Building, 7 Rolls Buildings, Fet-

ter Lane, London EC4A 1NL quoting the case number. The telephone number is 0207 947 66903.

Where the order is made in the Queen's Bench Division

Room E07, Royal Courts of Justice, Strand, London WC2A 2LL quoting the case number. The telephone number is 020 7947 6924.

Where the order is made in the Commercial Court

7 Rolls Building, Fetter Lane, London, EC4A 1NL quoting the case number. The telephone number is 0207 947 6826.

The offices are open between 10 a.m. and 4.30 p.m. Monday to Friday.

Schedule A

The Premises

P7-06   ...

Schedule B

The Listed Items

...

Schedule C

Undertakings Given to the Court by the Applicant

(1)   If the court later finds that this order or carrying it out has caused loss to the Respondent, and decides that the Respondent should be compensated for that loss, the Applicant will comply with any order the court may make. Further if the carrying out of this order has been in breach of the terms of this order or otherwise in a manner inconsistent with the Applicant's solicitors' duties as officers of the court, the Applicant will comply with any order for damages the court may make.

[(2)   As soon as practicable the Applicant will issue a claim form [in the form of the draft produced to the court] [claiming the appropriate relief].]

(3)   The Applicant will [swear and file an affidavit] [cause an affidavit to be sworn and filed] [substantially in the terms of the draft affidavit produced to the court] [confirming the substance of what was said to the court by the Applicant's counsel/solicitors].

(4)   The Applicant will not, without the permission of the court use any information or documents obtained as a result of carrying out this order nor inform anyone else of these proceedings except for the purposes of these proceedings (including adding further Respondents) or commencing civil proceedings in relation to the same or related subject matter to these proceedings until after the return date.

[(5)   The Applicant will maintain pending further order the sum of £ [ ] in an account controlled by the Applicant's solicitors.]

[(6)   The Applicant will insure the items removed from the premises.]

Schedule D

Undertakings Given by the Applicant's Solicitors

(1)   The Applicant's solicitors will provide to the Supervising Solicitor for service   **P7-07**
on the Respondent—
  (i)   a service copy of this order;
  (ii)   the claim form (with defendant's response pack) or, if not issued, the draft
          produced to the court;
  (iii)   an application for hearing on the return date;
  (iv)   copies of the affidavits [or draft affidavits] and exhibits capable of being
          copied containing the evidence relied upon by the applicant;
  (v)   a note of any allegation of fact made orally to the court where such allega-
          tion is not contained in the affidavits or draft affidavits read by the judge;
          and
  (vi)   a copy of the skeleton argument produced to the court by the Applicant's
          [counsel/solicitors].

(2)   The Applicants' solicitors will answer at once to the best of their ability any
question whether a particular item is a listed item.

(3)   Subject as provided below the Applicant's solicitors will retain in their own
safe keeping all items obtained as a result of this order until the court directs
otherwise.

(4)   The Applicant's solicitors will return the originals of all documents obtained
as a result of this order (except original documents which belong to the Applicant)
as soon as possible and in any event within [two] working days of their removal.

Schedule E

Undertakings Given by the Supervising Solicitor

(1)   The Supervising Solicitor will use his best endeavours to serve this order upon   **P7-08**
the Respondent and at the same time to serve upon the Respondent the other documents required to be served and referred to in paragraph (1) of Schedule D.

(2)   The Supervising Solicitor will offer to explain to the person served with the
order its meaning and effect fairly and in everyday language, and to inform him of
his right to take legal advice (such advice to include an explanation that the
Respondent may be entitled to avail himself of [the privilege against self-
incrimination or][legal professional privilege]) and to apply to vary or discharge this
order as mentioned in paragraph 27 above.

(3)   The Supervising Solicitor will retain in the safe keeping of his firm all items
retained by him as a result of this order until the court directs otherwise.

(4)   Unless and until the court otherwise orders, or unless otherwise necessary to
comply with any duty to the court pursuant to this order, the Supervising Solicitor
shall not disclose to any person any information relating to those items, and shall
keep the existence of such items confidential.

(5)   Within [48] hours of completion of the search the Supervising Solicitor will
make and provide to the Applicant's solicitors, the Respondent or his solicitors and

to the judge who made this order (for the purposes of the court file) a written report on the carrying out of the order.

Schedule F

Affidavits

P7-09   The Applicant relied on the following affidavits— [name] [number of affidavit] [date sworn] [filed on behalf of]
(1)
(2)

Name and Address of Applicant's Solicitors

The Applicant's solicitors are: [Name, address, reference, fax and telephone numbers both in and out office hours.]

8. GENERAL FORM OF APPLICATION FOR INJUNCTION: COUNTY COURT

Application for Injunction
(General Form)

Click here to reset form	Click here to print form
Name of court	Claim No.
Claimant's Name and Ref.	
Defendant's Name and Ref.	
Fee Account no.	

Notes on completion

Tick which boxes apply and specify the legislation where appropriate

(1) Enter the full name of the person making the application

(2) Enter the full name of the person the injunction is to be directed to

(3) Set out any proposed orders requiring acts to be done. Delete if no mandatory order is sought.

(4) Set out here the proposed terms of the injunction order (if the defendant is a limited company delete the wording in brackets and insert 'whether by its servants, agents, officers or otherwise').

(5) Set out here any further terms asked for including provision for costs

(6) Enter the names of all persons who have sworn affidavits or signed statements in support of this application

(7) Enter the names and addresses of all persons upon whom it is intended to serve this application

(8) Enter the full name and address for service and delete as required

☐ By application in pending proceedings

☐ Under Statutory provision _____

☐ This application is made under Part 8 of the Civil Procedure Rules

This application raises issues under the Human Rights Act 1998 ☐ Yes ☐ No

Seal

The Claimant[1]

applies to the court for an injunction order in the following terms:

The Defendant[2]

must[3]

The Defendant

be forbidden (whether by himself or by instructing or encouraging or permitting any other person)[4]

And that[5]

The grounds of this application are set out in the written evidence of[6]   sworn (signed) on

This written evidence is served with this application.

This application is to be served upon[7]

This application is filed by[8]
(the Solicitors for) the Claimant (Applicant/Petitioner)
whose address for service is

Signed   Dated

* Name and address of the person application is directed to

To*
of

This section to be completed by the court

This application will be heard by the (District) Judge
at
on   the   **day of**   20   at   o'clock

If you do not attend at the time shown the court may make an injunction order in your absence
If you do not fully understand this application you should go to a Solicitor, Legal Advice Centre or a Citizens' Advice Bureau

The court office at

is open between 10am and 4pm Mon - Fri. When corresponding with the court, please address all forms and letters to the Court Manager and quote the claim number.

N16A General form of application for injunction (05.14)   © Crown copyright 2014

9. COUNTY COURT GENERAL FORM OF INJUNCTION ORDER

Injunction Order

Between .... Claimant

and .... Defendant

Name of court	
Claim No.	
Claimant's Ref.	
Defendant Ref.	
For completion by the court **Issued on**	

Seal

If you do not comply with this order you may be held in contempt of court and imprisoned or fined, or your assets may be seized.

[1]The name of the person the order is directed to

On the   of   20   the court considered an application for an injunction

The Court ordered that[1]

[2]The terms of any orders requiring acts to be done. Delete if no mandatory order is made.

must[2]

on or before[3]

[3]Enter time (and place) as ordered

[4]The terms of the injunction order. If the defendant is a limited company, delete the words in brackets and insert "whether by its servants, agents, officers or otherwise"

[and] is forbidden (whether by himself or by instructing or encouraging or permitting any other person) [4] from

This order will remain in force until the   of   20   at   o'clock

unless before then it is revoked by a further order of the court

[5]The terms of any orders, costs etc.

It is further ordered that[5]

(i) A power of arrest be attached to clauses [   ] above[6]

(ii) The applicant do pay the costs of the application

[6]State the clause numbers to which the power of arrest relates

[Notice of further hearing

The court will re-consider the application and whether the order should continue at a further hearing at:

on the   day of   20   at   o'clock

[7]Use when order is temporary and made without notice; otherwise delete.

If you do not attend at the time shown the court may make an injunction order in your absence.

You are entitled to apply to the court to re-consider the order before that day]**[7]

If you do not understand anything in this order you should go to a Solicitor, Legal Advice Centre or a Citizens' Advice Bureau

The court office at

is open between 10 am and 4 pm Monday to Friday. When corresponding with the court, please address forms or letters to the Court Manager and quote the claim number.

N16 General form of injunction for interim application or originating application (10.12)

Injunction Order - Record of Hearing   Claim No.

On _____ the _____ day of _____ 20 ____

Before (H   Honour)(District) judge _____

The court was sitting at _____

_____

The	☐	**Claimant**	**(Name)**
was	☐	represented by Counsel	
	☐	represented by a Solicitor	
	☐	in person	
The	☐	**Defendant**	**(Name)**
was	☐	represented by Counsel	
	☐	represented by a Solicitor	
	☐	in person	
	☐	did not appear having been given notice of this hearing	
	☐	not given notice of this hearing	

The court read the written evidence of

☐   the Claimant   (sworn)(signed) on _____

☐   the Defendant   (sworn)(signed) on _____

And of _____ (sworn)(signed) on _____

The court heard spoken evidence on oath from

_____

_____

The Claimant gave an undertaking (through his counsel or solicitor) promising to pay any damages ordered by the court if it later decides that the Defendant has suffered loss or damages as a result of this order*

*Delete this paragraph if the court does not require the undertaking

Signed _____ Dated _____
                    (Judges Clerk)

N16 General form of injunction for interim application or originating application

10. COUNTY COURT GENERAL FORM OF UNDERTAKING

P10-01

General form of undertaking

Between	Claimant Applicant Petitioner
and	Defendant Respondent

Name of court	
Claim No.	
Claimant's Ref.	
Defendant's Ref.	

This form is to be used only for an undertaking not for an injunction

(1) Name of the person giving undertaking

(2) Set out terms of undertaking

(3) Give the date and time or event when the undertaking will expire

(4) The Judge may direct that the party who gives the undertaking shall personally sign the statement overleaf

(5) Set out any other directions given by the court

(6) Address of the person giving undertaking

On the   day of   [19   ][20   ]

(1)

[appeared in person] [was represented by Solicitor / Counsel]

and gave an undertaking to the Court promising (2)

Seal

And to be bound by these promises until (3)

The Court explained to (1)

the meaning of his undertaking and the consequences of failing to keep his promises,

And the Court accepted his undertaking (1) [and *if so ordered* directed that

(1)   should sign the statement overleaf].

And   (enter name of Judge) **ordered that** (5)

Dated

To (1)
of (6)

Important Notice

- If you do not comply with your promises to the court you may be held to be in contempt of court and imprisoned or fined, or your assets may be seized.

- If you do not understand anything in this document you should go to a Solicitor, Legal Advice Centre or a Citizens' Advice Bureau

The Court Office at

is open from 10 am to 4 pm. When corresponding with the court, address all forms and letters to the Court Manager and quote the claim number.

N117 General form of undertaking (10.12)   © Crown copyright 2012

The Court may direct that the party who gives the undertaking shall personally sign the statement below.

Statement

I understand the undertaking that I have given, and that if I break any of my promises to the Court I may be fined, my assets seized or I may sent to prison for contempt of court.

Signed

To be completed by the Court

Delivered

☐ By posting on:

☐ By hand on:

☐ Through solicitor on:

Officer:

---

11. CLAIM FORM SEEKING PROHIBITORY AND MANDATORY INJUNCTIONS: CHANCERY DIVISION

P11-01 IN THE HIGH COURT OF JUSTICE

Claim no: HC199079

CHANCERY DIVISION

Fee Account No:

BETWEEN:

HERBERT HOUSEHOLDER

Claimant

—and—

NORMAN NEIGHBOUR

Defendant

Brief Details of Claim

The claim is for:

(1) An injunction to restrain the Defendant (whether by himself or through others acting on his behalf or on his instructions or with his encouragement) from trespassing on the Claimant's land at 2 Parkfields, Barchester by erecting or allowing any building to remain thereon

(2) An order that the Defendant do forthwith demolish and remove so much of the extension recently added to the East side of his dwelling house at 2 Parkfields aforesaid as overhangs or is erected upon any part of the Claimant's land

(3) Damages for trespass to the Claimant's land

(4) Interest pursuant to section 35A of the Senior Courts Act 1981

(5) Further or other relief

(6) Costs

Value

P11-02 I expect to recover more than £15,000.

Preferred County Court Hearing Centre

Amount Claimed:
Court Fee:
Legal Representative's Costs:

Defendant's name and address

Norman Neighbour, 4 Parkfields, Barchester, BA1 1AA
Does, or will, your claim include any issue under the Human Rights Act 1998?
No
Particulars of Claim to follow.

Statement of Truth

I believe that the facts stated in these particulars of claim are true.
Full name: Herbert Householder
Signed..........(Claimant)

12. APPLICATION NOTICE TO CONTINUE INTERIM INJUNCTION GRANTED WITHOUT NOTICE: QUEEN'S BENCH DIVISION

IN THE HIGH COURT OF JUSTICE

Claim No: HQ19C7534

QUEEN'S BENCH DIVISION
BETWEEN:

OMNIPERM LIMITED

Claimant/Applicant

—and—

SAMUEL SMART

Defendant/Respondent

APPLICATION NOTICE

Part A: We, Grabber & Co, on behalf of the Claimant Omniperm Limited, apply for an order, a draft of which is attached [use Precedent 2], renewing until after judgment in this claim or further order the injunction granted in this case on 15 January 2019 forbidding the Defendant from being (whether by himself or as principal, director, manager, assistant or in any other capacity) in any way concerned or interested in the business of ladies' hairdresser within one mile of 8 Cavendish Avenue, Barchester.

We wish to have the application dealt with at a hearing before a Judge with an agreed time estimate of 3 hours.

This application will be heard on 22 January 2019 at 10.30 a.m. in a court to be notified, at the Royal Courts of Justice, Strand, London WC2A 2LL. See also directions given for the hearing, attached.

Part B: We wish to rely on the attached witness statement of Dennis Dryer.

Dated the 11th day of January 2019.

13. WITNESS STATEMENT ON APPLICATION FOR AN INTERIM INJUNCTION

Made on behalf of the Applicants
Witness: D Dryer
1st statement of witness
Exhibits: DD1-3
Dated: 8 January 2019

IN THE HIGH COURT OF JUSTICE

Claim no: HQ19C7534

QUEEN'S BENCH DIVISION
BETWEEN:

OMNIPERM LIMITED

Claimant/Applicant

—and—

SAMUEL SMART

Defendant/Respondent

Witness Statement of Dennis Dryer

I, DENNIS DRYER, of 121 Graham Road, Barchester, Managing Director of Omniperm Limited, the above-named Applicant, will say as follows:

(1) I am the Applicant's Managing Director and am duly authorised to make this witness statement on its behalf. The facts set out below are true to the best of my knowledge and belief.

(2) The Defendant entered into a contract of employment with the Applicant as a ladies' hairdresser on 21st October 2017. A copy of his contract is now produced and shown to me marked "DD1". It will be seen that Clause 4(4) of that contract provided that the Defendant should not, for a period of one year after leaving the service of the Applicant, work in a hairdressing establishment within one mile of the Applicant's premises, which are at 8 Cavendish Avenue, Barchester. The restriction is a reasonable one in all the circumstances and necessary in order to protect my business because [set out circumstances].

(3) The Defendant left the Applicant's employment voluntarily and without giving any notice on 21st December 2018 and on 7th January 2019 he commenced employment with Multiperm Limited at 28 Cavendish Avenue, Barchester, less than 200 metres from the Applicants' premises.

(4) By letters to the Defendant dated 8th January and 14th January 2019 I requested him to cease working for Multiperm Limited in breach of his covenant mentioned above. The Defendant telephoned me on 15th January 2019 and told me not to waste my time writing letters as he would ignore them. Copies of these letters have been shown to me and I produce them marked "DD2", "DD3".

(5) The Defendant threatens and intends unless restrained by the Court to continue working for Multiperm Limited at 28 Cavendish Avenue in breach of his covenant. Many of the Applicant's customers are transferring their custom to Multiperm Limited and the Applicant is suffering damage accordingly. For instance I am told and believe that [details of lost customers and lost profit].

(6)   I respectfully request this Honourable Court to grant the Order sought in the Application. The Applicant is a profitable company with net current assets exceeding £250,000 and are willing to give the usual undertaking in damages. I produce the latest management/audited accounts marked "DD4".

STATEMENT OF TRUTH

I believe that the facts stated in the witness statement are true.

[Signed]

[Dated]

14. MODEL INTERIM NON-DISCLOSURE ORDER WITH GUIDANCE NOTES

P14-01
Model Order

IN THE HIGH COURT OF JUSTICE

Claim No: [ ]

[QUEEN'S BENCH/CHANCERY] DIVISION
BEFORE THE HONOURABLE [MR][MRS] JUSTICE [ ] [(IN PRIVATE)]
Dated: [ ]
B E T W E E N :

"AAA"

Intended Claimant/Applicant

— and —
(1) "BBB"
(2) [ ] NEWSPAPERS LIMITED
(3) THE PERSON OR PERSONS UNKNOWN

who has or have appropriated, obtained and/or offered or intend to offer for sale and/or publication the material referred to in Confidential Schedule 2 to this Order

Intended Defendant(s)/Respondent(s)

PENAL NOTICE

IF YOU THE RESPONDENT DISOBEY THIS ORDER YOU MAY BE HELD TO BE IN CONTEMPT OF COURT AND MAY BE IMPRISONED (IN THE CASE OF THE FIRST AND THIRD DEFENDANTS) OR FINED OR HAVE YOUR ASSETS SEIZED.

ANY PERSON WHO KNOWS OF THIS ORDER AND DISOBEYS THIS ORDER OR DOES ANYTHING WHICH HELPS OR PERMITS ANY PERSON TO WHOM THIS ORDER APPLIES TO BREACH THE TERMS OF THIS ORDER MAY BE HELD TO BE IN CONTEMPT OF COURT AND MAY BE IMPRISONED, FINED OR HAVE THEIR ASSETS SEIZED.

NOTICE TO ANYONE WHO KNOWS OF THIS ORDER

You should read the terms of the Order and the Practice Guidance on Interim Non-Disclosure Orders very carefully. You are advised to consult a solicitor as soon as possible. This Order prohibits you from doing the acts set out in Paragraphs 6 [, 7] and 10 of the Order and obliges you to do the acts set out in Paragraphs 8, 9, and 11 of the Order. You have the right to ask the Court to vary or discharge the Order. If you disobey this Order you may be found guilty of contempt of court and you may be sent to prison or fined or your assets may be seized.

This Order

P14-02 1.   This is an Injunction, with other orders as set out below, made against the Defendants on [insert date] by the Judge identified above (the Judge) on the application (the Application) of the Claimant. The Judge:

(a)   read the witness statements referred to in Schedule A at the end of this Order, as well as the witness statements referred to in Confidential Schedule

1 [or "was given information orally by Counsel on behalf of the Claimant"];
(b) accepted the undertakings set out in Schedule B at the end of this Order; and
(c) considered the provisions of the Human Rights Act 1998 (HRA), section 12.

2. [This Order was made at a hearing without-notice to those affected by it, the **P14-03** Court having considered section 12(2) HRA and being satisfied:
(a) that the Claimant has taken all practicable steps to notify persons affected; and/or
(b) that there are compelling reasons for notice not being given, namely: [set out in full the Court's reasons for making the order without-notice]. The Defendants (and anyone served with or notified of this Order) have a right to apply to the Court to vary or discharge the Order (or so much of it as affects them): see clause 17 below.]
[ONLY TO BE GRANTED IN AN EXCEPTIONAL CASE WHERE ANONYMITY IS STRICTLY NECESSARY]

Anonymity

3. Pursuant to section 6 HRA, and/or CPR 39.2 the Judge, being satisfied that it **P14-04** is strictly necessary, ordered that:
(a) the Claimant be permitted to issue these proceedings naming the Claimant as "AAA" and giving an address c/o the Claimant's solicitors;
(b) the Claimant be permitted to issue these proceedings naming the [First] Defendant as "BBB" [and the Third Defendant as "Person or Persons Unknown" and, once it is known to the Claimant, notifying the Defendant's home address by filing the same in a sealed letter which must remain sealed and held with the Court office subject only to the further order of a Judge or the Senior Master of the Queen's Bench Division/Chief Chancery Master];
(c) there be substituted for all purposes in these proceedings in place of references to the Claimant by name, and whether orally or in writing, references to the letters "AAA"; and
(d) if necessary, there be substituted for all purposes in these proceedings in place of references to the Defendant[s] by name once identified and whether orally or in writing, references to the letters "BBB" [and any subsequent letters of the alphabet].
[ONLY TO BE GRANTED IN AN EXCEPTIONAL CASE WHERE A RESTRICTION ON ACCESS TO DOCUMENTS IS STRICTLY NECESSARY]

Access to Documents

4. Upon the Judge being satisfied that it is strictly necessary:

(a)(i) no copies of the statements of case; and
(ii) no copies of the witness statements and the applications, will be provided to a non-party without further order of the Court.
(b) Any non-party other than a person notified or served with this Order seeking access to, or copies of the abovementioned documents, must make an application to the Court, proper notice of which must be given to the other parties.

Service of Claim Form where Defendant not Known or Whereabouts not Known

P14-05 5.(a) The Claim Form should be served as soon as reasonably practicable and in any event by [ ] at the latest, save that there shall be liberty for the Claimant to apply to the Court in the event that an extension is necessary; and

(b) Any such application referred to in 5(a) must be supported by a witness statement. Such application may be made by letter, the Court having dispensed with the need for an application notice.

Injunction

P14-06 6. Until [ ] (the return date) / the trial of this claim or further Order of the Court, the Defendants must not:

(a) use, publish or communicate or disclose to any other person (other than (i) by way of disclosure to legal advisers instructed in relation to these proceedings (the Defendants' legal advisers) for the purpose of obtaining legal advice in relation to these proceedings or (ii) for the purpose of carrying this Order into effect) all or any part of the the information referred to in Confidential Schedule 2 to this Order (the Information);

(b) publish any information which is liable to or might identify the Claimant as a party to the proceedings and/or as the subject of the Information or which otherwise contains material (including but not limited to the profession [or age or nationality of the Claimant]) which is liable to, or might lead to, the Claimant's identification in any such respect, provided that nothing in this Order shall prevent the publication, disclosure or communication of any information which is contained in [this Order other than in the Confidential Schedules] or in the public judgments of the Court in this action given on [insert date].

[ONLY TO BE GRANTED IN AN EXCEPTIONAL CASE WHERE A REPORTING RESTRICTION IS STRICTLY NECESSARY]

Reporting Restriction/Super-Injunction

P14-07 7. Until service of the Order/ the return date/ [ ] the Defendants must not use, publish or communicate or disclose to any other person the fact or existence of this Order or these proceedings and the Claimant's interest in them, other than:

(a) by way of disclosure to the Defendants' legal advisers for the purpose of obtaining legal advice in relation to these proceedings; or

(b) for the purpose of carrying this Order into effect.

Information to be Disclosed

P14-08 8. The Defendants shall within [24] hours of service of this Order disclose to the Claimant's solicitors the following:

(a) the identity of each and every journalist, press or media organisation, press agent or publicist or any other third party with a view to publication in the press or media, to whom the Defendants have disclosed all or any part of the Information [since [insert date]]; and

(a) the date upon which such disclosure took place and the nature of the information disclosed.

9. The Defendants shall confirm the information supplied in paragraph 8 above in a witness statement containing a statement of truth within 7 days of complying

with paragraph 8 and serve the same on the Claimant's solicitors and the other parties.

Protection of Hearing Papers

10.   The Defendants [, and any third party given advance notice of the Application,] must not publish or communicate or disclose or copy or cause to be published or communicated or disclosed or copied any witness statements and any exhibits thereto and information contained therein that are made, or may subsequently be made, in support of the Application or the Claimant's solicitors' notes of the hearing of the Application (the Hearing Papers), provided that the Defendants[, and any third party,] shall be permitted to copy, disclose and deliver the Hearing Papers to the Defendants' [and third party's/parties'] legal advisers for the purpose of these proceedings.

P14-09

11.   The Hearing Papers must be preserved in a secure place by the Defendants' [and third party's/parties'] legal advisers on the Defendants' [and third party's/parties'] behalf.

12.   The Defendants [, and any third party given advance notice of the Application,] shall be permitted to use the Hearing Papers for the purpose of these proceedings provided that the Defendants' [third party's/parties'] legal advisers shall first inform anyone, to whom the said documents are disclosed, of the terms of this Order and, so far as is practicable, obtain their written confirmation that they understand and accept that they are bound by the same.

Provision of Documents and Information to Third Parties

13.   The Claimant shall be required to provide the legal advisers of any third party [where unrepresented, the third party] served with advance notice of the application, or a copy of this Order promptly upon request, and receipt of their written irrevocable undertaking to the Court to use those documents and the information contained in those documents only for the purpose of these proceedings:

P14-10

(a)   a copy of any material read by the Judge, including material read after the hearing at the direction of the Judge or in compliance with this Order [save for the witness statements referred to in Confidential Schedule 1 at the end of this Order] [the witness statements]; and/or

(b)   a copy of the Hearing Papers.

[ONLY TO BE GRANTED IN AN EXCEPTIONAL CASE WHERE HEARING THE APPLICATION IN PRIVATE IS STRICTLY NECESSARY]

Hearing in Private

14.   The Judge considered that it was strictly necessary, pursuant to CPR 39.2(3)(a),(c) and (g), to order that the hearing of the Application be in private and there shall be no reporting of the same.

P14-11

Public Domain

15.   For the avoidance of doubt, nothing in this Order shall prevent the Defendants from publishing, communicating or disclosing such of the Information[, or any part thereof, as was already in, or that thereafter comes into, the public domain in England and Wales [as a result of publication in the national media] (other than as a result of breach of this Order [or a breach of confidence or privacy]).

Costs

16. The costs of and occasioned by the Application are reserved.

Variation or Discharge of this Order

P14-12 **17.** The parties or anyone affected by any of the restrictions in this Order may apply to the Court at any time to vary or discharge this Order (or so much of it as affects that person), but they must first give written notice to the Claimant's solicitors. If any evidence is to be relied upon in support of the application, the substance of it must be communicated in writing to the Claimant's solicitors in advance. The Defendants may agree with the Claimant's solicitors and any other person who is, or may be bound by this Order, that this Order should be varied or discharged, but any agreement must be in writing.

Interpretation of this Order

P14-13 **18.** A Defendant who is an individual who is ordered not to do something must not do it himself or in any other way. He must not do it through others acting on his behalf or on his instructions or with his encouragement.

19. A Defendant which is not an individual which is ordered not to do something must not do it itself or by its directors, officers, partners, employees or agents or in any other way.

[In the case of an Order the effect of which may extend outside the jurisdiction]
PERSONS OUTSIDE ENGLAND AND WALES

20.(1) Except as provided in paragraph (2) below, the terms of this Order do not affect or concern anyone outside the jurisdiction of this Court.

(2) The terms of this Order will affect the following persons in a country or state outside the jurisdiction of this Court—
    (a) the Defendant or his officer or agent appointed by power of attorney;
    (b) any person who—
        (i) is subject to the jurisdiction of this Court;
        (ii) has been given written notice of this Order at his residence or place of business within the jurisdiction of this Court; and
        (iii) is able to prevent acts or omissions outside the jurisdiction of this Court which constitute or assist in a breach of the terms of this Order; and
    (c) any other person, only to the extent that this Order is declared enforceable by or is enforced by a court in that country or state.

Parties Other than the Claimant and the Defendant

P14-14 **21.** Effect of this Order
It is a contempt of court for any person notified of this Order knowingly to assist in or permit a breach of this Order. Any person doing so may be imprisoned, fined or have their assets seized.

Name and Address of the Claimant's Legal Representatives

22. The Claimant's solicitors are—
[Name, address, reference, fax and telephone numbers both in and out of office hours and e-mail]

Communications with the Court

23. All communications to the Court about this Order should be sent to:
Room E07, Royal Courts of Justice, Strand, London, WC2A 2LL, quoting the case number. The telephone number is 020 7947 6010.
The offices are open between 10 a.m. and 4.30 p.m. Monday to Friday.

Schedule A

The Claimant relied on the following witness statements:　　　　　　　　　**P14-15**
1.　　.........
2.　　.........

Schedule B

Undertakings Given to the Court by the Claimant

(1) If the Court later finds that this Order has caused loss to the Defendants, and decides that the Defendants should be compensated for that loss, the Claimant will comply with any order the Court may make.

(2) If the Court later finds that this Order has caused loss to any person or company (other than the Defendants) to whom the Claimant has given notice of this Order, and decides that such person should be compensated for that loss, the Claimant will comply with any Order the Court may make.

[(3) By 4.30pm on [ ] the Claimant will (a) issue a Claim Form and an Application Notice claiming the appropriate relief [and (b) cause a witness statement or witness statements to be made and filed confirming the substance of what was said to the Court by the Claimant's Counsel and exhibiting a copy of the Hearing Papers].

[(4) The Claimant will use all reasonable endeavours to identify and serve the Defendants within four months of the date of this Order and in any event will do so by [ ] at the latest. Once identified the Claimant will serve upon the Defendant together with this Order copies of the documents provided to the Court on the making of the Application and as soon as practicable the documents referred to in (3) above.]

(5) On the return date the Claimant will inform the Court of the identity of all third parties that have been notified of this Order. The Claimant will use all reasonable endeavours to keep such third parties informed of the progress of the action [insofar as it may affect them], including, but not limited to, advance notice of any applications, the outcome of which may affect the status of the Order.

(6) If this Order ceases to have effect or is varied, the Claimant will immediately take all reasonable steps to inform in writing anyone to whom he has given notice of this Order, or whom he has reasonable grounds for supposing may act upon this Order, that it has ceased to have effect in this form.

Schedule C

This should contain details of who the Claimant has given advance notice of the application to, including how and when and by what means this was done.

Schedule D

The detail required by paragraph 20 of the Guidance Note should go in here.

Schedule E

The detail required by paragraph 38 of the Guidance Note should go in here.

Confidential Schedule 1

The Claimant also relied on the following confidential witness statements:
1.   ....
2.   ....

Confidential Schedule 2

Information referred to in the Order

Any information or purported information concerning:
(1)   [Set out the material sought to be protected]
(2)   [Any information liable to or which might lead to the identification of the
       Claimant (whether directly or indirectly) as the subject of the proceedings
       or the material referred to above, [the fact that he has commenced these
       proceedings or made the application herein].]

Model order—guidelines for applicants

P14-16   The following guidelines should be read in conjunction with the model interim
nondisclosure order.

Penal Notice

P14-17   The penal notice should make clear that where the intended defendant or
respondent is an individual they may be imprisoned as well as being liable to a fine
or asset seizure. Where the intended defendant or respondent is a corporate defendant or respondent it should make clear that they can be fined or have their assets
seized.

The penal notice should also make clear the effect it may have on non-parties
who know of the order under the *Spycatcher* principle. The order will only bind
nonparties who are notified of it while it is in force: *Jockey Club v Buffham* [2003]
QB 462.

Clause 2(b)

P14-18   Reference should be made to paragraphs 18–28 of the Practice Guidance.

Clause 3 (Anonymity)

P14-19   This clause is optional. Reference should be made to paragraphs 9–14 of the
Practice Guidance. Anonymity is an exception to the principle of open justice. It
can only be ordered where it is strictly necessary. Guidance is set out in *JIH* at [21].

Clause 4(a)(ii) (Access to documents)

The court may need to decide which documents, e.g., statements of case, should **P14-20** not be available for public inspection. This decision may be prospective since there may be little if any opportunity to apply to court before some documents are served. While it may be the case that the claim form could be made anodyne by reference to a confidential schedule (subject to anonymity), subsequent statements of case or other documents in a case are unlikely to be dealt with so easily giventhat the purpose of the action, amongst other things, will be to seek a permanent injunction relating to the material protected on an interim basis under the order, and will involve a specific explanation of the material, how it is said to engage the applicant's Article 8 Convention rights and the effect such threatened disclosure would have if it is not so restrained (*Terry* at [23]; *G & G v Wikimedia* [2010] EMLR 14 at [14], [17] and [20]; *ABC Ltd v Y* [2010] EWHC 3176 (Ch) at [8]–[10].

(In respect of any non-party notified or served with the order CPR PD 25A 9.2 applies: see clause 13 of the Model Order.)

Clause 5(a) (Service of the claim form where defendant is not known or whereabouts unknown)

Where the respondent or defendant's identity is not known, or their whereabouts **P14-21** are unknown, there may be considerable problems in locating them in order to serve the claim form. This may necessitate an extension of time for service beyond the four month period. The court, by way of active case management, is required to ensure that the action is pursued with expedition. Indefinite extensions of time for service cannot be granted: *Terry* at [143]. A long-stop date may be inserted instead.

Clause 6 (Injunction)

CPR PD 25A 5 states that unless the court orders otherwise, the order must **P14-22** provide for a return date if the application was made without-notice. The need for, and importance of, a return date as a means to ensure the court can monitor the claim's progress and ensure it progresses properly was considered *G & G v Wikimedia* [2010] EMLR 14 at [21]–[27]; and in *Terry* at [134]–[136]. Reference should be made to paragraphs 37–41 of the Practice Guidance.

While there may be considerable practical and costs reasons which might render a return date in a claim against persons unknown unnecessary, especially given the safeguard of the liberty to vary or discharge provisions (*X & V v Persons Unknown* [2007] EMLR 290 at [73]), the court should ensure that the order contains provision for periodical review by the court to ensure that the claim progresses, for instance, to default judgment, summary judgment, or to a trial in the absence of the persons unknown.

Clause 6(b)

This clause is optional. See clause 3 above. This provides a possible solution to **P14-23** the problem which arises from a jigsaw identification of the Claimant if the fact of the injunction is not prevented from being published: *DFT* at [36]–[39]. Thereshould be a clear delineation in the order of what information can be released as to the fact of an order having been made.

Clause 7 (Reporting Restriction)

P14-24   This is the super-injunction element. It is an optional clause. It is only likely to be necessary for example to prevent the respondent or a third party being tipped-off before the order is served, possibly precipitating disclosure of the information or destruction of evidence: see *Terry* at [138]; *G & G v Wikimedia* [2010] EMLR 14 at [41].

If the proceedings are anonymised, and an injunction is granted restraining disclosure or publication of the private information, there is generally no reason in principle to prohibit in addition any report of the fact that an order has been made: Ntuli. Consideration should be given to the risk of jigsaw identification if no reporting restriction is imposed: *DFT*.

Clause 13 (Provision of documents and information to third parties)

P14-25   CPR PD 25A 9 requires any person served with the order not present at the application hearing to be provided with the order and supporting material read by the judge, and a note of the hearing.

This is the norm. Such notice is an elementary principle of natural justice:

Kelly v BBC [2001] Fam. 59 at 94–95, '... if one party wishes to place evidence or other persuasive material before the court the other parties must have an opportunity to see that material and to address the court about it. One party may not make secret communications to the court. It follows that it is wrong for a judge to be given material at an ex parte, or without notice, hearing which is not at a later stage revealed to the persons affected by the result of the application.';

G & G v Wikimedia [2009] EWHC 3148 (QB) at [30], '... where an order relates to freedom of expression, or may have the effect of interfering with freedom of expression, those applying for interim relief at a hearing at which the respondent or defendant is not present should generally provide the respondent with a full note, whether or not the respondent asks for it.'

Exceptions to the norm are exceptions to the principle of open justice, and natural justice, and are therefore only permissible where strictly necessary. If there is concern that information is particularly sensitive or confidential, it can be included in a separate witness statement which the court may agree should be specifically exempted from having to be provided under the CPR 25A PD 9, thus enabling as much information as possible to be provided to those, such as non-parties who request a hearing note under PD 9.2(2), not present at the application hearing.

Clause 13 Irrevocable written undertaking

P14-26   The following standard wording should be used by third parties in respect of the irrevocable undertaking to be given to the Court under paragraph 24 of the Practice Guidance and in respect of clause 13 of the Model Order. Breach of the undertaking may amount to contempt of court. The wording provides for a Claimant to agree to information and material subject to the undertaking provided by the third party to be supplied, by the third party, to other parties in order, for instance, to ensure that the prohibition on disclosure is not inadvertently breached by that other party.

Undertaking to the Claimant and to the Court

P14-27   The title of action or intended action is ....

1.   I, [insert name, occupation] [for and on behalf of ....] (hereinafter "the

receiver") promise that in consideration of the Claimant disclosing the material to the receiver, the receiver: will preserve the material in a secure place; use any material or information contained therein, or derived from such material or information, only for the purposes of the Proceedings except where:

(a) the information has been read to or by the court, or referred to, at a hearing which has been held in public;

(b) the court gives permission; or

(c) there is agreement in writing by the Claimant and by any other person who claims to be entitled to rights of property, privacy or confidentiality in respect of the information or the documents in which it is recorded;

and will only copy, disclose or deliver the material, or information contained therein or derived from such material or information, to the receiver's legal advisers, or as required by law, by order of the court or by agreement of the Claimant and by any other person who claims to be entitled to rights of property, privacy or confidentiality in respect of the information or the documents in which it is recorded.

2. Save as provided in para 1, this undertaking is irrevocable, and shall continue in force both before and after the conclusion of the Proceedings.

3. The receiver will give to the court an undertaking in writing in the same terms as herein, as soon as a judge is available to receive that undertaking.

4. For the purpose of this undertaking,

"Material" refers to: i) any claim form or application notice or statement of case (whether in draft or final form); ii) any evidence, whether in the form of witness statements or otherwise, in support of the proceedings, and any exhibits thereto; iii) and the material specified in CPR PD 25A para 9.2;

"Claimant" includes an intended claimant;

"Proceedings" means the proceedings identified above.

5. For the avoidance of doubt this promise only applies to those parts of the Material which contain the information alleged by the Claimant to be private and does not preclude the receiver (or anyone else) from making lawful use of any information that was already known to them prior to it being disclosed to the receiver pursuant to this undertaking, or of any information which is, or shall have come into, the public domain.

Clause 14 (Hearing in private)

This clause is optional. Reference should be made to paragraphs 9–14 of the **P14-28** Practice Guidance.

Private hearings can be reported without fear of contempt unless the material comes within the protection of the Administration of Justice Act 1960 s12. A specific order is required to prevent reporting under the Contempt of Court Act 1981 s.11: Clibbery v Allan [2002] 2 W.L.R. 151; *McKennitt v Ash* [2008] QB 73. Section 11 orders should only be made when strictly necessary.

This also incorporates the proviso, referred to in *JIH* at [42], regarding disclosure of material etc referred to in open court or in open judgments.

Clause 15 (Public Domain)

Orders will not usually, but may sometimes in cases of private information, **P14-29** prohibit publication of material which is already in the public domain. See *Terry* at [50].

Confidential schedule 2, paragraph 2

P14-30   See the notes to Clause 13 (Provision of documents and information to third parties).

15. MODEL EXPLANATORY NOTE TO INTERIM NON-DISCLOSURE ORDER

Smith v Jones

or

AAA v BBB

Application for an Interim Non-Disclosure Order

EXPLANATORY NOTE

1. The applicant is a well known professional sportsperson who has been in a long-term relationship with another person [XX]. A person [BBB/YY as appropriate] [or persons unknown] have threatened to take a story to the media about a relationship the applicant is alleged to have had with another person [YY], since the relationship with XX commenced.

2. An Interim Non-Disclosure Order has been [applied for/made] to protect the applicant's [right to privacy and/confidentiality] in respect of the information referred to in paragraph 1. This does not [will not] restrict publication of information which was in the public domain in England and Wales prior to this application being made or which is permitted by any order of the court to the extent permitted by the court

3. The [applicant applies for the application to be heard/the application was heard] in private. Judgment [will be/was] given in [public/private]. [The proceedings were anonymised.] [A private hearing/anonymity was applied for/granted on the grounds of strict necessity because …].

4. On [insert date] the application [will be heard by/was heard by] [Mr/Mrs Justice] in the High Court of Justice, [Queen's Bench Division/Chancery Division].

16. REGISTERED LAND: RESTRICTION IN THE LAND REGISTER

P16-01   Using Land Registry Form RX1

The applicant applies to enter a restriction in standard form AA against the estate/ charge referred to in panel 3 in the following words:

Under an order of the High Court of Justice (Queen's Bench Division) dated 11th February 2019 in an action entitled *John Bull v Shifti Enterprises SA* claim number HQ183456X no disposition or other dealing by the proprietor of the registered estate is to be registered except with the consent of John Bull of [address] or under a further Order of the Court.

17. ORDER NOT TO LEAVE THE COUNTRY

(1)   The Respondent be restrained from leaving England and Wales without the   P17-01
leave of the Court for a period of [two] days after service upon him of this Order

(2)   The Respondent do forthwith deliver up his passport to the solicitor serving
this Order upon him, such passport to be returned after the expiry of the said period
of [two] days

18. ORDER TO TIPSTAFF

P18-01 In the High Court of Justice No:
Family Division
THE CHILD ABDUCTION AND CUSTODY ACT 1985
COUNCIL REGULATION (EC) No. 2201/2003
THE SENIOR COURTS ACT 1981
THE CHILDREN ACT 1989
THE FAMILY LAW ACT 1986

Delete or Adapt as appropriate

The Child(ren) AA (a boy/girl born on dd/mm/yyyy)
BB (a boy/girl born on dd/mm/yyyy)
CC (a boy/girl born on dd/mm/yyyy)

After hearing [name the advocate(s) who appeared]....

DIRECTION ORDER TO THE TIPSTAFF MADE BY [NAME OF JUDGE] ON [DATE] SITTING IN PRIVATE

The Parties

1.   The applicant is XX
The respondent is YY
Specify any additional respondents
Specify if any adult party acts by a litigation friend
Specify if the children or any of them act by a children's guardian

2.   Unless otherwise stated, a reference in this order to 'the respondent' means all of the respondents.

Recital

3.   This direction order to the Tipstaff was made at the same hearing at which a Passport order was made against the respondent YY in respect of the child/children AA, BB and CC ("the Passport order").

IT IS ORDERED AND DIRECTED THAT:-

4.   The Tipstaff of the High Court of Justice, whether acting by himself or his deputy or an assistant or a police officer, shall:
   (a)   obtain the documents referred to in paragraph 10 of the Passport order;
   (b)   enter, if necessary by force, and search the premises in which he has reasonable cause to believe that any such document will be found and which, after taking all reasonable steps to do so, he remains unable to secure other permission to enter;
   (c)   whilst one or more of the entries referred to in sub-paragraph (f) below remains operative, arrest any person whom he has reasonable cause to believe has been served with the Passport order and has disobeyed any of the obligations imposed by paragraphs 11 or 12 of it, and shall explain to that person the ground for the arrest and shall bring him or her before the court as soon as practicable and in any event no later than the working day immediately following the arrest;
   (d)   cause any person arrested pursuant to paragraph 4(c) above to be detained

until he or she is brought before the court and, as soon as practicable during any such period of detention, give to that person the opportunity to seek legal advice;

(e) keep safely, until further direction of the court, any document handed over to him pursuant to paragraph 10 of the Passport order;

(f) initiate in respect of this direction and the Passport order entries of a Port Alert and on the PNC and WICU systems that are to remain operative until further order of the court or until the Tipstaff is satisfied that he has fully executed his primary duties under the Passport order whereupon he may cancel or amend the entries on the expiration of at least two business days from the date upon which he notifies the applicant either personally or through solicitors in writing of his intention to do so; and

(g) inform the National Ports Office and the police of the powers conferred by this direction on the Tipstaff acting by a police officer.

5. The Tipstaff must not disclose any information or provide a copy of any document obtained by the Tipstaff pursuant the Passport order to any person other than those listed in paragraph 6.

6. Subject to further direction of the court and notwithstanding any request that he should not do so the Tipstaff shall provide all information obtained by him pursuant to the Passport Order to:

(a) the court,

(b) the applicant's solicitors Messrs ZZZ on the basis of their undertaking set out in paragraph 9 of the Passport Order unless he has been notified of a proposed application for a direction that he should not do so.

7. If the Tipstaff has not obtained the documents referred to in paragraph 10 of the Passport order by [the date 6 months after the making of the order] this order shall lapse in its entirety.

A Justice of the High Court
Mr(s) Justice
Dated

19.   FREEZING INJUNCTION UNDER THE CIVIL JURISDICTION AND JUDGMENTS ACT 1982: ENDORSEMENT ON THE CLAIM FORM

P19-01   The Applicant applies for an order pursuant to section 25(1) of the Civil Jurisdiction and Judgments Act 1982 to restrain the Respondent whether by himself from transferring, dealing with, charging, disposing of or removing from the jurisdiction any of his assets within the jurisdiction until after the determination of proceedings brought against him by the Applicant in the Division for Civil Matters of the Regional Court of Luneburg, Germany, and the execution or enforcement whether in Germany or in England and Wales of any judgment or order in such proceedings.

20. MANDATORY ORDER FOR DISCLOSURE OF INFORMATION ("NORWICH PHARMACAL ORDER")— QUEEN'S BENCH DIVISION

IN THE HIGH COURT OF JUSTICE   P20-01
QUEEN'S BENCH DIVISION
Before The Honourable Mr Justice Quip

Claim No.
Dated 2019

Applicant John Smith
Respondents (1) Bloggs Bank PLC (2) Chancers Building Society PLC
  Name, address and reference of Respondents

PENAL NOTICE

If you do not comply with this order you may be held in contempt of court and imprisoned or fined, or your assets may be seized.

THE ORDER

This is a disclosure order made against Bloggs Bank PLC and Chancers Build-   P20-02
ing Society PLC ("the Respondents") on 4th January 2019 on the application of
John Smith ("the Applicant") to Mr Justice Quip who heard the application.

The Judge read the witness statements set out in Schedule A and accepted the undertaking(s) set out in Schedule B at the end of this Order.

And Upon Hearing Counsel for the Applicant

IT IS ORDERED that;   P20-03

1.   the First Respondent do by 11th January 2019 disclose to the Applicant
      i.   all bank account statements, instructions and cheques paid in in
            respect of an account in the name of Joe Green number 00112233,
            sort code 60-50-40 from the time the account was set up to date
      ii.   the sum or balance at present standing to the account
2.   the Respondents do by 11th January 2019 disclose to the Applicant the
      identity of any other accounts held in the name of Joe Green and the sum
      or balance at present standing to that account
3.   except for the purpose of obtaining legal advice and taking any steps in these
      proceedings, the Respondents must not directly or indirectly inform anyone
      of the application or this Order or warn anyone that proceedings have been
      or may be brought against them by the Applicant until 1st February 2019
      without the consent in writing of the Applicant's solicitors or the permis-
      sion of the court

Interpretation of this Order

(1)   A Respondent who is an individual who is ordered not to do something must not do it himself or in any other way. He must not do it through others acting on his behalf or on his instructions or with his encouragement.

(2)   A Respondent which is a corporation and which is ordered not to do something must not do it itself or by its directors, officers, employees or agents or in any other way.

Variation or discharge of this Order

The Respondents (or anyone notified of this Order) may apply to the Court at any time to vary or discharge this Order (or so much of it as affects that person), but anyone wishing to do so must first inform the Applicant or his legal representatives.

Communications with the Court

All communications to the Court about this Order should be sent to Room E07, Royal Courts of Justice, Strand, London WC2A 2LL (020 7947 6010). The offices are open between 10 am and 4.30 pm Monday to Friday.

Schedule A

P20-04   ....

Affidavits

....

Schedule B

Undertakings given to the Court by the Applicant:—
(1) To pay the reasonable costs of the Respondents incurred as a result of this Order
(2) ....
Name and address of Applicant's Legal Representatives
The Applicant's legal representatives are:—

Ref: Tel: Fax:

[Name and Address of Applicant]

21. NOTICE OF APPLICATION FOR INTERIM INJUNCTION: COUNTY COURT

IN THE BARCHESTER COUNTY COURT

Claim No. B9079

BETWEEN:

PHILIP MICHAEL TENNANT

Claimant/Applicant

—and—

LESLIE LANDLORD

Defendant/Respondent

By application in pending proceedings.

This case raises no issues under the Human Rights Act 1998.

The Applicant Philip Michael Tennant applies to the Court for an injunction order in the following terms:

That the Respondent Leslie Landlord be forbidden (whether by himself or by instructing or encouraging any other person) to harass the Applicant or to disturb his quiet enjoyment of the first floor flat at 113 Palmerston Road, Barchester or to interfere with the Applicant's access to the said flat

And that the Respondent do forthwith allow the Applicant to return to and occupy the said first floor flat at 113 Palmerston Road, Barchester

And for an order that the Respondent pay the Applicant's costs of this application

The grounds of this application are set out in the witness statement of the Applicant Philip Michael Tennant signed on 28th January 2019. This witness statement is served with this application.

This application is to be served upon Leslie Landlord of 113 Palmerston Road, Barchester.

This application is filed by Barritt & Co of 19 Foley Street, Barchester, Solicitors for the Applicant.

(Signed)   DATED the 29th January 2019

TO Leslie Landlord of 113 Palmerston Road, Barchester

This application will be heard by the [District] Judge at [place] on [date] at [time] o'clock. If you do not attend the court may make an injunction order in your absence.

If you do not fully understand this application you should go to a Solicitor, a Legal Advice Centre or a Citizens' Advice Bureau

22.   INTER PARTES INJUNCTION AGAINST HARASSMENT: COUNTY COURT

P22-01   IN THE BARCHESTER COUNTY COURT

Case No. B9079

BETWEEN:

PHILIP MICHAEL TENNANT

Claimant/Applicant

—and—

LESLIE LANDLORD

Defendant/Respondent

INJUNCTION ORDER (PROTECTION FROM HARASSMENT ACT 1997)

TO Leslie Landlord
OF 113 Palmerston Road, Barchester
If you do not comply with this order you may be held in contempt of court and imprisoned or fined, or your assets may be seized.

On the 5th day of February 20162019 the Court considered an application for an injunction.

The Court ordered that Leslie Landlord is forbidden (whether by himself or by instructing or encouraging any other person) to harass Philip Michael Tennant or to disturb his quiet enjoyment of the first floor flat at 113 Palmerston Road, Barchester or to interfere with his access to the said flat.

This Order shall remain in force until further order of this Court.

And it is ordered that Leslie Landlord do allow Philip Michael Tennant to return toand occupy the said first floor flat at 113 Palmerston Road, Barchester by 4 pm on the 8th day of February 20162019.

It is further ordered that Leslie Landlord pay the Applicant's costs of this application, to be assessed if not agreed.

If you do not understand anything in this Order you should go to a Solicitor, Legal Advice Centre or Citizens' Advice Bureau.

23. NON-MOLESTATION ORDER UNDER THE FAMILY LAW ACT 1996 S.42

IN THE FAMILY COURT

sitting at BARCHESTER...............CASE NUMBER: FL1804762

THE FAMILY LAW ACT 1996

MARY SMITH...............Applicant...............

and

..........JOHN SMITH...............Respondent

AFTER HEARING the advocate for the Applicant and/the Respondent/the Respondent in person

AFTER READING the statement/s of -------- and hearing the oral evidence of ----------

NON-MOLESTATION ORDER MADE BY DISTRIRCT JUDGE XY / HHJUDGE AB ON -------- 2018 SITTING IN PRIVATE

IMPORTANT NOTICE TO THE RESPONDENT, JOHN SMITH OF 39 MONT-CLAIR DRIVE BARCHESTER

YOU MUST OBEY THIS ORDER. You should read is carefully. If you do not understand anything in this order you should go to a solicitor, Legal Advice Centre or Citizens Advice Bureau. You have a right to apply to the court to change or cancel the order.

WARNING: IF WITHOUT REASONABLE EXCUSE YOU DO ANYTHING WHICH YOU ARE FORBIDDEN FROM DOING BY THIS ORDER, YOU WILL BE COMMITTING A CRIMINAL OFFENCE AND LIABLE ON CONVICTION TO A TERM OF IMPRISONMENT NOT EXCEEDING FIVE YEARS OR TO A FINE OR BOTH.

ALTERNATIVELY, IF YOU DO NOT OBEY THIS ORDER, YOU WILL BE GUILTY OF CONTEMPT OF COURT AND YOU AY BE SENT TO PRISON, BE FINED, OR HAVE YOUR ASSETS SEIZED.

The parties:

The Applicant is Mary Smith

The Respondent is John Smith

The relevant children are:

Joseph Smith a boy born on 14th December 2008

Alice Smith a girl born on 15th September 2010

Jane Smith a girl born on 24th July 2016

The family home is: 27 Seymour Road Barchester

(Any other property covered by the order should be identified separately)

This order was made at a hearing without notice/ on short notice to the Respondent. The order was made without notice /on short notice because ----------. The Respondent has the right to apply to the court to vary or discharge the order

IT IS ORDERED(BY CONSENT):

1. The Respondent John Smith must not use or threaten to use violence against the Applicant Mary Smith and must not instruct, encourage or in any way suggest that any other person should do so.

2. The Respondent John Smith must not intimidate, harass or pester the Applicant Mary Smith and must not instruct, encourage or in any way suggest that any other person should do so.

3. The Respondent John Smith must not telephone, text, email or otherwise

contact or attempt to contact the Applicant Mary Smith, including via social networking websites or other forms of electronic messaging(except for the purpose of making arrangements for contact between the Respondent and the relevant children) (except through his legal representatives (include the contact details of the firm)).

4. The Respondent John Smith must not damage, attempt to damage, or threaten to damage any property in the possession of or owned by the Applicant Mary Smith and must not instruct, encourage or in any way suggest that any other person should do so.

5. The Respondent John Smith must not damage attempt to damage or threaten to damage the property or contents of 27 Seymour Road Barchester and must not instruct, encourage or in any way suggest that any other person should do so.

6. The Respondent John Smith must not go to, enter or attempt to enter 27 Seymour Road Barchester or any property where he knows or believes the applicant Mary Smith to be living and must not go within 100 metres of Seymour Road except that the Respondent may go to the property but not enter it / go along Seymour Road for the purpose of collecting the children for and returning them from such contact with the children as may be agreed in writing between the Applicant and the Respondent or as may be ordered by the court.

7. The Respondent John Smith must not use or threaten to use violence against the relevant children and must not instruct, encourage or in any way suggest that any other person should do so.

8. The Respondent John Smith must not intimidate, harass or pester the relevant children and must not instruct, encourage or in any way suggest that any other person should do so.

9. The Respondent John Smith must not telephone, text, email or otherwise contact or attempt to contact the relevant children, including via social networking websites or other forms of electronic messaging (except for such contact as may be agreed in writing between the Applicant and the Respondent or as may be ordered by the court.)

10. The Respondent John Smith must not between the hours of ------------- go to or attempt to enter the school premises known as CD Primary School and EF Secondary School and must not go within 100 metres of it/ along Church Street unless invited to do so in writing and in advance by the school or with the written agreement in advance of the Applicant Mary Smith.

11. Paragraphs 1-10 of this order shall be effective against the Respondent John Smith once it is personally served on him (and/or once he is made aware of the terms of this order whether by personal service or otherwise.

12. Paragraphs 1-10 of this order shall last until 17th September 2018 unless it is set aside or varied before that date by an order of the court.

13. The Respondent has the right to apply to the court at any time to set aside, vary or revoke this order. (If the court specifies the number of days' notice to be of the application to set aside etc it should be set out here). Any evidence which the

Respondent intends to rely on to set aside or to oppose the continuation of the order at the next hearing must be provided in writing to the Applicant / the Applicant's solicitors in advance of the hearing.

14. If the Respondent intends to oppose the continuation of the order on the return date he must notify the court in writing no later than 10th September 2018 that he intends to attend the hearing on the return date and oppose the continuation of the order. If the Respondent does not notify the court by that date the court may make an order dispensing with the need for the Applicant and her solicitors to attend on the return date and may make an order on the return date extending the injunction.

15. The application is listed for further hearing on 17th September 2018 at 10am time estimate 1 hour (the return day)which may include giving directions for further evidence and a further hearing. At this hearing the court will consider whether the orders should continue/ the application be granted.

16. If the Respondent does not attend the hearing on 17th September 2018 at 10am the court may make an order in his absence.

17. The costs of the application are reserved to the judge hearing the case on 17th September 2018.

NOTE TO ARRESTING OFFICER:
Under section 42A of the Family Law Act 1996 breach of a non-molestation order is a criminal offence punishable by up to five years' imprisonment. It is an arrestable offence and it is not necessary to obtain a warrant.
A person who without reasonable excuse does anything that he is prohibited from doing by a non-molestation order is guilty of an offence.
FAMILY LAW ACT 1996 SECTION 42A(1).

24. OCCUPATION ORDER UNDER THE FAMILY LAW ACT 1996 SECTION 33

P24-01   IN THE FAMILY COURT....................CASE NUMBER: FL1804763
sitting at BARCHESTER
Applicant..........MARY SMITH
Respondent..........JOHN SMITH

After hearing the advocate for the Applicant and the Respondent

After reading the statement(s) and hearing the following witnesses

OCCUPATION ORDER MADE BY DISTRICT JUDGE ----/HHJUDGE ---- on 1ˢᵗOCTOBER 2018 SITTING IN PRIVATE

IMPORTANT NOTICE TO THE RESPONDENT JOHN SMITH OF 39 MONT-CLAIR DRIVE BARCHESTER

YOU MUST OBEY THIS ORDER. You should read it carefully. If you do not understand anything in this order you should go to a solicitor, Legal Advice Centre, or Citizens Advice Bureau. You have a right to apply to the court to change or cancel the order.

WARNING: IF YOU DO NOT OBEY THIS ORDER YOU WILL BE GUILTY OF CONTEMPT OF COURT AND YOU MAY BE SENT TO PRISON, BE FINED OR HAVE YOUR ASSETS SEIZED.

The parties:

The Applicant is Mary Smith

The Respondent is John Smith

The relevant children within the meaning of the Family Law Act 1996 are:

Joseph Smith a boy born on 14ᵗʰ December 2008

Alice Smith..........a girl born on 15ᵗʰ September 2010

Jane Smith..........a girl born on 24ᵗʰ July 2016

The family home is the property at 27 Seymour Road Barchester including its gardens, and outbuildings

Any other property to be covered by the order should be identified separately

This is an occupation order made against the Respondent on 1ˢᵗ October 2018 by District Judge Y on the application of the Applicant Mary Smith.

(If made without notice) The judge read the following witness statements and heard oral evidence from Mary Smith and Margaret Thomas

(If made without notice) This order was made at a hearing without notice/ on short notice to the Respondent. The reason why the order was made without notice /on short notice is -------. The Respondent has the right to apply to vary or discharge the order.

IT IS ORDERED (BY CONSENT):

The court declares that the Applicant Mary Smith is entitled to occupy the family home including its gardens and outbuildings as her home.

The court declares that the Applicant Mary Smith has home rights in the family home and/or the court declares that the Applicant's home rights in the family home shall not end when the Respondent dies or their marriage is dissolved and shall continue until ------- /the determination of the Applicant's financial provision claims under case number or a further order is made.

The Respondent John Smith shall permit the Applicant Mary Smith to occupy the family home including its gardens and out buildings.

The Respondent John Smith shall leave the family home including its gardens and outbuildings by ---- /within 48 hours of this order being personally served on him / being made aware of the terms of this order by personal service or any other means.

Having left the family home including its gardens and outbuildings the Respondent John Smith must not return to, enter or attempt to enter or to go within 50 metres of it except without entering it for the purpose of collecting or returning the children in respect of such contact as may be agreed in writing between the Applicant and the Respondent or as may be ordered by the court.

The Respondent must not obstruct, harass or interfere with the occupation by the Applicant of the family home including its gardens and outbuildings.

The above paragraphs of this order shall continue until --------- /further order/ it is set aside or varied by a further order of the court.

A power of arrest is attached to paragraphs ------- of this order and shall continue until ---------

The costs of the application shall be ---------

(NOTE: This precedent does not contain all of the possible variations for the different types of application that can be made for an occupation order under sections 35-38 Family Law Act 1996 and the above precedent should be adapted for use in those cases.)

If a power of arrest is attached to the occupation order a copy of the order must be delivered to the officer in charge of the police station for the Applicant's address or such other police station as the court may direct and must be accompanied by a statement showing that the Respondent has been served with the order or informed of its terms.

25.   UNDERTAKING: FAMILY COURT

P25-01   IN THE FAMILY COURT sitting at
BARCHESTER.....................CASE NUMBER:FL1804763
THE FAMILY LAW ACT 1996
Between:

MARY SMITH

Applicant

and

JOHN SMITH

Respondent

AFTER HEARING

AFTER READING the statements of MARY SMITH and JOHN SMITH and after hearing the oral evidence of both parties

ORDER MADE BY DISTRICT JUDGE ----- ON ----------SITTING IN PRIVATE

PENAL NOTICE

IMPORTANT NOTICE TO JOHN SMITH

YOU MUST OBEY THE TERMS OF THE UNDERTAKINGS YOU HAVE GIVEN TO THE COURT SET OUT IN PARAGRAPH ------ OF THIS ORDER.

IF YOU DO NOT, YOU MAY BE SENT TO PRISON, FINED OR HAVE YOUR ASSETS SEIZED

1.   The court has considered it is appropriate on the facts of the case to accept the undertakings offered by the Respondent and that a power arrest is not necessary to support the exclusion of the Respondent from the family home and the provisions of section 42A are not required for the protection of the Applicant and the children of the family.

2.   The court explained the penal consequences of any breach by the Respondent of his undertakings given to the court today.

3.   The Respondent has given the following undertakings:
   a.   Not to use or threaten to use violence against the Applicant Mary Smith and not to instruct, encourage or in any way suggest that any other person should do so.
   b.   Not intimidate, harass or pester the Applicant Mary Smith and must not instruct, encourage or in any way suggest that any other person should do so.
   c.   Not to telephone, text, email or otherwise contact or attempt to contact the Applicant Mary Smith, including via social networking websites or other forms of electronic messaging (except for the purpose of making arrangements for contact between the Respondent and the relevant children) (except through his legal representatives (include the contact details of the firm)).
   d.   Not to damage, attempt to damage, or threaten to damage any property in the possession of or owned by the Applicant Mary Smith and not to instruct, encourage or in any way suggest that any other person should do so.
   e.   Not to damage attempt to damage or threaten to damage the property or contents of 27 Seymour Road Barchester and not to instruct, encourage or in any way suggest that any other person should do so.
   f.   To vacate 27 Seymour Road Barchester by ----------and after that date not to live in that property.

g. Not to go to, enter or attempt to enter 27 Seymour Road Barchester or any property where he knows of believes the applicant Mary Smith to be living and not to go within 100 metres of Seymour Road except that the Respondent may go to the property but not enter it / go along Seymour Road for the purpose of collecting the children for and returning them from such contact with the children as may be agreed in writing between the Applicant and the Respondent or as may be ordered by the court.

h. Not to use or threaten to use violence against the relevant children and not to instruct, encourage or in any way suggest that any other person should do so.

i. Not to intimidate, harass or pester the relevant children and not to instruct, encourage or in any way suggest that any other person should do so.

j. Not to telephone, text, email or otherwise contact or attempt to contact the relevant children, including via social networking websites or other forms of electronic messaging (except for such contact as may be agreed in writing between the Applicant and the Respondent or as may be ordered by the court.)

k. Not between the hours of ------------- to go to or attempt to enter the school premises known as CD Primary School and EF Secondary School and not to go within 100 metres of it/ along Church Street unless invited to do so in writing and in advance by the school or with the written agreement in advance of the Applicant Mary Smith.

IT IS ORDERED THAT:

4. The application for a non-molestation order and an occupation order is adjourned to --------- with permission to restore before that date on not less than 48 hours notice.

5. If no party attends on the adjourned hearing the application will be dismissed. Any party who intends to appear shall notify the court in writing not less than 5 working in advance of the hearing.

6. No order for costs between the parties.
   Dated
   Notice pursuant to PD 37A paragraph 2.1
   You JOHN SMITH MAY BE SENT TO PRISON FOR CONTEMPT OF COURT IF YOU BREAK THE PROMISES THAT HAVE BEEN GIVEN TO THE COURT
   Statements pursuant to PD37A paragraph 2.2 (2)
   I understand the undertakings that I have given to the court and that if I break any of my promises to the court I may be sent to prison for contempt of court
   JOHN SMITH
   ....

26. NOTICE OF APPLICATION TO COMMIT: COUNTY COURT

P26-01 IN THE BARCHESTER COUNTY COURT

Case No: B4762

BETWEEN:

MARY SMITH

Applicant

—and—

JOHN SMITH

Respondent

TO John Smith of 27 Seymour Road, Barchester

On the 5th February 2019, you gave an undertaking as follows:

Whether by yourself or by instructing or encouraging any other person

(1) not to use any violence against Mary Smith or the children of the family

(2) not to threaten or molest Mary Smith or the children of the family

(3) not to communicate with Mary Smith by letter, telephone text message email or other means of communication except for the purpose of making arrangements for contact between the Respondent and [name(s) of child[ren]]

(4) to vacate the matrimonial home at 27 Seymour Road, Barchester on or before noon on 8th February 2019 and not to reside in nor enter nor approach within 100 yards of 27 Seymour Road, Barchester, except with the prior permission of the Applicant

and to be bound by these promises until 5th May 2019.

Mary Smith has applied for an order that you should be committed to prison. It is alleged that you have broken the undertaking by

(1) Entering 27 Seymour Road, Barchester on 9th February 2019 without Mary Smith's permission and beating her around the face

(2) Threatening to "punch her lights out" on the 10th February 2019 after approaching her in the Odeon Cinema, Barchester.

(3) Sending her 100 text messages between 11.30 pm on 10th February and 1 am on 11th February 2019 which accused her of seeing another man and taking him back to 27 Seymour Road Barchester after leaving the Odeon Cinema on 10am February 2019

YOU MUST ATTEND COURT at the Court House, High Street, Barchester on Friday the 15th day of February 2019 at 10.30 o'clock to show good reason why you should not be sent to prison.

Important Notice

The court has power to send you to prison, to fine you or seize your assets if it finds that any of the allegations made against you are true and amount to a contempt of court. YOU MUST ATTEND COURT on the date shown on the front of this form. It is in your own interest to do so. You should bring with you any witnesses and documents which you think will help you put your side of the case. If you consider the allegations are not true you must tell the court why. If it is established that they are true you must tell the court of any good reason why they do not amount to a contempt of court, or if they do, why you should not be punished. If you need advice, you should show this document at once to your solicitor or go to a Citizens Advice Bureau or similar organisation."

The Applicant's Solicitors are Crichton & Co of 1 Cathedral Close, Barchester (ref CH)

The Court Office at High Street, Barchester is open from 10 am to 4 pm Monday to Friday.

27. REPORTING RESTRICTION ORDER

P27-01   The standard form of draft order in reporting restriction cases has been agreed between representatives of the national media and the Official Solicitor and CAFCASS. It is as follows:

Case Number: [..........]
IN THE HIGH COURT OF JUSTICE
FAMILY DIVISION [PRINCIPAL REGISTRY]
BEFORE [JUDGE] IN PRIVATE
IN THE MATTER OF THE COURT'S INHERENT JURISDICTION
BETWEEN
[..........]
and
[..........]

Reporting Restriction Order

IMPORTANT
If you disobey this order you may be found guilty of contempt of court and may be sent to prison or be fined or have your assets seized. You should read the order carefully and are advised to consult a solicitor as soon as possible. You have the right to ask the Court to vary or discharge the order.

Explanation

A.   On [date] the Court considered an application for a reporting restriction order.
B.   The following persons and/or organisations were represented before the Court: [describe parties and their advocates]
C.   The Court read the following documents: [list the documents]
    and/or
    The Court directed the [Applicant/Claimant] to file a statement no later than [date] setting out the information presented to the court at the hearing.
    and/or
    The Court directed that copies of the attached Explanatory Note and [list any other documents] be made available by the [Applicant/Claimant] to any person affected by this Order.
D.   In a case where an undertaking in damages is required by the Court:
    The Applicant gave an undertaking that if the Court later finds that this Order was obtained as a result of any deliberate or careless misrepresentation by the Applicant, and that this has caused loss to any person served with the Order, and that that person should be compensated, the Applicant will comply with any order the Court may make.]
E.   In the case of an order made without notice:
    This order was made without notice to those affected by it, the Court having considered section 12(2) Human Rights Act 1998 and being satisfied (i) that the [Applicant/Claimant] has taken all practicable steps to notify persons affected and/or (ii) that there are compelling reasons for notice not being given, namely: [set out the Court's reasons for making the order without notice]
F.   In the case of an application by a local authority:
    The Court granted permission to the Applicant to apply for the exercise of the Court's inherent jurisdiction.]

Order

1. Duration

Subject to any different order made in the meantime, this order shall have effect [in the case of an adult] during the lifetime of the [Defendant], whose details are set out in Schedule 1 to this order.

[in the case of a child] until [date], the 18th birthday of the child whose details are set out in Schedule 1 to this order ("the Child").

2. Who is bound

This order binds all persons and all companies (whether acting by their directors, employees or agents or in any other way) who know that the order has been made.

3. Publishing Restrictions

This order prohibits the publishing or broadcasting in any newspaper, magazine, public computer network, internet website, sound or television broadcast or cable or satellite programme service of:

a.   The name and address of
     i.   the [Defendant/Child];
    ii.   [in the case of a child] the Child's parents ("the parents"), whose details are set out in Schedule 2 to this order;
   iii.   any individual having day-to-day care of or medical responsibility for the [Defendant/Child] ("a carer"), whose details are set out in Schedule 3 to this Order;
    vi.   any residential home or hospital, or other establishment in which the [Defendant/Child] is residing or being treated ("an establishment");

b.   any picture being or including a picture of either the [Defendant/Child], a carer or an establishment;

c.   any other particulars or information relating to the [Defendant/Child];

IF, BUT ONLY IF, such publication is likely to lead to the identification of the [Defendant/Child] as being [set out the feature of the situation which has led to the granting of the order].

4.   No publication of the text or a summary of this order (except for service of the order under paragraph 7 below) shall include any of the matters referred to in paragraph 3 above.

5. Restriction on seeking information

This Order prohibits any person from seeking any information relating to the [Defendant/Child] [or the parents] or a carer from any of the following:

a.   the [Defendant/Child];
b.   the parents];
c.   a carer;
d.   the staff or residents of an establishment.]

6. What is not restricted by this Order

Nothing in this Order shall prevent any person from:

a. publishing information relating to any part of a hearing in a court in England and Wales (including a coroner's court) in which the court was sitting in public and did not itself make any order restricting publication.

b. seeking or publishing information which is not restricted by Paragraph 3 above.

c. inquiring whether a person or place falls within paragraph 3(a) above.

d. seeking information relating to the [Defendant/Child] while acting in a manner authorised by statute or by any court in England and Wales.

e. seeking information from the responsible solicitor acting for any of the parties or any appointed press officer, whose details are set out in Schedule 4 to this order.

f. seeking or receiving information from anyone who before the making of this order had previously approached that person with the purpose of volunteering information (but this paragraph will not make lawful the provision or receipt of private information which would otherwise be unlawful).

g. publishing information which before the service on that person of this order was already in the public domain in England and Wales as a result of publication by another person in any newspaper, magazine, sound or television broadcast or cable or satellite programme service, or on the internet website of a media organisation operating within England and Wales.

7. Service

Copies of this Order endorsed with a notice warning of the consequences of disobedience shall be served by the [Applicant/Claimant] (and may be served by any other party to the proceedings)

a. by service on such newspaper and sound or television broadcasting or cable or satellite or programme services as they think fit, by fax or first class post addressed to the editor (in the case of a newspaper) or senior news editor (in the case of a broadcasting or cable or satellite programme service) or website administrator (in the case of an internet website) and/or to their respective legal departments; and/or

b. on such other persons as the parties may think fit, by personal service.

8. Further applications about this Order

The parties and any person affected by any of the restrictions in paragraphs 3-5 above may make application to vary or discharge it to a Judge of the High Court on not less than [48 hours] notice to the parties.

Schedule 1

[The [Defendant/Child] 's Full Name:
Born:
Address:]
Or
[Information enabling those affected by order to identify the Defendant/Child]

Schedule 2

[Similar details of parents]

Schedule 3

[Similar details of carers or other persons protected]

Schedule 4

[Contact details of responsible solicitor and/or press officer]
Date of Order:[..........]

URGENT COURT BUSINESS OFFICER NUMBERS FOR OUT-OF-HOURS INJUNCTION APPLICATIONS

London (Royal Courts of Justice)		0207 947 6000
South Eastern Circuit outside London		07471 141 742
Midland Circuit:	West side	07748 613 886
	East side	07748 542 966
Northern Circuit:	Cumbria & Lancs	07554 459606
	Greater Manchester	07554 459626
	Merseyside & Cheshire	07876 034775
North Eastern Circuit:	Durham & Northumbria	07917 270988
	Humber & S Yorkshire	07867 327865
	Leeds & Bradford	01399 618082
	Newcastle	01399 618083
	N & W Yorkshire	07810 181828
Wales	Cardiff	07699 618086
Western Circuit:	Avon, Glos & Somerset	07795 302944
	Devon, Cornwall & Dorset	07795 800420
	Hants & Wilts	07795 801293

INDEX

This index has been prepared using Sweet and Maxwell's Legal Taxonomy. Main index entries conform to keywords provided by the Legal Taxonomy except where references to specific documents or non-standard terms (denoted by quotation marks) have been included. These keywords provide a means of identifying similar concepts in other Sweet & Maxwell publications and on-line services to which keywords from the Legal Taxonomy have been applied. Readers may find some minor differences between terms used in the text and those which appear in the index. Suggestions to *sweetandmaxwell.taxonomy@tr.com*.